LEARNING ON THE JOB: PARENTING IN MODERN IRELAND

Edited by Colm O'Doherty and Ashling Jackson

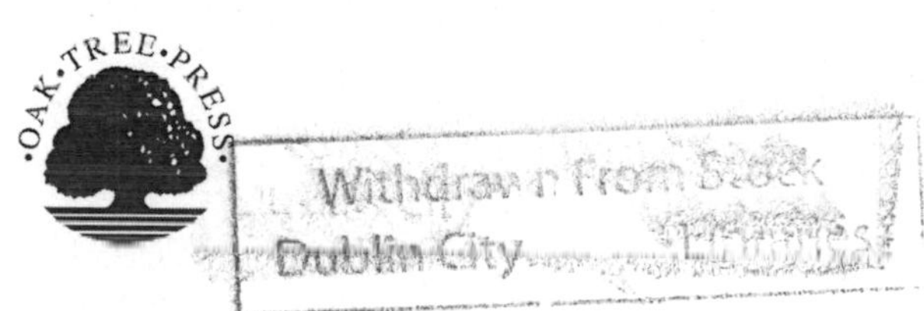

Published by Oak Tree Press, 19 Rutland Street, Cork, Ireland

www.oaktreepress.com / www.SuccessStore.com

A catalogue record of this book is available from the British Library.

ISBN 978 1 78119 187 3 (paperback)
ISBN 978 1 78119 188 0 (ePub)
ISBN 978 1 78119 189 7 (Kindle)
ISBN 978 1 78119 199 6 (PDF)

Cover design: Kieran O'Connor Design
Cover illustration: kudryashka / 123rf.com

Printed in Ireland by SPRINT-print Ltd.

Contents

Part Two: Discourse on Parenting and Emerging Family Issues

Figures

Tables

EDITORS

Dr Colm O'Doherty is a lecturer in Applied Social Studies at the Institute of Technology Tralee. He began his professional career as a social worker in Coventry and developed a family support service in the inner city there. After leaving Coventry Social Services, he worked as a social worker in West Wales and Cork city and county where he continued his involvement in family support and community development practice. After 18 years' frontline practice in social work, family support and community development, he took on a pivotal role in community and social work education at University College Cork. He left University College Cork and moved to the Institute of Technology Tralee, where he developed the Department of Social Sciences. His PhD, completed in 2004, critically examined the national deployment of family support services. He is the author of *A New Agenda for Family Support – Providing Services that Create Social Capital* (2007) and co-editor (with Dr Ashling Jackson) of *Community Development in Ireland – Theory, Policy and Practice* (2012). His current research interests are in the development of social entrepreneurship as a force for positive social change.

Dr Ashling Jackson is a Senior Lecturer in Social Care at Athlone Institute of Technology, where she lectures in the areas of sociology/social policy, community development and research methods. Her PhD examined premarital cohabitation as a pathway to marriage and how premarital cohabitation is changing the social institution of marriage in Ireland today. She has worked extensively with disadvantaged groups in community settings, most notably with the Traveller community. Prior to joining Athlone Institute of Technology, in 2001, Ashling was a Public Health Research Officer with the Health Service Executive – Dublin Mid-Leinster region, where she was responsible for the qualitative research function of the Dept. of Public Health. She has researched and published on family change, community education, health and experiences of the Irish Traveller community.

AUTHORS

Dr Anna Moore Asgharian is a senior clinical psychologist within the Health Service Executive in County Wexford. Anna trained at Royal Holloway, University of London where she received a Doctorate in Clinical Psychology. She has worked in the areas of mental health, intellectual disability and autism with adults and children for over 20 years. Her special interests include parent capacity assessments and how they relate to attachment theory.

Gertrude Cotter is a PhD candidate at University College Cork and holder of the Irish Research Council's National Forum Postgraduate Scholarship for Teaching and Learning in Higher Education. She studies at the School of Education in the field of development, intercultural and social justice education. She has seven post-graduate qualifications, including three Master's, and 30 years' experience of working in the academic and in the community and voluntary sectors at home and in South America. She worked for almost a decade as CEO of a leading refugee and migrant-support organisation in Ireland, where she bore witness to the many challenges faced by migrant families. She led several research projects documenting the experiences of migrants and asylum-seekers in Ireland and edited a number of publications. She campaigns extensively on migrant and refugee rights. She has lectured in University College Cork and Institute of Technology Tralee in international development management, community development, social care, Latin American history and international relations.

Rosemary Crosse is completing her doctoral studies in the School of Political Science and Sociology at NUI Galway. Her doctoral research examines Irish mothers' experiences of marital dissolution and the effectiveness of public policy and value of service provision in this area. Her research also focuses on gender inequality and public policy, with an emphasis on those parenting alone in contemporary Ireland.

Dr Tom Farrelly is a parent of two adult children and also has been a foster parent. In addition to working as a social science lecturer, he works as an educational developer with Institute of Technology Tralee's E-

Learning unit. He describes himself as a 'critical technophile', who appreciates the potential benefits presented by modern communications technology while at the same maintaining a questioning attitude to its unqualified use.

Sandra Irwin Gowran is Director of Education Policy with GLEN (Gay and Lesbian Equality Network). GLEN is a policy- and strategy-focused non-governmental organisation that aims to deliver ambitious and positive change for lesbian, gay and bisexual people in Ireland, ensuring full equality, inclusion and protection from all forms of discrimination. As well as education policy, Sandra's role at GLEN also has involved working extensively on the pursuit of equality in the areas of equal recognition of lesbian and gay relationships and LGBT-headed families.

Jennifer Kavanagh obtained a first class honours degree in social care in 2008 and went on to work as a support worker in various agencies, where she gained experience working with vulnerable adults. Through this work, her understanding of the impact of parental well-being on children was generated, alongside a passion to enhance the lives of both children and parents through parent support work. Jennifer went on to carry out her Master's by research on the topic of parenting in 2012 and has developed a new gateway model of parenting support that could enhance the lives of both children and parents universally. This gateway model is hoped to be influential in the structure of developing family and social services alongside providing life skills training for children and parents equally.

Liz Kerrins has held social research and social policy development and analysis roles in Irish third-level institutions and non-governmental organisations, and was Senior Policy Officer with the Children's Research Centre, Trinity College Dublin (TCD). She continues to work as an independent researcher. Liz is a graduate of TCD and University College Dublin.

Olaniyi Kolawole holds an MA in Contemporary Migration and Diaspora Studies from University College Cork (UCC). Currently, he is a final year PhD Social Science candidate in the College of Arts, Celtic Studies and Social Science in UCC. His areas of interest are in the dynamics of migration, social, economic and cultural integration of migrants, social exclusion, citizenship, identity, equality, multiculturalism and management of cultural diversity. He lectures in the Department of Sociology and the School of Applied Social Studies in UCC.

Edel Lawlor has an honours degree in social care, a Diploma in play therapy, a diploma in sand tray therapy and is currently studying for her Master's in humanistic and integrative psychotherapy. Edel is a mother of three children and has 18 years' experience of working with children and families, which began in a women's refuge in 1996. From there, Edel began to notice the significant benefits of therapeutic play for children and went on to further studies to enhance her professional understanding and capacity to help children and their parents. In 2005, Edel opened her own therapy centre, called 'Expressive Play', which was expanded and moved to Kilflynn, County Kerry, in 2008. Edel provides play therapy and parent support to a wide variety of families and facilitates children's camps, training to students in therapeutic play skills and inspired the Kilflynn fairy festival. Throughout her career, Edel has worked in a parenting support role alongside children's play therapy and also worked as a parent support worker in a resource centre. Her experience in parenting support work led her to develop her own parenting support programme, 'Creative Parenting', which is delivered at the centre, as well as in schools and resource centres nationwide.

Karen Leonard (B.Soc.Sc., M.Soc.Sc., M.Sc.Psychotherapy) originally studied social work at University College Dublin (UCD). On qualifying, she worked first as a child protection social worker and then as a family worker in Dublin. She has been a Lecturer of Applied Social Studies in Social Care at Athlone Institute of Technology since 2000. She studied family therapy at the Mater Family Therapy Unit and UCD and is a Registered Family Therapist with FTAI, ICP and EAP. She has experience working with children, adolescents and their families in a number of family centres in Dublin, in the West of Ireland and in her own private practice in County Roscommon.

Dr Maria Lohan is a Senior Lecturer in the School of Nursing and Midwifery at Queen's University Belfast and is currently a Visiting Professor at the School of Nursing, University of British Columbia. She is a sociologist specialising in critical men's health research, with a particular focus on men's reproductive and sexual health and fatherhood. Her research is informed by critical studies in men and masculinities and she has published extensively in leading international journals. She also specialises in knowledge translation and is currently leading NIHR- and HSE-funded studies evaluating an intervention targeting teenage men in relation to unintended pregnancy in Ireland and Northern Ireland: www.qub.ac.uk/sites/IfIWereJack/.

Dr Michelle Millar has extensive expertise in funded social policy research and analysis. She is a Senior Lecturer in Public and Social Policy at the School of Political Science and Sociology and Research Fellow at the UNESCO Child and Family Research Centre, NUI Galway. Michelle was the Principal Investigator of the Child and Family Research Centre study on the Labour Market Needs and Social Inclusion of One Parent Families in Galway City and County project.

Dr Elizabeth Nixon is Assistant Professor in Developmental Psychology in the School of Psychology, and Senior Research Fellow at the Children's Research Centre, Trinity College Dublin. Her research interests are in the areas of parenting, family processes and children's development, particularly within the context of parental separation, lone parenting and stepfamilies. She has been funded by the Department of Children and Youth Affairs and the Irish Research Council to conduct several projects on parenting and is a Co-Investigator on *Growing Up in Ireland*, the first national longitudinal study of children in Ireland.

Stella Owens holds a Bachelor's degree in Psychology from University College Dublin (UCD), a Master's degree in Social Work from Queen's University Belfast and a PhD also from UCD. Her PhD explored family involvement in family support services in Ireland. Stella has a background in social work practice and management, and has worked in residential, child protection and therapeutic family support services. She joined the Centre for Effective Services in January 2009 and her main work areas include: the development of Children and Young People's Services Committees; supporting implementation of services and programmes, including area-based initiatives in socially disadvantaged communities; synthesising evaluation findings from the Prevention and Early Intervention Initiative; the implementation and application of an evidence informed approach to practice; supporting the development of the Children's Research Network for Ireland and Northern Ireland; and leading the Special Interest Group on Supporting Parents.

Dr Noel Richardson is director of the National Centre for Men's Health at Institute of Technology Carlow. He has extensive experience in the area of men's health at a research, policy and advocacy level. He is the principal author of the first-ever National Policy on Men's Health, which was published in Ireland in 2009, and is also co-author of the first European Union report on men's health, published in 2011. He is a board member of the Men's Health Forum in Ireland and the European Men's Health Forum.

Colin Shaw is a doctoral candidate in Queen's University Belfast's School of Sociology, Social Policy and Social Work. His research interests centre on the changing ideals and practices of fatherhood. Colin's PhD project is an intergenerational study of fathering, with a particular focus on the experience of being fathered, drawing on contemporary and retrospective accounts to better understand how men's lives and family lives intersect.

Declan Smith is married to Ann and they have four daughters – Vicki, Amy, Rachel and Michelle – as well as six grandchildren – Lucas, Jamie, Kyle, Charlotte, Fionn and Noah. They have been fostering since 2000. Declan is an Air Traffic Controller, currently based at Cork Airport, while Ann looks after all the family 24/7 in the home. Declan completed his honours degree in Applied Social Studies in the Institute of Technology, Tralee and was awarded a BA(Hons) in 2009. For the last number of years, he has been a member of the Irish Foster Care Association's Voluntary Support and Advocacy team. In 2013, he completed a Master's degree in Counselling and Psychotherapy in the Irish College of Humanities and Applied Science (ICHAS), Limerick for which he was awarded an MA. An avid Munster Rugby fan, he enjoys numerous sporting activities and spending time with the family.

Michelle Share is a senior research fellow at the Children's Research Centre, School of Social Work and Social Policy, Trinity College Dublin. She is a sociologist with extensive experience in research management and the conduct of multi-site research and evaluation projects in child and youth settings. She has researched and published on the role of grandparents in childcare provision; children and parents who use intellectual disability services; educational access programmes at second and third level; and on young people's food and nutrition in second level and alternative education settings.

ACKNOWLEDGEMENTS

We hope the ideas, concepts and experiences in this book will increase our readers' understanding of the importance of parenting, in all its diverse forms, in contemporary Irish society.

The book would not have been possible without the help and support of many people. We are deeply grateful to all our contributors for their hard work, creativity and commitment to the project. Their generosity and expertise has enhanced the quality of the book as a whole.

We are indebted to Professor Mary Daly for the excellent **Foreword** she has written for the book. It is very clear, succinct and sets out the key debates in a straightforward and comprehensive fashion. It really complements the material in the book.

We also thank the Katharine Howard Foundation for the financial support that made this publication possible. In particular, we thank Noelle Spring, who enthusiastically supported the book from the outset.

We are grateful to our publisher, Brian O'Kane, for his assistance and commitment in producing the book. He has encouraged, inspired and painlessly guided us through the editing and publishing tasks required to complete it.

Dedication

This book is dedicated to Anna, Luke, Ellen and Molly O'Doherty; David, Saoirse and Nathan Jackson. To each of you, thank you so much for your invaluable love and support.

> "I can no other answer make but thanks, and thanks, and ever thanks ...". William Shakespeare (1564-1616), English playwright and poet, from: *Twelfth Night*, Act III, Scene 3.

Foreword

Parenting is firmly on the agenda today. Governments are striving to put in place measures oriented to parenting support and parents and parenting practices are popular topics of public discourse and debate. Ireland is no exception to this pattern. The developments are coming both from the ground up – from parents themselves, local organisations and self-help initiatives – and also from the top down – through government policy and the channelling of public and private funding. While the nature of the debate and the actual remedies and programmes put in place vary, at their core they signal an increasing state and societal interest in how people carry out their parenting roles. In some ways, what we are seeing is the ordinary made extraordinary. In the process, a new set of skills is said to be needed by today's parents, a new generation of professional experts is emerging and a new field of research and public policy is opening up in an area that we more or less took for granted up until recent years.

One of the remarkable elements today is the turn to parental agency. In some distinction to policies and debates in the past that concentrated on parenthood as a legal status or set of responsibilities, or indeed the parent as meriting some financial and other resources for the task of childrearing, contemporary provisions and debates are firmly focused on the practice of the parental role. The term 'parenting' connotes a focus on the 'doing' of parenthood, the quotidian practices and approaches whereby parents relate to their children and rear them to be adults.

Why parenting? Basically, there is a series of developments and factors that are all pushing for change in more or less the same direction. I see four main driving considerations.

First, there is a sense that parental knowledge and skill either have deteriorated or are inadequate to meet the exigencies of parenting in today's complex world. Not alone are parents faced with more moral dilemmas regarding childrearing, but the gap or distance between the generations also seems to be growing. Even parents themselves increasingly voice a need for support and guidance, conveying a sense that they just do not know how to manage the pressures of raising children whose culture they do not fully understand and, at the same time, engage in demanding jobs or other activities to earn sufficient money to raise a family. People have never been more invested in their children's behaviour but the result seems to be more, rather than less, anxiety for everyone: parents, children, communities, states and societies. But, beyond the challenges experienced by parents, there is also a general sense that parents are not performing the role as they should. This dovetails with – and, in turn, is occasioned by – a relatively critical public climate, in which elements of a culture of blame of parents seem to lurk beneath the surface. In a word, there are very high expectations of today's parents.

Second, public authorities and opinion leaders are trying to act upon the insights conveyed by the latest research. There is a very strong convergence in the messages from diverse fields of scientific research. Neuroscience is telling us about the plasticity of the infant brain and the short window for early intervention. Equally, economists make the argument that money spent early will have a strong future return from a prevention perspective. The educationalists extol the virtues of early education, so much so that what used to be childcare has now become much more like early education. And sociologists are busy constructing children as a risk group and childhood as a period defined primarily by risk. Such a strong and, in some ways, surprisingly singular set of messages conveys a sense of limited time for intervention and an urgency about the ways in which our children are being reared.

Third, there is a concern about child protection and child welfare. As more and more revelations come to light about the difficulties faced by many children and the complicit role played by adults and indeed our core societal institutions in this, the sense of needing to make radical changes to improve children's childhoods is underlined. There is also the parallel move to child rights and the treatment of the child as a person whose voice and perspective should be heard. This is very much in the spirit of the United Nations *Convention on the Rights of the Child*, which has been adopted by almost all countries from 1989 on. Viewing the situation from the perspective of the child, we can see in the discussions of parenting elements of a genuine attempt to protect children and to improve their experiences and life chances. It is in some ways a project of hope of a better life for future generations.

Finally, the discourses and practices around refashioning parenting are trying to rebuild a sense of family and of family solidarity in a context where families seem more fragile and less likely to endure. This fear is prevalent at home and abroad. It rests on a recognition of the important role that family plays in supporting people in everyday life and keeping societies stable. But it also sees family as playing a key role in helping to prevent social ills and social problems, such as antisocial behaviour and social exclusion. In this context, it is seen as important to inculcate parental responsibilities not only in individuals but also in society more broadly.

We should approach these developments with a questioning and critical orientation. Are parents being blamed for societal failures and is what is going on a way of loading more responsibilities on parents rather than helping to share the load? Is there one best way of parenting and who gets to say what that is? Is there a bias towards the parenting behaviours and preferences of particular sections of the population, whose practice is seen to be the norm or model to follow? How are low income and minority parents placed in the debate? Is the research evidence strong enough to promote particular approaches? Is the increased surveillance of children, parents and families – by the media, social services, education and health authorities – justified?

So far there has been little material available on Ireland and little analysis of the significance of the turn to parenting in an Irish context. This book fills that gap. It makes an original contribution in three main ways. First, through research on how people actually parent in today's Ireland, it fills a knowledge vacuum. In this regard, as well as revealing the general contours of parenting in today's Ireland, it shines a welcome light on parenting in particular conditions or situations (such as in cases of fostering, grandparenting, parenting alone and multicultural parenting). Second, the book considers and reviews strategies, techniques and programmatic approaches to parenting that are being developed and applied in Ireland. Third, the book builds on the insights and knowledge generated to outline a social vision on how to make society function better for parents and children. The three pillars of its unique vision of a parent-centred society are: equality of social relations, economic security and inter-generational solidarity. Throughout, the different chapters offer the kind of measured critique needed, at once uncovering key developments and changes but also examining them in a way that allows their deeper significance, intent and implications to be laid bare.

Mary Daly
Professor of Sociology and Social Policy
University of Oxford

INTRODUCTION

Ashling Jackson and Colm O'Doherty

This book is not about how to become a perfect parent. It is not about setting standards for parenting, nor is it a parenting manual. Rather, it is a reflection on general parenting issues in Ireland and parenting for a variety of 'new' emerging parent groups. Why is a book like this necessary, and why now?

Ireland has undergone significant social change in recent decades (Share *et al*, 2012). The immediate social context in which we now all live is very fluid and we no longer necessarily follow traditional pre-determined paths or trajectories. The loosening of the traditional hold of the Catholic Church on morality, state and family life means that there are now more liberal attitudes to sex before marriage (Layte *et al*, 2006). Fertility rates outside marriage increased in Ireland steadily in the last few decades (Central Statistics Office, 2013). Premarital cohabitation has emerged as the fastest-growing family form in Ireland (Central Statistics Office, 2012a). Of the 17,958 births recorded in *Census 2011*, there were 6,164 births registered as outside marriage/civil partnership, accounting for 34% of all births (Central Statistics Office, 2012b, p.1). Of these, 3,449 births were to unmarried parents with the same address – 19% of all births (Central Statistics Office 2012b, p.1). Marriage rates also are increasing, but marriage is happening later (Jackson, 2011).

We now live in an Ireland where there are a variety of social opportunities, such as increased female labour force participation and more career paths for men and women (Central Statistics Office, 2007). Until recently, this was framed by a high unemployment rate, characteristic of the economic recession that Ireland experienced from 2008 to 2013. In September 2014, the unemployment rate in Ireland was at 11.1% (Central Statistics Office, 2014), its lowest value since 2009. This means that there are increased job opportunities available for people. Increased educational opportunities (Department of Education and

Science, 2006) also mean that parenting takes place in the midst of multiplicity of choice and life situations.

Parenting is the ultimate lifelong learning curve, where learning can be seen as something that takes place on an on-going basis from our daily interactions with others and with the world around us. This book is intended to be a way of charting a course through parenthood, by recognising that there is no 'one size fits all' approach, but rather that parenthood is a process through which we negotiate a relationship with children in the midst of all our cultural, religious, social, familial and life demands. As the primary function of parenthood is socialisation of children, and in effect, rearing the next generation, the importance of it cannot be overstated. Yet, it remains a role in which there is no prior training and one has to be an expert in everything!

As this book makes clear, parenting should now be, more than ever, a joint enterprise between the state and citizens, where wellbeing is co-produced. It is not a technocratic project to be run according to the belief that 'the experts know best'. Indeed, recent research (2012), carried out by Angela Davis at the University of Warwick into 50 years of motherhood manuals, calls into question the value of expert advice. She talked to women about the advice given by published childcare 'experts' and found that experts presented their advice in the form of orders and prescribed impossibly high standards of behaviour for new mothers. A narrow focus on delivering measurable outcomes neglects the importance of human relationships and supports a target-driven culture that risks reducing the complexity and texture of parenting experiences to a simple number. This in turn leads to policies and services that do not enable people to engage in positive parenting activity. Critical human relationships need to be given greater priority as a goal of policy. As long as most parenting policy initiatives are directed towards standardisation and regulation, those who are parenting are almost certain to feel beleaguered and criticised if they are not up to the mark. In line with Bettelheim's (1995) view that perfection is not within the grasp of ordinary human beings, this book considers that 'good enough' is a more realistic ambition.

A Note on the Structure of This Book

We have structured this book in two parts. **Part 1: The Social Context of Parenting in Ireland** aims to review and discuss the social terrain in which parenting takes places at the moment in Ireland. As this terrain has changed for the family unit, the composition of that unit is now more diverse, the role of parents and children has changed and increasingly has to be negotiated within the family unit (Halpenny *et al*, 2010). The opening chapter *A Quiet Revolution: Modernity, Social Change and New Parenting Opportunities* addresses these issues. To really appreciate the influences on parenting and the varied environments in which parenting takes place, we have to explore changing family patterns and parenting in Ireland. In **Chapter 2**, *In with the New; Out with the Old: Changing Family Patterns in Ireland,* a new context for parenting in Ireland, changes to family life and the consequences for parenting are analysed. In **Chapter 3**, *The Value of Parenting,* consideration is given to the hidden value of parenting and its contribution to well-being. **Chapter 4,** *Happy Parenting* makes the case for parenting as a shared purposeful activity that is central to all our lives. **Chapter 5**, *Supporting Parents: Evidence-informed and Evidence-based Policy and Practice* provides a critical commentary on the programmes, initiatives and policy approaches that have been developed in Ireland and internationally to support parents. In addition, it benchmarks the research knowledge and theoretical understandings that underpin parenting support practice.

Part 2: Discourse on Parenting and Emerging Family Issues is a reflection on key parenting issues in Ireland at the moment. **Chapter 6**, *Parenting and Children's Development in Ireland: Lessons from Psychology* gives an overview of key issues of parenting from 0 to 18 years. **Chapter 7**, *"You Don't Understand!" – Navigating the Parenting Contours of Adolescence* focuses specifically on teenage parenting challenges and provides solutions for parents to effectively navigate this time in a teenager's life.

Part 1 of this book acknowledges the fluid social environment in which parenting takes place. However, we also live in a digital age, which means children increasingly have access to a plethora of technological devices and information across a wide variety of mediums. **Chapter 8**, *"There's an App for That!" – Parenting in a Digital Age* examines this in more detail.

Census 2011 results show a 100% increase in same-sex couples living together in Ireland (Central Statistics Office, 2012a). Acknowledged by Kieran Rose (2012), the Chair of GLEN, Gay and Lesbian Equality Network (Dublin) as an important step forward in gay and lesbian couples being more open about their living arrangements, he also emphasises that it is probably an under-representation of the numbers of gay/lesbian couples who live together. The *Civil Partnership and Certain Rights and Obligations of Cohabitants Act,* which was passed in Ireland in July 2010, heralds much lobbied for macro social change in response to the diversity of relationship preferences in individuals' lives. Importantly, it is a distinctive piece of rights-based legislation, providing people in cohabiting and same-sex relationships with many of the rights of married couples, such as succession rights and eligibility for similar social welfare provision. As a consequence, one would expect to see living arrangements for gay/lesbian/bi-sexual/transgender couples becoming more formal and parenting in these family units to increase. Therefore, **Chapter 9**, *Legal Gaps Impacting on Children of Lesbian, Gay and Bisexual Parents in Ireland* makes an important contribution to our understanding of the social and legal issues that confront gay and lesbian parents in modern Ireland. Parenting in one-parent family environments poses particular parenting challenges. **Chapter 10**, *Parenting Alone in Contemporary Ireland* establishes the position of one-parent families in Irish society, their social circumstances and the institutional barriers that serve to marginalise and separate them from mainstream Irish society. In **Chapter 11**, *Parents with Intellectual Disability,* parenting with intellectual disability is explored from an historical, legal and social perspective. How to promote best practice when working with parents with intellectual disability is expounded upon.

The demands of working and being a parent often can be difficult to synchronise. This, in turn, has meant that grandparents are assuming an active surrogate parental role for their grandchildren. This new third age role will be discussed in **Chapter 12**, *Grandchildcare: Grandparents and Childcare in Ireland*. The relationship between fathers and their children and fathers and wider society has rarely (if ever) been as comprehensively outlined as it is in **Chapter 13**, *Fathers and Parenting.*

Chapter 14, *Working on Parenting* describes the experiences of a play therapy practitioner, who has adopted a holistic approach to supporting her clients through the struggles of parenting. Parenting is not a linear process: **Chapter 15**, *Advancing Parenting – A New Perspective on Parenting Support* presents the findings of a research study that critically reviews existing parenting programmes and assesses their relevance and function in supporting all parents in rearing their children.

There also has been another phenomenal demographic change to Irish society in recent years, most notably the changes to the Irish ethnic landscape, particularly in Dublin and other large cities of Cork, Limerick and Galway, where immigrants progressively populate (Barrett and McCarthy, 2006). Barrett and McCarthy (2006) also noted that Ireland was unusual in terms of the speed with which the non-national percentage of its population had risen. The research evidence presented in **Chapter 16**, *Parenting in a Multicultural Society: Migrants and Their Experiences of*

Parenting in Ireland, makes it clear that many migrant parents do not have a salutary experience of Irish society and its institutions.

The joys and challenges of being a foster parent are reflected upon by a foster parent in **Chapter 17**, *Foster parenting.* Fostering is a form of alternative care that involves caring for someone else's child in your own home. Foster parents provide a family life for a child or young person, who for one reason or another cannot live with his or her own parents. In this reflective chapter, the reader will get a real insight into the foster parenting experience from the perspective of a foster parent.

At the start of this *Introduction,* we stated that this book is not a manual. We also stated that this book is intended to be a way of charting a course through parenthood, by recognising that there is no 'one size fits all' approach, but rather that parenthood is a process through which we negotiate a relationship with children in the midst of all our cultural, religious, social, familial and life demands. Therefore, each chapter in this book is like a piece in a jigsaw puzzle, all of which combine to present a picture of the changing nature of parenting in modern Ireland. In so doing, it is our intention, that you, the reader, will gain a clear understanding of the complexity of parenting in a variety of family forms, an awareness of current issues and challenges in this area, as well as effective solutions to address these issues and challenges.

References

Barrett, A. and McCarthy, Y. (2006). 'Immigrants in a Booming Economy: Analysing their Earnings and Welfare Dependence', IZA Discussion Papers 2457, IZA (Institute for the Study of Labour), *Labour*, Vol.21, No.4.

Central Statistics Office (2007). *Women and Men in Ireland 2007, Female Employment Rate Exceeds EU 2010 Target,* press release, retrieved 3 January 2013 from www.cso.ie/statistics/bthsdthsmarriages.htm.

Central Statistics Office (2012a). *Census 2011 Results, Profile 5, Households and Families – Living Arrangements in Ireland,* press release, retrieved 15 July 2014 from www.cso.ie/en/newsandevents/pressreleases/ 2012pressreleases/ pressreleasecensus2011profile5householdsandfamilies/.

Central Statistics Office (2012b). *Births, Deaths and Marriages in Quarter 2, 2012,* retrieved 3 January 2013 from www.cso.ie/en/newsandevents/pressreleases/ 2012pressreleases/pressreleasevitalstatisticssecondquarter2012/Pg. 1.

Central Statistics Office (2013). *Marriages and Civil Partnerships 2011,* press release, retrieved on 10 July 2014 from www.cso.ie/en/newsandevents/pressreleases/ 2013pressreleases/pressreleasemarriagesandcivilpartnerships2011/.

Central Statistics Office (2014). *Live Register 2014,* retrieved 6 November 2014 from www.cso.ie/en/releasesandpublications/er/lr/liveregisterseptember2014/#.VF-HIMJFCUk.

Davis, A. (2012). *Modern Motherhood: Women and Family in England, 1945-2000*, Manchester: Manchester University Press.

Department of Education and Science (2006). *Education Trends: Key Indicators on Education in Ireland and Europe*, retrieved 3 January 2013 from www.education.ie/admin/servlet/blobservlet/des_educ_trends_chapter08.htm#hd08_10.

Halpenny, A.M., Nixon, E., Watson, D. (2010). *Parenting Styles and Discipline: Parents' and Children's Perspectives: Summary Report*, Dublin: Office of the Minister for Children and Youth Affairs.

Jackson, A. (2011). *Premarital Cohabitation as a Pathway into Marriage: An Investigation into How Premarital Cohabitation is Transforming the Institution of Marriage in Ireland: Athlone as a Case Study*, PhD in Social Science (Sociology), Maynooth University, Ireland.

Layte, R., McGee, H., Quail, A., Rundle, K., Cousins, G., Donnelly, C., Mulcahy, F. and Conroy, R. (2006). *The Irish Study of Sexual Health and Relationships*, Dublin: Crisis Pregnancy Agency and the Department of Health and Children.

Rose, K. (2012). *Census Shows Almost 100% Increase in Cohabiting Same-sex Couples*, press release, 29 March, retrieved from www.glen.ie/attachments/GLEN_Press_Release_Census_Results_March_2012.PDF.

Share, P., Corcoran, M. and Conway, B. (2012). *A Sociology of Ireland*, Dublin: Gill and Macmillan.

Part One

The Social Context of Parenting in Ireland

1: A Quiet Revolution: Modernity, Social Change and New Parenting Opportunities

Ashling Jackson

We have come to know that an individual lives, from one generation to the next, in some society; that he lives out a biography, and that he lives it out within some historical sequence. By the fact of his living he contributes, however minutely, to the shaping of society and to the course of its history, even as he is made by society and by its historical push and shove. (Mills, 1959, p.7)

Introduction

This chapter will focus on the sociological perspective of modernity as the social context in which we live. Modernity is a post traditional order (Giddens, 1991) that reflects a 'categorical break' between the modern situation and historical times (Beck and Beck-Gernsheim, 2002). It is a way of describing how industrialised or Western societies have developed socially, culturally and economically. How modernity is defined, how Irish modernity is characterised, how we parent in modernity and what happens after we reach modernity as a stage of development in society will be discussed.

As macro social change gives people more choice and options generally in society, we start to see more choices and options emerging in family formation patterns and parenting opportunities for the individual. Likewise, when innovative behaviour replaces habitual or traditional patterns of behaviour in relationship development, family formation patterns and parenting opportunities, we see an eventual change at the macro level in society. This means that private lives have public significance, and correlatively, that social trends have individual consequences (Collard and Mansfield, 1991). In this chapter, I also will review the current debates on the role of social structure and/or human agency in decision-making and how as parents we create ourselves and frame our decision-making. This is very important to capture the complexity of life as parents in the modern social order in which we all live.

Modernity

Giddens describes modernity as:

> ... a shorthand term for modern society, or industrial civilisation. Portrayed in more detail, it is associated with (1) a certain set of attitudes towards the world, the idea of the world as open to transformation, by human intervention; (2) a complex of economic institutions, especially industrial production and a market economy; (3) a certain range of political institutions, including the nation-state and mass democracy. Largely as a result of these characteristics, modernity is vastly more dynamic than any previous type of social order. It is a society – more technically, a complex of institutions – which, unlike any preceding culture, lives in the future, rather than the past (Giddens and Pierson, 1998, p.94).

As used in classical sociological theory, the concept of modernity has its roots in the attempt to come to grips with the meaning and significance of the social changes occurring in Europe in the latter half of the 19th century, namely, the effects of industrialisation, urbanisation, and political democracy on essentially rural and autocratic societies (Eyerman, 1992). Modernity referred to a world constructed anew through the active and conscious intervention of actors and the new sense of self that such active intervention and responsibility entailed. In modern society, the world is experienced as a human construction, an experience that gives rise both to an exhilarating sense of freedom and possibility, as well as to a basic anxiety about the openness of the future (Eyerman, 1992). It is characterised by:

- Transformation of time and space (alteration of the conditions for social relations across wide spans of time-space, up to and including global systems);
- Dis-embedding mechanisms (the separation of interaction from the particularities of locales and the move of social life away from the hold of pre-established precepts and practices);
- Reflexivity, which is continuous revision in the light of new information or knowledge (Giddens and Pierson, 1998).

Schmidt (2006) refers to the existence of multiple modernities. The idea of multiple modernities means that there are not only many different varieties of modernity outside the Western hemisphere, but also within it. Thus, French modernity differs from German modernity, differs from Scandinavian (or Nordic) (Strath, 2004) modernity, differs from English modernity, differs from American modernity and so forth. The trajectory of a modernisation process cannot be predetermined, due to cultural and institutional differences between different countries. Caplow's 'Principle of Singularity' states that the sharing of trends by national societies does not imply shared outcomes, because of differences in institutional contexts and other considerations (historical context, for example) (Caplow, 1998). Schmidt's (2006) concept of 'multiple modernities' proposes that modernity and social change are unique to the institutional context in which they occur. This implies that characteristics of modernity, such as changing family patterns and pathways to parenthood, are unique to the country in which they occur.

Irish Modernity

Ireland has undergone significant social change in recent decades (Share *et al*, 2012). However, in comparison to the rest of Europe, Ireland was a late developer. Modernisation really only started in Ireland in the 1960s, when we moved from being an agrarian-based economy to a more industrialised one. This progressed to the rapid economic growth experienced in Ireland in the Celtic Tiger years (1990s to 2001/2002, continuing intermittently to 2008). It also was characterised by increased consumerism, reflected in an insatiable demand for housing and mortgage debt (Central Statistics Office, 2005). However, the demise of the Celtic Tiger heralded difficult times for Ireland, which experienced a recession from 2008 to the end of 2013. The impact of this was captured succinctly on 1 January 2009, in an editorial in *The Irish Times*. It declared that:

> We have gone from the Celtic Tiger to an era of financial fear with the suddenness of a Titanic-style shipwreck, thrown from comfort, even luxury, into a cold sea of uncertainty.

More recently, signs of economic recovery are evident. In the first quarter of 2014, Ireland's unemployment rate was 12.2%, reflecting a steady decline in unemployment (Central Statistics Office, 2014), reaching 11.7% in April 2014. This is the lowest level in nearly five years (Central Statistics Office, 2014). Ireland is still experiencing a budget deficit. *Budget 2014* (Department of Finance, 2013) was characterised by a continuation of public sector cuts and reduced social welfare provision. This was balanced somewhat by a less harsh *Budget 2015* (Department of Finance, 2014).

Significant social change in Ireland (Share *at al*, 2012) is not all about economic change. It also encapsulates a move away from traditional values and norms. The immediate social context in which we make our family decisions is now more fluid and we do not necessarily follow traditional predetermined trajectories. For example, in the 1990s, the Celtic Tiger replaced outward emigration with inward migration and 'high levels of respect for authority gave way to an increasing awareness of corruption in the institutional Church, the economic system and the State' (O'Connor, 2006, p.6). The loosening of the traditional hold of the Catholic Church on morality, state and family life means that there are now more liberal attitudes to sex before marriage (Layte *et al*, 2006). Marriage rates are also increasing (Central Statistics Office, 2013), but marriage is happening later (Jackson, 2011). Fertility rates outside marriage increased steadily in the last few decades (Central Statistics Office, 2013), premarital cohabitation is the fastest-growing family form (Central Statistics Office, 2013), and lesbian, gay, bisexual and transgender families are emerging as the newest family form in Ireland (Central Statistics Office, 2013). We now live in an Ireland where there are a myriad of social opportunities, such as increased female labour force participation and more career paths for men and women (Central Statistics Office, 2014), as well as more educational opportunities (Department of Education and Science, 2006).

Parenting takes place in the midst of this multiplicity of choice and life situations. Do we/I have children? When is a good time to have children? Do we/I go back to work afterwards? Who minds the children? How do we/I want our children reared? How is the home organised/managed? What values are important to us/me in childrearing? What is not important? What other demands are there on my time/expectations of us/me? These self-reflection questions constantly posed by parents are endless. As Giddens puts it:

> What to do? How to act? Who to be? These are focal questions for everyone living in circumstances of late modernity – and ones which, on some level or another, all of us answer, either discursively or through day-to-day social behaviour (1991, p.70).

The reflexive project of the self, therefore, incorporates numerous contextual happenings and forms of mediated experience, through which a course must be charted (Giddens, 1991). It follows that we may not necessarily pass through stringent and clearly-marked stages of the life course, but instead we constantly make choices and negotiate risks surrounding any of the questions referred to at the beginning of this paragraph. How this plays out in parents' lives will be discussed in the next section.

Parenting in Modernity

Self-actualisation, realising one's own identity through personal and social encounters, precisely because tradition and custom no longer guarantee who we are, is a basic condition of modern social life. It is a condition that promotes personal autonomy from socially-embedded expectations and thereby means a break from tradition. Whilst earlier societies with a social order based firmly in tradition would provide individuals with (more or less) clearly defined roles, in post-traditional societies we have to work out our roles for ourselves. Self-actualisation is possible by being authentic and true to oneself. It includes references to other people only within the sphere of intimate relationships – although this sphere is highly important to the self. With modernity has come the emergence of the 'rhetoric of intimacy' (Giddens and Pierson, 1998, p.119), a characteristic of a post-traditional world where emotional communication becomes crucial to the sustaining of relationships inside and outside of family life. In struggling with intimate problems, individuals help actively to reconstruct the universe of social activity around them (Giddens 1991, p.12).

Because we live in a society with increased choice, there is also increased risk. Beck (1992) sees individualisation as fundamental to the development of contemporary society. He also calls this a 'risk society'. In a risk society, the restrictions and restraints of ascribed status and the associated conventional ways of doing things no longer constrain people. There is a 'compulsion to lead your own life and the possibility of doing it' (Beck, 2000, p.165). Underpinning Beck's emerging 'risk' society is reflexive modernisation, a social form involving continuing self-consciousness or self-reflection. There are, therefore, numerous opportunities to self-actualise – 'to become more and more what one is, to become everything that one is capable of becoming' (Maslow, 1943) – but that also means there has to be a balance between opportunity and risk (Giddens, 1991) on an individual level. We no longer have to pass through stringent and clearly-marked stages of the life course, but make choices and negotiate risks. Accepted patterns of behaviour such as meeting, having a relationship, getting engaged and then marrying is no longer the 'only way' for relationships and families to develop. Family life in Ireland has undergone significant change. It is now typified by a variety of family forms, such as cohabiting families, lone parent families, single sex families, blended families, nuclear families and multicultural families (Central Statistics Office, 2013). However, if one is constantly negotiating and re-negotiating risk and decisions about relationship/ family trajectories as parents that heretofore were predetermined and not really flexible, while being aware of the range of options available and all the other social factors that can affect parenting decisions such as the needs of children, household income, employment, career progression, formal education for children and for oneself as a parent, can that not become overwhelming? The lifestyle options made available by modernity offer many opportunities for appropriation, but can also generate feelings of powerlessness (Giddens, 1991). How will this work out? Is this the best decision for my/our children? What is the best way? There seems to be no best way! Help!

With the 'disenchantment of the world' (Weber, 1985) comes a new state of 'inner homelessness', of being all alone in the vastness of the cosmos (Berger *et al*, 1973). If self-actualisation (realising one's own identity through personal and social encounters) is to be achieved, then it seems that we have to find a way to cope with the multiplicity of choice, while maintaining and deriving emotional satisfaction from our personal relationships. It is the process of negotiation and re-negotiation in the face of increased opportunities that can determine the types of parenting choices that we make.

The self forms a trajectory of development from the past to the anticipated future. The individual appropriates his past by sifting through it in the light of what is anticipated for an (organised) future. The trajectory of the self has a coherence that derives from a cognitive awareness of the various phases of the life-span. Any analysis of parenting then must be done with a look back on what has happened to date and what one hopes will happen in the future. As Beck puts it: individuals:

> ... must learn, on pain of permanent disadvantage, to think of themselves as action centres, as planning offices in relation to their own lives, their own capacities, orientations, relationships and so on (Beck, 1992, p.217).

For Beck and Beck-Gernsheim (2002), this means individuals are 'forced into the future' and it would seem that calculative personal relationships are a consequence of this.

> Where everything is uncertain, where old norms and traditions have less and less currency, people want to create commitment, security and reliability in their own domain (that is, in their personal life as a couple). Here at least, they want to make the future calculable (Beck and Beck-Gernsheim 2002, p.50).

In a world of alternative lifestyle options, strategic life planning becomes of special importance. Life planning is a means of preparing a course of future actions mobilised in terms of the self's biography (Giddens, 1991). As parents, this may include engaging with education to secure employment/desired career, securing employment to acquire a mortgage and/or obtaining investment plans for the future education of children.

Is Modernity It?

Post-modernists advocate that we have moved into a new period of development (post-modernism). For Lyon (2013, p.7), the 'inflated characteristics of modernity', which give rise to post-modern premonitions, relate above all to communication and information technologies and the shift towards consumerism. The preponderance of sociological writing on post-modernity places an emphasis on the economic and technological changes that have profoundly impacted the cultural sphere. Castells (1989) for example, sees the emerging post-modern order resting upon the dual pillars of consumerism and information technologies. For Bauman (1992), the developing economic system is not just about consumption *per se,* but a cultural transformation that emphasises choice. Consumer choice, in turn, has become the criterion for much more than shopping. The skills acquired for consumer choice are called upon in different spheres of life including education, health and the family. The cultural notion of 'choice' also has impacted the life course in many important respects. Therefore, it is not surprising that multiple pathways to parenthood have emerged, giving individuals and couples choices and options.

A number of social theorists (Beck, 1992; Giddens, 1991; Lash, 1990) critique the idea that some contemporary societies have moved beyond modernisation as a stage of development. Giddens does not dispute that important changes have occurred, but he says that we have not really gone beyond modernity. He uses a variety of terms such as 'high', 'reflexive' or 'late' modernity (Giddens, 1991) to describe how modernised countries are. These terms are interchangeable. Continued social change in industrialised societies reflects developed, radicalised, 'high', 'reflexive' or 'late' modernity – but it is still modernity. Whatever this stage of modernity is called – 'high', 'reflexive' or 'late' modernity – there is agreement that it is a more advanced form of modernity. Its identifying features, including the re-organisation of time and space, globalisation, and the radicalisation of pre-established institutional traits of modernity, transform the content and nature of day-to-day social life (Giddens, 1991, p.2).

Referring to the issue of modernities and post-modernities, Matthewman and Hoey argue that 'terms of convenience may be disposable, but the issues they stand as proxy for persist' (2006, p.542). This implies that the categorisation of changing social times into stages of modernity is perhaps not as crucial as the observation of the effect of changing social conditions on family patterns and parenting scenarios, as they exist, and are created, in this emerging social order.

Social Structure and/or Human Agency in Parenting

The issue of whether social structure and/or human agency is paramount in decision-making is the subject of perennial sociological debate. Classical social theorists emphasised the importance of social context in all human activity and sought to analyse the characteristics of emergent modern society (King, 2004). Comte's (1798-1857) sociology, for example, seeks to demonstrate the decisive role that the social context plays in all human activity. For Durkheim (1858-1917), social relations are 'sacred'; humans develop a powerful emotional attachment to each other, which binds them together, inspiring them to particular forms of activity. In the course of social interaction, humans mutually transform each other to produce a completely new level of reality. Weber (1864-1920) described sociology as 'a science concerning itself with the interpretive understanding of "social" action' (Weber, 1978, p.4). He specified that 'action is "social" insofar as its subjective meaning takes account of behaviour of others and is thereby oriented in its course' (Weber, 1978, p.4). Marx (1818-1883) argued that humans could never be considered separately from the social relations, in which they existed:

> … for only to social man is nature available as a bond with other men, as the basis of his own existence for others and theirs for him, and as the vital element in human reality (Marx, 1990, p.90).

In classical social theory, therefore, we get a sense of the importance of social relations between humans as being a primary focus of sociology.

Contemporary social theory emerged as a distinctive sub-discipline within sociology in the 1970s to become particularly prominent in the 1980s and 1990s and with it, the focus of sociology changed. Much of the contemporary social theory debate centres on the primacy of social structure or human agency in the reproduction of the social order. Realism, represented most prominently in Britain by Roy Bhaskar and Margaret Archer, has an increasingly important position. From their perspective, society consists of a dual or stratified ontology in which the individual reproduces an already existing social structure. Thus, Archer (1995, p.75) insists that 'it is fully justifiable to refer to structures (being irreducible to individuals or groups) as pre-existing them both'. Bhaskar (1979, p.46) also emphasises that 'there is an ontological hiatus between society and people'. Blau's (1964, p.338) dialectical social theory argues that the social structure is reproduced and transformed by the individual in the process of social exchange: 'structural change, therefore, assumes a dialectical pattern'. Stones (1996) advocates that social theorists must recognise that individuals are reflexive about the objective conditions of their existence, but that these individuals are themselves confronted by certain real structural conditions. This seems to imply that, while individuals can be reflexive about the conditions of their existence, they are restrained however by the structural conditions in which they find themselves, so therefore they do not really have autonomy.

Giddens' (1984) theory of structuration proposes that it is human agency that continuously reproduces social structure. It is a prime example of the ontological dualism of contemporary social theory. He suggests human agency and social structure are in a relationship with each other, and it is the repetition of the acts of individual agents that reproduces the structure. This means that there is a social structure – traditions, institutions, moral codes, and established ways of doing things; but it also means that these change when people start to ignore them, replace them, or reproduce them differently. Certainly we see this in the emergence of premarital cohabitation as the fastest-growing family type and lesbian, gay, bi-sexual and transgender families as the newest family type in Ireland (Central Statistics Office, 2013).

Other theorists such as Luhmann (1995) accept that any social system is comprised of individuals and their actions, but reject the argument that sociological analysis can limit itself merely to human social interaction (Luhmann, 1997, p.47). Decisions are not just the result of macro-sociological forces on an individual, nor are they solely the product of micro-sociological forces, such as individual agency. Luhmann (1997) is concerned ultimately with the dialectic between the social system and the environment in which that system exists. For Callinicos (2004), society consists of structure and agents and the purpose of social theory is to reconcile the two distinct elements. Sztompka's (2008) development of a third sociology perspective is a way of doing that. First sociology is the sociology of 'social wholes – organisms, systems' (Sztompka, 2008, p.25). These organisms and systems determine social life. In comparison, second sociology sees social life as a collection of behaviours and actions (Sztompka, 2008). In reality, we are neither completely determined, nor are we completely free. Third sociology takes as its ultimate 'object of inquiry social events: human action in collective contexts, constrained on the one hand by the agential endowment of participants and on the other hand by structural and cultural environments of action' (Sztompka, 2008, p.25). It looks at the level between structures and actions, where the constraints of structures and dynamics of action produce the real, experienced and observable social events. It is here that we can see the interplay between structural constraints and individual agency and how that plays out in people's lives – the choices they make, how these fulfil their needs, the options people feel are available to them and the ones that should be created, or made available.

However, decisions to engage in different kinds of relationships, whether parenting or not, rebound on the state's policies, the behavioural expectations and the communal networks that are the social contexts and conditions of personal life.

> The transformation of intimacy signals positive changes in personal relationships even at the same time as the changes generate difficulties and problems for people and institutions alike. (Martin, cited in Giddens and Pierson, 1998, p.22)

Some of Jackson's (2011) findings in a study examining premarital cohabitation in Ireland as pathway to marriage can be applied here. Fieldwork for this study comprised of 41 in-depth interviews with cohabiting couples with plans to marry, cohabiting couples with no plans to marry, as well as couples who married without living together first. Fieldwork took place in Athlone in 2007. Respondents also filled in an event history calendar, recording key events in their lives since the age of 16 years. The study employed a life course methodology by analysing the social, structural, person-historic, and individual issues that merge when individuals in a couple engage in a decision to live together and then a decision to marry. Jackson (2011) contended that the social reality of cohabitation in Ireland is not just about the institutional framework and how that facilitates relationship development, neither is it collective individual action in relationship development, which brings about premarital cohabitation as a stage in relationship development. It also is not just about the dialectic between the social system and the environment in which that system exists that creates premarital cohabitation as a new family form in Ireland. Rather, it is *how* an individual experiences and interprets social events, in the context of their own personal history, and their current relationship, that determines whether a couple will live together or not before marriage, and whether they will marry or not in that relationship. Therefore, it is the relationship between structural constraints *and* individual agency, how that plays out in individual lives, and how individuals interpret them, that determine a couple's relationship trajectory, and the decisions they will make in the evolving social order in which we live. Similarly, it could be inferred that the social reality of parenting in Ireland is not just about the institutional framework and how that facilitates pathways to parenting and parenting opportunities, neither is it collective individual action in relationship development, which brings about new parenting scenarios. It also not just about the dialectic between the social system and the environment in which that system exists that creates alternative parenting opportunities. Rather, it is *how* an individual experiences and interprets social events, in the context of their own personal history, as well as those of their significant others and children that determine what their parenting experience for them and their family unit will be. Again, it is the relationship between structural constraints *and* individual agency, how that plays out in individual lives, and how individuals interpret them, that determine how new parenting opportunities develop in our evolving social world.

Conclusion

In this chapter, I discussed modernity as the pervading social context in which we all live our lives. The current debates on the role of social structure and/or human agency in decision-making and how as parents we create ourselves and frame our decision-making also were reviewed. The relationship between structural constraints *and* individual agency, how that plays out in individual lives, and how individuals interpret them, was put forward as a way of determining how new parenting opportunities develop. This chapter provided some sociological observations on the changing social environment and how that affects parenting in Ireland. In so doing, it provides a social context for the chapters in **Part 2** of this book that will specifically examine parenting expression and challenges in new and emerging family forms in Ireland.

References

Archer, M. (1995). *Realist Social Theory: The Morphogenetic Approach*, Cambridge: Cambridge University Press.

Bauman, Z. (1992). *Intimations of Post-modernity*, London: Routledge Kegan Paul.

Beck, U. (1992). *Risk Society: Towards a New Modernity*, London: Sage.

Beck, U. (2000). 'Living Your Own Life in a Runaway World: Individualisation, Globalisation and Politics' in Hutton, W. and Giddens, A. (eds.), *On the Edge: Living with Global Capitalism*, London: Jonathan Cape.

Beck, U. and Beck-Gernsheim, E. (2002). *Re-inventing the Family: In Search of New Lifestyles*, Oxford: Wiley-Blackwell.

Berger, P., Berger, B. and Kellner, H. (1973). *The Homeless Mind: Modernization and Consciousness*, New York: Vintage.

Bhaskar, R. (1979). *The Possibility of Naturalism*, Brighton: Harvester Press.

Blau, P. (1964). *Exchange and Power in Social Life*, New York: Wiley and Sons.

Callinicos, A. (2004). *Making History: Agency, Structure, and Change in Social Theory*, Köln: Brill.

Caplow, T. (1998). 'Trends and Contexts: The Principle of Singularity' in Sasaki, M. (ed.), *Values and Attitudes Across Nations and Time: International Studies in Sociology and Social Anthropology, Vol.69*, Köln: Brill.

Castells, M. (1989). *The Informational City: Information Technology, Economic Restructuring, and the Urban-Regional Process*, Oxford: Basil Blackwell.

Central Statistics Office (2005). *Construction and Housing in Ireland*, Dublin: Government Publications.

Central Statistics Office (2013). *Vital Statistics, Quarter 1*, Dublin: Government Publications.

Central Statistics Office (2014). *Quarterly National Household Survey, Quarter 1, 2014*, Dublin: Government Publications.

Collard, J. and Mansfield, P. (1991). 'The Couple: A Sociological Perspective' in Hooper, D. and Dryden, W. (eds.), *Couple Therapy*, Milton Keynes: Open University.

Department of Education and Science (2006). *Education Trends: Key Indicators on Education in Ireland and Europe*, retrieved 1 July 2014 from www.education.ie/admin/servlet/blobservlet/des_educ_trends_chapter08.htm#hd08_10.

Department of Finance (2013). *Budget 2014*, Dublin: Government Publications.

Department of Finance. (2014). *Budget 2015*, Dublin: Government Publications.

Eyerman, R. (1992). 'Modernity and Social Movements' in Haferkamp, H. and Smelser, N. (eds.), *Social Change and Modernity*, Berkeley: University of California Press.

Giddens, A. (1984). *The Constitution of Society: Outline of the Theory of Structuration*, Cambridge: Polity Press.

Giddens, A. (1991). *Modernity and Self Identity: Self and Society in the Late Modern Age*, Cambridge: Polity Press.

Giddens, A. and Pierson, C. (1998). *Conversations with Anthony Giddens*, Cambridge: Polity Press.

Jackson, A. (2011). *Premarital Cohabitation as a Pathway into Marriage: An Investigation into How Premarital Cohabitation is Transforming the Institution of Marriage in Ireland: Athlone as a Case Study*, PhD in Social Science (Sociology), Maynooth University, Ireland.

King, A. (2004). 'Structure and Agency' in King, A., *The Structure of Social Theory*, London: Routledge, retrieved 14 June 2014 from www.eric.exeter.ac.uk/exeter/bitstream/10036/69294/2/AfterStructCh1.pdf.

Lash, S. (1990). *The Sociology of Post-modernism*, London: Routledge.

Layte, R., McGee, H., Quail, A., Rundle, K., Cousins, G., Donnelly, C., Mulcahy, F. and Conroy, R. (2006). *The Irish Study of Sexual Health and Relationships*, Dublin: Crisis Pregnancy Agency and the Department of Health and Children.

Luhmann, N. (1995). *Social Systems*, Stanford, CA: Stanford University Press.

Luhmann, N. (1997). *Die Gesellschaft der Gesellschaft*, Frankfurt: Suhrkamp.

Lyon, D. (2013). *Jesus in Disneyland: Religion in Postmodern Times*, Oxford: Polity Press.

Marx, K. (1990). *Capital: A Critique of Political Economy*, London: Penguin Books.

Maslow, H. (1943). 'A Theory of Human Motivation', *Psychological Review*, Vol.50, No.4, pp.370-96.

Matthewman, S. and Hoey, D. (2006). 'What Happened to Post-modernism?', *Sociology*, Vol.40, No.3, pp.529-47.

Mills, C.W. (1959). *The Sociological Imagination*, London: Oxford University Press.

O'Connor, P. (2006). 'Private Troubles, Public Issues: The Irish Sociological Imagination', *Irish Journal of Sociology*, Vol.15, No.2, pp.5-22.

Schmidt, V. (2006). 'Multiple Modernities or Varieties of Modernity', *Current Sociology*,Vol.54, No.1, pp.77-97.

Share, P., Corcoran, M. and Conway, B. (2012). *A Sociology of Ireland*, Dublin: Gill and Macmillan.

Stones, R. (1996). *Sociological Reasoning: Towards a Past-Modern Sociology*, Basingstoke: Palgrave Macmillan.

Strath, B. (2004). 'Nordic Modernity: Origins, Trajectories and Prospects', *Thesis Eleven*, Vol.77, pp.5-19.

Sztompka, P. (2008). 'The Focus on Everyday Life: A New Turn in Sociology', *European Review*, Vol.16, No.1, pp.23-37.

The Irish Times (2009). 'No time for whingers', Editorial, 1 January, retrieved 3 July 2013 from www.irishtimes.com/newspaper/opinion/2009/0103/1230842387565.html.

Weber, M. (1978). *Economy and Society*, Berkeley: University of California.

Weber, M. (1985). *The Protestant Ethic and the Spirit of Capitalism*, London: Unwin Paperbacks.

2: Out with the Old, In with the New: Changing Family Patterns in Ireland

Ashling Jackson

> *There is more to a boy than what his mother sees. There is more to a boy than what his father dreams. Inside every boy lies a heart that beats. And sometimes it screams, refusing to take defeat. And sometimes his father's dreams aren't big enough, and sometimes his mother's vision isn't long enough. And sometimes the boy has to dream his own dreams and break through the clouds with his own sunbeams.* (Behunin, 2009)

Introduction

The family is a changing social institution (Heffernan, 2005). The sociological concept of 'institution' refers to relatively stable normative patterns of individual behaviour. It implies 'the existence of agencies that regulate behaviour as well as models of normality that function as background expectations for such regulations' (Leisering and Schumann, 2003, p.193). If the family is a changing social institution, then we can expect that normative patterns of individual behaviour exist, but that these can change periodically. In this chapter, I will use the following well-documented changes to family life in Ireland: changing marriage patterns, trends in fertility outside marriage and the emergence of premarital cohabitation as a new family form as a lens through which to appreciate the depth of change to fundamental aspects of family life in Irish society. These are a particularly effective way to do this as the *Irish Constitution* defines the family as 'founded on the institution of marriage' (Government of Ireland, 1937, Article 41). The All-Party Oireachtas Committee on the Constitution in 2006 decided against changing this definition. Implied here is that marriage precedes living together, having children, becoming and being parents. Vital statistics from the first quarter of 2013 show that people now live together before marriage, they marry later, rates of fertility outside the institution of marriage are at an historic high, and people will avail of a divorce if a married relationship no longer meets their expectations for whatever reason (Central Statistics Office, 2013a). Although no constitutional change was recommended by the All-Party Oireachtas Committee on the Constitution in 2006, it appears that, for a growing number of people, the Irish family is no longer 'founded on the institution of marriage' (Government of Ireland, 1937, Article 41). From a parenting perspective, this is very important. We now have a different social environment for family development, which means that numerous parenting opportunities have emerged and are emerging in Irish society.

Ireland as the Late Starter

'Two demographic trends, known as demographic transitions' (Heffernan, 2005, p.2) capture trends in marriage and family formation patterns. These demographic changes occurred in Western Europe and the United States during the 19th and 20th centuries. The first demographic transition was characterised by large declines in mortality and fertility (van de Kaa, 1987). By the 1930s, the industrialised world had reached the last stages of this first demographic transition that began around the 1870s, from high birth rates and high death rates to a pattern of low birth and death rates (Kennedy, 2001, p.3). At the time of Irish Independence in 1922, Britain was the most industrialised country in Europe, while Ireland was predominantly an agrarian society, in which the small farm provided the economic base for a majority of families. Marriage and family formation were synonymous in Ireland. Marriage rates in Ireland were especially low in the 1930s in Ireland, when over half of the 30 to 34 year olds in Ireland and 27% of the 50 to 54 year olds were single (Fahey and Layte, 2007, p.167). Fahey and Layte (2007, p.168) emphasise that, in the 1930s, when the marriage rate dropped in Ireland, the average age at marriage was 33 years for men and 28 years for women. So not only were marriage rates historically low in the 1930s in Ireland, people also were older when marrying. Indeed, whether marriage took place or not, or at a later stage in peoples' lives, often was interpreted as a reaction to economic conditions (Guinnane, 1997). Other Western countries experienced a surge in marriage rates in the 1950s, as did Ireland, but not on the same scale.

Lesthaeghe and van de Kaa (1986) and Lesthaeghe (1995) propose that the mid-1960s marked the beginning of a second demographic transition in

Europe, because of the large-scale family changes that subsequently occurred. This second demographic transition comprised several elements:

- The transition from the 'golden age of marriage' to the 'dawn of cohabitation';
- The transition from the child as the main element of a family to the couple as the main element;
- The transition from 'preventative contraception' (to avoid third and fourth children) to 'self-fulfilling conception' (whenever conception is desirable) (Raley, 2001, p.60).

Each of these transitions also happened in Ireland, but slightly later than the rest of Europe. Heffernan (2005) argues that the Republic of Ireland for much of the 20th century had been struggling to complete the initial demographic phase, even though the rest of Europe had completed, or was in the process of completing, the second demographic transition. The characteristics that marked family life until the 1960s in Ireland – low marriage rates combined with high fertility of those who did marry, together with a high incidence of permanent bachelorhood and spinsterhood – marked Irish demography as unique (Government of Ireland, 1956; Coleman, 1992). Relationship development typically followed the pattern of couple meet, engagement, marriage, post-marital cohabitation and children. Emigration, late marriages and the form of morality advocated by the Catholic Church controlled family formation patterns. However, while the distinctiveness of family patterns in Ireland meant that Ireland at one point was categorised as 'a special case' (Ardagh, 1995, p.1), as we will see below, Ireland is now better described as a 'late starter' (Kennedy, 2001, p.3).

Changing Marriage Patterns in Ireland

Ireland has experienced very rapid economic, social and cultural change, in recent decades (O'Connor, 2006; Fahey and Layte, 2007; Share *et al*, 2012). The year 1958 was 'one of the most significant milestones in the evolution of Irish society. A turning point in the nature and rule of the Irish state' (Breen *et al*, 1990, p.1). It was the year in which the *First Programme for Economic Expansion* was published (Department of Finance, 1958), signifying direct government intervention in the economy and the creation of a job market in Ireland to stem the increasing rates of emigration from Ireland. It opened the economy to foreign investment, committed the state to free trade and began a process of offering generous incentive packages of capital grants and tax concessions to foreign industry to locate in Ireland. Education and employment opportunities improved in Ireland, especially employment in the industries that had been targeted by the Industrial Development Authority, such as pharmaceuticals and chemicals. By 1979, the *Financial Times* described Ireland as the 'miracle economy' of Europe (cited in Lee, 1989, p.154).

The marriage rate peaked in Ireland in 1974, with the 'highest annual figure, of 22,833 recorded' (Central Statistics Office, 2006a, p.76). At this time, the age at marriage was younger (just over 26 years of age for men and 24 years of age for women) (Fahey and Layte, 2007, p.168), compared to previous decades. However, by the mid-1980s, Ireland was in a recession and high outward migration characterised this period until the mid-1990s. The number of marriages subsequently fell from 21,792 in 1980 to 18,174 in 1989 and the trend continued downward until the mid-1990s (Central Statistics Office, 2007a, p.1). In the 1980s, the most dramatic decrease in marriage rates was in the 25 to 29 year age group (55.8% to 18.5%) (Central Statistics Office, 2007a, p.1). This is markedly different to the 1930s, for example, which saw an overall low marriage rate and an older age at first marriage. In the 1980s, we start to see the beginning of marriage postponement, rather than the start of a marriage abandonment trend.

Postponement of marriage is evident in Ireland since 1996. Interestingly though, it also has been accompanied by an increase in the marriage rate. Almost half (49%) of females marrying for the first time were aged 30 or over, compared with 44% and 28% in 2002 and 1996 respectively. Almost two-thirds of males marrying for the first time (64%) were aged 30 or over in 2005 compared with 59% in 2002 and 42% in 1996 (Central Statistics Office, 2005, p.1). 'This is probably best interpreted as a consequence of catch-up among those who deferred marriage during the 1980s and early 1990s and then crowded into marriage from the mid-1990s onward' (Fahey and Layte, 2007, p.168). The catch-up achieved was not complete, since it did not prevent the proportion of those single among those aged in their 20s and early 30s, which had started to rise in the early 1980s, to continue to rise throughout the 1990s. However, between 2002 and 2005, the increase in single-hood began to slow down and among those aged over 35 actually turned into a decline (Central Statistics Office, 2008). This highlights that marriage is occurring, but is happening later (early 30s) rather than sooner (mid-20s), for couples in Ireland.

Overall, during the 1990s, the marriage rate fluctuated in Ireland, but has been rising steadily since 2000 (Central Statistics Office, 2007a). However, with the revised description of Ireland as a first world industrial economy (Allen, 1997, 2000; Kirby, 1997, 2002), and the unprecedented economic growth in the years of the Celtic Tiger (1990s to 2001/2002, continuing intermittently to 2008), it is also interesting to note that, during this time, marriage rates overall increased, as they did during the good economic times of the 1970s. In 2007, the number of marriages in Ireland was 22,544 (Central Statistics Office, 2007a, p.1). While Fahey and Layte (2007, p.168) argue 'the rise in marriage rates followed hard on the heels of the economic boom and makes it hard to avoid the conclusion that the latter was a major cause of the former' (Fahey and Layte, 2007, p.168), the economic boom is not the only cause. Divorce, for example, was introduced into Ireland in 1997, which meant that marriages registered after that year could include second marriages (where at least one of the spouses had been married previously). Therefore, some of the increase in marriages is a result of the now available option to marry again. Divorce also has an effect on the rising rates of premarital cohabitation, where people may choose to live with a new partner, rather than re-marrying. The *Census of Ireland 2011* shows a continuation of this trend – the married population increased by 9.2% between 2006 and 2011, growing from 1,565,016 to 1,708,604 (Central Statistics Office, 2012a).

The implications of all these changes on family life are significant. They are significant because marriage is no longer a defining characteristic of family life. It is also no longer a socially acceptable prerequisite for parenting. We will see this in the increase in fertility outside of marriage, as well as the emergence of premarital cohabitation as a new family type.

Trends in Fertility Outside Marriage

Marriage traditionally facilitated sexual activity and childbearing. However, sexual activity before marriage is now customary. Between 1980 and the end of the 1990s, non-marital births as a proportion of all births increased six-fold, rising from 5% in 1980 to 31% in 2000 (Fahey and Layte, 2007, p.169). Hannan and Ó Riain (1993) in the 1990s showed that non-marital fertility was associated with early school-leaving and poor employment prospects among young mothers and young fathers. Since 2000, the surge in non-marital births has levelled out at between 31% and 32% (Central Statistics Office, 2008, p.4). However, statistics published in 2013 by the Central Statistics Office document an increase to 36.5% (Central Statistics Office, 2013b, p.4). Some of the reasons for this reflect more general trends.

Following a peak rate of births in Ireland in 1980 (74,064) (Central Statistics Office, 2007b, p.1), a decline set in that continued until 1994, when births decreased to 48,255 for that year (Central Statistics Office, 2008, p.14). Then a recovery occurred, and by 2004, annual births had risen to almost 62,000, an increase of 26% since 1994 (Central Statistics Office, 2007b, p.1). The *Central Statistics Office (Ireland) Vital Statistics Report 2013 (Quarter 1)* indicates an annual birth rate of 15.3 per 1,000 of the population (Central Statistics Office, 2013a). The increase in Ireland was due in part, to an expansion of the numbers of women of child-bearing age, which in turn 'reflected the maturation of the large baby boom generation of the 1970s' (Fahey and Layte, 2007, p.162).

Along with changing migration patterns, the average age of women at first birth also has been increasing (to 30.2 years) and there were a greater number at that age in 2011 (Central Statistics Office, 2013a). This is higher than the average age of first-time mothers in 1998 (27.1 years) (Central Statistics Office, 2007c, p.1).

Premarital Cohabitation – An International Perspective

'Since the 1970s, alternative pathways to marriage and alternative forms of partnering have become more accepted' (Penman, 2005, p.34). Many sociologists and demographers who foresee a continuation of the upward trend in alternative family forms (Smock, 2000) have documented the growth of premarital cohabitation in industrialised societies. Premarital cohabitation is a relatively new phenomenon in Ireland. It is defined here as living together as a couple, without being married, at a shared address. Until recently, relationships went through very clear stages of development. Boyfriend/girlfriend was the first stage, followed by engagement, marriage, living together, setting up home, having children and becoming parents. Now, that is not necessarily the case. Increasingly, couples live together before marriage, while some couples continue to live together without marrying. As children are very often part of this cohabiting family unit, parenting also takes place within this emerging family environment.

Popenoe (2008, p.2), when comparing couples cohabiting as a percentage of all couples, shows that the highest rate of premarital cohabitation in Europe is in the Nordic countries, such as Sweden at 28.4%, followed by Denmark at 24.4% and Canada at 18.4%. In the Nordic countries, premarital cohabitation has emerged as an alternative to marriage, rather than a precursor, amongst a substantial proportion of the population. Many Northern and Western European countries seem to be following the Swedish and Danish patterns of rising premarital cohabitation (Prinz, 1995). In the United States, the proportion of all first unions that started as premarital cohabitation rose from 46% for unions formed between 1980 and 1984 to almost 60% for those formed between 1990 and 1994 (Bumpass and Lu, 2000). The number of cohabiting couples almost tripled between 1977 and 1994 (Casper and Cohen, 2000). For Seltzer (2000), approval of premarital cohabitation in the US is also likely to increase in the future, as younger cohorts who are supportive of premarital cohabitation experience replace the older ones. Studies of British respondents suggest a similar tendency (Seltzer, 2000; Barlow *et al*, 2005).

Ermisch and Francesconi (2000), using data from the *British Household Panel Survey* collected during the last quarter of 1992, completed histories of all spells of marriage and premarital cohabitation from a representative sample of 9,459 adults aged 16 years and over throughout Great Britain. The study focused on people born since 1930. They found that co-habitation has become a much more important route into first partnership. By their 24th birthday, more than two-fifths of the women in the most recent cohort (1963 to 1976) had entered premarital cohabitation, compared with a fifth of the previous cohort. The proportion of women who went directly into marriage fell from 54% to 21%. Similarly, in Australia, 75% of all partners married in 2003 had cohabited before marriage (Australian Bureau of Statistics, 2004). This dropped to 61% in 2006 (Healey, 2010). Some reasons suggested for this are the trend towards partnering at a later age, and the increased financial and social independence of women, as well as legal changes in recent decades in Australia that have improved access to divorce (Healey, 2010).

Emerging Cohabitation Patterns in Ireland

According to the *Census of Ireland 2011*, cohabiting couples with or without children were the fastest-growing type of family unit (Central Statistics Office, 2012a). Cohabiting couples represented 11.6% of all family units in Ireland in 2006 (Central Statistics Office, 2006b, p.1). By 2011, this had increased by a further 18% (Central Statistics Office, 2012b). The number of children living with cohabiting parents increased from 51,700 in 2002 to 74,500 four years later (Central Statistics Office, 2006b). The majority of cohabiting couples without children (81.7%) were unions in which both partners were single, while in a further 5% of cases, both partners were either separated or divorced (Central Statistics Office, 2006b). Given that divorce was legalised in Ireland in 1997, this is not surprising. Over the 15 years since 1996, the proportion of the population aged 15 years and over who were divorced grew significantly from 0.4% in 1996 (9,787 people) to 2.4% (87,770) in 2011 – an increase of almost 800% over the period (Central Statistics Office, 2012b). It may be the case that marriage deferral, rather than 'marriage avoidance' (Fahey and Layte, 2007, p.169), is a more appropriate description of what has been happening in the Irish context.

Halpin and O'Donoghue (2004, p.6), in their analysis of *Labour Force Survey* data and *European Community Household Panel Survey* data, conclude that premarital cohabitation is becoming more frequent in Ireland. When they analysed 238 distinct relationship histories in the *Irish European Community Household Panel Survey* data, they found that, for four out of every five relationships, where premarital cohabitation was a feature of that relationship, marriage followed premarital cohabitation. Premarital cohabitation in Ireland tends to be a feature of younger cohorts and has a much shorter duration than marriage (Halpin and O'Donoghue, 2004). Premarital cohabitation 'is most often a temporary arrangement found mainly among young urban adults that either dissolves after a relatively short period or leads on to marriage' (Fahey and Layte, 2007, p.169). The fact that marriage is still occurring, indeed even rising in Irish society, gives credence to the view that marriage is still an important part of a relationship development (Jackson, 2011), but so too is premarital cohabitation. With it, new parenting opportunities are emerging in society.

Premarital Cohabitation and Parenting

Premarital cohabitation has emerged as an optional pathway in relationship development and may or may not include parenting experiences. Halpin and O'Donoghue (2004) emphasised that cohabiting couples are far more likely than married couples to be childless, though less likely than the never-married. Of the 17,958 births recorded in *Census 2011*, 6,164 (34%) were registered as outside marriage/civil partnership. Of these, 3,449 births (19%) were to unmarried parents with the same address (Central Statistics Office, 2012b, p.1).

According to Reed (2006), there was a close relationship between pregnancy and premarital cohabitation for couples. Reed used a sub-sample of 44 couples who were cohabiting around the time of their child's birth, from the *Time, Love and Cash in Couples with Children Study*, a qualitative, longitudinal, intensive interview study of 48 unmarried and 26 married couples who had a child together in 2000. This study is itself a sub-sample of the *Fragile Families and Child Well-being Study*, which investigates non-marital births in the urban United States. Although all the couples surveyed were living together around the time of their child's birth, a substantial majority (73%) began their premarital cohabitation experience with a 'shotgun' cohabitation, moving in during their first pregnancy together, or just after the child's birth. For them, premarital cohabitation was not a relationship decision, but instead a response to pregnancy. A study by Gibson-Davis *et al* (2005), exploring barriers to marriage among unmarried parents, provides an important context for the present analysis. Similar to Reed (2006), their sample draws from the 2000 *Time, Love and Cash in Couples with Children Study*. Although Gibson-Davis *et al* (2005) do not limit their sample to cohabiting couples, about three-quarters of their unmarried parents are cohabitees, making the samples quite similar. On the basis of interviews conducted shortly after their child's birth, Gibson-Davis *et al* found unmarried parents have a high regard for marriage and would like to marry, yet feel they need to overcome financial obstacles and reach a high level of relationship quality first. Fear of divorce also emerged as an additional barrier to marriage. The authors (Gibson-Davis *et al*, 2005) also note that unmarried parents view premarital cohabitation as a test for marriage and that children do not feature in their parents' discussions about marriage.

There are, however, mixed views on this. These are discussed in the next section.

The Influence of Children on Cohabiting Relationships

Raley (2001), using data from the 1987-1988 *National Survey of Families and Households* and the 1995 *National Survey of Family Growth* for the US, shows that most of the growth in the proportion of births to those cohabiting is the result of increases in the proportion of women cohabiting, rather than changes in union formation behaviours surrounding pregnancies. Therefore, premarital cohabitation occurs in its own right and is not just a reactive response to pregnancy.

Porter *et al* (2004) found that the actual or anticipated effects of children on a cohabiting relationship are different for parent and non-parent couples who are cohabiting. Non-parents tend to see cohabiting relationships as a space for developing and testing their relationships before marrying and having children. In contrast, those who already have biological or stepchildren acknowledge that a pregnancy may speed up the marriage process for them, but few think they should marry simply because children are involved in the relationship (Porter *et al*, 2004).

Unmarried parents usually disapprove of 'shotgun' marriages (Edin *et al,* 2003).

Recent research (Jackson, 2011) in Ireland investigating how premarital cohabitation is transforming the institution of marriage in Ireland confirmed that, although there are various pathways to marriage in the current, fluid social environment in which we live, the institution of marriage was still highly normatively valued for respondents in this study. Based on a sample of 41 in-depth interviews in 2007, as well as detailed event history calendar analysis with cohabiting couples with plans to marry, cohabiting couples with no plans to marry, as well as couples who married without living together first, the study yielded an unexpected finding – that parents often feel a pressure or obligation to marry from their children. This can be fuelled simply by children asking when their parents will marry and/or asking them to marry. While Jackson (2011) emphasised that the emotional needs of the couple are crucial in relationship decision-making and a decision to marry will only come about if it is *also* a positive decision for children, children can actively encourage a relationship to move from one stage to the next. Therefore, rather than being passive in relationship development, children can be instrumental to it. In this, we can see children as being 'active, creative social agents who produce their own unique children's cultures while simultaneously contributing to the production of adult societies' (Cosaro, 2005, p. 3).

Responsive Social Policy Development

As referred to previously, premarital cohabitation, while recognised by the institutional framework in Ireland, is not recognised in the *Constitution.* The *Civil Partnership and Certain Rights and Obligations of Cohabitants Act, 2010,* passed by the Oireachtas in July 2010, allows same-sex couples to register their civil partnership. It also provides cohabiting couples with succession rights, protection of a home that couples share, plus maintenance rights in the event of a separation. On registration, civil partners have the same entitlements to social welfare as a married couple. Social policy provision has always been a 'grey' area for cohabiting couples, with cohabiting couples not receiving recognition in the same way as married couples. The Minister for Justice, Dermot Ahern, described the *Civil Partnership and Certain Rights and Obligations of Cohabitants Act, 2010* as 'one of the most important pieces of civil rights legislation to be enacted since Independence. This Act provides enhanced rights and protections for many thousands of Irish men and women. Ireland will be a better place for its enactment' (cited in Taylor, 2010, p.1).

The *Civil Partnership and Certain Rights and Obligations of Cohabitants Act, 2010* formally endorses the range of relationship trajectories and types of relationships occurring in Irish society now and facilitates them. The institutional framework in Ireland supports premarital cohabitation as a viable relationship trajectory, but *still* places a higher value on marriage, so much so that marriage remains enshrined in the Irish *Constitution* as being integral to family life. However, social change as provided for by legislative reform is itself a response to collective individual behaviour change. Developments in the field of life course research suggest that, to produce social change, an innovative individual has to depart from the norm, substituting constructive alternative patterns. In the process, they must exercise their own agency in the face of powerful social forces that otherwise would reproduce the existing social order (Giele and Holst, 2004). While a person's own agency has serious implications in the context of social structure, the power of human agency itself is a reflection of the social order in which it occurs. This was explored in the previous chapter, *A Quiet Revolution: Modernity, Social Change and New Parenting Opportunities*, where the influence of the social structure and our own agency (individual decision-making abilities and capacity) was considered in determining parenting outcomes. Suffice it to mention here that traditional societies are characterised by pre-determined relationship patterns, whereas modern/post-traditional societies emphasise the importance of human agency through the effort of individuals to take control in a world of choice.

Conclusion

At the beginning of this chapter, I referred to the sociological concept of 'institution' as meaning relatively stable normative patterns of individual behaviour. I also stated that this implies 'the existence of agencies that regulate behaviour as well as models of normality that function as background expectations for such regulations' (Leisering and Schumann, 2003, p.193). If the family is a changing social institution, then we can expect that normative patterns of individual behaviour exist, but that these can change periodically. In this chapter, we see numerous examples of how this has happened. The family is no longer merely a production unit, facilitating reproduction, providing care for its dependent members, where there may or may not be emotional satisfaction for those involved, especially the parents. Now, we have flexible family formation trends that *potentially* accommodate the needs of all, depending on life situation and lifestyle preferences. 'Potentially' is a key word here, because, of course, in reality, this does not occur in all family units. However, we now have a social situation where family formation preferences and, as a result, parenting preferences are likely to be more fluid. The essential point, therefore, is that there is now social potential for this to occur in Ireland and it is increasingly becoming an expected normative pattern in relationship and family development processes.

References

Allen K. (1997). *Fianna Fáil and Irish Labour: 1926 to the Present*, London: Pluto Press.

Allen, K. (2000). *The Celtic Tiger: The Myth of Social Partnership in Ireland*, Manchester: Manchester University Press.

Ardagh, J. (1995). *Ireland and the Irish: Portrait of a Changing Society*, Harmondsworth: Penguin.

Australian Bureau of Statistics (2004). *Marriages Australia*, Catalogue No. 3306.0.55.001, Canberra: Australian Bureau of Statistics.

Barlow, A., Duncan, S., James, G. and Park, A. (2005). *Cohabitation, Marriage and The Law*, Oregon: Hart Publishing.

Behunin, B. (2009). *Remembering Isaac: The Wise and Joyful Potter of Niederbipp*, Salt Lake City, UT: Abendmahl Press.

Breen, R., Hannan, D.F., Rottman, D.B. and Whelan, C.T. (1990). *Understanding Contemporary Ireland: State, Class and Development in the Republic of Ireland*, Dublin: Gill and Macmillan.

Bumpass, L.L., and Lu, H. (2000). 'Trends in Cohabitation and Implications for Children's Family Contexts in the US', *Population Studies*, Vol.54, pp.29-41.

Casper, L.M. and Cohen, P.N. (2000). 'How does POSSLQ Measure Up? New Historical Estimates of Cohabitation', *Demography*, Vol.37, pp.237-45.

Central Statistics Office (2005). *Vital Statistics: Marriages Report for 2005*, retrieved 20 June 2014 from www.cso.ie/statistics/bthsdthsmarriages.htm.

Central Statistics Office (2006a). *Statistical Yearbook of Ireland, 2006*, Dublin: Government Publications.

Central Statistics Office (2006b). *Census 2006, Vol. 3: Household Composition and Family Units and Fertility*, Dublin: Government Publications.

Central Statistics Office (2007a). *Marriages 2005*, retrieved 15 June 2014 from www.cso.ie/releasespublications/documents/vitalstats/current/marriages.pdf.

Central Statistics Office (2007b). *Principal Statistics*, retrieved 10 July 2014 from www.cso.ie/statistics/bthsdthsmarriages.htm.

Central Statistics Office (2007c). *Vital Statistics, Quarter 1 2007: Births, Deaths and Marriages in Quarter 1 2007: Average Age of First-Time Mothers Continues to Rise*, press release, retrieved 25 June 2014 from http://www.cso.ie/newsevents/pressrelease_vitalstatisticsquarter12007.htm.

Central Statistics Office (2008). *Vital Statistics, Quarter 2, 2007*, Dublin: Government Publications.

Central Statistics Office (2012a). *Census 2011 Results, Profile 5 Households and Families – Living Arrangements in Ireland*, press release, retrieved 15 July 2014 from www.cso.ie/en/newsandevents/pressreleases/2012pressreleases/pressreleasecensus2011profile5householdsandfamilies/.

Central Statistics Office (2012b). *Census 2011 Results, Profile 5 Households and Families – Living Arrangements in Ireland*, Dublin: Government Publications.

Central Statistics Office (2013a). *Vital Statistics, Quarter 1, 2013*, Dublin: Government Publications.

Central Statistics Office (2013b). *Marriages and Civil Partnerships 2011*, press release, retrieved 10 July from www.cso.ie/en/newsandevents/pressreleases/2013pressreleases/pressreleasemarriagesandcivilpartnerships2011/.

Coleman, D.A. (1992). 'The Demographic Transition in Ireland in International Context', in Goldthorpe, J.H. and Whelan, C.T. (eds.), *The Development of Industrial Society in Ireland*, Oxford: Oxford University Press.

Cosaro, W. (2005). *The Sociology of Childhood*, second edition, Thousand Oaks, CA: Pine Forge Press.

Department of Finance (1958). *First Programme for Economic Expansion*, Dublin: Government Publications.

Edin, K., England, P. and Linnenberg, K. (2003). 'Love and Distrust Among Unmarried Parents', paper presented at the *National Poverty Center Conference on Marriage and Family Formation Among Low-Income Couples*, September, Washington, D.C.

Ermisch, J. and Francesconi, M. (2000). 'Cohabitation in Great Britain: Not for Long But Here to Stay', *Journal of the Royal Statistical Society – Series A*, Vol.63, No.2, pp.153-71.

Fahey, T. and Layte, R. (2007). 'Family and Sexuality' in Fahey, T., Russell, H. and Whelan, C.T. (eds.), *Best of Times? The Social Impact of the Celtic Tiger*, Dublin: Institute of Public Administration.

Gibson-Davis, C., Edin, K. and McLanahan, S. (2005). 'High Hopes but Even Higher Expectations: The Retreat from Marriage among Low-Income Couples', *Journal of Marriage and the Family*, Vol.67, pp.1301-12.

Giele, J.Z. and Holst, E. (eds.). (2004). *Advances in Life Course Research, Vol.8: Changing Life Patterns in Western Industrial Societies*, Amsterdam: Elsevier Science.

Government of Ireland (1937). *Constitution of Ireland (Bunreacht na hÉireann)*, retrieved 6 May 2014 from www.taoiseach.gov.ie/attached_files/Pdf%20files/Constitution%20of%20IrelandNov2004.pdf.

Government of Ireland (1956). *Reports of the Commission on Emigration and Other Population Problems 1948-1954*, Dublin: Government Publications.

Guinnane, T. (1997). *The Vanishing Irish: Households, Migration, and the Rural Economy in Ireland, 1850-1914*, Princeton: Princeton University Press.

Halpin, B. and O'Donoghue, C. (2004). 'Cohabitation in Ireland: Evidence from Survey Data', *SAI Annual Conference*, Athlone, 23 April.

Hannan, D. and Ó Riain, S. (1993). *Pathways to Adulthood in Ireland: Causes and Consequences of Success and Failure in Transitions amongst Irish Youth*, Dublin: Economic and Social Research Institute.

Healey, J. (2010). *Issues in Society, Vol.304: Marriage and Cohabitation*, Thirroul, NSW: The Spinney Press.

Heffernan, C. (2005). 'Gender, Cohabitation and Marital Dissolution: Are Changes in Irish Family Composition Typical of European Countries?', *IRISS Working Paper Series*, No.2005-03.

Jackson, A. (2011). *Premarital Cohabitation as a Pathway into Marriage: An Investigation into How Premarital Cohabitation is Transforming the Institution of Marriage in Ireland: Athlone as a Case Study*, PhD in Social Science (Sociology), Maynooth University, Ireland.

Kennedy, F. (2001). *Cottage to Crèche: Family Change in Ireland*, Dublin: Institute of Public Administration.

Kirby, P. (1997). *Poverty amid Plenty: World and Irish Development Reconsidered*, Dublin: Gill and Macmillan / Trócaire.

Kirby, P. (2002). *The Celtic Tiger in Distress: Growth with Inequality in Ireland*, Basingstoke: Palgrave.

Lee, J. (1989). *Ireland, 1912-1985: Politics and Society*, Cambridge: Cambridge University Press.

Leisering, L. and Schumann, K.F. (2003). 'How Institutions Shape the German Life Course' in Heinz, W.R. and Marshall, V.W. (eds.), *Social Dynamics of the Life Course: Transitions, Institutions, and Interrelations*, Berlin: Aldine De Gruyter.

Lesthaeghe, R. (1995). 'The Second Demographic Transition in Western Countries: An Interpretation' in Mason, K.O. and Jensen, A.M. (eds.), *Gender and Family Change in Industrialised Countries*, Oxford: Clarendon Press.

Lesthaeghe, R. and van da Kaa, D.J. (1986). 'Twee Demografische Transities' in Lesthaeghe, R. and van da Kaa, D.J. (eds.), *Groie of Krimp?, Beokuitgave Mens en Maatschappij*, Deventer: Van Loghum Slaterus.

O'Connor, P. (2006). 'Private Troubles, Public Issues: The Irish Sociological Imagination', *Irish Journal of Sociology*, Vol.15, No.2, pp.5-22.

Penman, R. (2005). 'Current Approaches to Marriage and Relationship Research in the United States and Australia', *Family Matters*, No.70.

Popenoe, D. (2008). *Cohabitation, Marriage and Well-being: A Cross-National Perspective*, New Brunswick, NJ: Rutgers University, National Marriage Project.

Porter, M.J., Manning, W.D. and Smock, P.J. (2004). 'Cohabitors' Prerequisites for Marriage: Individual, Relationship and Sociocultural Influences', Working Paper No.2004-09, Bowling Green, OH: Bowling Green State University, Center for Family and Demographic Research.

Prinz, C. (1995). *Cohabiting, Married, or Single: Portraying, Analyzing, and Modeling New Living Arrangements in the Changing Societies of Europe*, Aldershot: Avebury.

Raley, R. (2001). 'Increasing Fertility in Cohabiting Unions: Evidence for the Second Demographic Transition in the United States', *Demography*, Vol.38, No.1, pp.59-66.

Reed, J. (2006). 'Not Crossing the "Extra Line": How Cohabitors with Children View Their Unions', *Journal of Marriage and Family*, Vol.68 (December), pp.1117-31.

Seltzer, J. (2000). 'Families Formed Outside of Marriage', *Journal of Marriage and the Family*, Vol.62, pp.1247-68.

Share, P., Corcoran, M. and Conway, B. (2012). *A Sociology of Ireland*, Dublin: Gill and Macmillan.

Smock, P.J. (2000). 'Cohabitation in the United States: An Appraisal of Research Themes, Findings and Implications', *Annual Review of Sociology*, Vol.26, pp.1-20.

Taylor, C. (2010). 'Civil Partnership Bill Signed into Law', *The Irish Times*, 19 July.
van de Kaa, D. (1987). 'Europe's Second Demographic Transition', *Population Bulletin*, Vol.42 (March), pp.1-57.

3: The Value of Parenting

Colm O'Doherty

Nothing is more flexible, contingent, ever-changing, particular or beyond control than a proper rewarding human relationship. Relationships which are mapped, dissected, analysed and shaped according to standard patterns rarely exhibit that emotional warmth that we require. (Stears, 2012)

Introduction

This chapter identifies parenting as a relationship activity that generates well-being and significant social return on investment.

Social progress depends on successful financing and investment in social reproduction. Parents meet the psychological and financial costs involved in raising the next generation. Employers and taxpayers are the beneficiaries of parental services that create and sustain human capital. While economists often see education as the defining investment in human capital, it is important to point out that, if parents do not create and nurture children, schools have no function and employers have no staff to hire. Parents, communities and taxpayers invest in children and the costs and benefits of these investments affect the economic system as a whole. The benefits of spending directly or indirectly on children can be measured precisely in terms of improved educational outcomes, reduced social expenditure on social problems, such as crime and drugs, and enhanced productivity. Benefits that can accrue from investment in education include improved citizenship, enhanced parenting and earning abilities. Benefits that accrue from 'democratic and responsible parenting' are vast and can only be fully understood from differing perspectives that acknowledge the centrality of relationships. A narrow focus on measuring parenting outcomes and the acquisition of parenting skills runs the risk of neglecting the importance and intrinsic worth of human relationships.

POLICY AND PARENTING

Overview

Historically, in Ireland, children's needs and interests have been concealed within the private sphere of the family and, as a result, to a large degree, they have been invisible in the policy process.

Policy provision has been skewed by the familisation of children and an ambivalent relationship between the state and the family. The familisation of children has meant that policies that are directed towards meeting the needs of families take precedence over policies that directly respond to children's needs. Furthermore, familisation assumes that the interests of children are best served by social policies that are focused on the broader needs of the family. Based on the assumption that children's best interests are indistinguishable from their family's best interests, the 1937 *Constitution* favoured the rights of parents over children (Government of Ireland, 1937). This imbalance between the rights of children and parents has been reduced by the recent successful children's rights amendment to the *Constitution*. Some progress has been made on separating the needs and interests of children from the needs and interests of parents. However, the relationship between the state and the family continues to be influenced by the differing political and ideological views held by successive governments. Strains and tensions evident in the relationship between the state and the family have crystallised around issues of child protection and welfare. Underpinning these tensions and strains is the fundamental issue of whether children are recognised as social assets or private concerns.

Figure 3.1: Children – Social Assets/Private Concerns

Children are Social Assets	Children are Private Concerns
Every young person has a gift, talent, knowledge or skill ready to be given, contributed or marketed now. Every community is in need of these capacities if it is to be a healthy place to live (McKnight, 2010, p.75).	Parents anxious about their children's happiness, health, achievements, or personal development are encouraged by today's risk-averse parenting culture to see other parents (and their children) as a threat as well as a potential source of solidarity (Bristow, 2014, p.123).

Emerging Issues

Increased labour force participation has also skewed social provision – this time in the direction of defamilisation policies. The employment rate for women in Ireland was 60.3% in 2007, compared with 45.9% in 1997.

Following the economic crash, the female employment rate dropped back to 55.2% in 2012 but has risen over the past two years to stand at 55.9% in 2014 (Central Statistics Office, 2014). Core parenting has been left to professional and public providers in order to facilitate labour market activation policies. Recent changes to the One Parent Family Payment mean that recipients with children over a particular age threshold – currently seven – must transfer to Jobseeker's Allowance and be actively seeking work to qualify for a benefit (see **Chapter 10** for details). Defamilisation policies reflect the low value of parenting and the high value attached to labour market activation in modern Ireland. The creeping commodification of care-giving is associated with a life course-transforming trend that is widely supported across the EU.

> According to Esping-Andersen, many women today hesitate to have children until they have secured a stable job. Flexible and precarious employment and high female unemployment have become major impediments to motherhood. But even women with more stable careers find it increasingly difficult to reconcile work with family life. In Southern Europe, this has led to a huge drop in fertility and a rise in childlessness, in particular among well-educated women in Italy and Spain, exacerbating the dynamic of demographic aging (Hemerijck, 2013, p.64).

While Ireland may have the highest birth rate of any EU country at 15.6 births per 1,000 population, compared to the EU average of 10.4 per 1,000, figures released by the Economic and Social Research Institute (*The Irish Times*, 2013a) pointed to a declining birth rate as an indication that childbearing is being postponed during the economic downturn (also see UNICEF, 2014).

Irish social policy also has been affected by processes of incremental but transformative change with far-reaching consequences for parenting. The relationship between familisation and welfare policies that existed from the beginning of the Irish state until the 1980s has been thrown off balance by internal societal challenges and the feminisation of the labour market. The rise of 'maternal breadwinning', where working wives and partners earn as much or more than their male partners and single mothers provide the sole income for their family has contributed to the decline of the male breadwinner model of welfare, associated with the key social risk of job loss. Recent research evidence makes it clear that maternal breadwinning stands at 30% in the UK (Institute for Public Policy Research, 2013) and 41.4% in the US (Glynn, 2012). Across comparable European welfare regimes, the 'new social risks' attached to changing family formation, divorce, gender equality, career, and family reconciliation have impacted primarily on young people and young families. A narrow social investment agenda, which views public policy as a key provider for labour markets, has been actively pursued in Ireland in the critical policy arena of childcare. Viewed through a social investment policy lens, the position of children and families until recently has been seen as a resource for the state – human capital – rather than as future citizens.

> The 'social investment state' entails a movement away from traditional welfare policies towards policies built on investment in social and human capital. In this welfare strategy, children are central to future economic success; they are the citizen-workers of the future. In the 'social investment state' children are valued for the adults they will become and policies are explicitly targeted towards ensuring that their potential is developed to ensure the economic prosperity of the country in the future in order to maintain national economic prosperity in a competitive global market. Therefore, childhood and the development of healthy and educated/skilled children are too important for the economic future of the country to be left solely in the hands of parents. (Ridge, 2012)

Childcare provision has been developed as a service for working family members in general and, in particular, as a means to encourage mothers back into the labour market. Ireland's first Minister for Children, Frances Fitzgerald, made it clear that she intended to 'shift the focus of childcare from being a support for women in the workforce, to what it is doing for the child' (*The Irish Times*, 2013b). At the heart of this debate is a fundamental question as to how the state perceives children. Should children be viewed as private or public goods? Viewed as a private good, children are primarily seen through a family policy lens. When children are recognised as public goods, they are more directly engaged as entitled citizens in the co-production of state services.

In truth, because they are both 'beings' (children in childhood) and 'becomings' (future adults and citizen workers), a balanced approach to their care, education and training is required. As Ridge argues:

> … too strong a focus on children as future adults is unbalanced without an equal concern for the well-being of children in childhood, and the quality of their social lives and opportunities for self-realisation (Ridge, 2012).

Future Policy

The national policy framework for children and young people – *Better Outcomes, Brighter Futures* (Department of Children and Youth Affairs, 2014) – asserts the importance of supporting children and young people 'to realise their maximum potential now and in the future' (p.20). Outlined in the document are transformational goals that will deliver five national outcomes for children and young people.

Figure 3.2: *Better Outcomes, Brighter Futures* Policy Framework

Transformational Goals	Better Outcomes
Support parents Earlier intervention and prevention Listen to and involve children and young people Ensure quality services Strengthen transitions Cross-Government and interagency collaboration and co-ordination	Active and healthy Achieving In all areas of learning and development Safe and protected from harm Economic security and opportunity Connected, respected and contributing

Within the new 'joined up' policy domain represented in the framework, explicit goals are predicated on evidence-based claims that the state should invest in children and young people.

> Investment in children and young people is a social responsibility and it makes good economic sense, but it needs to be guided by a medium to long-term perspective. Investment in children and young people is akin to a capital investment from which significant returns flow. Hence the focus in this Policy Framework on an agreed and enduring set of outcomes to guide decisions and monitor progress. (Department of Children and Youth Affairs, 2014, p.3)

A balanced policy focus requires child-centred social investment that recognises the financial benefits of supporting parents but is not determined solely by economic considerations.

From Well-becoming to Well-being

Children know normal better than anyone. (Ford, 2012)

It is impossible to place a value on parenting unless we are clear about the kind of people we want our children to grow into. Desired 'outcomes' for children and young people have been conceptualised as indicators that enable measurement of different dimensions of child well-being. Much has been written about child well-being in recent times: what it is and how can it be achieved. Internationally, well-being approaches have become associated with a new understanding of how best to support the optimal development of children and adolescents – see **Table 3.1**.

> This new conceptual approach is explicitly strengths-based, focusing on cultivating children's assets, positive relationships, beliefs, morals, behaviours, and capacities to give children the resources they need to grow successfully across the life course. There has been a shift from an adult perspective on child well-being to a child perspective, with broad acceptance for children's subjective perspectives on their own well-being and for children as reporters as a preferred method of assessing their well-being. (Ben-Arieh, 2008)

A well-being approach to child welfare policy-making poses challenges for the Irish state's longstanding policy orientation of overvaluing the labour market's claim on childhood and regarding it as principally a source of human capital. However, an observable trend, since the publication of the *National Children's Strategy* (Department of Health and Children, 2000), has been the foregrounding of child well-being as a policy concern in its own right rather than within the context of family and parental rights or obligations and labour activation strategies.

There is increasing recognition, across diverse states, that the true measure of a nation's standing is how it values its children and how it attends to their well-being (UNICEF, 2007). In Ireland, the employment of a well-being framework, which acknowledges the multi-dimensional nature of children's lives, to inform new service delivery structures, is strong evidence of the state adopting more child-centred social investment strategies. These strategies have found expression in the Children's Services Committees established since 2007.

Children's Services Committees (now re-titled Children and Young People's Services Committees) have developed and been influenced by three major government policy documents: *The National Children's Strategy* (Department of Health and Children, 2000), the 10-year Social Partnership Agreement *Towards 2016* (Department of the Taoiseach, 2006) and *The Agenda for Children's Services: A Policy Handbook* (Department of Health and Children, 2007).

This policy push for the development of new local policy and practice structures capable of co-ordinating and integrating services for children originates from an understanding of child well-being that reflects the multi-dimensional nature of children's lives. Child well-being, within this policy framework, is generally represented by how children are doing in a number of different domains of their life. The 'whole child' perspective of the *National Children's Strategy* in turn is derived from the holistic view of the child encapsulated in the *Convention on the Rights of the Child* (United Nations, 1989). Thus, the current Irish policy position, which recognises the agency of children and their capacity to influence their own lives and to form positive relationships while being supported by their families, their communities and formal supports and services, is underpinned by the *Convention on the Rights of the Child* (United Nations, 1989). A set of 42 national indicators was developed and is published every two years in the *State of the Nation's Children* reports (Office of the Minister for Children, 2006; Office for the Minister for Children and Youth Affairs 2008, 2010). These indicators were developed by drawing on existing research in the area (Brooks and Hanafin, 2005), on the expertise of multiple stakeholders and the input of children themselves on what they consider important in their lives (Nic Gabhainn and Sixsmith, 2005) – see **Table 3.1**.

In the UK, a research report from the University of Central London Institute of Health Equity – *An Equal Start: Improving Outcomes in Children's Centres* (University of Central London, 2012) – developed an outcomes framework for Children's Centres to help inform their activities and priorities. The priority outcomes identified in the report are evidence-based and informed by the views of a steering group comprised of highly-skilled academics, government representatives, practitioners and commissioners. The research also was discussed with parents. Building on a previous policy document that articulated a vision for Children's Centres, which encompassed working with the most disadvantaged families in order to reduce inequalities in child development, the outcomes framework proposed in *An Equal Start* prioritises three areas: children's health and development; parenting; and parent's lives.

Once the welfare and safety of children is assured, Children's Centres should focus on specific areas and work towards achieving key outcomes associated with child development and parenting. Children develop well when cognition, communication and language, social and emotional development and physical health are secured through a dynamic interaction with their parents and a dynamic interaction between parents and their environment.

> Dynamic interaction between parent and child, and in particular the type of home communication and learning environment that parents establish and nurture for their children from birth, is critical. Parenting must also generate attachment between parents and their

> children. Children's Centres can offer a range of interventions and opportunities to support parents to improve their own approaches and skills based on an understanding of what is most important. There are particular factors that sit outside the immediate parent-child relationship but exert powerful influence over parenting. Parent's health, social networks, financial resources and knowledge about parenting collectively act as enablers or barriers to nurturing their children's development. (University of Central London, 2012)

International efforts to assess and monitor children's well-being have developed rapidly over the past 25 years. The International Society for Child Indicators (www.childindicators.org) has a membership drawn from many countries and walks of life, including academicians, researchers, government officials, data collectors, policy-makers, child advocates, data users, funders, practitioners and journalists. Its primary goal is to contribute to improving the well-being of the world's children. The Society held an inaugural conference in the USA in June 2007 and launched its *Child Indicators Research* journal in June 2008.

Frameworks for assessment of child well-being have now become a significant and accepted part of the political and policy landscape in many countries. While there is no doubt that such frameworks are evidence of positive ambitions for children, it is important to note that, for most children, the achievement of desired outcomes expressed in them is heavily dependent on their parenting experiences and the tangible measures provided by the state to assist carers in their role as parents. Support for parenting and parent's lives is therefore particularly important in improving early-years experiences and later-life chances. Parenting against the headwinds of social inequality and personal difficulties is particularly challenging. Parents' capacity to be positive parents is challenged if they have limited or inadequate incomes, lack networks of support and do not experience mental well-being.

Table 3.1: Frameworks for Assessment of Child Well-being

Child Well-being Indices	Indicators	Domains
Child Well-being Index (US)	28	Material well-being Health Safety / behavioural concerns Productive activity (educational attainment) Place in community (participation in schooling or work institutions) Social relationships (family, peers) Emotional / spirit well-being
Every Child Matters Index (UK)	25	Be healthy Stay safe Enjoy and achieve Make a positive contribution Achieve economic well-being
Multi-National Project for Monitoring and Measuring Children's Well-being	50	Safety and physical status Personal life Civic life Children's economic resources and contributions Children's activities
State of the Nation's Children Reports (Ireland)	42	Socio-demographics Children's relationships Children's outcomes (education outcomes; health outcomes; and social, emotional and behavioural outcomes) Formal and informal supports
Australia's Children: Their Health and Well-being (Australia)	78	Demographics Mortality, morbidity, disability and burden of disease Maternal, perinatal and infant conditions Vaccine-preventable and other communicable diseases Chronic diseases Oral health Injury Risk and preventive factors Health services
UNICEF (comparisons across OECD countries)	21	Material well-being Health and safety Education Peer and family relationships Subjective well-being Behaviour and risk

Source: O'Doherty *et al* (2012).

THE VALUE OF PARENTING FOR CHILDREN

> Relationships are central to child well-being and are highly valued by children themselves. Positive indicators of relationships include eating and talking together with family members, and having friends and pets. Risks to good relationships and well-being include living in disruptive and conflicted families, in poor families, living in care, having burdensome caring responsibilities, spending a lot of time outside the home in the evenings and contact through electronic media substituting for personal social interaction. (National Economic and Social Council, 2009)

There is an extensive research literature on parent-child relationships and their long-term outcomes for children and young people. It is not my intention, in the context of this chapter, to attempt to do justice to this vast research literature on parent-child relationships and their importance for children's development. It is, however, appropriate to present some of the research evidence that provides theoretical and practical justification for programmes and services directed towards improving outcomes for children and young people through support for their parents. Utting (2009), building on the work of Moran *et al* (2004), identified seven relationship arenas that influence critical outcomes for children and young people. Positive outcomes can be encouraged and poorer ones avoided by delivery at the frontline of programmes supporting parental activity and behaviours that are socially valued.

Positive parental well-being lies at the heart of child well-being. Positive parental well-being creates parent-child relationships that offer protection against generalised risk factors such as poverty and community crime. Children also can be exposed to risk factors at an individual level such as having a disability, at family level such as a parent or parent(s) with mental health difficulties or at neighbourhood level such as living without community facilities/amenities. Positive well-being and resilience lies at the heart of parenting. Adult well-being or happiness is driven by a variety of factors across three domains:

- **Self:** The way people feel about their own lives;
- **Support:** The quality of social supports and networks within the community;
- **Structures and systems:** The strength of the infrastructure and environment to support people to achieve their aspirations and live a good life (Mguni and Bacon, 2010, p.7).

Table 3.2: Relationship Arenas

Relationship Arenas	Critical Outcomes Linked to these Arenas
1. Learning and educational attainment	Parental involvement in children's learning, both in the home and the school, is associated with achievement (O'Connor and Scott, 2007; Barrett, 2006).
2. Social skills	The presence or absence of bonds of attachment between children and their parents during infancy and early childhood has been linked by a number of studies to the quality of later friendships and relationships (O'Connor and Scott, 2007; Barrett, 2006).
3. Self-efficacy and self- worth	There is evidence that the way children view themselves, from an early age, is associated with attachment and the quality of parenting they receive (Toth *et al*, 2000).
4. 'Externalised' behaviour problems and criminality	Prospective longitudinal research in Britain, the United States and other Western countries – following children's development from an early age – has shown that poor parent-child relationships are consistently associated with aggressive 'externalising' behaviour and an increased risk that young people will become involved in crime and other anti-social activities, including substance misuse (Utting *et al*, 1993; Rutter *et al*, 1998; Anderson *et al*, 2005; Farrington and Welsh, 2007).
5. 'Internalised' problems, including depression	Large-scale population studies, as well as clinical and child development research, has consistently demonstrated an association between the quality of parent-child relationships and depression, anxiety and other 'internalised' problems where physical symptoms are related to emotional stress and social withdrawal (Dadds *et al*, 1996; Garber *et al*, 1998; Wood *et al*, 2003).
6. Risky health behaviours and poor physical health	Affectionate, authoritative relationships with parents who hold clear expectations concerning tobacco, alcohol and drug misuse are protective for children and young people (Green *et al*, 1990).
7. Adolescent brain development	Where it was once thought that the brain was fully developed by early adolescence, it is now increasingly understood that improved cognitive skills, as well as typical teen 'problems' like mood swings, rebelliousness and risk-taking behaviour, relate to biochemical and structural changes in the brain. The latest indications that the adolescent brain is less developed and more malleable than once assumed place additional emphasis on the nurturing role of parents in supporting the development of cognitive and other skills (Blakemore and Choudhury, 2006; Kuhn, 2006).

Adapted from Utting (2009).

Resilience and well-being are closely connected. Resilient individuals are capable of bouncing back and flourishing in the face of adversity or risk. Resilient communities also are influenced by the interaction of these three domains. Social capital – relationships of trust and reciprocity with family, friends, neighbours, colleagues and the wider community – support the ability to bounce back or withstand adversity. Some practical resources, such as good transport links and availability of key educational and welfare service, also contribute to a resilient community. Sites and opportunities for meaningful engagement – community buildings and organisations – also are important, as they facilitate collective action and generate trust amongst community members.

The Value of Parenting for Society

Poor parenting contributes to social breakdown. One of the key findings of Power and Barnes' (2011) research into crime and community safety in certain communities in Limerick city was the identification by residents of the corrosive effects of poor parenting on the social fabric:

> The issue of poor parenting united the residents across all of the estates. These concerns centre around the growth in the numbers of young parents who are disengaged from the community, disengaged from work, and who are seen as either unable or unwilling to discipline and educate their children. Residents clearly see a cyclical process of neglect and the subsequent impact it has on their communities (2011, p.74).

Poor parenting contributes to child abuse and neglect (Halpenny, 2012; Skehill, 2008; Munro, 2012).

> The association between parental problems, such as poor mental health, domestic violence and substance misuse, and abuse and neglect is well-established. (Munro, 2012)

Communitarians (Etzioni, 1994) and social capitalists (Putnam, 2000) present a strong case for the decline in community being linked to a parenting deficit.

Cherti and McNeil's research (2012) alerts us to the importance of everyday activities, such as parenting, in advancing social integration amongst diverse populations.

The New Economics Foundation and Action for Children, in its research report, *Backing the Future: Why Investing in Children is Good for Us All* (2009), calculated the economic and social costs of failing to address preventable social problems across 16 European countries. The report benchmarked the financial cost of negative outcomes where parents facing adverse circumstances or lacking the support they needed were unable to prevent their children becoming exposed to unemployment, crime, teenage pregnancies, substance misuse, mental health problems, family breakdown, inequality and child abuse.

Table 3.3: The Cost of Social Problems Relating to Poor Parenting across 16 Countries

Countries	Costs in £bn
Finland	44.55
Denmark	84.94
Sweden	88.54
Austria	90.97
The Netherlands	97.24
Spain	98.70
France	108.11
Norway	107.03
Belgium	101.80
Germany	110.41
Ireland	116.07
Luxembourg	118.33
Greece	121.29
Portugal	118.16
Italy	118.87
United Kingdom	161.31

Source: New Economics Foundation and Action for Children (2009).

Furlong *et al* (2012), in their review of the effectiveness of behavioural and cognitive-behavioural group-based parenting programmes, found that they achieved good results at a cost of approximately $2,500 (£1,712 or €2,217) per family. These are modest costs when compared with the long-term social, educational and legal costs associated with childhood conduct problems.

Better Outcomes, Better Futures (Department of Children and Youth Affairs, 2014) asserts that:

> The case for investing in children and young people on both social and economic grounds is supported by a body of international evidence, across a range of policy areas, using a variety of evaluation methods and spanning different policy interventions (p.16).

Examples of financial and social returns accruing from investment are listed:

- Each euro (€1) spent on early years programmes gives a greater return on investment than the same spending on schooling (OECD, 2012);
- An American study found that society is better off by $7 for every $1 invested in preschool (Reynolds *et al*, 2002);
- Across OECD countries, one year in preschool significantly improved reading outcomes for children (OECD, 2013);
- Good quality early years services can activate social gains and benefits, including better health, reduced likelihood of engagement in risky behaviours and stronger civic and social engagement (OECD, 2012);
- In Ireland, for every €1 invested in youth work, there is a €2.20 return (Indecon, 2012);
- In Ireland, for every €1 invested in universal early years services, there is a €7 return (National Economic and Social Forum, 2005);
- For every €1 invested in the Headstrong Jigsaw model of Youth Mental Health services, there is a €3 return (Headstrong, 2013).

On a cautionary note, McKeown *et al*'s research study (2014) of child outcomes in preschool found that the state-funded free preschool year, introduced in 2010, is not narrowing the gap in outcomes for children from different social classes. The preschool year – which costs about €165 million a year and is availed of by 65,000 children – was seen as an investment in the early years that would improve overall child incomes, especially for disadvantaged children. McKeown *et al*'s research study found that socio-economic background is a major influence on children's participation within the early years services being provided under the free preschool year scheme:

> A robust finding of the study is that socially-generated disparities between children observed at the beginning of the year tend to be maintained over the course of that year. In fact, what happens to a child before the Free Preschool Year has a much greater influence on the distribution of skills at the end of that year compared to what happens during that year (2014, p.*xiii*).

The implications of this finding are that the state's economic investment in the early years services in its current form does not have the capacity to narrow or eliminate developmental gaps between children from different socio-economic backgrounds. The existing free preschool year is ineffective because:

- It is not a multi-year programme;
- It does not meet the same standards of quality found in landmark studies of effective preschool programmes;
- Additional support services for vulnerable families are not a routine part of the programme (McKeown *et al*, 2014, p.10).

Green and Hayes (2014) also are critical of the lack of progress in implementing a quality-improvement agenda in early childhood care and education services.

The Value of Parenting for Parents

> Families are, ideally at least, communities, and conversely the idea of community is analysed as 'family writ large'. (Frazer, 1999)

Parenting in this sense is about increasing well-being through membership of an intimate community. Members are offered unconditional solidarity, respect and care in the face of individualised responsibility for their own fate and the fate of the state.

> Left increasingly to their own resources and acumen, individuals are expected to devise individual solutions to socially generated problems, and to do it individually, using their own individual skills and individually possessed assets. Such an expectation sets individuals in mutual competition, and renders communal solidarity (except in the form of temporary alliances of convenience: that is of human bonds tied together and untied on demand and with 'no strings attached') to be perceived as by and large irrelevant, if not downright counterproductive. (Bauman, 2011, p.17)

Parents are responsible for bringing another being into the world and, ideally, parents should have a long-term commitment to each other as well as to the welfare of the child (Layard and Dunn, 2009, p.28). Pursuit of goals that benefit immediate family and others in the community leads to higher levels of well-being than pursuit of the goals of career advancement and material gain (Headley, 2007). However, traditional parenting – a task-oriented activity delivered on behalf of the state and/or a religious doctrine – often was regarded as a duty rather than an opportunity for promoting collective well-being and social cohesion. Traditional parenting took place within a narrow and idealised two-adult nuclear family framework that imposed certain socialisation responsibilities on the two adults. Irish society is gradually adjusting to an understanding of parenting as a gift relationship (Titmuss, 1971) that embraces difference and diversity. Kessler makes the case for community parenting as a transformative force for social cohesion and individual fulfilment:

> Today's families are characterised by increased fluidity, a loosening of the state's hold on family life, and the delegation of caregiving tasks to individuals and institutions outside the formal, legal family (Kessler, 2007, p.1).

Community parenting operates as an effective source of civic cohesion when families look outwards as well as inwards. The story of modern parenting is one of healthy proliferation. Children's well-being can be entrusted to socially-integrated married or unmarried heterosexual adults, married or unmarried gay adults, lone parents and multiple parents. When family relations are part of the wider fabric of life, parenting provides adults with a rewarding social dividend.

It must be acknowledged that the value of parenting for many parents is unquestionably diminished by the financial burden they are required to bear in current recessionary times. Material costs of parenting in Ireland have been documented by the Vincentian Partnership for Social Justice (MacMahon *et al*, 2012).

Figure 3.3: The Cost of Parenting (per week)

Age/Life-stage of Child	Location: Rural	Location: Urban
Baby	At home €92.98 In childcare €260.31	At home €91.13 In childcare €296.13
Preschool	At home €50.03 In childcare €183.44	At home €48.29 In childcare €223.87
Primary school	At home €83.04 In childcare €134.72	At home €78.66 In childcare €130.30
Secondary school	At home €140.20	At home €144.92

According to this report, the costs associated with parenting in recessionary times are not adequately covered by state income supports (MacMahon *et al*, 2012). Reductions in universal income supports such as child benefit will transfer further the costs of parenting from the state to hard-pressed individuals. 'Households with two children have spending needs that are, on average, 40% higher than comparable families without children' (UNICEF, 2014).

THE VALUE OF SERVICES

There are a number of different ways that parenting support services can be focused, structured, organised and delivered. One of the most widely-used typologies for classifying operational levels of parenting support is the Hardiker *et al* (1991) model for preventive child care practice:

- Level one services are intended to promote health and well-being, prevent negative outcomes and often will equate with universal services being offered to any parent(s) within a defined geographical area;
- Level two services seek to prevent problems escalating and often are targeted at individual parents or all families living in a disadvantaged neighbourhood. Programme interventions, delivered on a group or one-to-one basis, are more intensive than universal services;
- Level three services are a response to problems that are categorised as severe and where children and parents are deemed to be at risk of highly undesirable outcomes. These services are often intensive and focused on crisis situations;
- Level four services are intended to stabilise chronic family behaviours and commonly require targeted services to be sustained at a high level of intensity.

A number of parenting support services operate at just one of these levels, while other interventions are designed to operate at several levels of intensity, with different components building on the same basic approach. In addition to Irish programmes, there is a growing range of interventions that originated in the US, the UK and Australia now being offered in Ireland.

While there is undoubtedly a value in parenting support being delivered in different contexts, at varying levels of intensity and at different stages in children and young people's development, the downside of such a scattergun approach to service delivery is that widespread variations in the quality and availability of support occur. Whether parents can access support in their locality is arbitrarily dependent on the commitments and choices of different service providers in different sectors with different agendas. Programmes currently are being delivered by the Health Service Executive, family resource centres, schools and private individuals and organisations.

Table 3.4: Parenting Programmes Operating in Ireland

Programme	Age of Child	Mode of delivery	Hardiker Level
Community Mothers	0-2	Individual parent	1/2
Homestart	0-5	Individual parent	1
Triple P	0-18	Group of parents	1/2/3/4
Incredible Years	2-12	Group of parents	1/2
Strengthening Families	12-15	Group of parents and Children	1/2
Expressive Play and Parenting Support	0-18	Group of parents	1/2/3/4
Preparing for Life	0-5	Individual parent	1/2
Growing Child Parenting Programme	0-5	Individual parent	1
Parenting UR Teen	11-18	Group of parents	1

There is clearly a need for a unified, universal service delivery approach to be mainstreamed across the entire state. The advent of a new national structure for the delivery of child and family services represents an opportunity to mainstream parenting support programmes as a core well-being activity of the state. The Minister for Children and Youth Affairs established a Task Force to assist her Department in the work of preparing for the establishment of the Child and Family Support Agency on a statutory basis in early 2013. A new approach offering a collaborative environment was proposed for the Child and Family Support Agency (Department of Children and Youth Affairs, 2012). In its work with children of school and preschool age, the new agency is charged with working closely with the early childhood care and education sector, as well as primary and secondary schools. Rogers *et al* (2008), in their research into the relationship between parenting programmes and schools in the UK, found that headteachers and teachers were generally unaware of parents' attendance and participation in support programmes.

The new agency, Tusla, is in a unique position to offer a progressive alignment between parent support programmes and educational activities in schools. Sneddon and Owens (2012), in their review of parenting programmes, conclude that interagency partnership and collaboration may reduce unnecessary duplication of services and also facilitate greater involvement and participation from all of the key stakeholders.

The Task Force Report, in outlining the scope, function and vision for the new agency, recognised that :

- The role of specific professionals or services place them in a unique position *vis-à-vis* prevention and early intervention for children and families, which is strongly aligned to the mission and vision of the Agency;
- Some services operate in a universal setting, which positions them as part of a critical interagency interface (in particular schools and primary care teams / networks);
- Because of the 'universal' aspects of some services. they provide a non-stigmatising 'face' for the new agency, casting it as an organisation that supports and assists parents in their parenting role. These services have the potential to assist the Agency in providing earlier, more accessible and responsive interventions'
- The Agency should **provide services to and support families at all levels along a continuum** from children in need to children in the care of the state. The Hardiker model is an internationally-recognised model for understanding the needs of children within a population. The model must recognise that children have universal needs but they may migrate to higher levels of needs / response and the need for ongoing family support and further preventive measures continues. Clarity on the scope for supportive services, respective roles of family support and child protection, and the critical thresholds for escalation to higher levels of intervention / protection are essential to keep the correct balance and ensure the right responses for children and families on an individual basis (Department of Children and Youth Affairs, 2012, p.*x*, *xii*).

Universal parenting support programmes will offer egalitarian provision that is appealing and non-stigmatising to all parents across all social boundaries. A universal service delivery model stresses social unity rather than divergence and is relatively free from disincentives. It is important to point out that utilisation of universal services can still be highly selective, in that certain groups within the 'universe' may use the services more or less than other groups. The direct parenting support services provided by the new agency can be aligned with private or not-for-profit 'interface services' in a defined and mutually accountable framework.

The Value of Childhood

> If generations have defining moments, this is certainly one of them. (UNICEF, 2014)

Children's well-being has declined in many countries since the beginning of the economic recession in 2008. Their well-being has been compromised by the impact of the crisis on their parents' employment and the depleted capacity of states to protect families. Across a range of indicators, parents in Ireland have been hit harder by the recession than in many other EU countries (UNICEF, 2014). Between 2008 and 2012, the child poverty rate in Ireland has increased significantly: from 18.0% in 2008 to 28.6% in 2012 (UNICEF, 2014). Austerity measures imposed since the economic crash have cost Irish parents the equivalent of 10 years of income progress (UNICEF, 2014). According to UNICEF, this 'great leap backward' for Irish childhood might not have been so pronounced if the Irish state had stronger social protection policies for families in place before the economic crash. According to UNICEF (2014), Irish policy choices made since the beginning of the recession have weighed heavily on children and parents – trapping many of them in a cycle of poverty:

> '… children rarely manage to sidestep the stress and suffering of parents enduring unemployment or a significant reduction in income. They experience downturns in family fortunes in both subtle and painfully evident ways' (p.15).

Conclusion

This chapter has established that investing in parenting support is good for society, for children and for parents. In short, it is good for everyone. However, despite the fact that the family is regarded as a basic institution of the state, parenting as an activity only becomes an issue when it is deemed to be dysfunctional or problematic. This orthodox thinking is reflected in the unsystematic organisation and availability of parenting support services. Parenting is neither a problem to be solved nor a source of raw material for the labour market. The focus should be on supporting **all** parents and enriching family relationships. At present, many parents feel under siege and, in their everyday lives, feel like they are in conflict with both the market and state bureaucracy. Better parenting support will produce better outcomes for children, parents, communities and wider society. Tusla, the new Child and Family Agency, can become the hub for programmes co-producing generalised well-being through collaboration between the state or service providers and citizen parents.

In an uncertain future, children must be treated as ends not means, because if they are treated as ends then they will become the means to a more hopeful future.

References

Anderson, B., Beinart, S., Farrington, D., Longman, J., Sturgis, P. and Utting, D. (2005). *Risk and Protective Factors*, London: Youth Justice Board.

Barrett, H. (2006). *Attachment and the Perils of Parenting: A Commentary and a Critique*, London: National Family and Parenting Institute.

Bauman, Z. (2011). *Collateral Damage: Social Inequalities in a Global Age*, Cambridge: Polity Press.

Ben-Arieh, A. (2008). 'The Child Indicators Movement: Past, Present and Future', *Child Indicators Research*, Vol.1, No.1, pp.3-16.

Blakemore, S-J. and Choudry, S. (2006). 'Brain Development during Puberty: State of the Science', *Developmental Science*, Vol.9, pp.11-14.

Bowers, A., Strelitz, J., Allen, J. and Donkin, A. (2012). *An Equal Start: Improving Outcomes in Children's Centres: An Evidence Review*, London: University of Central London Institute of Health Equity.

Bristow, J. (2014). 'Who Cares for Children? The Problem of Intergenerational Contact' in Lee, E., Bristow, J., Faircloth, C. and Macvarish, J. (eds.), *Parenting Culture Studies*, Basingstoke: Palgrave Macmillan.

Brooks, A.M. and Hanafin, S. (2005). *The Development of a National Set of Child Well-being Indicators*, Dublin: National Children's Office.

Central Statistics Office (2014). *Women and Men in Ireland 2013*, press release, July.

Cherti, M. and McNeil, C. (2012). *Rethinking Integration*, London: Institute for Public Policy Research.

Dadds, M.R., Barrett, P.M., Rapee, R.M. and Ryan, S. (1996). 'Family Process and Child Anxiety and Aggression: An Observational Analysis', *Journal of Abnormal Child Psychology*, Vol.24, pp.715-34.

Department of Children and Youth Affairs (2012). *Report of the Task Force on the Child and Family Support Agency*, Dublin: Government Publications.

Department of Children and Youth Affairs (2014). *Better Outcomes, Brighter Futures: The National Policy Framework for Children and Young People 2014-2020*, Dublin: Government Publications.

Department of Health and Children (2000). *The National Children's Strategy*, Dublin: Government Publications.

Department of Health and Children (2007). *The Agenda for Children's Services : A Policy Handbook*, Dublin: Government Publications.

Department of the Taoiseach (2006). *Towards 2016: The Ten Year Social Partnership Framework Agreement*, Dublin: Government Publications.

Etzioni, A. (1994). *The Spirit of Community: The Re-invention of American Society*, New York: Touchstone.

Farrington, D.P. and Welsh, B.C. (2007). *Saving Children from a Life of Crime: Early Risk Factors and Effective Interventions*, Oxford: Oxford University Press.

Ford, R. (2012). *Canada*, New York: Bloomsbury.

Frazer, E. (1999). *The Problems of Communitarian Politics*, Oxford: Oxford University Press.

Furlong, M., McGilloway, S., Bywater, T., Hutchings, J., Smith, S.M. and Donnelly, M. (2012). 'Behavioural and Cognitive-behavioural Group-Based Parenting Programmes for Early-Onset Conduct Problems in Children Aged 3 to 12 Years (Review)', *Cochrane Database of Systematic Reviews*.

Garber, J., Little, S., Hilsman, R. and Weaver, K.R. (1998). 'Family Predictors of Suicidal Symptoms in Young Adolescents', *Journal of Adolescence*, Vol.21, pp.445-57.

Glynn, S.J. (2012). *The New Breadwinners: 2010 Update*, Washington, DC: Center for American Progress.

Government of Ireland (1937). *Constitution of Ireland (Bunreacht na hÉireann)*, Dublin: Government Publications.

Green, G., Macintyre, S., West, P. and Ecob, R.(1990). 'Do Children of Lone Parents Smoke More because Their Mothers Do?', *British Journal of Addiction*, Vol.85, pp.1497-500.

Green, S. and Hayes, N. (2014). 'No sign of a radical overhaul of crèche standards', *The Irish Times*, 3 July.

Halpenny, A. (2012). 'Parenting and Family Support for Families at Risk – Implications from Child Abuse Reports', *Irish Journal of Applied Social Studies*, Vol.12, Iss.1, Art.8.

Hardiker, P., Exton, K. and Barker, M. (1991). *Policies and Practices in Preventative Child Care*, Aldershot: Avebury.

Headley, B. (2007). *The Set-Point Theory of Well-being Needs Replacing: On the Brink of a Scientific Revolution*, DIW Berlin Discussion Papers, No.753, Berlin: Impressum.

Headstrong (2013). *Cost Analysis of the Jigsaw Programme*, Dublin: Headstrong, The National Centre for Youth Mental Health.

Hemerijck, A. (2013). *Changing Welfare States*, Oxford: Oxford University Press.

Indecon (2012). *Economic Value of Youth Work*, Dublin: National Youth Council of Ireland.

Institute for Public Policy Research (2013). *Who's Breadwinning? Working Mothers and the New Face of Family Support*, London: Institute for Public Policy Research.

Kessler, L. (2007). 'Community Parenting', *Washington University Journal of Law and Policy*, Vol.24, pp.47-77.

Kuhn, D. (2006). 'Do Cognitive Changes Accompany Developments in the Adolescent Brain?', *Perspectives in Psychological Science*, Vol.1, pp.59-67.

Layard, R. and Dunn, J. (2009). *A Good Childhood*, London: Penguin.

McKeown, K., Haase, T. and Pratschke, J. (2014). *Evaluation of National Early Years Access Initiative and Siolta Quality Assurance Programme: A Study of Child Outcomes in Preschool*, Dublin: Pobal.

McKnight, J. (2010). 'Asset Mapping in Communities', in Morgan, A., Davies, M. and Ziglio, E. (eds.), *Health Assets in a Global Context*, New York: Springer.

McMahon, B., Weld, G., Thornton, R. and Collins, M. (2012). *The Cost of a Child*, Dublin: Vincentian Partnership for Social Justice.

Mguni, N. and Bacon, N. (2010). *Taking the Temperature of Local Communities: The Well-being and Resilience Measure (WARM)*, London: The Young Foundation.

Moran, P., Ghate, D. and van der Merwe, A. (2004). *What Works in Parenting Support? A Review of the International Evidence*, London: Department for Education and Skills.

Munro, E. (2012). *The Munro Review of Child Protection: Final Report: A Child-centred System*, London: Department for Education.

National Economic and Social Council (2009). *Well-being Matters: A Social Report for Ireland*, Dublin: National Economic and Social Council.

National Economic Social Forum (2005), *Early Childhood Care and Education: Report 31*, Dublin: National Economic and Social Forum.

New Economics Foundation and Action for Children (2009). *Backing the Future: Why Investing in Children is Good for Us All*, London: New Economics Foundation.

Nic Gabhainn, S. and Sixsmith, J. (2005). *Children's Understanding of Well-being*, Dublin: NUI Galway and National Children's Office.

O'Connor, T.G. and Scott, S. (2007). *Parenting and Outcomes for children*, York: Joseph Rowntree Foundation.

O'Doherty, C., Farrelly, T. and O'Leary, D. (2012). *The Kerry Children's Services Committee Child Well-being Indicators Report*, Tralee: Institute of Technology and Kerry Children's Services Committee.

OECD (2012). *Investing in High-quality Early Childhood Education and Care*, Paris: OECD Publishing.

OECD (2013), *How Do Early Childhood Education and Care (ECEC) Policies, Systems and Quality Vary across OECD Countries?*, Education Indicators in Focus, No. 11, Paris: OECD Publishing.

Office of the Minister for Children (2006). *State of the Nation's Children*, Dublin: Government Publications.

Office of the Minister for Children and Youth Affairs (2008). *State of the Nation's Children*, Dublin: Government Publications.

Office of the Minister for Children and Youth Affairs (2010). *State of the Nation's Children*, Dublin: Government Publications.

Power, M. and Barnes, C. (2011). *Feeling Safe in Our Community*, Limerick: University of Limerick Department of Sociology.

Putnam, R.D. (2000). *Bowling Alone*, New York: Simon and Schuster.

Reynolds, A.J., Temple, J.A., Robertson, D.L. and Mann, E.A. (2002). 'Age 21 Cost-benefit Analysis of the Title 1 Chicago Child-parent Centers', *Educational Evaluation and Policy Analysis*, Vol.24, No.4, pp.267-303.

Ridge, T. (2012). 'Children', in Alcock, P., May, M. and Wright, S. (eds.), *The Students Companion to Social Policy*, Chichester: Wiley-Blackwell.

Rogers, L., Hallam, S. and Shaw, J. (2008). 'Do Generalist Parenting Programmes Improve Children's Behaviour and Attendance at School? The Parents' Perspective', *British Journal of Special Education*, Vol.35, No.1, pp.16-25.

Rutter, M., Giller, H., and Hagell, A. (1998). *Antisocial Behaviour by Young People*, Cambridge: Cambridge University Press.

Skehill, C. (2008). 'Socio-legal Practices in Child Welfare and Protection in Northern Ireland and the Republic of Ireland: Histories of the Present and Possibilities for the Future', in Burns, K. and Lynch, D. (eds.), *Child Protection and Welfare Social Work*, Dublin: A. and A. Farmar.

Sneddon. H. and Owens, S. (2012). *Prevention and Early Intervention in Children and Young People's Services: Parenting*, Dublin: Centre for Effective Services.

Stears, M. (2012). 'The Case for a State that Supports Relationships, Not a Relational State', in Cooke, G. and Muir, R. (eds.), *The Relational State: How Recognising the Importance of Human Relationships could Revolutionise the Role of the State*, London: Institute for Public Policy Research.

The Irish Times (2013a). 'Immigration appears key factor for high birth rate', 20 November.

The Irish Times (2013b). 'Other countries pay people to have children', 2 January.

Titmuss, R. (1971). *The Gift Relationship*, New York: Pantheon Books.

Toth, S.L., Cicchetti, D., Macfie, J., Maughan, A. and Van Meenen, K. (2000). 'Narrative Representations of Caregivers and Self in Maltreated Preschoolers', *Attachment and Human Development*, Vol.2, pp.271-305.

UNICEF (2007). *An Overview of Child Well-being in Rich Countries*, Florence: UNICEF.

UNICEF (2014). *Children of the Recession: The Impact of the Economic Crisis on Child Well-being in Rich Countries*, Florence: UNICEF.

United Nations (1989). *Convention on the Rights of the Child*, Geneva: United Nations.

University of Central London (2012). *An Equal Start: Improving Outcomes in Children's Centres*, London: University of Central London Institute of Health Equity.

Utting, D. (2009). *Parenting Services: Filling the Gaps, Assessing and Meeting the Need for Parenting Support Services: A Literature Review*, London: Family and Parenting Institute.

Utting, D., Bright, J. and Henricson, C. (1993). *Crime and the Family: Improving Childrearing and Preventing Delinquency*, London: Family Policy Centre.

Wood, J.J., McLeod, B.D., Sigman, M., Hwang, W.O. and Chu, B.C. (2003). 'Parenting and Child Anxiety: Theory, Empirical Findings and Future Directions', *Journal of Child Psychology and Psychiatry*, Vol.44, pp.134-51.

4: Happy Parenting

Colm O'Doherty

> *To say that parenthood is all happiness, and that children represent nothing but joy, would be a gross misrepresentation of the facts. Parenthood represents the last frontier in American society, for the great majority of young people approach parenthood with as little formal training and knowledge of the conditions involved as the early pioneers had when they first chopped their way through the wilderness of North America.* (Womble, 1966, pp.443-44)

Introduction

Is parenting in 21st century Ireland an activity for pioneering amateurs on a quest for personal fulfilment and personal utopias? Thomas Moore coined the word *utopia* in the early 16th century to describe a dream-world that is perfectly secure and morally correct. Parents rearing the next generation are in the market for utopian experiences that will secure their happiness. The widespread belief that parenting forges personal utopias and settings for happiness is challenged by research evidence.

> The social conditioning of happiness starts in the family. Most cultural traditions see childhood as the model for innocent happiness, and parenthood as an ideal model of this – worldly and virtuous fulfilment. Yet happiness scholarship in modern societies has repeatedly produced a disturbing finding: parenting, which nowadays is increasingly seen as a life choice freely entered into as part of the pursuit of happiness, appears to be *inversely* correlated with self-reported happiness (Powdthavee, 2009; Keizer *et al*, 2010). (Thin, 2012, pp.151-52)

This chapter debates our understandings of happiness, explores its relationship with childrearing, considers the downsides of parenting and suggests how parenthood can be a happier experience.

What is Happiness?

Happiness is generally associated with pleasure, purpose and meaning. It is one of those loaded terms that cover a multitude of feelings, experiences and reciprocities. Layard (2005) puts the emphasis on feelings: 'So by happiness I mean feeling good – enjoying life and wanting the feeling to be maintained'. Ben-Shahar (2008) defines happiness as 'the overall experience of pleasure and meaning'. For Thin (2012), 'happiness is best understood not as definable entity but as an evaluative kind of "conversation" (broadly conceived to include internal dialogues) concerning how well our lives go'. Carr highlights the distinction between hedonic and eudaimonic philosophies of happiness: 'The hedonic approach defines happiness and the good life in terms of pleasure seeking and pain avoidance. The eudaimonic tradition in contrast defines happiness and the good life in terms of achieving one's full potential' (Carr, 2011). Some psychologists (Lyubomirsky *et al*, 2005; Carr, 2011) argue that three factors influence a person's level of happiness: a genetically determined set point for happiness, life circumstances and intentional activities. The idea of a happiness set point is associated with the observation that some people are born with a happier disposition than others and that differences in disposition are partially determined by genetic factors. This perspective assumes that individuals can exercise control over certain aspects of their lives but have no influence whatsoever over their genetic predisposition and only limited influence over their circumstances. A further consideration is the notion that happiness is all in the mind and that a person can be happy whatever their circumstances if they adopt a positive attitude. Removing cognitive barriers gives free rein to our positive emotions. Thin (2012) describes this as 'thinking ourselves happy' by controlling our own thoughts and feelings.

Finding Happiness

In contemporary Ireland, happiness is increasingly located within the 'gated' utopias of individuals. People now choose to set up subjective happiness camps that can act as bulwarks against wider unhappiness-triggering insecurities. Consequently, utopian goals have moved away from the 'big tent' ideas of shared improvement towards notions of individual survival.

Figure 4.1: The Happiness Matrix

Factors Influencing Happiness Levels	Approaches to Happiness	Strategies for Achieving Happiness	Happiness Indicators	Happiness Locations
1. Genetic predisposition 2. Life circumstances 3. Intentional activities	1. Pleasure seeking and pain avoidance – hedonic approach – utilitarianism 2. Achieving one's full, potential – eudaimonic approach	1. Subjective strategy – mind over matter – thinking ourselves happy 2. Objective strategy – changing our circumstances by changing our physical and social environments	1. Feeling good 2 .Enjoying life 3. Pleasure 4. Meaning 5. Positive reflections 6. Flourishing	1. Personal utopias 2. Real utopias

Unlike 'gated' utopias, real utopias embrace the tensions between happiness ambitions and real world practices. Whereas 'gated' utopias are intended to secure better places in the world for their occupants, real utopias hope to make the world a better place to live in for everybody. 'Gated utopias' crystallised in the boom years when personal ambitions were fanned by the flames of red-hot capitalism. Despite the harmful effects of the crash, they still represent the utopias of those who view capitalism as a benign social order within which humanity will flourish. Taken to an extreme, this worldview casts parents as rational economic agents buying and selling in competitive markets. Decisions to parent represent 'decisions to invest in a form of capital, like consumer durables, that yields a future flow of valuable resources' (Folbre, 2008, p.27).

Using capitalist thinking means parenting becomes an imagined perfect project with utilitarian ends. Viewing parenting through an economic lens like this is questionable, despite the acknowledged truth that 'children are an expensive crop' (Folbre, 2008, p.65). As Jordan (2010) and Sen (2009) make clear, the utilitarian perspective encourages parents to fasten their responsibilities to their happiness. Parenting commitments resemble investments and are regulated by contracts protecting the freedom of individuals from unwanted social interferences. Sen (2009) questions the contracterian argument that the commitment of parents to the pursuit of happiness excuses them from cultural and moral regulation for the sake of the common good. His argument suggests that, because parents have the capability to order their lives in ways that can make a significant contribution to levels of collective happiness, they are accountable for what they do.

Parenting promotes many opportunities for happiness and because it involves caring for others, its unique value, as a social institution, stems from its commitment to creative altruism. Creative altruism involves promoting the interests of the other in ways that go beyond our social roles. The role of being a parent is constructed around recognising and fulfilling socially-specified caring responsibilities and mobilising altruism exclusively in the service of social utility. But, as Scott and Seglow point out:

> Much of the moral appeal of altruism is lost once it is put exclusively in the service of social utility (Scott and Seglow, 2007, p.119).

Creative altruism allows us to transcend our established parental roles and creates space, beyond obligation, where happiness will occur. For happy parenting to flourish, altruism must be re-loaded with morality. As Etzioni states:

> Making a child is a moral act. Obviously it obligates the parent to the child. But it also obligates the parents to the community. Therefore, *parents have a moral responsibility to the community to invest themselves in the proper upbringing of their children, and communities – to enable parents to so dedicate themselves* (Etzioni, 1993, p.54).

Everyday exchanges in social life can form the basis for a reliable set of social and political relationships and a moral order where parenting commitments are fostered and cherished. This moral order sustains a virtuous circle of creative altruism where parents are encouraged to see the parent in every person they encounter and to practice generalised reciprocity – 'I'll do this for you now, without expecting anything immediately in return and perhaps without even knowing you, confident that down the road you or someone else will return the favour' (Putnam, 2000, p.134).

The social institution of parenting fits uncomfortably within an economic system that does not recognise its real value. Through creative altruism and generalised reciprocity, parents form emotional connections with their own children, other children, their parents, and the wider community. As Jordan (2010, p.17) puts it: 'simply in communicating meanings and purposes we construct a moral order, however ephemeral, in our everyday exchanges'. Parents and children become attached to each other regardless of future payback. Decisions and choices around parenting are at odds with the dominant idea of life being lived as a self-regulating profit and loss venture. Most people are reluctant to commit themselves in advance to relationships that they think will make them unhappy and parenting is no different. Cultural messages and perceptions of what others are doing make people aware of the moral standing of parenting as a social institution. Conventional Irish cultural norms present people with a mental image of parenthood as a vital cog in the operation of a good society. In reality, many people are not affirmed or happy as a result of choosing to become a parent. They find that there is a gap between their experiences and the public image of parenting as a utopian project that will secure their happiness.

The Happiness Gap

Thin is critical of the parenting-as-misery proposition, which is rooted in academic and populist understandings of dysfunctional families:

> Most of the scholarly and therapeutic attention to childrearing and education addresses childhood pathologies and subsequent adverse outcomes or therapeutic treatments, rather than carefully studying what goes right in childhood and what can be done to facilitate both happy childhoods and good life prospects (Thin, 2012, p.150).

Thin does have a point, though he overstates the degree to which childrearing is portrayed as a cheerless activity. His plea for greater study of the joys of parenting and what can be done to facilitate happy childhoods has merit but, in suggesting that an inquiry such as *A Good Childhood* (Layard and Dunn, 2009), which focuses our attention on the context in which childrearing is happening, is all 'doom and gloom', he is being somewhat misleading. Parenting is shaped by biology and the environment. *A Good Childhood* acknowledges the widespread unease that exists around childrearing and makes inquiry into the experiences that children need to flourish and the obstacles to their flourishing:

> Flourishing means above all social engagement and the enjoyment of life-fulfilling our capacity to live in harmony with others and ourselves. Children flourish when they have a sense of meaning in their lives, which comes from both social engagement and from enthusiastic development of their own interests and talents. Children who grow up like this are likely to lead happy lives (Layard and Dunn, 2009, p.9).

Obviously what is needed is a balanced appreciation of parenting as a complicated enterprise where happiness ebbs, flows and changes over time. Parents often do not know what will make them happy, change their minds about what they want and face insecure and uncertain futures. Society can be thought of as a complex interdependent ecosystem. Parenting takes place within this ecosystem where social forces emanating from institutions, structures and cultural standpoints are continually in play. A National Economic and Social Council report (2013) made it clear that the economic crash has diminished the happiness of many parents.

Unhappy Parenting

> Few of us commit ourselves in advance to relationships that we think will make us unhappy (Folbre, 2008, p.34).

According to Lee (2014), there has been a 'growing momentum from the 1970s onwards towards the targeting of parental behaviour as deficient and also "parenting" as something of a joyless task or "job", to be conducted under the watchful gaze of experts' (p.8).

An unintended consequence of the expansion and diversification of parenting advice is the promotion of parenting expertise as a marketable commodity, sold by different vendors (parenting experts, psychologists and other professionals) to increasingly disempowered learner parents. Learner parents also must come to terms with an inflation of their role and responsibility in modern society. Furedi (2002), cited in Faircloth (2014), has suggested that parenting has become an increasingly significant aspect of adult identity:

> Adults do not simply live their lives through children, but in part, develop their identity through them ... parents are also inventing themselves (p.46).

The activity of parenting provides a counterbalance to the existential uncertainties of an insecure world. Parenting becomes a meaningful project in a world characterised by fluid relationships and economic insecurity. Faircloth (2014, p.48), drawing on the work of Villalobos (2009) and Hays (1996), contends that overinvestment in parenting to compensate for limited or non-existing channels for self-actualisation through work or relationships is a cultural phenomenon that has led to the emergence of a particular parenting style in European and American societies:

> It is broadly one that is child-centred, expert-guided, emotionally-absorbing, labour-intensive and financially-expensive (Hays, 1996, p.*x*).

Faircloth refers to the syndrome of 'new momism' in the US 'where motherhood is presented as ultimately fulfilling and an almost sacred endeavour' (2014, p.28). New momism represents a media-driven idealisation of motherhood, which is based on the lifestyles of celebrity 'moms' fused with what Wolf (2011) refers to as a doctrine of total motherhood whereby mothers are required to become experts on all aspects of parenting. This portrayal of idealised intensive parenting as the norm can produce strong feelings of failure amongst women who do not parent at that level. According to Faircloth (2014, p.29), intensive parenting requires mothers to strive to:

> … become experts on all aspects of childrearing – making sure that those mealtimes, stories and playing are not only safe, but also optimal, for infant development: lay paediatricians, psychologists, consumer product safety inspectors, toxicologists, and educators. Mothers must not only protect their children from immediate threats but are also expected to predict and prevent any circumstance that might interfere with putatively normal development' (Wolf, 2011, p.*xv*).

Defensive parenting and overparenting are manifestations of the intensive parenting syndrome. The practice of defensive parenting is linked to the role of parents as 'risk managers', where the focus is on dangers that might threaten the safety and well-being of children. Notions of 'stranger danger' and the suspicion of other adults that accompanies it can lower social capital levels and make parenting a solitary and lonely activity. The parental responsibility for keeping children safe becomes the prime concern and relationships characterised by reciprocity and trust between adults are replaced by a generalised sense of anxiety and a climate of suspicion that drives a wedge between parents and other adults. Overparenting stifles young children's capacity to take the risks necessary to grow up and is creating a generation of 'cotton wool kids'. 'Helicopter' overparenting prevents older children from gaining personal independence. Bristow has detailed the characteristics and activities of the different forms taken by parental over-protectiveness and relates them to the 'extent to which the orthodoxy of intensive parenting culture takes a toll on parents' time, emotional energy, and capacity to pursue their ambitions in the adult world' (2014, p.202).

Cultural norms are susceptible to economic pressures and during the boom years a combination of economic arrangements and individualisation of social life ensured that parenting in Ireland was valued more as a production line for human capital than as an essential feature of a good society. Parenting as a collective social activity was undermined by an excessive individualism, which held that a person's main duty was to make the most of themselves. Gilligan captures this social confusion about parenting in modern Ireland: 'In the Ireland of the new, the exact nature of what it means to be a parent is becoming more difficult to define' (2008, p.1). Parenting is influenced not only by our own views of what it is to be a parent, but also by family factors, societal factors, cultural factors and parenting traditions (accepted parenting views and practices passed on to us from previous generations). Parents are unsure about their capabilities and role as parents in the face of these fast changing ideas, beliefs and practices about childrearing. Confusion around the heartbeat of parenting is understandable today when there is constant reference being made within social circles, communities and the media to dysfunctional families and inept parenting. To paraphrase Franklin D. Roosevelt, there are as many opinions on parenting as there are experts. There is a belief today that parenting is simply a matter of learning certain rules that can be generally applied – like learning to drive a car. One of the most popular books on parenting, *The Rules of Parenting* (Templar, 2013), provides its readers with 109 rules for parenting. Templar casts parents as novices learning survival rules for action. Parents are portrayed as problem-solving novices who follow a model of reasoning that is slightly mechanistic and separates the whole of parenting into parts. Parents need to acquire skills through expert help. Rearing children is less and less about instinct or intuition and more and more about scientific research and evidence-based approaches to parenting. Micro-managing the minutiae of parent-child relations becomes a finger in the dyke activity keeping insanity at bay. Given the precarious position of parenting in modern Ireland and the ambivalent attitudes it inspires – idealised in general but criticised in particular – it should come as no surprise that many parents are unhappy. In recent times, there has been little or no systematic gathering of information on unhappiness that is triggered by or related to the parenting role. Instead, as Thin (2012, p.150) points out, scholarly and therapeutic attention is mainly focused on what parents do badly rather than on how unhappy they are: 'parents can be forgiven for believing that all the experts are eagerly waiting to document their failures'. Some of this relates to the fact that, as Daly suggests, an overemphasis on the instrumental or utilitarian side of family life – the family as an economic or welfare institution – can blind us to the reality that:

> ... family relations are not just or even functional but are, rather, based on emotion and affect and embedded in systems of meaning that have a cultural base. As such family relations involve exchanges and reciprocities that are not primarily interpretable in an instrumental idiom (Daly, 2011, p.145).

The moral values influencing family altruism define parenting. Familial altruism requires a moral compass created and sustained by moral energy. Moral energy is, however, variable and uneven as it is culturally regulated. Therefore a balance is required in society between contractual utilitarianism, which is market-driven, and moral regulation, which enables parents to act together and separately in pursuit of their own well-being and the well-being of their children. Moral energy is diminished and parental unhappiness is magnified in a social landscape dominated by regulation that prioritises the market economy.

Sites and sources of unhappiness declared by parents attending an independent support programme (Lawlor, 2013) are wide-ranging:

- Bed times;
- In-law pressure;
- Your own pressures;
- Being a 'bad' parent;
- Depression;
- Shopping with children;
- Waiting for help (getting a social, health or education service involves long waiting periods);
- Family conflict;
- Family breakups;
- Addiction problems;
- Conflict between siblings;
- Behaviour of children;
- The weight of responsibility involved in parenting;
- Social isolation;
- Meeting emotional needs of children;
- Disciplining children;

- Social expectations;
- Time poverty;
- School problems;
- Material poverty and costs attached to parenting.

Happy Parenting

> One of the myths of modern-day living is the perception that if it is to be done right parenting must be stressful and intense. Parenting, in itself, is neither demanding or stressful – it is the myriad other demands on a parent's time and energies that cause the difficulties. (Gilligan, 2008, p.5)

While nobody is a perfect parent and there are no objective standards that can be employed to rank quality, it is important to acknowledge that incompetent parenting and the damage it can cause to a child's welfare can be assessed. In the final analysis, however, only parents and their children can be witnesses to the quality of their relationships. The caregiving relationship is influenced by the self-awareness of parents and insight into their parenting strengths, weaknesses and responsibilities. Thin's (2012) idea of happiness as an internal evaluative conversation, helping parents to reflect on how well their parenting is going, is relevant here. Commitment to parenting involves both the personal politics (politics is about vying for scarce resources) of behaviour change and the realisation of culturally-defined moral commitments. Why should I become a parent? Is it worth it? Do I want to invest my limited resources of time, energy, money and effort in parenting? What competes for my attention? How strong are these competing goals? Who are likely to be my allies in this venture? Becoming a parent may be considered as an accident or outcome forced on us by somebody else. Alternatively, we might choose to create a parenting contract with a partner and be disappointed by this partner and their attitudes when the realities of parenting are encountered. Our level of happiness is influenced by how we rate ourselves and our current parenting behaviour, not only in comparison with our own values, but also in comparison with those of others. Personal choices are informed by social values and images. Societal beliefs and instructions on parenting are constantly presented to us by individuals and organisations. In general, however, sites and sources of happiness stem from the emotional satisfactions, fresh experiences and meanings germinated through relationships characterised by creative altruism.

Emotional Satisfaction

Parenting elicits emotional satisfactions that could not be possible in any other way. Not only do children represent joyful futures, but they also enhance the present in unique ways. It is possible for parents to explore aspects of their own childhood experiences and to relive aspects of their own early lives. Parents, however, should not take this too far, for it is not possible or advisable to live completely through their children. Children's complete dependence on their parents also can be a source of emotional satisfaction as everyone, in a sense, likes to feel needed. Children are a source of companionship, especially when they are older. Examples/ instances of emotional satisfactions declared by parents attending the independent support programme facilitated by Lawlor are:

- Unconditional love;
- Being needed;
- Love you get;
- Bonding;
- Play time;
- Watching movies;
- Christmas/Santa;
- Parties;
- Best friends;
- Going places together (2013).

Fresh Experiences

Parenting is a continuously new experience in life. All children, according to Kellmer-Pringle (1986), have four basic emotional needs – love and security; new experiences; praise and recognition; and responsibility – which must be met if they are to develop from infancy to mature adulthood. Because no two children are exactly alike and no two situations with the same child are exactly alike, the status of these needs and their relative importance is constantly changing. Managing and responding to these spontaneous situations, which arise on a daily basis, keeps parents alert and prevents them falling into rigid patterns of habit. Examples/instances of fresh experiences declared by parents attending the independent support programme facilitated by Lawlor are:

- Different stages – glad to see them growing;
- Development;
- School reports;
- Giggles, laughs, fun;
- 'Ah' moments;
- Getting dirty;
- Watching them grow;
- Firsts (school, walking) (2013).

New Meaning to Life

Taking responsibility for another person allows parents to invest in society in a special way. For most people, their interest in the future is stimulated and heightened by the advent of children. What is happening domestically and around the world may have a new relevance with the arrival of parenthood. As a parent, a person may feel that they have an increased stake in the future and that, therefore, they should be contributing more directly to social affairs. Parents are incentivised to become active. As active citizens, parents will get involved with others to pursue interests and goals relating to the welfare and development of their children and to challenge the way society deals with parents and children. Parenting does not take place in isolation from broader society and parents are not solely responsible for the welfare of children. Society and societal factors have a significant influence on the extent to which parents are integrated and supported in communities. Parents, as active citizens, may become 'awkward' and vocal citizens pushing for social changes that will be beneficial for them and their communities. Creating a more parent-friendly society is a pre-condition for ensuring that children's welfare is prioritised and parenting is supported at every level. Intergenerational solidarity needs to be promoted. As Putnam (2000, p.296) stated: 'Child development is powerfully shaped by social capital'.

Making Happiness Happen

It is difficult, if not impossible, to directly measure parental happiness. The happiness of a parent cannot be regarded as an indicator of the happiness of the parent's child. This is because children are active participants in the parenting process. A child, no matter what his or her age, has rights, views, beliefs and feelings that need to be integrated into the parenting process. Ignoring a child's individualism and personality results in a passive parenting relationship that can be directed more towards care and control at the expense of happiness. Gilligan (2008) recommends that the involvement of children as active participants in the parenting process should be guided by a set of principles that encourage children to freely express their views and opinions in a safe, secure and democratic environment. By forging and nurturing altruistic relationships based on these principles, parents create opportunities for children to increase the collective happiness of the entire family. It can be hard for parents to find the right balance between their own desires and those of their children. Altruism – understood as our readiness to help others – is a central measure of social capital, according to Putnam (2000). Social capital within families is increased by the development of trust relations between parents and children. Parents are happy to do things for their children because they trust them to reciprocate. And they do reciprocate, with love and emotional capital, because they want to maintain their relationship with their parents. However familial altruism cannot be turned on and off like a switch. Parents become more altruistic and 'sensitive to their children when their levels of stress are reduced and they experience an increase in their own felt security, confidence, self-esteem, self-efficacy and social understanding' (Howe *et al*, 1999, p.268). Where parents enjoy close supportive relations with other adults and wider society, such relationships act as a buffer against life stressors. Levels of familial altruism and the fostering of trusting relations between parents and children can be guided and enhanced through the promotion of a more parent-centred society.

Supporting Happiness

> Parenting Support refers to a range of information, support, education, training and counselling and other measures or services that focus on influencing how parents understand and carry out their parenting role. (Daly, 2011, p.1)

Bristow criticises the culture of intensive parenting, which 'works against the idea that childrearing should be conceptualised as a generational responsibility whereby all adults can and should play a positive role in shaping the next generation' (2014, p.102). Adult social solidarity is missing in an over-regulated and expert-led parenting culture. What is lost is the social capital-derived sentiment that all adults should be prepared and willing to engage in supporting childrearing as a good and necessary part of everyday life.

Figure 4.2: An Integrated System of Parenting Support

Strategy	Policy	Action
A resourced national policy framework for parenting supports in Ireland and Northern Ireland either integrated into the policy framework (for example, for children and young people) or as a stand-alone strategy/framework (for example, *National Parenting Strategy*, Scotland 2012). A co-ordinated approach to ensure that parenting support services are available to all families who want or need them, through a combination of universal and targeted supports.	A higher value placed on parenting, with parenting a recognised issue on the national policy agenda. A widespread recognition that the state has a role in supporting parenting. A widespread recognition that parenting supports should be seen as normal.	A range of publicly-financed parenting programmes and supports provided through a planned and strategic approach. A requirement that publicly-supported parenting programmes are evidence-based or evidence-informed. Identification of mainstream services through which parenting supports and practice approaches can be delivered. A quality framework for delivering parent support should be developed. Cross-sectoral and cross-departmental (Justice, Education, Health and Children) co-operation and collaboration between parenting programmes/supports and health services, early years, community development, youth services and family and educational supports. Public information campaigns emphasising the importance of parenting.

Source: Special Interest Group on Parenting (2013).

Parenting does not take place in some kind of social vacuum. Society and societal factors have a significant influence on the welfare and well-being of parents. Many parents feel that they are targeted by a blaming culture. Creating a more parent-centred society is important to ensure that the happiness of parents is prioritised and supported at every level. A parent-centred society, through its legislation, policies and programmes, will value and support parenting. Support for parenting is based on a belief that interventions that support parents in their parenting role should:

- Empower parents by developing their confidence and competence;
- Enable parents to foster optimal child well-being and development outcomes;
- Increase the enjoyment and satisfaction of parenting (Special Interest Group on Parenting, 2013).

If support is not based on these principles, an unintended consequence of some programmes may be to increase the stress levels of participants – particularly where programmes are used to solve other problems such as child abuse. By making happiness a more explicit focus in support programmes, public policy can become a transformative force for a new kind of 'choice architecture' around parenting. The Special Interest Group on Parenting, which was established under the aegis of the Centre for Effective Services in 2010, brought together an all-island cross-section of managers, researchers, public officials, academics, practitioners and funders from relevant sectors to create a new social family contract that recognises the importance of parental happiness as a policy objective.

Conclusion

Happy parenting is oxymoronic to many people, given the low status of parenting in Irish society and the widespread portrayal of childrearing as a joyless activity.

This chapter has examined this proposition and considered the cultural and social construction of happy parenting. In the eudaimonic tradition, where happiness comes from doing what is morally worth doing and achieving one's full potential through living a meaningful life, parenting is a social and public good, not just a private and individual concern. Widespread deficits in parental flourishing are not simply the result of genetic limitations, Acts of God, or variations in people's problem-solving attributes, but are the result of social causes.

By attending explicitly to the social dimension of parenting, through the provision of mainstream support programmes, Irish society can ensure that the majority of parents have access to the conditions needed to live flourishing lives.

References

Ben-Shahar, T. (2008). *Happier*, Maidenhead: McGraw-Hill.

Bristow, J. (2014). 'The Double Bind of Parenting Culture: Helicopter Parents and Cotton Wool Kids', in Lee, E., Bristow, J., Faircloth, C. and Macvarish, J. (eds.), *Parenting Culture Studies*, Basingstoke: Palgrave Macmillan.

Carr, A. (2011). *Positive Psychology: The Science of Happiness and Human Strengths*, Hove: Routledge.

Daly, M. (2011). *Welfare*, Cambridge: Polity Press.

Etzioni, A. (1993). *The Spirit of Community: The Re-invention of American Society*, New York: Touchstone Books.

Faircloth, C. (2014). 'Intensive Parenting and the Expansion of Parenting' in Lee, E., Bristow, J., Faircloth, C. and Macvarish, J. (eds.), *Parenting Culture Studies*, Basingstoke: Palgrave Macmillan.

Folbre, N. (2008). *Valuing Children: Rethinking the Economics of the Family*, Cambridge, MA: Harvard University Press.

Gilligan, P. (2008). *Keeping Your Child Safe: A Manual for Parents*, Dublin: Gill and Macmillan.

Hays, S. (1996). *The Cultural Contradictions of Motherhood*, New Haven and London: Yale University Press.

Howe, D., Brandon, M., Hinings, D., and Schofield, G. (1999). *Attachment Theory, Child Maltreatment and Family Support*, Basingstoke: Palgrave.

Jordan, B. (2010). *Why the Third Way Failed – Economics, Morality and the Origins of the 'Big Society'*, Bristol: The Policy Press.

Keizer, R., Dykstra, P.R. and Poortman, A.-R. (2010). 'Life Outcomes of Childless Men and Fathers', *European Sociological Review*, Vol.26, No.1, pp.1-15.

Kellmer-Pringle, M. (1986). *The Needs of Children*, London: Hutchinson.

Lawlor, E. (2013). *Creative Parenting Workshop*, Kilflynn, County Kerry.

Layard, R. (2005). *Happiness: Lessons from a New Science*, London: Penguin.

Layard, R. and Dunn, J. (2009). *A Good Childhood: Searching for Values in a Competitive Age*, London: Penguin.

Lee, E. (2014). 'Experts and Parenting Culture', in Lee, E., Bristow, J., Faircloth, C. and Macvarish, J. (eds.), *Parenting Culture Studies*, Basingstoke: Palgrave Macmillan.

Lyubomirsky, S., Sheldon, K.M. and Schkade, D. (2005). 'Pursuing Happiness: The Architecture of Sustainable Change', *Review of General Psychology*, Vol.9, pp.111-131.

National Economic and Social Council (2013). *The Social Dimensions of the Crisis: The Evidence and its Implications*, Dublin: National Economic and Social Development Office.

Powdthavee, N. (2009). 'Think Having Children Will Make You Happy?', *The Psychologist*, Vol.22, pp.308-11.

Putnam, R.D. (2000). *Bowling Alone*, New York: Simon and Schuster.

Scott, N. and Seglow, J. (2007). *Altruism*, Maidenhead: McGraw-Hill.

Sen, A. (2009). *The Idea of Justice*, London: Penguin.

Special Interest Group on Parenting (2013). 'Supporting Parents in their Parenting Role', position paper presented at *Towards a Parenting Strategy: An All-island Symposium*, Dublin, 1 July.

Templar, R. (2013). *The Rules of Parenting*, New Jersey: Pearson Education.

Thin, N. (2012). *Social Happiness: Theory into Policy and Practice*, Bristol: The Policy Press.

Villalobos, A. (2009). *Motherload: How Mothers Bear the Weight of Societal Insecurity*, PhD thesis, University of California, Berkeley.

Wolf, J. (2011). *Is Breast Best? Taking on the Breastfeeding Experts and the New High Stakes of Motherhood*, New York: New York University Press

Womble, W.L. (1966). *Foundations for Marriage and Family Relations*, New York: The Macmillan Company.

5: Supporting Parents – Evidence-informed and Evidence-based Policy and Practice

Stella Owens

Introduction

This chapter provides critical evidence-informed and evidence-based understandings of parenting support and discusses the implications for policy and practice. It begins with a brief exploration of the current international policy and practice context in which parents are supported and how this leads to better outcomes for children and families. Policies, initiatives and the key stakeholders in Ireland are discussed, and this is followed by a summary of the burgeoning evidence base of approaches to supporting parenting currently being delivered in Ireland and Northern Ireland. Challenges to supporting parents are examined also and recommendations made for the development of a national parenting action plan to address the issues presented.

International Context

It is widely recognised that parents are crucial to their child's well-being, and supporting parents plays a significant role in achieving good outcomes for children and young people. The United Nations *Convention on the Rights of the Child* (United Nations, 1989) places particular emphasis on supporting the family in carrying out its caring and protective functions and Articles 3, 5, 18 and 27 relate specifically to parental responsibilities. The *Convention* identifies parents as central to realising children's rights within the context of the family, with the state giving sufficient support to families generally (Henricson and Bainham, 2005; Pecnik, 2007).

In response to this, the last 15 years has seen an unprecedented increase in the quantity of children and family support services internationally, all aimed at intervening effectively and improving the lives of children and families. International trends have seen a focus on specific higher order outcomes to be achieved for children, through strengthening universal services – that is, services to all children and families – and then targeting services at those most vulnerable (Department of Children and Youth Affairs, 2014; Office of the Minister for Children and Youth Affairs, 2007a; Parton, 2006; Hardiker *et al*, 1991; Hardiker, 2002). This 'outcomes-focused' approach to children's services aims to encourage service providers and delivery agents to focus their service planning and delivery around how their interventions can improve outcomes for children (Barlow and Scott, 2010; Office of the Minister for Children and Youth Affairs, 2007a).

Policy directives to achieve outcomes have resulted in a focus on prevention and early intervention, concepts that translate in practice as providing services and supports for parents and children aimed at intervening early in children's lives to prevent situations escalating, and also intervening early in the development of a psychological or social problem (Allen, 2011; Fernandez, 2004). A framework for understanding the different 'levels of need' of families and how services can be planned to meet these needs has been developed by Hardiker and colleagues in the UK (Hardiker *et al*, 1991), and adopted and adapted by the government in Ireland (Office of the Minister for Children and Youth Affairs, 2007a). It is a planning framework that assists in understanding different levels of need within a population of children, and facilitates partnership working with statutory, voluntary and community services, by providing clarity about which services are needed for children at each level and how each agency can contribute to providing these services (Hardiker, 2002) – see **Figure 5.1**.

Progress towards outcomes-focused, needs-led services with an emphasis on early intervention and prevention is reflected in major children's reform programmes taking place in many jurisdictions. Scotland provides a good example of strategies, policies and reform programmes that include parent support initiatives. *Getting it Right for Every Child* (Scottish Government, 2006) is Scotland's overarching policy for children's services. It promotes action to improve the well-being of all children and young people in eight outcome areas (in this policy, the outcomes are framed as indicators of well-being), and is an approach to delivering children's services based around a common co-ordinating framework for assessment, planning and action across all agencies working with children and young people.

Figure 5.1: The Hardiker Model

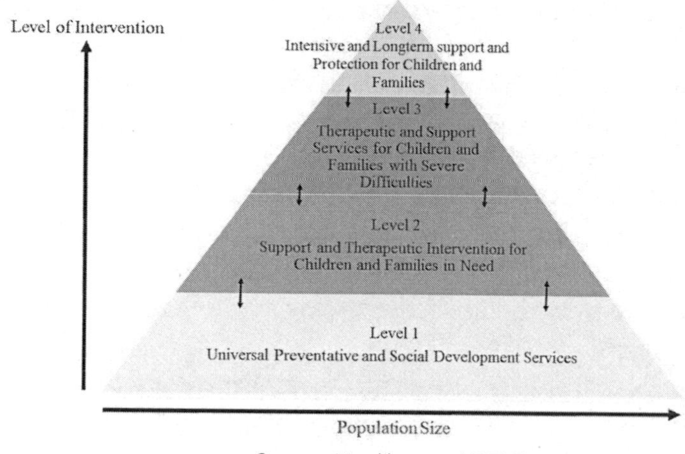

Source: Hardiker *et al* (1991).

The Scottish Government developed an *Early Years Framework* (2008), which seeks to maximise positive opportunities for children to get the best start in life. Specifically in relation to supporting parents, the framework states that:

- Parents are given appropriate support to help them understand the responsibilities and sustained commitment associated with bringing up a child and to develop the skills needed to provide a nurturing and stimulating home environment free from conflict;
- Parents have access to world-class antenatal, maternity and postnatal care that meets their individual needs;
- Parents are involved in their children's learning and are given learning opportunities that will help them support their child's learning and development. Parents are supported to access employment and training to help reduce the risk of child poverty, including through the provision of flexible, accessible and affordable childcare;
- Parents and children have integrated support from services to meet a range of needs they may have. This includes help for parents to develop relationships with their child and to address stresses that may impact on their ability to perform their parenting role (Scottish Government, 2008).

In October 2012, Scotland launched its *National Parenting Strategy* (Scottish Government, 2012). The Strategy aims to address the need to:

- Ensure all parents have easy access to clear, concise information on everything from pregnancy to the teenage years and beyond;
- Offer informed, co-ordinated support to enable parents to develop their parenting skills, whatever their need, wherever they live, whether they live together or apart;
- Take steps to improve the availability of – and access to – early learning, childcare and out-of-school care, taking into account parents in rural areas and those who work irregular hours;
- Provide targeted support to families facing additional pressures that impact on day-to-day parenting;
- Acknowledge and address the wider issues that can affect parents' abilities to provide a nurturing environment and care for their child.

Policies, Initiatives and Stakeholders in Ireland

From a policy perspective in Ireland, in recent years we have witnessed a significant cultural and philosophical shift in our thinking with respect to the role of parents in children's lives. In Ireland, we have had no agreed approach to supporting parents and our efforts in this area have been predominantly based on intervening to remedy deficits rather than building on strengths in a timely way (Special Interest Group, 2013). The concept of parenting support has evolved considerably over the decades and is understood in various ways. For the purposes of this chapter, the following definition will be used:

> Parenting Support refers to a range of information, support, education, training and counselling and other measures or services that focus on influencing how parents understand and carry out their parenting role (Daly, 2012, p.1)

Children and Parents in Ireland in the 21st Century

This section outlines a chronology that sets out the context in which policy in relation to supporting parents has been developed. First, let us look at what we know about children and parents in Ireland in the 21st century. The table below provides some key facts and figures relating to children and families in Ireland.

Table 5.1: Socio-demographic and Other Key Information Relating to Children and Families

1. In 2011, **the number of children aged 0 to 6** in Ireland was **486,242,** which represented 11% of the population. This represents a **16% increase** of this population group since 2006 (Central Statistics Office, 2011).
2. In 2011, 9.3% of children lived in consistent poverty – up from 6.3% in 2008; 63% of all children in consistent poverty are in jobless households (Department of Children and Youth Affairs, 2014).
3. 26% of children live in jobless households (Department of Children and Youth Affairs, 2014).
4. 32.1% of children experienced basic deprivation in 2011 (Department of Children and Youth Affairs, 2014).
5. **17%** of children aged 0 to 4 and **18%** of children aged 5 to 9 **live in lone-parent families** (Department of Children and Youth Affairs, 2012).
6. In the *Growing Up in Ireland* study, 57% of mothers of infants aged 9 months and 91% of fathers were employed outside the home. The **proportion of parents working outside the home has reduced over time.** At 3 years of age, 53% of mothers were working outside the home and there was an increase in unemployment among fathers from 6% to 14% (McGinnity *et al*, 2011).
7. **38%** of infants aged 9 months in the *Growing Up in Ireland* study were in some form of regular **non-parental childcare**, which **rose to 50%** at 3 years (McGinnity *et al*, 2011).
8. At 9 months, 3 years and 5 years, mothers with lower levels of education were the most likely to be 'looking after the home/family' and the least likely to be employed (Nixon, 2012).
9. Family income was strongly related to the mother's education. Where the mother had left school with the Junior Certificate or less, 45% of the families were in the lowest income group and just 5% of these families were in the highest income group (Nixon, 2012).
10. Educational attainment of mothers is strongly correlated to employment prospects, as well as to a range of children's outcomes, including risk of poverty and deprivation. Thus, measures to improve maternal educational attainment and access to employment will have an effect on child poverty (Department of Children and Youth Affairs, 2014).
11. Parent-child relationships are a significant influence on children's social and emotional skills and language and cognitive skills. The mother's well-being is the main influence on the parent-child relationship, which, in turn, is influenced by her social class, support networks and non-English speaking background (McKeown *et al*, 2014).
12. 35% of the mothers of 9-month-old infants did not have any family living locally (Nixon, 2012).
13. Parents of 3 year olds tended to have a positive view of themselves in their parenting role. Just under 40% of mothers and 27% of fathers rated themselves

as 'average', with the majority feeling they were either 'better than average' or 'very good' (Nixon, 2012).

14. Among fathers of infants, greater parental relationship satisfaction was associated with lower levels of parenting stress, which in turn had a positive effect on their feelings towards the infant (Nixon, 2012).
15. Approximately 85% of infants in the infant cohort are living in a two-parent family, while 78% of children in the child cohort are living in a two-parent family. For both cohorts, about 4% of children changed from a one-parent to a two-parent family structure, and *vice versa*, in the four-year gap between data collections (Nixon, 2012).
16. In both 2012 and 2013, there were over 40,000 referrals to child welfare and protection services in Ireland (Department of Children and Youth Affairs, 2014).
17. There are presently 6,400 children in the care of the state; 90% of children in the care of the state in 2011 were in foster care, of whom 32% were fostered with relatives (Department of Children and Youth Affairs, 2014).

The Report of the Commission on the Family

The policy environment in Ireland has altered substantially in the years since the final report of the Commission on the Family, *Strengthening Families for Life* (1998), made substantive recommendations for supporting parents in Ireland. The main recommendations of the report were presented as desirable outcomes relating to:

- **Building strengths in families:** This required greater investment in family support work at a preventative level in the statutory health boards through which both health and welfare were delivered;
- **Supporting families in caring for children:** In considering the role of the state in the above, the Commission recommended that policies should support parents in their choices in relation to the care of their children, enable them to be the best parents they can by giving them practical help with childrearing, and equipping them with parenting skills and knowledge;
- **Protecting and enhancing the position of children and vulnerable dependent family members:** The needs of families bringing up children in difficult circumstances, the unemployed or low income families, lone parents and teenage parents, were to be prioritised.

The *National Children's Strategy*

The *National Children's Strategy* (Department of Health and Children, 2000) set out a 10-year strategic plan for children in Ireland within the context of a 'whole child perspective'. The central tenet was the belief that a coherent and inclusive view of childhood was crucial to the success of the strategy. It not only provided a means of identifying a range of children's needs but helped to identify how best to meet those needs by empowering families and communities and improving the quality of children's lives through integrated delivery of services in partnership with children, young people, their families and their communities. The strategy sought to establish this 'whole child' perspective, based on the ecological model (Bronfenbrenner, 1979), at the centre of policy development and service delivery. The ecological model or ecological perspective provides a framework to understand the multiple influences – or risk and protective factors – that impact on children. According to Bronfenbrenner, how a child develops is a function of interactions between the individual child and his or her environment over the period of time that the child is developing. The model takes a systems perspective on family functioning, and it provides a framework for understanding how critical factors that influence development nest together within a hierarchy of four levels:

- The socio-cultural level ('macro-system' factors);
- The community ('exo-system' factors);
- The family ('micro-system' factors);
- The level of the individual parent or child ('ontogenic' factors).

Investing in Parenthood

Investing in Parenthood (Best Health for Children, 2002), a strategy document produced by Best Health for Children, an initiative led by the Health Services Executive, focused on identifying a strategic approach to support parents to achieve best health for their children. It called for both universal and targeted supports for parents, and multi-agency and cross-departmental working. It advocated the use of people-centred and community development approaches and emphasised the promotion of children's rights.

Agenda for Children's Services

Although the objectives of the *Investing in Parenthood* strategy were not delivered on, the document did have an influence on a major policy document produced some years later. In late 2007, the Office of the Minister for Children and Youth Affairs, now the Department of Children and Youth Affairs, published *The Agenda for Children's Services: A Policy Handbook* (Office of the Minister for Children and Youth Affairs,

2007), which sets out the strategic direction and key goals of public policy in relation to children's health and social services in Ireland. Following international trends, the policy focused on specified outcomes as goals to improving children's lives and well-being. It identified seven (now five) national outcomes for children in Ireland. These will be named later in this chronology.

State of the Nation's Children Reports

The development of a national set of child well-being indicators was identified as a key action under the *National Children's Strategy*, published in 2000 (Department of Health and Children, 2000). Following a year of research, the indicator set – which now comprises approximately 50 child well-being indicators and seven demographic indicators – was launched by the National Children's Office in 2005 (Hanafin and Brooks, 2005). The national child well-being indicators inform the biennial *State of the Nation's Children* reports in Ireland. The *State of the Nation's Children* reports (Department of Health and Children, 2006, 2008, 2010; Department of Children and Youth Affairs, 2012) provide updated statements of key indicators of children's well-being and essentially describe how children in a population are doing. Through the work of the Research Unit of the Department of Children and Youth Affairs, in collaboration with the Central Statistics Office, the national child well-being indicators have been matched to the five national outcomes for children – each of the five outcomes has a number of associated child well-being indicators.

Growing Up in Ireland Study

Growing Up in Ireland, the National Longitudinal Study of Children in Ireland, which commenced in 2007 and is being extended to 2019, is the largest research activity being undertaken by Department of Children and Youth Affairs as part of its research strategy agenda. This study is monitoring the development of 18,000 children, a birth cohort of 10,000 and a 9 year old cohort of 8,000 children. The aim of *Growing Up in Ireland* is to examine the factors that contribute to, or undermine, the well-being of children in contemporary Irish families, and through this to contribute to the setting up of effective and responsive policies relating to children and to the design of services to children and their families (Office of the Minister for Children and Youth Affairs, 2007). Findings from the most recent report on parent relevant components of the study are outlined below (Nixon, 2012).

Table 5.2: How Families Matter for Social and Emotional Outcomes of 9 year old Children

The *Growing Up in Ireland* report (Department of Children and Youth Affairs, 2007) is based on data collected from 8,568 9 year old children, their parents and teachers. The key findings are:

- The majority of 9 year olds are developing well without any significant social, emotional or behavioural difficulties.
- 15% to 20% of children are displaying significant levels of social, emotional or behavioural difficulties, as reported by mothers and teachers.
- Certain parenting styles, particularly authoritarian and neglectful, were associated with social and emotional difficulties in children.
- High levels of mother-child and father-child conflict were associated with social and emotional difficulty.
- Maternal depression impacts on the mother-child relationship and is associated with increased conflict with children.
- Low levels of mother's marital satisfaction were associated with more presenting difficulties with their children and also impacted on the mother-child relationship.
- Children living in one-parent households displayed more difficulties than those in two-parent households.
- The quality of the parent child relationship is more important for children's development than the family income or structure.

These two major data and research initiatives, *State of the Nation's Children's* Reports and the *Growing Up in Ireland* study, which include both parental well-being and child well-being indicators, are facilitating the development of a more comprehensive understanding and picture of children's and parents' lives in Ireland. Outputs from these studies and reports should inform policy development and service planning, and facilitate the cross-comparison of data on how our children are doing across a number of sectors and geographical regions.

Department of Children and Youth Affairs

The prospects of succeeding in implementing the new policy directives of 1) early intervention and prevention, 2) services across the lifecycle and, 3) the promotion and delivery of more integrated collaborative services for children and families has been bolstered significantly by the appointment, in 2010, of the first cabinet level Minister of Children and Youth Affairs and a new government department, the Department of Children and Youth Affairs.

Better Outcomes, Brighter Futures

Among the many achievements of the fledgling Department has been the publication of *Better Outcomes, Brighter Futures: The National Policy Framework for Children and Young People 2014-2020* (Department of Children and Youth Affairs, 2014). This document builds on the *National Children's Strategy* and aims to deliver a whole-of-government cross-sectoral approach to improving outcomes for children and young people based on the five national outcomes (see **Figure 5.2**).

Figure 5.2: The Six Transformational Goals and The Five National Outcomes

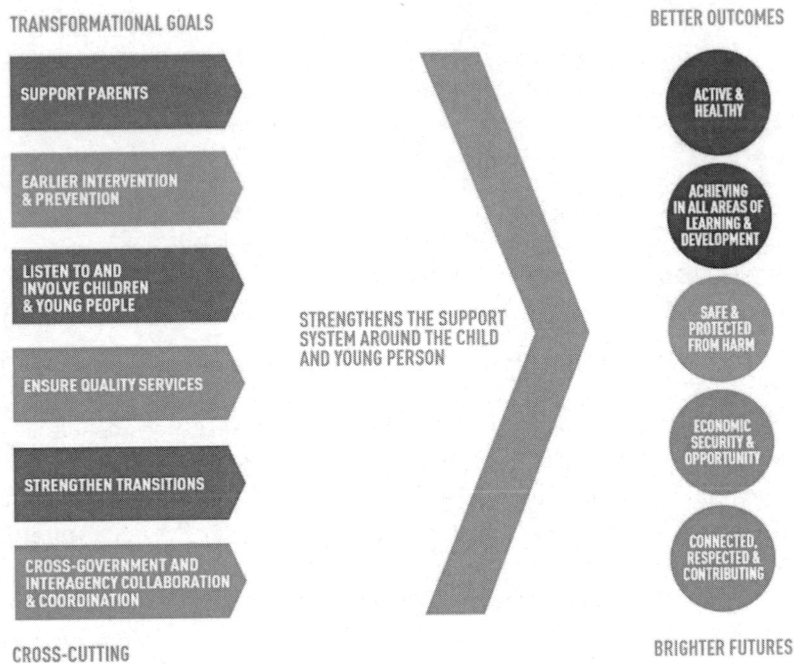

Source: Department of Children and Youth Affairs (2014, p.*iv*).

To ensure more children and young people achieve these outcomes, the policy identifies six transformational goals that, with focused and collective effort over the next seven years, have the potential to transform the effectiveness of existing policies, services and resources. The first transformational goal is to *support parents*, which represents a significant acknowledgement and growing understanding of the critical role of parents. In relation to this transformational goal, the policy states:

> This Framework seeks to ensure that parents in Ireland are equipped and supported to raise their families, to play their role as their children's primary carers, to promote the best possible outcomes for their children and to meet all challenges that may arise. This priority will be delivered through commitments made to increase the provision of supports to all parents through universal access to good-quality parenting advice and programmes, and access to affordable quality childcare, as well as targeted, evidence-based supports to those parents with greatest needs (Department of Children and Youth Affairs, 2014, p.*x*).

The government's commitments under the *support parents* goal, including the production of a 'high level policy statement on parenting and family support', will ensure that, when implemented, there will be greater co-ordinated planning for services and programmes for parents at both universal and targeted level.

Tusla, The Child and Family Agency

On foot of a number of recent damning reports into the care and protection of children in Ireland (Shannon and Gibbons, 2012; Health Service Executive, 2011; Roscommon Child Care Inquiry, 2010) the Minister and the Department of Children and Youth Affairs announced the establishment of a new Child and Family Agency, Tusla, which became operational in January 2014.

Recommendations to the government on the development of the agency included the need for a child-centred service delivery model based on the five national outcomes, strengthened universal services and emphasis on the provision of community-based early intervention services delivered through an integrated service delivery model, and to families at all levels along a continuum (Department of Children and Youth Affairs, 2012). Tusla has developed a suite of documents to support parents and those delivering services to parents as part of its Service Delivery Framework (available at www.tusla.ie).

Children and Young People's Services Committees

The continued development of Children and Young People's Services Committees (CYPSCs), an important policy of the Department of Children and Youth Affairs, and which loom large in the policy framework, provides a strong basis for interagency working and for the planning, co-ordinating and delivering of services at local level

(Department of Children and Youth Affairs, 2012b; Department of Children and Youth Affairs, 2014). The functions of the CYPSCs are:

- Co-ordinating the implementation of national and regional policies and strategies that relate to children, young people and families;
- Planning and co-ordinating services for children and young people in the area covered by the CYPSC;
- Eliminating fragmentation and duplication of services by ensuring more effective collaboration between children, young people and family services within the area;
- Influencing the allocation of resources;
- Strengthening the decision-making capacity at local level.

CYPSCs involve collaboration between Tusla, local authorities, the Health Service Executive, and other partners such as the local Education and Training Boards, the Education Welfare Service, the National Educational Psychological Service, school principals and principals' representatives at primary and post primary, probation services, An Garda Síochána, City and County Childcare Committees and the community and voluntary sector. Each CYPSC is required to produce a comprehensive three-year Children and Young People's Plan to direct its work in the local authority area. Currently in Ireland there are 22 CYPSCs in operation, with a further four to be established to give full national coverage by mid-2015. A primary subgroup of each CYPSC is the parenting subgroup, which facilitates the co-ordination and planning of parenting supports in the county or local authority area.

Area-based Childhood Programme

The *Programme for Government* (Department of the Taoiseach, 2011) promised '… to adopt a new area-based approach to child poverty, which draws on best international practice and existing services to tackle every aspect of child poverty'. In April 2013, €30 million was allocated for the Area-based Childhood Programme (ABC), involving 13 sites of social and economic deprivation, jointly funded by the Department for Children for Youth and Affairs and Atlantic Philanthropies (a philanthropic organisation headed by Chuck Feeney, which has invested substantially in Ireland and Northern Ireland over the past two decades). The ABC programme's objective is breaking the cycle of child poverty within areas where it is most deeply entrenched and where children are most disadvantaged, through integrated and effective services and interventions in the following areas: child development, child well-being and parenting and educational disadvantage. Under the programme, the interventions and approaches within areas should be evidence-informed and integrated with mainstream statutory services such as health, education and the new Child and Family Agency, Tusla.

The ABC programme has been heavily influenced and informed by the learning from two previous initiatives, the Prevention and Early Intervention Initiative and the National Early Years Access Initiative (NEYAI). Atlantic Philanthropies, sometimes in partnership with government, invested €127m across the island into 52 programmes and services in the PEII, aimed at addressing a range of issues including children's learning, child behaviour, promoting inclusion, child health and development and parenting. NEYAI is a three-year programme (2011-2014) to improve quality and outcomes in the early years sector. NEYAI comprised 11 projects, mainly located in disadvantaged areas of Dublin, Cork and Limerick and two rural locations in Longford/ Westmeath and Donegal. Finally, the Parenting Support Initiative – funded by the Katharine Howard Foundation – is a small grants programme for organisations and services delivering parenting support to parents of children aged 0 to 3 years.

Key Themes

This rapid review of policy developments, nationally and internationally, shows that there has been substantial progress made in reforming children's services, and increased efforts to provide outcomes focused, needs led services to improve outcomes for children. A number of key themes emerge from the reform programmes referred to earlier, characterised by their emphasis on an outcomes-focused approach, with supports to parents identified as a significant contributor to achieving these outcomes. The reform programmes and policy frameworks:

- Have an increased focus on early intervention and prevention, and the use of evidence-based and evidence-informed programmes and practices;
- Focus on the provision of support and information to mothers both ante-natally and post-natally and additional support to disadvantaged and vulnerable families;
- Emphasise the need to provide integrated support services for children and families, particularly in the early years;
- Are provided on a cross-government departmental basis and almost always include children's services, health, education and justice;

- Emphasise a collective/shared responsibility for improved child well-being, with interagency collaboration central to improvement and progress – for example, CYPSCs;
- Have a children's workforce development strategy and provide interagency guidance and training – for example, professionals working with children and their parents, public health nurses and social workers;
- Are developing information sharing systems and associated IT systems to support this.

Supporting Parents: Reflecting on International and Irish Evidence

Government policies internationally have been directed at promoting research that can provide evidence for effective early interventions and prevention programmes to improve child and family well-being. International efforts to extract the constituent elements or active ingredients that contribute to effectiveness in terms of both programme-specific and service provision in general have been achieved to a good extent. The employment of rigorous evaluation methods is producing evidence for models and programmes that can be easily replicated across different services and settings (McAuley *et al*, 2006), and this is being combined with an increasing body of literature identifying key theoretical underpinnings and practice principles to support programme and service development.

The following provides a summary of international and national evidence relating to supporting parents to improve outcomes for their children. It is not an exhaustive review of the literature, rather it identifies theories and approaches to parenting that have proven to be effective, particularly those approaches and programmes that are being replicated and delivered as part of the Prevention and Early Intervention Initiative in Ireland and Northern Ireland.

Why Supporting Parents Matters – the Evidence

Recent arguments purport that the most effective way of dealing with chronic long-term disadvantage and the intergenerational cycles of social problems is through early childhood intervention and, in particular, policies and programmes aimed at supporting the family in early childhood development (Munro, 2011; Allen, 2011). There is emerging consensus from the breadth of research and literature conducted in recent decades that demonstrates the impact of supporting parents:

- **Parenting in early childhood:**
  - Early intervention to promote social and emotional development has been shown to significantly improve mental and physical health, education and employment opportunities, and prevent criminal behaviour, substance abuse and teenage pregnancy (Barlow *et al*, 2012; Allen, 2011);
  - Parents are key mediators in developing and supporting desirable health-related behaviours among children and addressing undesirable behaviours (Allen, 2011);
  - Although poor parenting practices potentially can have a detrimental effect on children of all ages, children are most vulnerable when their brains are being formed before birth and during the first two years of life. This is the stage when the part of the brain governing emotional development is forming. The ante-natal period is as important as infancy to the health and well-being of a child because maternal behaviour has such strong impacts on the developing foetus (Allen, 2011);
  - Children who develop secure attachments to their primary caregivers are less likely to have social and emotional difficulties and reduced likelihood of developing problems associated with substance abuse and domestic violence (Davies and Ward, 2012; Allen, 2011; Heckman, 2010);
  - A supportive home learning environment is positively associated with children's early achievements and well-being and influences social mobility (Allen, 2011);
  - How a child is parented is more important than family structure or income. A negative parenting style is strongly associated with aggressive behaviour, delinquency, depression, anxiety and high risk behaviours – for example, smoking, drug/alcohol misuse (O'Connor and Scott, 2007).
- **Impact of positive parenting:**
  - Children's social, emotional and physical development can be greatly enhanced by parenting that is warm, attentive and stimulating (Allen, 2011);
  - Effective quality parenting can guide a child from infancy to a self-determining, self-regulated adult with the competence and emotional health to achieve pro-social goals and to interact effectively with others (Baumrind *et al*, 2010);

- The provision to parents of positive parenting skills and practice promotes healthy child adjustment and mediates the effects of risk factors, such as genetic susceptibility and social disadvantage (Shaw and Winslow, 1997);
- Parenting programmes have been shown to have an impact on the emotional and behavioural adjustment of children and to reduce the likelihood of the early occurrence of child behavioural and emotional problems (Barlow *et al*, 2012);
- Meta-analyses and systematic reviews covering an evidence base of over 100 studies have concluded that behavioural parent training is effective in ameliorating childhood behaviour problems and can lead to a 60 to 70% improvement in children (Nock, 2003; Coren *et al*, 2002; Behan and Carr, 2000; Brestan and Eyberg, 1998).

- **Adverse effects of poor quality parenting:**
  - Emotional abuse and neglect can have serious adverse long-term consequences across all aspects of development, including children's social and emotional well-being, cognitive development, physical health, mental health and behaviour, and lead to high costs to society through burdens on health and other services (Davies and Ward, 2012);
  - Children growing up in families affected by parental substance misuse, inter-parental conflict and mental ill-health will require additional support and intervention. Such difficulties are particularly conducive to abusive and neglectful parenting when they occur in combination and/or are compounded by other stressors such as parental learning disability, financial or housing problems and unsupportive or inadequate social and familial networks (Davies and Ward, 2012).
- **Cost implications:**
  - There is widespread recognition from governments, policy-makers, service commissioners and service providers of the increasing cost implications and burden on services resulting from behavioural and conduct problems in children and young people and also familial and parenting difficulties, resulting in increased contact with a range of adult and children's services, often over protracted periods of time – for example, children coming into the care of the state (Edwards *et al*, 2007; Muntz *et al*, 2004);
  - The cost of using health and social services at age 28 was found to be 10 times higher for people with childhood conduct disorders than those without (Scott *et al*, 2001);

- o Indicators of childhood behavioural problems at age 7 have significant negative effects on school attendance and contact with police (with both outcomes measured at age 16), as well as on early school leaving (Gregg and Machin, 1999).

Prevention and Early Intervention Initiative

Since 2004, a number of large-scale interventions have been funded and introduced in Ireland in an effort to assess the effectiveness of evidence-based prevention and early intervention programmes. The Prevention and Early Intervention Initiative (PEII) alluded to earlier provided – and continues to provide – services and programmes to support parents. A large number of these parenting programmes and initiatives have been the subject of rigorous evaluation and have demonstrated positive improvements in:

- Child behaviour;
- Parental self efficacy – confidence in completing the parenting task;
- Parenting skills;
- Levels of parental stress;
- Parental mental well-being;
- Social support for parents;
- The home learning environment.

A synthesis of the evaluations of all of the PEII was conducted by the Centre for Effective Services and the full outcomes reports, including parenting and improving child behaviour (Sneddon and Owens, 2012; Statham, 2013; Rochford *et al*, 2013) and briefing papers, can be found at www.effectiveservices.org/prevention/early-intervention.

Approaches to Supporting Parents and Parenting

The key messages in the literature and the increased focus on the economic and cost-effectiveness in children's services development and provision all point to the benefits, both short-term and long-term, of intervening early in children's lives. This has prompted the rapid development and implementation of a range of programmes and services to support children and families. Approaches to supporting parents to improve outcomes for children tend to be based on assessed need, using a tiered approach, and according to frameworks such as the Hardiker model mentioned previously. Supports and services for parents and children are provided at universal level or to families with additional needs, up to and including more intensive and specialist interventions and services at levels three and four with children and parents experiencing multiple difficulties.

Evidence-based and evidence-informed approaches to parenting range from population health approaches, which are universal and target the entire population and specific children and parents within that population, to individual home visiting programmes, which tend to target young mothers, parents with young children and those identified to be 'at risk'. Group-based parenting programmes can be offered to parents at universal services level and also provided to parents experiencing particular difficulties as parents themselves (substance abuse or mental illness) or with their children (emotional and behavioural difficulties). Intensive individual one-to-one approaches to supporting parents deemed hard to reach or who are less likely to benefit from participating in a group also have been developed.

Such services and interventions often are provided using a variety of methods, by different practice professionals, at varying levels of formality, and can take place in a variety of settings whether community-based clinics or family centres, schools and in the family home. Some services and interventions are directed solely at addressing the parenting process and the parent-child relationship, developing techniques and approaches for bringing up children (particularly parenting programmes). Other initiatives indirectly support parenting by providing parents with skills to promote and foster child development and well-being in specific areas, such as literacy or transition to secondary school.

Population Approaches

A population approach to parenting is non-stigmatising, more likely to reach families early and prevent escalation of childhood behaviour problems and parenting stress associated with this, and is more likely to reach those children whose needs or developing problems tend to pass unnoticed (Davies and Ward, 2012). Effective approaches include:

- Legislative changes – for example, physical chastisement ban (Durrant, 1999);
- Mass media public education programmes – for example, anti-bullying campaign (ISPCC);
- Universally accessible parenting programmes (Triple P) (Prinz *et al*, 2009).

The Triple P Positive Parenting Programme is a population-based approach that has been rigorously and extensively evaluated (Chu *et al*, 2012; Prinz *et al*, 2009; Sanders, 2008). Developed by Matt Sanders in Queensland, Australia, this is a multi-level parenting and family support strategy that aims to prevent severe behavioural, emotional and developmental problems in children by enhancing the knowledge, skills and confidence of their parents. The programme is based on a 'positive parenting' approach that aims to promote children's development and manage children's behaviour in a constructive manner. The five levels of intervention are:

- Level 1 – Universal Triple P targets the entire population and uses health promotion and public awareness and media strategies;
- Level 2 – Selected Triple P targets subgroups of parents deemed to be at greater risk than others;
- Level 3 – Primary Care Triple P targets children with mild to moderate behavioural difficulties;
- Level 4 – Group Triple P is designed for parents of children with more severe behavioural difficulties;
- Level 5 – Enhanced Triple P is a more intensive intervention programme aimed at parents experiencing conflict, depression or high levels of stress.

In Ireland, the Midlands Area Parenting Partnership (MAPP), which consists of a number of statutory and voluntary organisations, is currently responsible for the implementation of the Triple P programme in the counties of Longford, Westmeath, Laois and Offaly. The overarching goal of MAPP is to improve outcomes for children at risk of developing emotional and behavioural difficulties by strengthening collaborative relationships and referral pathways for children and their families. The implementation of Triple P in Longford/Westmeath was subject to evaluation, the findings of which indicate that this partnership approach to service delivery has resulted in improved outcomes for both parents and children (Fives *et al*, 2014).

Home-visiting Programmes

Home-visiting programmes, expanded and sustained health-visiting services and universal health care programmes for expectant mothers all have the potential to improve parents' ability to parent and promote positive parenting behaviours (Davies and Ward, 2012; Olds, 2002; Olds and Korfmacher, 1998). Home-visiting increasingly is being employed as an approach in preventive interventions designed to intervene with families with young children. In general, the goals of home-visiting programmes are to provide parents with information, emotional support, access to other community services, and direct instruction on parenting practices (Howard and Brooks-Gunn, 2009). Many home-visiting programmes target their service to socio-economically deprived, first-time, teenage parents. Such programmes allow service providers to more easily engage with hard-to reach populations, thus removing challenges that might deter families from participating in centre-based forms of intervention (Astuto and Allen, 2009). Meta-analyses of evaluations of home-visiting programmes (Kahn and Moore, 2010; Gomby, 2007), examining the effects across several domains such as overall physical health, externalising behaviour, cognitive development, social skills, mental/emotional health, parenting skills, parent/child relationship, child maltreatment, substance use and reproductive health, have concluded that:

- Early childhood home-visiting schemes are effective in improving a range of outcomes for children and demonstrate long-term cost-effectiveness;
- Home-visiting programmes can produce benefits for children and parents, but are most beneficial for families where either the need or the perceived need is greatest, with some studies suggesting that the mothers categorised as high risk (low income, teen mothers, those with low IQ or those with mental health problems) may benefit most;
- Programmes that offer home-visiting in conjunction with centre-based programmes produce the largest and most long-lasting results, compared to programmes that offer home-visiting services alone. In particular, centre-based programmes with a parenting training component have been found to improve child vocabulary, reading and mathematical skills, and overall IQ;
- Effective programmes include high-intensity early childhood interventions that last for more than a year, with an average of four or more home-visits per month, and programmes that use therapists/social workers to teach parenting skills;
- A significant finding is that some of these improvements have been found to last into the adolescent years;
- Parenting programmes that involve both parents and preschool staff are more successful in addressing behavioural problems than programmes that involve only parents.

The Nurse-Family Partnership has been a particularly successful early intervention home-visiting programme to improve outcomes for children and families. It is a home-visiting programme provided by nurses to low-income, first-time mothers, commencing at the prenatal stage and continuing during pregnancy. The aim is to improve pregnancy outcomes through better health-related behaviours, and to improve parenting both in the short-term and long-term by facilitating the development of better skills in the care of the child, planning and economic self-sufficiency. The programme employs a model based on theories of human ecology, self-efficacy and attachment. Nurses develop trusting relationships with mothers and other family members to review their childhood experience of being parented, to help them decide how they themselves want to parent, and to promote sensitive, empathetic care of their children.

The Nurse-Family Partnership was first developed in the US (Olds, 2002), where it has been shown to have lasting and wide-ranging impacts, including a reduction in children's injuries and in adolescent anti-social behaviour. Rigorous evaluations also have shown that the programme reduces physical abuse and neglect, and associated adverse outcomes such as injuries to the children of first-time, disadvantaged mothers. In recent years, the Public Health Agency in Northern Ireland has introduced the Family Nurse Partnership into voluntary and statutory organisations and the approach is widely used across Europe and North America.

The Community Mothers Programme, first established in Ireland in 1988, is facilitated by the Health Service Executive. For first-time and second-time parents of children from birth to 24 months, who live in disadvantaged areas, its aim is to develop the skills of parents of young children with a focus on health care, nutritional improvement and overall child development. It is a parent support programme in which local women known as Community Mothers carry out monthly structured visits by appointment to first-time parents during the first year of their babies' lives, providing information in a non-directive way to foster parenting skills and parental self-esteem. The programme is currently being delivered by 157 Community Mothers to 1,400 families. Home-visits also are being delivered to Travellers and refugees / asylum-seekers. Evaluations of the programme have found that it has significant beneficial effects for mothers and children (Johnson *et al*, 1993, 2000).

Other services employing a home-visiting component are being delivered and evaluated as part of the Prevention and Early Intervention Initiative and Area-based Childhood programme in Ireland and

Northern Ireland. These include Preparing for Life, a prevention and early intervention home-visiting programme that aims to improve levels of school-readiness of young children living in several designated disadvantaged areas of North Dublin; the Tallaght West Childhood Development Initiative; and Ready Steady Grow, a programme of youngballymun. The Lifestart Foundation is delivering the evidence-based programme, The Growing Child, to parents with children from birth to age 5 across numerous sites in Ireland and Northern Ireland. Home-visiting is also a key feature of the integrated and co-ordinated services being delivered as part of the Area-based Childhood programme in Limerick, Cork and Dublin.

Another key area is the potential for home-visiting programmes to influence and improve the home-learning environment (Melhuish, 2010; Sylva *et al*, 2004; Desforges and Abouchaar, 2003; Tizard and Hughes, 2002). Findings from the Effective Provision of Preschool Education (EPPE) project in the UK (Sylva *et al*, 2004) demonstrated that higher quality home-learning environments are positively associated with social, behavioural and cognitive development. The home-learning environment was a stronger predictor of child cognitive outcomes in preschool children than either social class or parental education. The authors concluded that engagement in activities in the home with their child that promote cognitive development could counteract the negative effects of social class or level of parental education. Follow up with these children at age 11 demonstrated that the home-learning environments still had a significant effect on social and behavioural scores (Melhuish, 2010).

An example of a home-learning programme being delivered in Ireland is the Parent-Child Home Programme, which is being implemented in the docklands and other areas of Dublin. This US model has been in existence for over 40 years and its operation and effectiveness has been subject to longitudinal multi-site randomised control studies showing positive results (Rafoth and Knickelbein, 2005; Levenstein *et al*, 1998; Lazar and Darlington, 1982). The model is focused on parents as the key to promoting school-readiness and academic success, and is aimed at strengthening parent-child verbal interaction through reading and play activities in the home.

Group-based Parenting Programmes

Providing support to parents is recognised as a significant factor in improving children's lives, and there is a growing emphasis on structured parenting programmes, often delivered in a group format, that aim to improve parenting and family relationships by providing advice, support and sometimes an opportunity to develop/practice skills. Research has suggested that positive outcomes following parental programmes can continue for up to four years post-intervention (Spoth *et al*, 2000; Spoth *et al*, 1999). This accumulating body of evidence indicates that parenting programmes have the potential to lead to better outcomes and lifestyles for parents, children and adolescents (Chu *et al*, 2012) and many large-scale international group parenting programmes have evolved, including the Incredible Years Programme (Webster-Stratton, 1998), which will be discussed in greater detail later in this section, and the Triple P Positive Parenting Programme (Sanders, 1999), described earlier.

In parallel, there are also a number of individual studies, meta-analyses and literature reviews analysing the effectiveness of these group parenting programmes. Findings from this extensive body of research are summarised below.

Parenting programmes delivered in group settings:

- Are effective in improving child conduct problems. Meta-analyses of randomised controlled trials show that group-based behavioural parent training is about twice as effective as individual therapy in reducing behaviour problems (McCart *et al*, 2006);
- Improve the development of positive parenting skills in the short-term, and also reduce parental anxiety, stress and depression, according to a recent Cochrane systematic review (Furlong *et al*, 2012);
- Can have positive effects on maternal psychosocial health. As maternal mental health has been shown to affect the parent-child relationship, which in turn can have both short-term and long-term consequences for the psychological health of the child, any programme that improves the mental health of parents also may improve child outcomes (Barlow and Parsons, 2003; Gross *et al*, 2003);
- Have been shown to be successful in improving maternal depression, anxiety/stress, self-esteem and relationships with spouse, but had little effect on maternal social support (Barlow *et al*, 2002). There is a lack of studies examining the long-term effectiveness of these programmes; the few studies that have been conducted in this area have found ambiguous results (Gross *et al*, 2003);
- Improve behaviour outcomes for children under the age of three years (Barlow and Parsons, 2003; Gross *et al*, 1995);
- Are successful in improving behavioural problems in 3 to 10 year old children (Barlow and Stewart-Brown, 2001). From 16 programmes reviewed, they found that the programmes were effective in creating positive changes in both parental perceptions and objective measures

of children's behaviour and that these changes were maintained over time.

The Incredible Years BASIC Preschool/Early School Years Parent Training (IYP) programme is a programme developed by Carolyn Webster-Stratton and is a brief, group-based intervention for parents of children aged 2 to 7 years, guided by the principles of behavioural and social learning theory. Considerable research has been undertaken in North America and Europe to assess the programme, and the evidence suggests that the programme significantly improves parent-child interactions and child behaviour outcomes (Furlong *et al*, 2012; Larsson *et al*, 2009; Hutchings *et al*, 2007; Gardner *et al*, 2006; Reid *et al*, 2003; Gross *et al*, 2003; Reid and Webster-Stratton, 2001; Scott *et al*, 2001; Webster-Stratton and Hancock, 1998). In Ireland, the IYP programme is being delivered mainly in disadvantaged areas nationally. Findings from the IYP evaluation demonstrated the effectiveness and cost-effectiveness of the programme as an intervention to reduce the early onset of conduct problems amongst young children in community-based settings, and significantly in improving parenting skills, competencies and the well-being of family members (McGilloway *et al*, 2012).

Another group-based parenting programme, developed in Ireland and currently being delivered in schools, Child and Adolescent Mental Health Services (CAMHS) and community-based settings across the country, is the Parents Plus parenting programme. Parents Plus is an evidence-based parenting programme developed by Professor Carol Fitzpatrick, Dr John Sharry and other Irish professionals in the Mater Child and Adolescent Mental Health Service. There are three programmes aimed at three different age groups:

- Parents Plus Early Years Programme (1 – 6 years);
- Parents Plus Children's Programme (6 – 11 years);
- Parents Plus Adolescent Programme (11 – 16 years).

The Parents Plus programmes have been subject to randomised control trials and independent evaluations in Ireland and the UK. The studies have shown that the programmes are effective in reducing behaviour problems in children, reducing parental stress and achieving high parent satisfaction (Nitsch, 2011; Coughlin *et al*, 2009; Beattie *et al*, 2007; Quinn *et al*, 2007; Quinn *et al*, 2006; Griffin *et al*, 2010; Sharry *et al*, 2005; Behan *et al*, 2001).

The Odyssey programme (formerly the Parenting UR Teen Programme) was developed by Parenting NI in response to the lack of programmes specifically targeted at parents of adolescents. The programme is a group-based intervention delivered over eight weeks in 2-hour sessions, using a variety of techniques, including presentations by programme facilitators, role plays, problem-solving and group discussions. The programme has provided strong evidence for an effective parenting programme for adolescents. The programme has had a positive effect on the mental health and well-being of parents, has enhanced the relationship between parents and their teenage children, and has reduced distress through lessening of conflictual situations (Higgins *et al*, 2012).

One-to-one Individual Parenting Programmes

Parenting programmes can lead to a reduction in children's behaviour problems and parental stress/mental health difficulties (Sanders, 2010; Gould and Richardson, 2006; Griffin *et al*, 2010; Barlow *et al*, 2002; Webster-Stratton and Hancock, 1998). Individual one-to-one programmes and approaches have been designed that promote and strengthen the quality of the parent-child relationship.

Parent-Child Interaction Therapy (PCIT) is an evidence-based behavioural training for parents of children aged 2 to 7 years and their caregivers (Eyberg and Pincus, 1999). It is used extensively in clinical services in Ireland and Northern Ireland. PCIT is aimed at young children experiencing emotional and behavioural disorders and places an emphasis on improving the quality of the parent-child relationship and changing parent-child interaction patterns. PCIT outcome research has demonstrated statistically and clinically significant improvements in the behaviour problems of preschool age children (Eyberg *et al*, 1995), is effective with children with autism (Masse *et al*, 2007) and oppositional defiant disorder (Zisser and Eyberg, 2009), and with physically abusing parents (Chaffin and Silovsky, 2004).

Another parenting programme being delivered in Ireland, with a focus on the parent-child relationship, is the Marte Meo programme. It is a video-based communication approach to child development that focuses on the quality of the interaction between child and caregiver. Marte Meo is most often conducted in the family home or residential setting and can be used with children from 0 to 18 years. Developed by Maria Aarts in The Netherlands, it is an evidence-informed approach to parenting being implemented in over 40 countries worldwide and has been delivered in Ireland through the Health Service Executive (HSE) since 1995, and is now centrally delivered through Tusla, the Child and Family Agency. There are currently 180 accredited Marte Meo therapists from a range of professional backgrounds using this parent training method in all HSE and Tusla regions. The Marte Meo programme is subject to evaluation in Ireland and Europe.

School-based Delivery or Complementary Support

It has been posited that consistency between the home and preschool setting is extremely important in order to provide a lasting change in children's behaviour as a result of a parenting intervention (Webster-Stratton and Reid, 2010). In this regard, parenting programmes for families at risk from multiple disadvantage are best delivered in a school or preschool setting as a strategic way of targeting more children in need (Webster-Stratton and Reid, 2010) and also a more diverse range of families (Cunningham *et al*, 1995). Family economic resources and quality of parenting have been found to play a unique role in children's cognitive abilities at 14, 24, and 36 months in an ethnically-diverse sample of 2,089 children from low-income families (Lugo-Gil and Tamis-LeMonda, 2008). This study suggests that preschool intervention programmes, including parenting programmes for low-income families, are imperative in preparing children for school. As the intervention is targeted at all families in a setting, the programme is non-stigmatising and it not only offers the chance to target children before problems escalate, it also allows children with more developed social skills to model appropriate behaviours for those that may benefit most from an intervention (Webster-Stratton and Reid, 2010).

Intensive Individual and Family-Based Interventions

Most of the programmes or interventions identified above are either universal or targeted at particular populations – for example, young mothers, parents of young children, children presenting with emotional and behavioural difficulties. However, children growing up in families affected by parental substance abuse, inter-familial conflict and mental illness will require more focused intervention that seeks to address both individual and family issues. Programmes that are designed to address adults' own experiences of poor parenting and/or the psychological consequences of abuse can make a valuable contribution. Parent-Child Interaction Therapy (Brinkmeyer and Eyberg, 2003) and the Enhanced Triple P Positive Parenting programme (Sanders *et al*, 2004) now include additional sessions on stress management and parental support.

Training in communication and problem-solving has been found to help families deal with conflict and enhance social functioning. Family-focused interventions concentrate on the interaction between all family members as well as the mental health of the individual. The Strengthening Families Programme (SFP) is a 14-session, science-based parenting skills, children's life skills, and family life skills training programme specifically designed for high-risk families. Parents and children participate in SFP, both separately and together. Positive results from over 15 independent research replicated studies and a Cochrane systematic review have demonstrated that the programme is robust and effective in increasing protective factors by improving family relationships, parenting skills, and improving youth's social and life skills (Kumpfer *et al*, 2010; Foxcroft *et al*, 2003). The SFP for 12 to 16 year olds is being delivered in Ireland through probation services and local drug and alcohol community groups in 52 sites covering all counties. The programme, designed for high-risk families of 3 to 6 year olds, has potential for use in the early years.

Challenges to Supporting Parents

Multiple Problem Families

Permeating throughout the research literature is the acknowledged difficulty of intervening effectively and achieving good outcomes for families most marginalised and disadvantaged, and engaging them in services (Tanner and Turney, 2006; Stevenson, 2007, 1998; Smith, 2006). The longstanding, complex problems associated with neglect require longer term, multi-dimensional and co-ordinated intervention, involving a combination of concrete and therapeutic services that target the particular issues in the family and include direct work with both children and parents (Thoburn *et al*, 2000). The literature further identifies that, whatever the approach, an empowering and empathic relationship between the worker and the parent must exist. A parent's own adverse childhood experiences are known to be associated with child abuse (Allen, 2011; Anda *et al*, 2006). Many parents will be unlikely to benefit from specific interventions to improve their parenting skills unless some of these and/or other underlying issues also have been addressed (Furlong *et al*, 2012; Cleaver *et al*, 2011). Parents are likely to require individual therapeutic intervention to deal with their own childhood difficulties that are impacting on their parenting capacity (Stevenson, 2007; Tanner and Turney, 2006; Iwaniec, 2004).

Engagement of Families

Recruitment and engagement of families to parenting programmes or services is a key component to producing improved outcomes for their children. Figures for dropping out of child and family support services, in international research, range from 20% to 50% (Staudt, 2007; Staudt, 2003; Daro and Donnelly, 2002; Daro and Harding, 1999; McKay *et al*, 1996; Kazdin and Mazurick, 1994). Research informs us that high attrition and low attendance and participation in services can lead to poor outcomes for children, with children who do not receive any form of intervention or service when identified as in need and being more likely to engage in delinquent activities later in life including involvement in violent crime, school drop-out, drug and alcohol abuse and unemployment, and to have mental health problems (Nock and Photos, 2006; Fergusson and Lynskey, 1998). A review of prevention research reported that, despite extensive efforts and a clear, strengths-based approach to service delivery, the majority of families reached by prevention programmes will leave before reaching their service goals or achieving the service levels articulated in a particular programme's model (Daro and Donnelly, 2002).

Parenting programmes, particularly those aimed at families presenting with multiple difficulties, tend to report relatively low participation and high drop-out rates. Research findings report that, where attrition data was collected, as many as half of all parents referred to behavioural parent training programmes may drop out prematurely (Spencer, 2003). Even in the case of programmes whose effectiveness has been robustly evaluated, it has been reported that up to two-fifths of parents will continue to experience problems with their children (Assemany and McIntosh, 2002). A meta-analysis of 31 studies found that socially-isolated parents with mental health problems and high levels of poverty-related stress benefited least from parent training (Reyno and McGrath, 2006). These parents require additional interventions aimed at addressing parental vulnerabilities. For many families, life circumstances dictate the use of multiple services, whether voluntarily sought out or recommended by others, and in many cases where child health and education, mental health or substance abuse difficulties are experienced, parents often are referred simultaneously to a number of different services providers, where weekly attendance is required. Without appropriate sequencing of service referrals, parents may well become overwhelmed by the demands and expectations placed upon them, resulting in disengagement from any or all of the multiple services on offer (Staudt, 2007, 2003).

The optimum approach to offering parenting support is to provide services to children and families where they are able to make a voluntary choice to receive them. Parents who voluntarily engage with support services tend to make more progress, while a more coercive approach by service providers can affect the relationship and block progress (Fauth *et al*, 2010). It is important that programmes and services aimed at parents develop strategies to increase the likelihood that parents will attend services – for example, conducting outreach visits, making convenient and flexible appointments and session times, providing transport assistance or other facilities to reduce potential barriers to engagement – for example, crèche facilities (Staudt, 2007).

The Way Forward – Recommendations for a National Parenting Action Plan

Special Interest Group: Supporting Parents in their Parenting Role

The Special Interest Group – Supporting Parents in their Parenting Role (Special Interest Group), chaired and established by the Centre for Effective Services since the end of 2010, has been contributing substantially to the supporting parents policy agenda. This all-island group currently includes agency directors or CEOs, funders and public officials, professional bodies and practitioners engaged in direct work and academics and professional researchers in the relevant sectors. The SIG warmly welcomes the commitment made by the Government in the *Children and Young People's Policy Framework* to develop a 'high-level policy statement on parenting and family support to guide the provision of universal evidence-informed parenting supports' (Department of Children and Youth Affairs, 2014; Special Interest Group, 2013).

The high-level policy statement is an opportunity for the Government to make clear its commitment to parents at the centre of children's lives, reflecting the Constitutional position of the family as the primary and natural educator of the child, and to set out the ways in which the state and other actors can support parents in their parenting role.

The SIG interprets parenting support to be practice approaches, services and interventions that:

- Empower parents by developing parenting confidence and competence;
- Enable parents to foster optimal child well-being and development outcomes;
- Increase enjoyment and satisfaction of parenting.

The work of the SIG has developed a number of key themes that should form the basis of a policy and subsequent parenting action plan to support parents in Ireland:

- Integrated planning;
- Reconfiguration of resources;
- Building on 'what works';
- Inter-agency workforce development, training and support;
- Data and knowledge collection and dissemination.

Integrated Planning

The Plan should draw together the range of services provided to support parents – for example, by public health nurses and wider primary care teams, Tusla, maternity hospitals, schools (for example, home-school community liaison), early years services, early intervention teams, family resource centres and community and voluntary sector organisations, as well as the delivery of specific evidence-based and evidence-informed parenting programmes and practices. Similarly, it should encompass both universal and targeted programmes and approaches. Co-ordination is needed also at local level – drawing together statutory, community and voluntary provision – and the plan should specify the local structures responsible. Children and Young People's Services Committees (CYPSCs) should be the structure for local co-ordination of parenting actions and approaches through the CYPSC itself and or subgroups within it.

Reconfiguration of Resources

Central to a successful parenting action plan will be reconfiguring what is already in place to work more effectively through co-ordinated commissioning, planning and work force development. Integrated planning of how services are commissioned and delivered is complex and requires inter-organisational co-operation at various levels in the system along with strong local collaboration.

Building on What Works

There is now a clear and ever-growing evidence base that indicates that appropriate interventions and supports, when implemented early in childhood, can improve child health and well-being and family functioning, and reduce the risks of poor long-term outcomes. Parenting clearly plays a key role in influencing child development and behaviour, and there is now a suite of fully evidence-based prevention and early intervention programmes and services being delivered in Ireland that target parenting as a means of tackling embedded childhood difficulties. Most notably these interventions also have been shown to significantly reduce the potential for early childhood problems to remain into late childhood, adolescence and adulthood.

Inter-agency Workforce Development, Training and Support

To facilitate the delivery of evidence-based programmes and services within local communities, a national inter-agency workforce development plan for parenting support needs to be developed, building on the work of the Health Service Executive's National Workforce Development Team and jointly co-ordinated by it and Tusla.

Data and Knowledge Collection and Dissemination

Knowledge, evidence and data collection, collation and dissemination are critical to understanding and developing a national picture of children's lives and those of their parents and families. This information and data helps to inform policy, research and practice and ensures that decision-making is informed by evidence. A number of large-scale and small-scale policy and practice initiatives currently being delivered and implemented in Ireland and referenced earlier in this chapter are contributing to a burgeoning evidence base about effective interventions, approaches and programmes to support parents (for example, the Prevention and Early Intervention Initiative, the Area-based Childhood programme, the Parenting Support Initiative, *Growing Up in Ireland*, *State of the Nation's Children* reports).

CONCLUSION

This chapter has presented evidence – both international and national – of the value in supporting parents to improve outcomes for children. It calls for the continued and effective development and implementation of policy and practice in adherence with the UN *Convention* and emphasises the necessity of the key underpinning principles in policy and practice of prevention and early intervention, focusing on proven approaches and more efficient co-ordination and collaboration in service delivery. In summary, if we support parents, we achieve the results shown in **Table 5.3**.

Table 5.3: Potential Results from Effective Support of Parents

Benefits for parents	Benefits for children	Benefits for society
Better family relationships. Better mental and emotional health. Better socio-economic prospects. More active community participation. More knowledgeable about their child's development. Better home learning environment. Increased understanding of the importance of play and interaction with their children.	Better child/parent bonding and attachment. Better social, emotional and cognitive outcomes. Better health outcomes – reduction in childhood obesity. Better self-identity and self-esteem. Better resiliency and school-readiness. Better outcomes in later life across a range of psycho-social dimensions.	Reduced social costs. Effective use of resources. Productive, well-educated workforce. Reduction of inequalities. Promoting active citizenship. Developing human and social capital. Improved cross-departmental and cross-sectoral co-operation.

Source: Ghate (2009).

REFERENCES

Allen, G. (2011). *Early Intervention: The Next Steps*, London: The Stationery Office .

Anda, R., Felitti, V., Walker, J., Whitfield, C., Bremner, J., Perry, B., Dube, S. and Giles, W. (2006). 'The Enduring Effects of Abuse and Related Adverse Experiences in Childhood: A Convergence of Evidence from Neurobiology and Epidemiology', *European Archives of Psychiatry and Clinical Neuroscience*, Vol.256, pp.174-86.

Assemany, A.E. and McIntosh, D.E. (2002). 'Negative Treatment Outcomes of Behavioural Parent Training Programs', *Psychology in the Schools*, Vol.39, pp.209-19.

Astuto, J. and Allen, L. (2009). 'Home-visitation and Young Children: An Approach Worth Investing In?', *Social Policy Report: Publication of the Society for Research in Child Development*, Vol.23, pp.1-22.

Barlow, J. and Parsons, J. (2003). 'Group-based Parent-training Programmes for Improving Emotional and Behavioural Adjustment in 0-3 year old Children', *Cochrane Database of Systematic Reviews 2003*, Iss.4.

Barlow, J. and Scott, J. (2010). *Safeguarding in the 21st Century – Where to Now?*, Dartington: Research in Practice.

Barlow, J. and Stewart-Brown, S. (2001). 'Understanding Parenting Programmes: Parents' Views', *Primary Health Care Research and Development*, Vol.2, pp.117-30.

Barlow, J., Coren, E. and Stewart-Brown, S. (2002). 'Meta-analysis of the Effectiveness of Parenting Programmes in Improving Maternal Psychosocial Health', *British Journal of General Practice*, Vol.52, pp.223-33.

Barlow, J., Smailagic, N., Huband, N., Roloff, V. and Bennett, C. (2012). 'Group-based Parent Training Programmes for Improving Parental Psychosocial Health', *Cochrane Database of Systematic Reviews 2003*, Vol.13, No.6.

Baumrind, D., Larzelere, R.E. and Owens, E. (2010). 'Effects of Preschool Parents' Power Assertive Patterns and Practices on Adolescent Development', *Parenting: Science and Practice*, Vol.10, No.3, pp.157-201.

Beattie, D., Fitzpatrick, C., Guerin, S. and O'Donoghue, P. (2007) *Parent Management Training for Adolescent Mental Health Disorders – A controlled trial*, Dublin: University College Dublin.

Behan, J. and Carr, A. (2000). 'Oppositional Defiant Disorder' in Carr, A. (ed.), *What Works With Children And Adolescents? A Critical Review of Psychological Interventions with Children, Adolescents and Their Families*, London: Routledge.

Behan, J., Fitzpatrick, C., Sharry, J., Carr, A. and Waldron, B. (2001). 'Evaluation of the Parents Plus Programme', *Irish Journal of Psychology*, Vol.22, No.3-4, pp.238-56.

Best Health for Children (2002). *Investing in Parenthood to Achieve Best Health for Children: The Supporting Parents Strategy*, Dublin: Best Health for Children.

Brestan, E.V. and Eyberg, S.M. (1998). 'Effective Psychosocial Treatments of Conduct-disordered Children and Adolescents: 29 years, 82 studies and 5,272 Kids', *Journal of Clinical Psychology*, Vol.27, pp.180-89.

Brinkmeyer, M. and Eyberg, S.M. (2003). 'Parent-child Interaction Therapy for Oppositional Children' in Kazdin, A.E. and Weisz, J.R. (eds.), *Evidence-based Psychotherapies for Children and Adolescents*, New York: Guilford Publications.

Bronfenbrenner, U. (1979). *The Ecology of Human Development*, Cambridge, MA: Harvard University Press.

Central Statistics Office (2011). *This is Ireland: Highlights from Census 2011: Part 1*, Dublin: Government Publications.

Chaffin, M. and Silovsky, J.F. (2004). 'Parent-Child Interaction Therapy with Physically Abusive Parents: Efficacy for Reducing Future Abuse Reports', *Journal of Consulting Clinical Psychology*, Vol.72, No.4, pp.500 10.

Chu, J.T.W., Farragia, S.P., Sanders, M.R. and Ralph, A. (2012). 'Towards a Public Health Approach to Parenting Programmes for Parents of Adolescents', *Journal of Public Health*, Vol.34 (Supplement 1), pp.141-47.

Cleaver, H., Unell, I. and Aldgate, J. (2011). *Children's Needs – Parenting Capacity: The Impact of Parental Mental Illness, Learning Disability, Problem Alcohol and Drug Use and Domestic Violence on Children's Safety*, second edition, London: The Stationery Office.

Commission on the Family (1998). *Strengthening Families for Life, Final Report*, Dublin: Government Publications.

Coren, E., Barlow, J. and Stewart-Brown, S. (2002). 'Systematic Review of the Effectiveness of Parenting Programmes for Teenage Parents', *Journal of Adolescence*, Vol.26, pp.79-103.

Coughlin, M., Sharry, J., Fitzpatrick, C., Guerin, S. and Drumm, M. (2009) (2009). 'A Clinical Evaluation of the Parents Plus Children's Programme: A Training Course for Parents of Children with Behavioural and / or Developmental Problems', *Clinical Child Psychology and Psychiatry*, Vol.14, No.4, pp.541-58.

Cunningham, C.E., Bremner, R.B. and Boyle, M. (1995). 'Large Group Community-based Parenting Programs for Families of Preschoolers at Risk for Disruptive Behaviour Disorders: Utilization, Cost-effectiveness and Outcome', *Journal of Child Psychology and Psychiatry*, Vol.36, pp.1141-59.

Daly, M. (2012). 'Parenting Support – A New Policy Domain in Northern Ireland and Elsewhere', briefing paper for *Knowledge Exchange Seminars*, Stormont, NI Assembly, 4 October.

Daro, D. and Donnelly, A. (2002). 'Charting the Waves of Prevention: Two Steps Forward, One Step Back', *Child Abuse and Neglect*, Vol.26, pp.731-42.

Daro, D. and Harding, K.A. (1999). 'Healthy Families America: Using Research to Enhance Practice', *Future of Children*, Vol.9, pp.152-76.

Davies, C. and Ward, H. (2012). *Safeguarding Children Across Services: Message from Research*, London: Jessica Kingsley Publishers.

Department of Children and Youth Affairs (2012). *Report of the Task Force on the Child and Family Support Agency*, Dublin: Government Publications.

Department of Children and Youth Affairs (2012). *State of the Nation's Children* Dublin: Government Publications.

Department of Children and Youth Affairs (2014). *Better Outcomes, Brighter Futures: National Policy Framework for Children and Young People 2014- 2020*, Dublin: Government Publications.

Department of Health and Children (2000). *Our Children, Their Lives: The National Children's Strategy*, Dublin: Government Publications.

Department of Health and Children (2006). *State of the Nation's Children: Ireland 2006*, Dublin: Government Publications.

Department of Health and Children (2007). *Growing Up in Ireland: National Longitudinal Study of Children*, Dublin: Economic and Social Research Institute, Trinity College Dublin and Office of the Minister for Children and Youth Affairs.

Department of Health and Children (2008). *State of the Nation's Children: Ireland 2008*, Dublin: Government Publications.

Department of Health and Children (2010). *State of the Nation's Children: Ireland 2010*, Dublin: Government Publications.

Department of the Taoiseach (2011). *Programme for Government 2011–2016*, Dublin: Government Publications.

Desforges, C. and Abouchaar, A. (2003). *The Impact of Parental Involvement, Parental Support and Family Education on Pupil Achievement and Adjustment: A Literature Review*, London: Department for Education and Skills.

Durrant, J.E. (1999). 'Evaluating the Success of Sweden's Corporal Punishment Ban', *Child Abuse and Neglect, Vol.23*, No.5, pp.435-48.

Edwards, R.T., Ó Céilleachair, A., Bywater, T., Hughes, D.A. and Hutchings, J. (2007). 'Parenting Programme for Parents of Children at Risk of Developing Conduct Disorder: Cost-Effective Analysis', *British Medical Journal*, Vol.334, No.682. doi:10.1136/bmj.39126.699421.55.

Eyberg, S. and Pincus, D. (1999). *Eyberg Child Behavior Inventory & Sutter-Eyberg Student Behavior Inventory-Revised: Professional Manual*, Odessa, FL: Psychological Assessment Resources.

Eyberg, S.M., Boggs, S. and Algina, J. (1995). 'Parent-child Interaction Therapy: A Psychosocial Model for the Treatment of Young Children with Conduct Problem Behavior and Their Families', *Psychopharmacology Bulletin*, Vol.31, pp.83-91.

Fauth, R., Jelecic, H., Hart, D., Burton, S. and Shemmings, D. (2010). *Effective Practice to Protect Children Living in 'Highly Resistant' Families*, London: C4EO.

Fergusson, D. and Lynskey, M. (1998). 'Conduct Problems in Childhood and Psychosocial Outcomes in Young Adulthood: A Prospective Study', *Journal of Emotional and Behavioural Disorders*, Vol.6, pp.2-18.

Fernandez, E. (2004). 'Supporting Children and Responding to their Families: Capturing the Evidence on Family Support', *Children and Youth Services Review*, Vol.29, pp.1368-94.

Fives, A., Pursell, L., Heary, C., Nic Gabhainn, S. and Canavan, J. (2014). *Parenting Support for Every Parent: A Population-level Evaluation of Triple P in Longford Westmeath: Summary Report*, Athlone: Longford Westmeath Parenting Partnership.

Foxcroft, D., Ireland, D., Lister-Sharp, D., Lowe, G. and Breen, R. (2003). 'Longer-term Primary Prevention for Alcohol Misuse in Young People: A Systematic Review', *Addiction*, Vol.98, No.4, pp.397-411.

Furlong, M., McGilloway, S., Bywater, T., Hutchings, J., Smith, S.M. and Donnelly, M. (2012). *Group Parenting Programmes for Improving Behavioural Problems in Children aged 3 to 12 Years*, Cochrane Database of Systematic Reviews.

Gardner, F., Burton, J. and Klimes, I. (2006). 'Randomised Controlled Trial of a Parenting Intervention in the Voluntary Sector for Reducing Child Conduct Problems, Outcomes and Mechanisms of Change', *Journal of Child Psychology & Psychiatry*, Vol.47, pp.1123-32.

Ghate, D. (2009). 'Messages from Research about Quality in Parenting Services', *Parents Advice Centre NI 30th Anniversary Conference*, Belfast, 22 May.

Gomby, D.S. (2007). 'The Promise and Limitations of Home-visiting: Implementing Effective Programs', *Child Abuse and Neglect*, Vol.31, pp.793-99.

Gould, N. and Richardson, R. (2006). 'Parent-training/Education Programmes in the Management of Children with Conduct Disorders: Developing an Integrated Evidence-based Perspective for Health and Social Care', *Journal of Children's Services*, Vol.1, No.4, pp.47-60.

Gregg, P. and Machin, S. (1999). 'Childhood Disadvantage and Success or Failure in the Labour Market' in Blanchflower, D. and Freeman, R. (eds.), *Youth Employment and Joblessness in Advanced Countries*, Cambridge, MA: National Bureau of Economic Research.

Griffin, C., Guerin, S., Sharry, J. and Drumm, M. (2010). 'A Multi-centre Controlled Study of an Early Intervention Parenting Programme for Young Children with Behavioural and Developmental Difficulties', *International Journal of Clinical and Health Psychology*, Vol.10, No.2, pp.279-94.

Gross, D., Fogg, L. and Tucker, S. (1995). 'The Efficacy of Parent Training for Promoting Positive Parent-toddler Relationships', *Research in Nursing and Health*, Vol.18, pp.489-99.

Gross, D., Fogg, L., Webster-Stratton, C., Garvey, C., Julion, W. and Grady, J. (2003). 'Parent Training of Toddlers in Day Care in Low-income Urban Communities', *Journal of Consulting and Clinical Psychology*, Vol.71, No.2, pp.261-78.

Hanafin, S. and Brooks, A. (2005). *Report on the Development of a National Set of Child Well-being Indicators in Ireland*, Dublin: Government Publications.

Hardiker, P. (2002). 'A Framework for Conceptualising Need and its Application to Planning and Providing Services' in Ward, H. and Rose, W. (eds.), *Approaches to Needs Assessment in Children's Services*, London: Jessica Kingsley Publishers.

Hardiker, P., Exton, K. and Barker, M. (1991). *Policies and Practices in Preventative Child Care,* Aldershot: Avebury.

Health Service Executive (2011). *Reports of the National Review Panel for Serious Incidents and Child Deaths,* Dublin: Government Publications.

Heckman, J.J. (2010). 'Building Bridges between Structural and Program Evaluation Approaches to Evaluating Policy', *Journal of Economic Literature,* Vol.48, No.2, pp.356-98.

Henricson, C. and Bainham, H. (2005). *The Child and Family Policy Divide: Tensions, Convergences and Rights,* York: Joseph Rowntree Foundation

Higgins, K., MacDonald, G., McLaughlin, K., O' Hara, L., McCann, M. and Moriarty, J. (2012). *Parenting UR Teen: A Randomised Trial of Implementation and Effectiveness,* Belfast: Parenting NI.

Howard, K.S. and Brooks-Gunn, J. (2009). 'The Role of Home-visiting Programs in Preventing Child Abuse and Neglect', *The Future of Children,* Vol.19, pp.119-46.

Hutchings, J., Bywater, T., Daley, D., Gardner, F., Whitaker, C., Jones, K., Eames, C. and Edwards, R.T. (2007). 'Parenting Intervention in Sure Start Services for Children at Risk of Developing Conduct Disorder: Pragmatic Randomised Controlled Trial', *British Medical Journal,* Vol.334(7595): 678.

Iwaniec, D. (2004). *Children Who Fail to Thrive: A Practice Guide,* Chichester: John Wiley & Sons.

Johnson, Z., Howell, F. and Molloy, B. (1993). 'Community Mothers Programme: Randomised Controlled Trial of Non-Professional Intervention in Parenting', *British Medical Journal,* Vol.306, pp.1449-52.

Johnson, Z., Molloy, B., Scallon, E., Fitzpatrick, P., Rooney, B., Keegan, T. and Byrne, P. (2000). 'Community Mothers Programme: Seven Year Follow-Up of a Randomised Controlled Trial of Non-Professional Intervention in Parenting', *Journal of Public Health Medicine,* Vol.22, No.3, pp.337-342.

Kahn, J. and Moore, K.A. (2010). *What Works for Home Visiting Programmes: Lessons from Experimental Evaluations of Programmes and Interventions?,* Washington DC: Child Trends.

Kazdin, A.E. and Mazurick, J.L. (1994). 'Dropping Out of Child Psychotherapy: Distinguishing Early and Late Dropouts over the Course of Treatment', *Journal of Consulting and Clinical Psychology,* Vol.62, pp.1069-74.

Kumpfer, K., Whiteside, H., Greene, J. and Allen, K. (2010). 'Effectiveness Outcomes of Four Age Versions of the Strengthening Families Program in Statewide Field Sites, *Group Dynamics: Theory, Research, and Practice,* Vol.14, No.3, pp.211-229.

Larsson, B., Fossum, S., Clifford, G., Drugli, M., Handegård, B. and Mørch, W. (2009). 'Treatment of Oppositional Defiant and Conduct Problems in Young Norwegian Children', *European Child & Adolescent Psychiatry,* Vol.18, pp.42-52.

Lazar, I. and Darlington, R. (1982). *Lasting Effects of Early Education: A Report from the Consortium of Longitudinal Studies,* monograph 47 (serial #195), Ann Arbor, MI: Society for Research in Child Development.

Levenstein, P., Levenstein, S., Shiminski, J.A. and Stolzberg, J.E. (1998). 'Long-term Impact of a Verbal Interaction Program for At-risk Toddlers: An Exploratory Study of High School Outcomes in a Replication of the Mother-Child Home Program', *Journal of Applied Developmental Psychology,* Vol.19, pp.267-85.

Lugo-Gil, J. and Tamis-LeMonda, C.S. (2008). 'Family Resources and Parenting Quality: Links to Children's Cognitive Development across the First 3 Years', *Child Development*, Vol.79, No.4, pp.1065-85.

Masse, J.J., Wagner, S.M., McNeil, C.B. and Chorney, D.B. (2007). 'Parent-Child Interaction Therapy and High Functioning Autism: A Conceptual Overview', *Journal of Early and Intensive Behavior Intervention*, Vol.4, pp.714-35.

McAuley, C., Pecora, P.J. and Rose, W. (2006). *Enhancing the Well-being of Children and Families through Effective Interventions: International Evidence for Practice*, London: Jessica Kingsley Publishers.

McCart, M.R., Priester, P., Davies, W.H. and Azen, R. (2006). 'Differential Effectiveness of Cognitive-behavioural Therapy and Behavioural Parent-training for Antisocial Youth: A Meta-analysis', *Journal of Abnormal Child Psychology*, Vol.34, No.4, pp.527-43.

McGilloway, S., Ní Mhaille, G., Furlong, M., Hyland, L., Leckey, Y., Kelly, P., Bywater, T., Comiskey, C., Lodge, A., O'Neill, D. and Donnelly, M. (2012). *The Incredible Years Ireland Study: Parents, Teachers, and Early Childhood Intervention. Long-term Outcomes of the Incredible Years Parent and Teacher Classroom Management Training Programme (Combined 12 month report)*, Dublin: Archways.

McGinnity, F., Murray, A. and McNally, S. (2011). *Growing Up in Ireland: Mothers' Return to Work and Childcare Choices for Infants in Ireland*, Dublin: Government Publications.

McKay, M.M., McCadam, K. and Gonzales, J.J. (1996). 'Addressing the Barriers to Mental Health Services for Inner City Children and their Caretakers', *Community Mental Health Journal*, Vol.32, pp.353-36.

McKeown, K., Haase, T. and Pratschke, J. (2014). *Evaluation of National Early Years Access Initiative and Siolta Quality Assurance Programme: A Study of Child Outcomes in Preschool*, Dublin: Pobal.

Melhuish, E. (2010). 'England: Sure Start', in Oates, J. (ed.), *Early Childhood in Focus: Supporting Parenting*, Milton Keynes: Open University.

Munro, E. (2011). *The Munro Review of Child Protection. Final Report: A Child-Centred System*, London: Department for Education and Skills.

Muntz, R., Hutchings, J., Edwards, R.T., Hounsome, B. and Ó Ceilleachair, A. (2004). 'Economic Evaluation of Treatment for Children with Severe Behavioural Problems', *Journal of Mental Health, Policy and Economics*, Vol.7, No.4, pp.177-89.

Nitsch, E. (2011). *Positive Parenting: A Randomized Controlled Trial Evaluation of the Parents Plus Adolescent Programme in Schools*, Limerick: University of Limerick Department of Psychology.

Nixon, E. (2012). *Growing Up in Ireland: How Families Matter for Social and Emotional Outcomes of 9 year old Children*, Dublin: Government Publications.

Nock, M.K. (2003). 'Progress Review of the Psychosocial Treatment of Child Conduct Problems', *Clinical Psychology: Science and Practice*, Vol.10, pp.1-28.

Nock, M.K. and Photos, V. (2006). 'Parent Motivation to Participate in Treatment: Assessment and Prediction of Subsequent Participation', *Journal of Child and Family Studies*, Vol.15, pp.345-358.

O'Connor, T.G. and Scott, S.B.C. (2007). *Parenting and Outcomes for Children*, York: Joseph Rowntree Foundation.

Office of the Minister for Children and Youth Affairs (2007a): *Growing Up in Ireland: National Longitudinal Study of Children*, Dublin: Government Publications.

Office of the Minister for Children and Youth Affairs (2007b). *The Agenda for Children's Services: A Policy Handbook*, Dublin: Government Publications.

Olds, D.L. (2002). 'Prenatal and Infancy Home-visiting by Nurses: From Randomised Trials to Community Replication', *Prevention Science*, Vol.3, pp.153-72.

Olds, D.L. and Korfmacher, J. (1998). 'Maternal Psychological Characteristics as Influences on Home-visitation Contact', *Journal of Community Psychology*, Vol.26, pp.23-36.

Parton, N. (2006). '"Every Child Matters": The Shift to Prevention whilst Strengthening Protection in Children's Services in England', *Children and Youth Services Review*, Vol.28, pp.976-92.

Pecnik, N. (2007). 'Towards a Vision of Parenting in the Best Interests of the Child', in Daly, M. (ed.), *Parenting in Contemporary Europe: A Positive Approach*, Strasbourg: Council of Europe Publishing.

Pecora, P.J., McAuley, C. and Rose, W. (2006). 'Effectiveness of Child Welfare Interventions: Issues and Challenges', in McAuley, C., Pecora, P.J. and Rose, W. (eds.), *Enhancing the Well-being of Children and Families through Effective Interventions: International Evidence for Practice*, London: Jessica Kingsley Publishers.

Prinz, R.J., Sanders, M.R., Shapiro, C.J., Whitaker, D.J. and Lutzker, J.R. (2009). 'Population-based Prevention of Child Maltreatment: The US Triple P System Population Trial', *Prevention Science*, Vol.10, No.1, pp.1-12.

Quinn, M., Carr, A., Carroll, L. and O'Sullivan, D. (2007). 'Parents Plus Programme: Evaluation of its Effectiveness for Preschool Children with Developmental Disabilities and Behavioural Problems', *Journal of Applied Research in Intellectual Disabilities*, Vol.20, pp.345-59.

Quinn, M., Carr, A., Carroll, L. and O'Sullivan, D.(2006). 'An Evaluation of the Parents Plus Programme for Preschool Children with Conduct Problems: A Comparison of Those with and without Developmental Disabilities', *The Irish Journal of Psychology*, Vol.27, No.3-4, pp.168-82.

Rafoth, M. and Knickelbein, B. (2005). *Cohort One Final Report: Assessment Summary for the Parent Child Home Program: An Evaluation of the Armstrong Indiana County Intermediate Unit PCHP Program*, Indiana, PA: University of Pennsylvania Center for Educational and Program Evaluation.

Reid, M.J. and Webster-Stratton, C. (2001). 'The Incredible Years Parent, Teacher and Child Intervention: Targeting Multiple Areas of Risk for a Young Child with Pervasive Conduct Problems Using a Flexible Manualized Treatment Programme', *Cognitive and Behaviour Practice*, Vol.8, pp.377-86.

Reid, M.J., Webster-Stratton, C. and Hammond, M. (2003). 'Follow-up of Children Who Received the Incredible Years Intervention for Oppositional Defiance Disorder: Maintenance and Prediction of 2 Year Outcome', *Behaviour Therapy*, Vol.34, pp.471-91.

Reyno, S. and McGrath, P. (2006). 'Predictors of Parent Training Efficacy for Child Externalizing Behaviour Problems – A Meta-analytic Review', *Journal of Child Psychology and Psychiatry*, Vol.47, pp.9-111.

Rochford, S., Doherty, N. and Owens, S. (2014). *Prevention and Early Intervention in Children and Young People's Services: Ten Years of Learning*, Dublin: Centre for Effective Services.

Roscommon Child Care Inquiry (2010). *Roscommon Child Care Case: Report of the Inquiry Team to the Health Service Executive*, available at http://hdl.handle.net/10147/113945.

Sanders, M.R. (1999). 'Triple P Positive Parenting Program: Towards an Empirically Validated Multi-level Parenting and Family Support Strategy for the Prevention of Behaviour and Emotional Problems in Children', *Clinical Child and Family Psychology Review*, Vol.2, pp.71-90.

Sanders, M.R. (2008). 'The Triple P-Positive Parenting Programme: A Public Health Approach to Parenting Support', *Journal of Family Psychology*, Vol.22, pp.506-17.

Sanders, M.R. (2010). 'Adopting a Public Health Approach to the Delivery of Evidence-based Parenting Interventions', *Canadian Psychology*, Vol.51, No.1, pp.17-23.

Sanders, M.R., Mazzucchelli, T.G. and Studman, L.J. (2004). 'Stepping Stones Triple P: The Theoretical Basis and Development of an Evidence-based Positive Parenting Program for Families with a Child Who Has a Disability', *Journal of Intellectual and Developmental Disability, Vol.29*, No.3, pp.265-83.

Scott, S., Knapp, M., Henderson, J. and Maughen, B. (2001). 'Financial Cost of Social Exclusion: Follow-up Study of Anti-social Children into Adulthood', *British Medical Journal*, Vol.323, pp.191.

Scott, S., Spender, Q., Doolan, M., Jacobs, B. and Aspland, H. (2001). 'Multicentre Controlled Trial of Parenting Groups for Childhood Antisocial Behaviour in Clinical Practice', *British Medical Journal*, Vol.323, pp.194-203.

Scottish Government (2006). *Getting It Right for Every Child*, Edinburgh: Scottish Executive.

Scottish Government (2008), *The Early Years Framework*, Edinburgh: Scottish Executive.

Scottish Government (2012). *National Parenting Strategy*, Edinburgh: Scottish Executive.

Shannon, S. and Gibbons, N. (2012). *Report of the Independent Child Death Review Group*, Dublin: Government Publications.

Sharry, J., Guerin, S., Griffin, C. and Drumm, M. (2005). 'An Evaluation of the Parents Plus Early Years Programme: A Video-based Early Intervention for Parents of Preschool Children with Behavioural and Developmental Difficulties', *Clinical Child Psychology and Psychiatry*, Vol.10, pp.3-6.

Shaw, D.S. and Winslow, E.B. (1997). 'Precursors and Correlates of Antisocial Behavior from Infancy to Preschool' in Stoff, D., Breiling, J. and Maser, J.D. (eds.), *Handbook of Antisocial Behaviour*, New York: John Wiley & Sons.

Smith, M. (2006). 'Early Interventions with Young Children and Their Parents in the UK, in McAuley, C., Pecora, P.J. and Rose, W. (eds.), *Enhancing the Well-being of Children and Families through Effective Interventions: International Evidence for Practice*, London: Jessica Kingsley Publishers.

Sneddon, H. and Owens, S. (2012). *Prevention and Early Intervention in Children and Young People's Services – Parenting*, Dublin: Centre for Effective Services.

Sneddon, H., Kehoe, S., Harris, M. Owens, S., Sheehan, A. and Mac Evilly, C. (2012). *Prevention and Early Intervention in Children and Young People's Services – Organisational Learning*, Dublin: Centre for Effective Services.

Special Interest Group: Supporting Parents in their Parenting Role (2013). *Position Paper*, Dublin: Centre for Effective Services.

Spencer, N. (2003). 'Parenting Programmes', *Archives of Disease in Childhood*, Vol.88, pp.99-100.

Spoth, R., Redmond, C. and Shin, C. (2000). 'Reducing Adolescents' Aggressive and Hostile Behaviors: Randomized Trial Effects of a Brief Family Intervention Four Years Past Baseline', *Archives of Pediatrics and Adolescent Medicine*, Vol.154, No.12, pp.1248-57.

Spoth, R., Redmond, C., Shin, C. and Lepper, H. (1999). 'Modelling Long-term Parent Outcomes of Two Universal Family-focused Preventive Interventions: One-year Follow-up Results', *Journal of Consulting and Clinical Psychology*, Vol.6, No.6, pp.975-84.

Statham, J. (2013). *Prevention and Early Intervention in Children and Young People's Services – Improving Child Behaviour*, Dublin: Centre for Effective Services.

Staudt, M. (2003). 'Helping Children Access and Use Services: A Review', *Journal of Child and Family Studies*, Vol.12, pp.49-60.

Staudt, M. (2007). 'Treatment Engagement with Caregivers of At-Risk Children: Gaps in Research and Conceptualization', *Journal of Child and Family Studies*, Vol.16, pp.183-96.

Stevenson, O. (2007). *Neglected Children and their Families*, Oxford: Blackwell.

Sylva, K., Melhuish, E.C., Sammons, P., Siraj-Blatchford, I. and Taggart, B. (2004). *The Effective Provision of Preschool Education (EPPE) Project: Final Report*, London: Department for Education and Skills/University of London Institute of Education.

Tanner, K. and Turney, D. (2006). 'Therapeutic Interventions with Children Who Have Experienced Neglect and Their Families in the UK' in McAuley, C., Pecora, P.J. and Rose, W. (eds.), *Enhancing the Well-being of Children and Families through Effective Interventions: International Evidence for Practice*, London: Jessica Kingsley Publishers.

Thoburn, J., Wilding, J. and Watson, J. (2000). *Family Support in Cases of Maltreatment and Neglect*, London: The Stationery Office.

Tizard, B. and Hughes, M. (2002). *Young Children Learning and Talking*, Oxford: Blackwell.

United Nations (1989). *Convention on the Rights of the Child*, Geneva: United Nations.

Webster-Stratton, C. (1998). 'Parent Training with Low-income Families: Promoting Parental Engagement through a Collaborative Approach' in Lutsker, J.R. (ed.), *Handbook of Child Abuse Research and Treatment*, New York: Plenum.

Webster-Stratton, C. and Hancock, L. (1998). 'Parent Training: Content, Methods and Processes' in Schaefer, E. (ed.), *Handbook of Parent Training*, second edition, New York: Wiley and Sons.

Webster-Stratton, C. and Reid, M.J. (2010). 'The Incredible Years Parents, Teachers and Children Training Series' in Weisz, J. and Kazdin, A. (eds.), *Evidence-based Psychotherapies for Children and Adolescents*, second edition, New York: Guilford Publications.

Zisser, A. and Eyberg, S. (2009). *Parent-Child Interaction Therapy and the Treatment of Disruptive Behavior Disorders*, Gainesville, FL: University of Florida.

Part Two

Discourse on Parenting and Emerging Family Issues

6: Parenting and Children's Development in Ireland: Lessons from Psychology

Elizabeth Nixon

'Parenting' – the care and nurturance of offspring – has been a focus of significant research and theorising within psychology for several decades. The field of psychology – among others – has made an important contribution to scientific and social knowledge regarding parenting. Drawing upon psychological research and theory about parenting, this chapter will describe the approaches that parents in Ireland adopt when rearing their children, how parenting in Ireland is related to children's development, and the factors that influence how parents in Ireland rear their children. In the opening section of the chapter, a brief overview of key concepts that have informed psychological research on parenting will be provided. Following this, attention will turn to a selection of psychological research on parenting within an Irish context. Here, consideration will be given to research on styles of parenting adopted by Irish parents, and the factors that influence how Irish parents rear their children.

A Psychological Perspective on Parenting

Child and developmental psychologists have long viewed parents and the family as the most significant influence on the developing child (Bjorklund *et al*, 2002), particularly during the early years of the child's life. A substantial body of psychological research has considered how parenting behaviours and approaches to childrearing shape children's development and well-being (Maccoby, 1992; Parke and Buriel, 1998). Among the dimensions of parenting most commonly assessed in the research are parental warmth and responsiveness to distress, and the manner and extent to which parents monitor and control their children's behaviour (O'Connor, 2002).

Parental Responsiveness and Warmth

Parental responsiveness refers to the degree of support, warmth and affection that parents display towards their children, and the nature of the parents' reaction when a child is upset or distressed. Negative, insensitive responses include being hostile or dismissive of a child's distress; sensitive responses include comfort and helping, while warmth involves expressing positive emotion and affection towards the child and deriving enjoyment from interacting with her/him (Davidov and Grusec, 2006). There are a number of ways in which parental warmth and responsiveness help promote positive developmental outcomes for children. Children whose parents are warm and positive when interacting with them are more likely to comply with parents' wishes and control their impulses in order to continue positive and satisfying parent-child interactions (Grusec and Davidov, 2007). Children whose parents respond positively to their distress can learn effective strategies for dealing with negative emotions and learn to trust in the availability of their parents. Responsive parents model empathy and compassion, which in turn promotes children's ability to understand the emotions of others and can facilitate pro-social behaviour, empathy and positive relationships with peers and friends (Eisenberg and Fabes, 1998).

On the other hand, children whose parents are insensitive or dismissive of their negative emotions tend to be less well able to manage their negative emotional states (Davidov and Grusec, 2006). Not surprisingly then, parental warmth and responsiveness to child distress have been associated with positive developmental outcomes, including good relationships with peers, high self-esteem, a strong sense of morality and low levels of behaviour problems (Hastings *et al*, 2000; Ladd and Pettit, 2002; von Suchodoletz *et al*, 2011). Indeed, arising from consistent warmth, responsiveness and emotional availability of the primary parent, children derive a sense of emotional security, whereby they feel safe and secure in the knowledge that their parent will be there for them if they become upset (Ainsworth *et al*, 1978).

Parental Control

Alongside the warmth/responsiveness dimension of parenting, parental control has been widely studied also. Parents who are controlling make demands of their children, place limits on their children's freedom and monitor their children's behaviour, while less controlling parents grant children considerable freedom and autonomy and place fewer demands on them (Nixon and Halpenny, 2010). While the research is clear that warm and responsive parenting is associated with positive developmental outcomes, the links between parental control and children's outcomes are less clear cut. For example, children whose parents who do not monitor their behaviour and who allow them extensive freedom engage in higher rates of problem behaviour (Kerr and Stattin, 2003), suggesting that it is important that parents have knowledge of their children's whereabouts and activities. However, when parents are overly controlling and do not grant their children age-appropriate freedom, this can lead to problems also. It appears that the manner in which parents enforce the rules and make demands matters in terms of their effectiveness for promoting positive development.

Parents employ various tactics when exerting control over their children, including the use of reason, persuasion, punishment or power assertion (Grusec and Davidov, 2007). When tactics are applied in a harsh and rejecting way, or when parents are inflexible and insensitive, negative outcomes tend to follow. For example, parents who use love withdrawal strategies (such as refusing to talk to a child) or attempt to induce guilt in their children are said to be psychologically controlling. High levels of psychological control have been found to be associated with a range of child difficulties, including anxiety, depression, loneliness, low self-esteem and low academic achievement (Barber and Harmon, 2002). On the other hand, when parents apply disciplinary tactics in a fair and consistent manner and engage in inductive discipline (such as reasoning, reminding children of rules, and explaining the impact of their behaviour and actions on others), they promote children's internalisation of parents' moral and social values (Kerr *et al*, 2004). This means that children's standard of moral conduct becomes guided by the self, and the need for external control of behaviour through parental reward and punishment is lessened (Hoffman, 2000).

Parenting Styles

Depending upon where parents lie along these two dimensions of parenting, they can be categorised as belonging to one of four parenting patterns or styles, as illustrated in the diagram:

- Authoritative [high-control, high-responsive];
- Authoritarian [high-control, low-responsive];
- Permissive-indulgent [low-control, high-responsive];
- Permissive-neglectful [low-control, low-responsive] (Baumrind, 1971; Maccoby and Martin, 1983).

Figure 6.1: A Two-dimensional Classification of Parenting Patterns

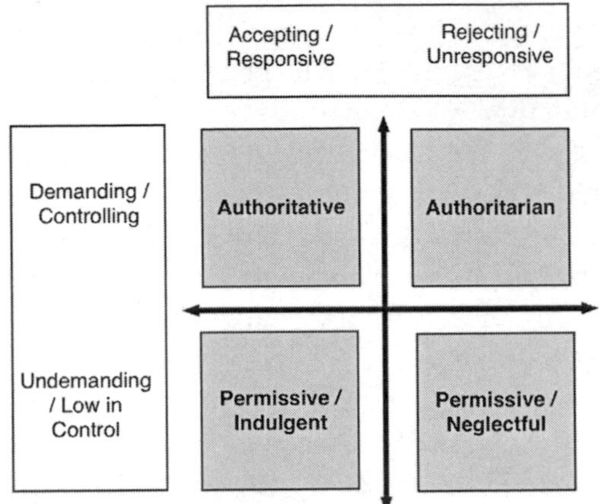

Source: Maccoby and Martin (1983, p.39).

Authoritative parenting is represented by expectations of mature behaviour from the child, firm enforcement of rules and standards using commands and sanctions when necessary. At the same time, these parents encourage the child's independence, and there is open communication between parents and children, with parents listening to the child's point of view. With authoritarian parenting, parents attach strong value to maintaining their authority, and rules are not arrived at by discussion or negotiation. When children deviate from parental requirements, severe punishment is employed. Overall, with this parenting style, parents' demands on their children are not balanced by their acceptance of demands from their children (Maccoby and Martin, 1983).

Permissive/indulgent parenting is a lax pattern of parenting – characterised by high levels of warmth and low levels of control and maturity demands. These parents take a tolerant, accepting attitude towards their child's impulses, and avoid asserting authority or making demands on their children. These children are allowed to regulate their own behaviour. Finally, with the permissive/neglectful style (also sometimes called the uninvolved parenting style), the parent is motivated to minimise interaction with the child and to keep the child at a distance (Maccoby and Martin, 1983). These parents are emotionally and physically disengaged from their children, and exhibit little monitoring and supervision and support of their children (Teti and Candelaria, 2002).

Studies on the impact of parenting styles have found that authoritative parenting most commonly has been associated with positive outcomes.

Children of authoritative parents display higher levels of independence and assertiveness, and are more co-operative with parents and friendly with peers, in comparison with children from authoritarian and permissive homes. In contrast, children with authoritarian parents are more hostile with peers and are overly dependent on parents. Similarly, children of permissive parents display characteristics like non-assertiveness, poor self-control and dependency. Finally, the abdication of parental responsibility, characteristic of a permissive/neglectful parenting style results in the worst outcomes of all, such as lower self-esteem, higher levels of psychological distress, delinquency and drug-use, and poorer academic grades. This suggests that even harsh parental involvement is better than none at all (Teti and Candelaria, 2002; Avenevoli *et al*, 1999).

Influences on Parenting

Efforts to understand the effects of parenting styles on children's development have broadened to take account of a range of other factors and characteristics that shape how parents approach childrearing tasks. It has been suggested that three factors seem to be important – the characteristics of:

- The children;
- The parents;
- The settings in which parenting takes place (Bornstein, 2001; Belsky, 1984).

First, children themselves affect parenting. The child's age and developmental stage will dictate the level of care that parents will be required to give to their child and will constrain the demands and expectations that parents can make of their child. Other child characteristics include child gender (parents may provide different opportunities to or interact differently with their sons and daughters) and child temperament, which is akin to the concept of adult personality. Some children with 'difficult' temperaments are more challenging to interact with sensitively – these children become easily aroused and can be difficult to soothe when upset, and so will require more patience and tolerance from the parent.

Secondly, parenting draws upon the personality, intellectual, physical and emotional characteristics of the parent himself or herself, as well as on the parent's own experiences of childrearing. One of the most widely studied parental characteristics is that of parental mental health, with substantial research supporting the idea that psychologically healthy parents provide more sensitive and responsive care to their children, thereby promoting children's positive development. Children whose parents experience depression, for example, display higher risk of having anxiety, mood and social difficulties themselves (Cummings *et al*, 2005). It has been suggested that symptoms of depression may make it more difficult for parents to engage in authoritative parenting and to create and maintain a positive parent-child relationship (Goodman and Gotlib, 2002), which in turn affects children's social and emotional development.

Finally, a full understanding of the influences on parenting involves looking beyond the individual child and parent to consider other relationships within and beyond the family. Such broader influences include the resources that parents can draw upon from the marital relationship and other community and work ties. Family structure and socio-economic class also represent important elements of the context that influences parenting. For example, having a supportive spouse can buffer the parent from stress, which presumably impacts positively upon the parent's psychological well-being, thereby enabling more responsive parent-child interactions, characteristic of an authoritative parenting style. On the other hand, high levels of marital conflict and dissatisfaction appears to negatively affect parents' ability to be responsive to their children's needs (Belsky, 1984; Grych, 2002). In addition to the marital relationship, the social and economic resources that parents have available to them also matter for the quality of parenting. For example, good quality relationships with relatives, friends and neighbours, and access to community resources and services can help to buffer parents from stress and to support them in their parenting role. Poverty and economic stress also diminish parents' capacities for responsive parenting and increases parents' tendencies to discipline children in a harsh and inconsistent manner. These parenting behaviours may stem partly from the depletion of parents' psychological resources, which renders them more susceptible to anxiety, depression, irritability and the effects of negative life events (Conger and Donnellan, 2007).

Having provided a brief overview of the key concepts that have informed psychological research on parenting, attention now turns to consider a selection of psychological research on parenting within an Irish context.

Parenting Styles among Parents in Ireland

Relatively little research on parenting from a psychological perspective has been conducted within an Irish context. One of the earliest psychological studies of parenting in Ireland, the Dublin Child Development Study initiated in 1985, was concerned with exploring the quality of parenting and its relationship to measures of the child's functioning within families defined as 'working class' (Wieczorek-Deering *et al*, 1991). Over three-quarters of the children were classified as securely attached at 18 months, which arises from high levels of parental warmth and responsiveness to the baby's distress. However, these mothers also engaged in higher levels of physical punishment, in comparison with levels found in other Western cultures at that time. Thus, Irish childrearing, within this sample at least, incorporated elements of authoritarian parenting (evidenced by the use of physical punishment) and authoritative parenting (reflected in the secure attachment of the babies). Greene (1994) suggested that inherent contradictions in parents' styles may indicate that parents were suspended between the certainties of a harsher traditional approach to childrearing and the uncertainties of newer more democratic approaches.

Substantial cultural and demographic changes have occurred since then and shifts in how children are thought about have been reflected at policy and legislative levels. Noteworthy among developments include: Ireland's ratification of the United Nations *Convention on the Rights of the Child* in 1992; the establishment of a Family Support Agency in 2003; the establishment of an Office of the Minister for Children and Youth Affairs in 2005; followed by the creation of a full ministerial position of Minister for Children and Youth Affairs in 2011; and the publication of policy and strategy documents pertaining to understanding and improving the lives of children and families in Ireland (such as the *National Children's Strategy, 2000-2010* and *Better Outcomes, Brighter Futures, the National Policy Framework for Children and Young People, 2014-2020*). More recently, the 31st amendment to the Irish *Constitution* gave more explicit expression to the rights of children, by identifying children as individuals who require child-specific rights that take into account that children are largely dependent upon adults for their care, and are sometimes powerless to vindicate their own rights (Children's Rights Alliance, 2012). Thus, at a national level, attention increasingly was given to what services and resources parents and families need in order for children to flourish and achieve their full potential as human beings.

However, the extent to which broader societal discourses about the nature of childhood and children has seeped into the psyche of parents and affected their practices remains somewhat unknown, although existing Irish research suggests that the nature of parenting has changed. For example, Halpenny *et al* (2010) telephone-surveyed a random sample of 1,343 parents (946 mothers, 417 fathers) across Ireland. The responses showed that 70% of parents were of the view that parenting was 'very different' when compared with 20 years ago; almost three-quarters of parents believed that they had 'less control' over their children than parents in the past; and 84% indicated that they experienced greater pressure in their parenting role when compared with parents 20 years ago. These findings suggest that parents in contemporary Ireland perceive the task of parenting to be distinct from previous generations.

Further evidence for how parenting in Ireland may have changed emerged from the aforementioned telephone survey in which parents' parenting styles and use of physical punishment with their children also were examined (Halpenny *et al*, 2010). Findings from the survey revealed that the use of physical punishment was low among the parents – 20% reported having used physical punishment on their child in the past year. Younger children more likely to have been physically punished in the past year than older children, with 26% of 0 to 4 year olds, 31.8% of 5 to 9 year olds, 12.1% of 10 to 14 year olds and 4.1% of 15 to 17 year olds having been physically punished in the past year. In contrast, a large majority (81%) of the parents in the study (average age 41 years) reported ever having experienced physical punishment as a child. While these rates are not directly comparable, they do point to generational shifts in approaches to childrearing. Interestingly, parents in the study did not view physical punishment as a particularly effective method of controlling children's behaviour – 40% of parents indicated that physical punishment was not effective in deterring the child's misbehaviour at the time, and a further 60% of parents believed that it was ineffective at preventing later misbehaviour. Almost two-thirds of parents believed that physical punishment was not necessary to bring up a well-behaved child, 28% believed that it was wrong and should never be used, and 43% believed that it could damage the parent-child relationship. Notwithstanding these attitudes, over half of the parents believed that parents should have the right to use physical punishment if they wish, and two-thirds were of the view that an occasional smack does not do a child any harm. Although some of these attitudes were patterned according to parents' actual use of physical punishment, the findings do reflect considerable ambiguity in how parents in Ireland today view the use of physical punishment. Indeed, the rates of physical punishment in the study were relatively low, when compared with other similar studies from Scotland and the United Kingdom (Anderson *et al*, 2002; Ghate *et al*, 2003).

Inductive responses to child discipline, which involve actions such as using reasoning with the child, or requesting the child take time out, predominated current discipline practices. Inductive approaches to discipline are consistent with an authoritative style of parenting, and focus upon teaching the child about right and wrong and avoiding power battles between parents and children. The survey with parents in Ireland revealed that mothers and parents of older children were more likely to use inductive responses to discipline than fathers and parents of younger children, respectively. There also appeared to be an association between parenting behaviours and children's behavioural outcomes. Parental use of physical punishment was highest in families where children were classified as having conduct or hyperactivity problems, but not emotional problems, while verbal hostility was highest in families where children were classified as having conduct or emotional problems, but not hyperactivity difficulties. Parents of children with conduct problems also scored higher on authoritarian parenting (Halpenny *et al*, 2010). Of course, the direction of effects is difficult to disentangle here – is it that children have conduct problems because their parents use physical punishment or adopt an authoritarian parenting style, or is it that parents are more likely to resort to harsher forms of control when their children are exhibiting behaviour problems? The likely answer lies somewhere in between: that harsh discipline and behaviour problems give rise to each other, and parent and child become entrenched in a cycle of negative interactions (Patterson and Fisher, 2002).

Perhaps the most significant effort to understand parenting and its relation to children's development within the Irish context arises from work of *Growing Up in Ireland*, which was initiated in 2006. This government-funded study, the first of its kind in Ireland, is a national longitudinal study of almost 20,000 Irish children and their families. A sample of 11,100 babies and their parents has been studied at 9 months (Wave 1), 3 years (Wave 2) and 5 years (Wave 3). A second sample of 8,568 children, along with their parents and teachers, has been studied when the children were 9 years (Wave 1) and followed up at 13 years (Wave 2) (Williams *et al*, 2009, 2010, 2013).

Information on parenting collected at Wave 1 from the 9 year old sample has yielded new and comprehensive insights into the nature of parenting in modern Ireland. Because *Growing Up in Ireland* is based upon a large and representative sample of families in Ireland, we can be reasonably confident that the picture that emerges reflects what is happening within the broader population of families. Both mothers and fathers reported upon the quality of their relationship with their children, while children themselves answered a series of questions tapping into parents' warmth and responsiveness, and use of control and discipline, from which parents could be classified into one of the four parenting styles. Mothers and teachers also reported upon children's emotional, social and behavioural functioning (Nixon, 2012).

The majority of both mothers (77%) and fathers (68%) engaged in an authoritative style of parenting, with mothers adopting this style more often than fathers. Following this, the most commonly used style was permissive/indulgent parenting, adopted by 16% of mothers and 20% of fathers. A minority of parents was classified as uninvolved/neglectful (3% mothers, 6% fathers) and as authoritarian (4% mothers, 6% fathers) (Williams *et al*, 2010). For the majority of children, these findings are encouraging because they suggest that most children in Ireland perceive their parents to be warm and responsive, and to exert control over them in a manner that is constructive and enables them to learn about right and wrong. However, it is also worrying that a sizeable minority of parents in Ireland are engaging with their children in a less than optimal fashion. The data also suggest that girls were more likely than boys to experience a permissive parenting style by both mothers and fathers, while boys were more likely than girls to experience authoritarian parenting by both mothers and fathers (Nixon, 2012).

The question about how parenting style relates to children's developmental outcomes also has been addressed using this data. The analysis suggests a relationship between style of parenting and children's levels of social and emotional and behaviour problems. Relative to children with authoritative mothers, children with authoritarian and neglectful mothers had higher levels of social and emotional difficulties, and the same pattern of findings emerged for fathers. Permissive parenting by either mothers or fathers was not associated with higher levels of difficulties for children (Nixon, 2012).

These findings suggest that both authoritarian parenting and neglectful parenting can be harmful for children's development, although the effects seem to operate slightly differently for boys and girls. Specifically, with respect to mothers' parenting style, there were no differences in girls' outcomes (such as levels of emotional or conduct problems or hyperactivity) when mothers are authoritative, authoritarian or permissive, but girls had worse outcomes when mothers are neglectful. For boys, there were no differences in their outcomes when mothers are authoritative or permissive, but boys had worse outcomes when mothers are authoritarian or neglectful. The parenting style that fathers adopt with their daughters did not seem to be related to their outcomes. For boys, however, this was not the case and boys seemed to fare poorly when their fathers adopt an authoritarian or neglectful style of parenting with them (Nixon, 2012).

Together these findings point to important pathways linking mothers' and fathers' styles of parenting to boys' and girls' development and well-being. It appears that authoritarian parenting seems to carry particularly negative consequences for boys, in ways that it does not for girls. Perhaps the control inherent in authoritarian parenting is difficult for boys to deal with, as it runs counter to their gender-typed expectations that boys should be dominant and assertive, rather than being dependent and submissive, which are known outcomes of authoritarian parenting. Boys also appear to be vulnerable to the impact of neglectful fathering, in ways that girls are not, suggesting that involvement by fathers is particularly important for boys.

Influences on Parenting in Ireland

Again drawing upon *Growing Up in Ireland* data, researchers have begun to explore the influence of factors like parental stress, psychological difficulties, marital distress, low socio-economic status, and single parenthood on parenting styles and parental sensitivity. Based on information collected on 11,100 infants and their parents, Nixon *et al* (2013) found that mothers and fathers who experienced high levels of stress and depression were less responsive when interacting with their babies. The effect of depression was somewhat stronger for mothers than it was for fathers, possibly because fathers tend to spend less time overall with their infants. Higher levels of support and higher levels of marital satisfaction were associated with lower levels of parental stress, which in turn was associated with greater responsiveness. The findings point to the potentially negative effect of parental stress on infant development – when parents are stressed, it is more difficult for them to be patient and tolerant with their babies, and this situation is compounded when infants themselves have 'difficult' temperaments.

A similar picture emerged when the families of the 9 year old children were examined. Mothers' depression was associated with higher levels of mother-child conflict and lower levels of mother-child closeness. Fathers' depression was associated with higher levels of father-child conflict, but did not affect father-child closeness. Mothers' and fathers' marital satisfaction also appeared to matter for the quality of the parent-child relationship. When mothers were dissatisfied in the marital relationship, there were higher levels of mother-child and father-child conflict, and lower levels of mother-child (but not father-child) closeness. Fathers' marital dissatisfaction was associated with higher levels of father-child conflict and lower levels of father-child closeness. However, the mother-child relationship did not appear to be affected by the father's marital satisfaction. Together, these findings support the idea that negative interactions in one type of relationship in the household (for example, marital relationship) can spill-over and affect other relationships in the household (for example, the parent-child relationship) (Nixon, 2012).

Finally, the effects of family structure (single parent *versus* couple-headed households) and household social class and income level also appear to be important influences on parenting style and quality of the parent-child relationship. While the majority of mothers engaged in authoritative or permissive parenting styles, mothers in larger single parent households (with three or more children) were more likely to be classified as neglectful (5.3%) in comparison with couple-headed families and smaller single parent families, where less than 3% of parents were classified as neglectful. Similarly, the likelihood of mothers in larger single parent households being authoritarian was also significantly higher than mothers in other households. Fathers from single parent households were more likely to engage in permissive parenting and less likely to engage in authoritative parenting than fathers from couple-headed households. The majority of these fathers from single parent households are non-resident fathers. Perhaps as a result of being non-resident, time spent with their children may be limited and so they opt for a parenting style that is indulgent and permissive, in order to ensure that their children enjoy themselves during their time together. Mothers and fathers in the lowest income groups also were slightly more likely to be use a neglectful parenting style, when compared with parents in the highest income groups.

Overall, the findings suggest that certain groups of parents may be at risk of engaging in less than optimal parenting styles with their children. However, when examining the links between family structure and income/social class and children's outcomes, the picture is somewhat more complicated. The data from *Growing Up in Ireland* suggests that family structure and income affect children's outcomes, primarily through the effect that these have on parental stress and the quality of parenting and parent-child relationship (Nixon, 2012). This is an encouraging finding and points to the fact that children do not face inevitable negative outcomes, just because they are growing up in a single parent or a low-income household. What matters more is sustaining positive parent-child relationships and helping parents to manage their stress, especially when they are parenting in the context of low social support and low economic resources. Children can be protected from the potentially negative influence of marital distress, parental depression, poverty and single parenthood, so long as parents can maintain responsiveness and positive interactions with their children.

Conclusion

The research presented in this chapter does not claim to be an exhaustive account of all psychological research on parenting conducted within an Irish context. The *Growing Up in Ireland* study and other research commissioned by the Department of Children and Youth Affairs are proving to be valuable resources for understanding the dynamics of parenting in Ireland, the effects of various parenting practices on children's development, and the factors that influence parents' approaches to childrearing. In addition to these research endeavours, numerous parenting support and intervention programmes are being implemented and evaluated across various sites in Ireland. Such programmes, including the Incredible Years Programme (McGilloway *et al*, 2012) and the Parents' Plus programmes (Sharry and Fitzpatrick, 1998, 2001), are underpinned by psychological approaches to behaviour management and aim to enhance parental responsiveness and provide parents with the skills to discipline their children in a manner consistent with authoritative parenting. The Incredible Years Programme involves weekly group sessions for parents where they engage in role play, group discussions, and learning about various aspects of child development. Similarly, the Parents' Plus programme uses techniques such as group discussions, role plays, and reviewing recordings of parent-child interactions to empower parents to attend to and reward their children for good behaviour, develop an inductive approach to discipline, and build a positive relationship with their child.

The findings arising from research on parenting in modern Ireland are encouraging and suggest that the majority of parents adopt an authoritative parenting style – a style known to promote positive developmental outcomes among children. However, it is concerning that a sizeable minority of parents use less than optimal strategies when interacting with their children, including the use of physical punishment as a disciplinary method. It appears that certain groups of parents, particularly those parenting within contexts of heightened stress and limited resources have a higher risk of being authoritarian or neglectful. As a society then, it behoves us to support parents who are vulnerable to help them engage positively and responsively with their children, thereby buffering children from the potentially negative effects of parental stress and promoting their optimal well-being.

References

Ainsworth, M.D.S., Blehar, M.C., Waters, E. and Wall, S. (1978). *Patterns of Attachment: A Psychological Study of the Strange Situation*, Hillsdale, NJ: Lawrence Erlbaum Associates Publishers.

Anderson, S., Murray, L. and Brownlie, J. (2002). *Disciplining Children: Research with Parents in Scotland*, Edinburgh: Scottish Executive Central Research Unit.

Avenevoli, S., Sessa, F.M. and Steinberg, L. (1999). 'Family Structure, Parenting Practices and Adolescent Adjustment: An Ecological Examination' in Hetherington, E.M. (ed.), *Coping with Divorce, Single Parenting and Remarriage: A Risk and Resiliency Perspective*, Mahwah, NJ: Lawrence Erlbaum Associates Publishers.

Barber, B.K. and Harmon, E.L. (2002). 'Violating the Self: Parental Psychological Control of Children and Adolescents' in Barber, B.K. (ed.), *Intrusive Parenting: How Psychological Control Affects Children and Adolescents*, Washington, DC: American Psychological Association.

Baumrind, D. (1971). 'Current Patterns of Parental Authority', *Developmental Psychology Monographs*, Vol.4, No.1, Pt.2.

Belsky, J. (1984). 'The Determinants of Parenting: A Process Model', *Child Development*, Vol.55, pp.83-96.

Bjorklund, D.R., Yunger, J.L. and Pelligrini, A.D. (2002). 'The Evolution of Parenting and Evolutionary Approaches to Childrearing' in Bornstein, M.H. (ed.), *Handbook of Parenting, Vol.2: Biology and Ecology of Parenting*, second edition, Mahwah, NJ: Lawrence Erlbaum Associates Publishers.

Bornstein, M.H. (2001). 'Parenting: Science and Practice', *Parenting: Science and Practice*, Vol.1, pp.1-4.

Children's Rights Alliance (2012). *Recognising Children's Rights in the Constitution: The 31st Amendment to the Constitution (children)*, Dublin: Children's Rights Alliance.

Conger, R.D. and Donnellan, M.B. (2007). 'An Interactionist Perspective on the Socio-economic Context of Human Development', *Annual Review of Psychology*, Vol.58, pp.175-99.

Cummings, E.M., Keller, P.S. and Davies, P.T. (2005). 'Towards a Family Process Model of Maternal and Paternal Depressive Symptoms: Exploring Multiple Relations with Child and Family Functions', *Journal of Child Psychology and Psychiatry*, Vol.46, pp.479-89.

Davidov, M. and Grusec, J.E. (2006). 'Untangling the Links of Parental Responsiveness to Distress and Warmth to Child Outcomes', *Child Development*, Vol.77, pp.44-58.

Eisenberg, N. and Fabes, R.A. (1998). 'Pro-social Development' in Damon, W. (series ed.), Eisenberg, N. (vol. ed.), *Handbook of Child Psychology, Vol.3: Social, Emotional and Personality Development*, fifth edition, New York: Wiley.

Ghate, D., Hazel, N., Creighton, S., Finch, S. and Field, J. (2003). *The National Study of Parents, Children and Discipline in Britain*, London: Policy Research Bureau.

Goodman, S.H. and Gotlib, I.H. (eds.) (2002). *Children of Depressed Parents: Mechanisms of Risk and Implications for Treatment*, Washington, DC: American Psychological Association.

Greene, S.M. (1994). 'Growing Up Irish: Development in Context', *Irish Journal of Psychology*, Vol.15, pp.354-71.

Grusec, J.E. and Davidov, M. (2007). 'Socialization in the Family: The Roles of Parents' in Grusec, J.E. and Hastings, P.D. (eds.), *Handbook of Socialization: Theory and Research*, New York: Guilford Press.

Grych, J.H. (2002). 'Marital Relationships and Parenting' in Bornstein, M.H. (ed.), *Handbook of Parenting: Vol.4: Social Conditions and Applied Parenting*, second edition, Mahwah, NJ: Lawrence Erlbaum Associates Publishers.

Halpenny, A.M., Nixon, E. and Watson, D. (2010). *Parents' Perspectives on Parenting Styles and Disciplining Children*, Dublin: Government Publications, retrieved from www.tcd.ie/childrensresearchcentre/assets/pdf/ Publications/ Parents'_Perspectives_on_parenting_styles.pdf.

Hastings, P.D., Zahn-Waxler, C., Robinson, J., Usher, B. and Bridges, D. (2000). 'The Development of Concern for Others in Children with Behaviour Problems', *Developmental Psychology*, Vol.36, pp.531-46.

Hoffman, M.L. (2000). *Empathy and Moral Development: Implications for Caring and Justice*, Cambridge: Cambridge University Press.

Kerr, D., Lopez, N., Olson, S. and Sameroff, J. (2004). 'Parental Discipline and Externalizing Behaviour Problems in Early Childhood: The Roles of Moral Regulation and Child Gender', *Journal of Abnormal Child Psychology*, Vol.32, pp.369-83.

Kerr, M. and Stattin, H. (2003). 'Parenting of Adolescents: Action or Reaction?' in Crouter, A.C. and Booths, A. (eds.), *Children's Influence on Family Dynamics: The Neglected Side of Family Relationships*, Mahwah, NJ: Lawrence Erlbaum Associates Publishers.

Ladd, G.W. and Pettit, G.S. (2002). 'Parenting and the Development of Children's Peer Relationships' in Bornstein, M.H. (ed.), *Handbook of Parenting: Vol.5: Practical Issues in Parenting*, second edition, Mahwah, NJ: Lawrence Erlbaum Associates Publishers.

Maccoby, E.E. (1992). 'The Role of Parents in the Socialisation of Children: An Historical Overview', *Developmental Psychology*, Vol.28, pp.1006-17.

Maccoby, E.E. and Martin, J.A. (1983). 'Socialisation in the Context of the Family: Parent-child Interaction' in Mussen, P.H. (series ed.) and Hetherington, E.M. (vol. ed.), *Handbook of Child Psychology: Vol.4: Socialization, Personality and Social Development*, fourth edition, New York: Wiley.

McGilloway, S., Ni Mhaille, G., Bywater, T., Leckey, Y., Kelly, P., Furlong, M., Comiskey, C. and Donnelly, M. (2012). 'A Parenting Intervention for Childhood Behavioural Problems: A Randomised Controlled Trial in Disadvantaged

Community-based Settings', *Journal of Consulting and Clinical Psychology*, Vol.80, pp.116-27.

Nixon, E. (2012). *Growing Up in Ireland: How Families Matter for Social and Emotional Outcomes of 9 year old Children: Child Cohort, Report 4*, Dublin: Government Publications.

Nixon, E. and Halpenny, A.M. (2010). *Children's Perspectives on Parenting Styles and Discipline: A Developmental Approach*, Dublin: Government Publications, retrieved from www.tcd.ie/childrensresearchcentre/assets/pdf/Publications/Children's_Perspectives_on_parenting_styles.pdf.

Nixon, E., Swords, L. and Murray, A. (2013). *Growing Up in Ireland: Parenting and Infant Development: Infant Cohort, Report 3*, Dublin: Government Publications.

O'Connor, T.G. (2002). 'Annotation: The "Effects" of Parenting Reconsidered: Findings, Challenges and Applications', *Journal of Child Psychology and Psychiatry*, Vol.43, pp.555-72.

Parke, R.D. and Buriel, R. (1998). 'Socialisation in the Family: Ethnic and Ecological Perspectives' in Damon, W. (series ed.) and Eisenberg, N. (vol. ed.), *Handbook of Child Psychology: Vol.3: Social, Emotional and Personality Development*, fifth edition, New York: Wiley.

Patterson, G.R. and Fisher, P.A. (2002). 'Recent Developments in our Understanding of Parenting: Bidirectional Effects, Causal Models and the Search for Parsimony' in Bornstein, M.H. (ed.), *Handbook of Parenting, Vol.5: Practical Issues in Parenting*, second edition, Mahwah, NJ: Lawrence Erlbaum Associates Publishers.

Sharry, J. and Fitzpatrick, C. (1998). *Parents Plus Programme: A Practical and Positive Video-based Course for Managing and Solving Discipline Problems in Children*, Dublin: Mater Hospital.

Sharry, J. and Fitzpatrick, C. (2001). *Parents Plus Adolescent Programme: A Parenting Guide to Handling Conflict and Getting On Better with Adolescents aged 11 to 15*, Dublin: Mater Hospital.

Teti, D.M. and Candelaria, M.A. (2002). 'Parenting Competence' in Bornstein, M.H. (ed.), *Handbook of Parenting, Vol.4: Social Conditions and Applied Parenting*, second edition, Mahwah, NJ: Lawrence Erlbaum Associates Publishers.

von Suchodoletz, A., Trommsdorff, G. and Heikamp, T. (2011). 'Linking Maternal Warmth and Responsiveness to Children's Self-regulation', *Social Development*, Vol.20, pp.486-503.

Wieczorek-Deering, D., Greene, S.M., Nugent, J.K. and Graham, R. (1991). 'Classification of Attachment and Its Determinants in Urban Irish Infants', *Irish Journal of Psychology*, Vol.12, pp.216-34.

Williams, J., Greene, S., Doyle, E., Harris, E., Layte, R., McCoy, S., McCrory, C., Murray, A., Nixon, E., O'Dowd, T., O'Moore, M., Quail, A., Smyth, E., Swords, L. and Thornton, M. (2009). *Growing Up in Ireland: The Lives of 9 year olds: Child Cohort, Report 1*, Dublin: Government Publications.

Williams, J., Greene, S., McNally, S., Murray, A. and Quail, A. (2010). *Growing Up in Ireland: The Infants and Their Families: Infant Cohort, Report 1*, Dublin: Government Publications.

Williams, J., Murray, A., McCrory, C. and McNally, S. (2013). *Growing Up in Ireland: Development from Birth to Three Years: Infant Cohort, Report 5*, Dublin: Government Publications.

7: "You Don't Understand!" – Navigating the Parenting Contours of Adolescence

Karen Leonard

> *Adolescents are not monsters. They are just people trying to learn how to make it among the adults in the world, who are probably not so sure themselves.* (Virginia Satir, n.d.)

This chapter focuses on the dilemmas that practitioners and parents experience when children reach adolescence. Adolescence as a stage of development is explored, along with a review of the developmental tasks a young person needs to negotiate at this stage. Common issues and tensions between adolescents and their parents are discussed. Finally, some solutions are put forward for practitioners and parents on how to manage these dilemmas through the use of a systemic perspective.

Adolescence as a Stage of Development

Adolescence is generally accepted as bringing biological, physical and relational changes. The teenager tries to make sense of these changes and the people around them – parents, professionals and carers – must find ways to relate to them in a new and different way. In my practice as a family therapist, I have often heard parents wonder where their little boy or girl has disappeared to when faced with a monosyllabic, hormonal and moody 'imposter'. As a newly qualified social worker in 1996, I remember being handed my first long-term caseload, which comprised a considerable number of teenagers. Some of the other more experienced social workers professed they found teenagers a difficult group to engage and work with. While at times very challenging, working with adolescents and their families or their foster parents/social care workers gave me invaluable experience in terms of my own professional confidence that has stood to me in terms of challenges in later work contexts. This fascination with adolescence as a stage of development, and my preference to work with young people and their parents continues in my work as a family therapist.

Figure 7.1: Erikson's Psychosocial Stages of Development

Stage	Main Task	Positive Outcome	Negative Outcome
1: Infancy to 1 year	Trust *versus* Mistrust	Infant learns to trust.	If needs are not met, they do not trust others.
2: 1 to 3 years	Autonomy *versus* Shame	Child uses their new motor skills to develop autonomy.	If parents do not encourage this, shame/doubt develops.
3: 3 to 6 years	Initiative *versus* Guilt	Child initiates and performs new tasks. Self-confidence develops.	If parents do not encourage this, then guilt develops.
4: 6 to 12 years	Industry *versus* Inferiority	Children learn skills and can work with others.	If this does not happen, they feel inferior to others.
5: 12 to 20 years	Identity *versus* Role confusion	Adolescents develop their own identity and role in society.	If not, it can lead to lack of a stable identity and confusion about adult roles.
6: 20 to 30 years	Intimacy *versus* Isolation	Young adults wish to develop relationships.	If they are unable to do this, they experience isolation.
7: 30 to 65 years	Generativity *versus* Self-absorption	Mature adults try to influence life for the next generation.	If they do not, they may become self-absorbed.
8: 65+	Integrity versus Despair	Reflection on their life and they have a sense of accomplishment.	If not, they may fear the end of their life.

In terms of the developmental tasks that need to be addressed in adolescence, the Life Cycle Theory as developed by Erik Erikson (1985) is a useful approach. This model suggests that there are different stages of development, each with its own features, which will not be experienced to the same extent at any other stage of the life cycle. Comer and Gould (2011) point out that this approach was one of the few theories of child development that spans the entire life course. This perspective sees adolescence as but one stage in the formation of our identity, each stage having its own challenges that must be addressed in order to deal with the next stage of development (see **Figure 7.1**). Erikson (1985) characterises adolescence as the fifth stage in the life cycle and terms the dilemma at this stage as 'identity *versus* role confusion' (p.263).

What this means is that there are particular developmental tasks that need to be negotiated as the young person moves towards adulthood. The task of the parent is to give the young person the space to begin this process of de-individuation from them and to support them as they begin to construct their own separate identity and involve themselves more in their peer relationships. Therein is the difficulty: the adult needs to interact with the young person in a different way to how they might have interacted with them when he/she was a child. Parents should encourage him/her to make some decisions and take on more responsibility for themselves.

From these ideas, it is clear that adolescence is a time of transition for the young person and their family. Erikson (1985) does not focus on the construction of identity as just an internal process of the individual but notes that there are social processes also involved in their identity formation. This model places a strong emphasis on social factors like the impact of external relationships on the individual's development and it is termed a psychosocial model of development (Comer and Gould, 2011).

Therefore, the importance of the peer group, fashion, music and technology for this age group cannot be underestimated. When parents complain in family sessions that their home is being treated 'like a B&B' where the teenager comes home to eat and sleep, in fact they are describing a very important developmental task! The challenge for teenagers seems to be the negotiation of their role in society with their family and peers while also developing their own identity. As parents and practitioners understand this, it may make it easier for us to deal with the issues and challenges more effectively.

It is often parenting dilemmas that lead to parents seeking help from a professional. The push and pull between teenager and parent of control *versus* independence is often negotiated within the therapeutic space. The adolescent wishes to spread their wings whereas parents may be concerned about this new freedom and the risks it may pose. Minuchin (1974) describes this in his renowned work with families, when he says 'parents cannot protect and guide without at the same time controlling and restricting. Children cannot grow and become individuated without rejecting and attacking' (p.58). Therefore, systemic practitioners/family therapists often help parents and adolescents manage these tensions, while opening up communication within a family session.

Dilemmas for Parents, Teenagers and Practitioners

A review of any research on family therapy will illustrate its effectiveness in dealing with a wide variety of serious adolescent and family problems as well as its cost-effectiveness as a treatment model in comparison to other approaches (Carr, 2014; Crane, 2014; Crane and Christenson, 2014). The usefulness and evidence base of systemic/family therapy interventions with parents and teenagers for a wide range of problems including attachment difficulties, substance abuse by the young person, conduct disorders, child abuse/neglect and somatic difficulties is well documented (Carr, 2014; Liddle, 2010). The use of a systemic perspective in the treatment of a wide variety of emotional and mental health difficulties of children and young people, including depression, anxiety, grief and eating disorders as well as family abuse and violence, are featured in the academic research on adolescents and their parents (Coogan, 2012).

While there is no doubt that these issues feature in the caseload of any health or social care professional, there are also less 'deadly serious problems' (White and Epston, 1990) that parents, teenagers and professionals grapple with on a regular basis that also require attention. Conflicts may arise in the family over the young person's school attendance, peer choice, socialising and resistance to parental boundaries. It is my experience that early intervention with adolescents and their parents by use of a systemic approach can prevent a tense situation escalating and ultimately may prevent family breakdown and the need for alternative care. It is the more ordinary trials and tribulations of caring for and parenting teenagers that may require some support and guidance from the extended family, community or in some instances a professional. It is these types of parenting dilemmas that are the focus of the rest of this chapter.

One model that attempts to plot the changes and transitions a family goes through is the Family Life Cycle Model as put forward by Carter and McGoldrick (1980). This model discusses the stages that an average family goes through in their lifetime. It includes milestones like the early couple relationship, the couple with young children and the family with adolescents. It then focuses on the young person leaving home or the infamous 'empty nest stage'. Other changes across the life course include the couple moving towards retirement and their children becoming parents themselves. And so the cycle continues.

However, the cycle is not simple as other life events cannot be predicted and these may complicate the adaptation of the family members to the different stages. Some examples of changes include sudden death, illness, redundancy and separation/divorce. In systemic therapy, it is believed that the emergence of problems coincides with the demands placed on families at these times of change (Dallos and Draper, 2010). So it would be usual for a family therapist to help families adapt, for example, to a death of a significant person in the family, negotiate issues around separation/divorce, or other significant events that a family may experience.

As well as changes within the family, a systemic therapist looks at the impact of the social, political and economic context or what is known as the suprasystem on the family (Burnham, 1986). In Ireland over the past number of years, a change in the economic fortunes of the country may have influenced family life leading to changing roles in the family in terms of the traditional gender roles. There may be pressure on parents from employers or business partners, financial stress, the commute to and from work, or in some cases the need to work abroad. In my experience, parents in therapy often talk about the pressure they are under and how they find it difficult to give time to their partner or children. This may take its toll on the individual, couple and family relationships as members try to adapt to these changing roles and economic difficulties.

More recently, other issues are emerging that are placing pressure on adolescents and their parents. While many of us rely on and embrace new technologies, there are some indications in family sessions that this ever-available culture may be impacting on family life. Some of my family sessions have been dominated by conversations about the use of phones, laptops, Xbox in the family and family members' concerns that these are taking away from family time and hindering family communication. This is not just the preserve of young people, who may complain that technology and online work communications equally distract their parents. Teenagers wish to have private access to their phones and social media but parents must balance this with their concerns regarding their young person's relationships. Recent research on the increase of cyberbullying in second level education (National Association of Principals and Deputy Principals, 2014) does little to allay parents' fears in this area.

A Systemic Perspective on Parenting Dilemmas in Adolescence

Hills (2013, p.10) explains that 'the given of any family or systemic approach is a belief in the gathering of family members of a family system together to look at what is going on'. Family therapy, as a model of psychotherapy, tries to help improve the communication between family members and works with families to bring about change. Sometimes, families have trouble dealing with changes or transitions. We probably all can relate to the stress of changing jobs, moving house or retiring. In the same way, some families need additional support to deal with situations like changing roles due to bereavement, parents separating or young people leaving home. A family generally likes to stay the same and do things as they have always been done. This tendency means that times of change – for example, adolescence – can sometimes be problematic for a family to deal with. Sometimes difficulties or symptoms a family member presents with may be signalling that there are wider family issues that may need attention with the help of a family therapist.

When a young person is referred by their parents/carers for therapy, there is a usually a concern regarding a young person's behaviour or emotional/psychological well-being. There may be other difficulties also, including a change in school performance/attendance, poor social relationships and conflict in the family. Unlike individual therapy, a systemic approach sees the problems as being connected to the family environment that the child is in and an observation of family interactions 'provides us with the clues to which a family system manages, contributes to and/or maintains emotional and behavioural disturbances in a child' (Geldard *et al*, 2014, p.78). Winek (2010) points out that a systemic perspective focuses not on why the problem has developed but on how the problem is being maintained – in other words, how the other members of the family are contributing to the problem and what changes may need to be made at family, rather than individual, level.

Therefore, in contrast to other models, family therapy looks specifically at the relationships and dynamics between family members. The problem one person has – be it anxiety, depression or behavioural problems – is seen as being a product of the dynamics in the family. It sees the problem as being located within the family relationships (Burnham, 1986). Likewise, problems teenagers present with are addressed within the family context and the broader system, including the extended family. Winek (2010) sees the goal of treatment as changing how the family members interact and communicate in the session. For that reason, professionals using a systemic approach may (but not always) involve the entire family in the therapeutic process.

Within a systemic perspective, a family unit is seen as a system. There may be a number of subsystems, which are like mini parts of the system – for example, the couple system or the sibling subsystem (**Figure 7.2**). There should be a boundary between the different subsystems, particularly between parents and children. For example, a child could show signs of anxiety if exposed to adults talking about money worries all the time. To counteract this, sometimes the parents may discuss the more 'adult' issues separately with the therapist/professional.

Figure 7.2: The Family System

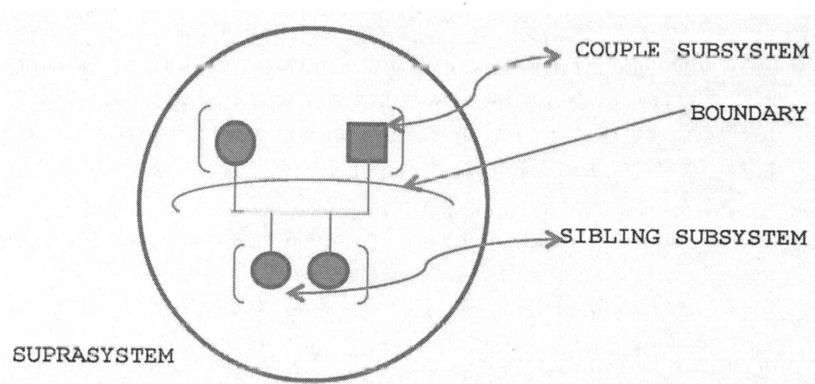

The suprasystem is the external context outside the family that may impact positively or negatively on the family. It is made up of other systems that influence the family, namely the political system, the educational system, the social system and the extended family, neighbourhood and community. For example, the economic system, whereby parents find it difficult to get work or if there are financial difficulties, may contribute to tension in the home. Likewise, the political or social system may affect the family members – for example, changes in social policy introduced by a new government may adversely impact on parents/carers, putting pressure on the family. Of course, the reverse is also possible. The education system or professionals working within the social system may support parents and children and help to bring about change or new opportunities, leading to better outcomes for family members.

The Therapeutic Work

When families ask for help or support in dealing with family difficulties, they have ideas about how they are, what their struggles are and a vision of how they would like things to be. There are a wide variety of techniques and concepts from family therapy at the disposal of a practitioner working with adolescents and their parents. Systemic theory and practice spans a vast range of theories and techniques.

While it is outside the capacity of this chapter to address all models of family therapy sufficiently, ideas and techniques from some approaches that I have found useful when working with parents and their teenagers will now be discussed.

Aspects of some of the systemic models that are drawn on here include ideas from Structural Family Therapy and the Milan Associates Systemic Therapy. Structural Therapy, as espoused by Salvador Minuchin (Minuchin *et al*, 1967), helps the family re-structure themselves in terms of more appropriate boundaries around parts of the family (subsystems) in order to improve family functioning (Burnham,1986). In this model, families are encouraged to be organised better in terms of each person's role – for example, parental role. Winek (2010, p.148) points out that 'if the family could maintain the new structures, then the change was more likely to be stable upon discharge from treatment'.

The Milan Associates Systemic Therapy was developed by four Italian psychiatrists – Palazzoli, Boscolo, Ceechin and Prata – in the 1970s and 1980s in Milan, Italy. This model focuses on the family's beliefs and rituals and how these guide family members' actions and the emergence of the symptom/problem for one member of the family (Dallos and Draper, 2010). The Milan team are renowned for their three guidelines to making a session systemic, namely hypothesising, circularity and neutrality (Palazzoli *et al*, 1980). Hypothesising means that the professional develops systemic suppositions on why the symptomatic behaviour has emerged or in other words they question what the function of the symptom is in terms of the family relationships. In the Duncan family example discussed later, we can see certain hypotheses being developed as I attempt to understand Zoe's behaviour within the family context. Circularity refers to the kinds of questions that are asked of members in the family session. Questions are circular rather than linear. For example, instead of asking a child (John) how he feels since his mother and father separated, his sister is asked: "Mary, how do you think John feels about mam and dad separating?". This means different perspectives may emerge and it stops the person having to answer a direct question they might be reluctant to answer in front of others. The third guideline that the Milan team put forward was neutrality. By that, they meant that the family members should feel that the therapist did not align themselves with any member of the family and the overall impression given to the family by the therapist should be that he/she is neutral (Palazzoli *et al*, 1980).

With these ideas in mind, in a family session relationships in the family are observed and spoken about within the therapeutic context (**Figure 7.3**).

Figure 7.3: The Focus of Therapeutic Work in a Family Session

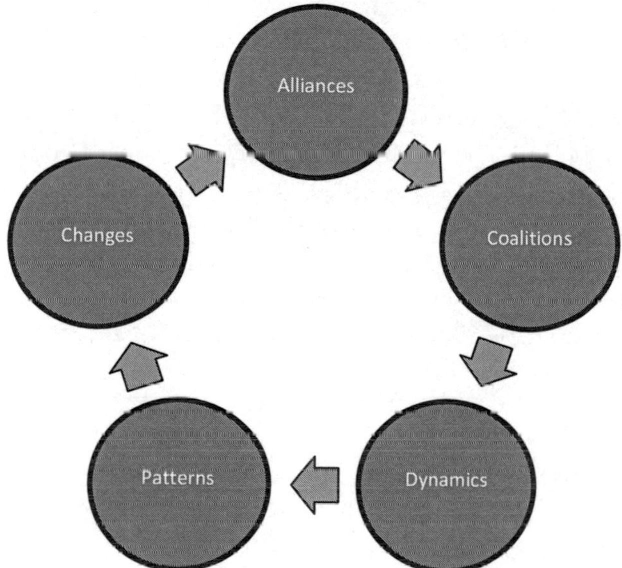

Coalitions are observed in a family therapy session, as they can give a lot of information on how a family is organised as well as display a variety of communication styles present in the family (Bateson, 1972). For example, a mother may take the adolescent daughter's side against the father. This family formation called 'triangulation' came from the Structural School and in particular Salvador Minuchin (1974). It refers to a young person being drawn in by the parents into tensions between the couple and taking the side of one of the parents against the other. The result is that the young person takes on a quasi-adult role that gives him/her an amount of power that keeps the other parent out of the family system (Dallos and Draper, 2010).

Of course, this is not a healthy role for the teenager to play as he/she needs the support of their parents and this adult role means their needs as a young person are not being met. Minuchin (1974, p.54) reminds us that 'for proper family functioning, the boundaries of subsystems need to be clear'. The therapeutic work therefore would focus on the parents being encouraged to be 'on the same page', establishing appropriate boundaries between parents and children and presenting a united front to the teenager and the other children in the family. The father would be encouraged to become more involved with the daughter and the mother would step back in terms of her overly close relationship to her son or daughter. This then negates the necessity for the young person to be in an adult role, as the adults are performing their roles effectively again.

Some Techniques from a Systemic Approach

When looking at a family across different generations, we may see certain patterns emerge – for example, the use of alcohol by a father and a grandfather. These patterns would be explored and alternative ways of being might be put forward in the therapeutic work. Life changes and transitions like job loss, illness or bereavement can see problems emerge at this time for family members. A useful tool to explore family patterns, alliances and transitions is the genogram as developed by Murray Bowen (Dallos and Draper, 2010). McGoldrick and Gerson (1985) expanded the model and applied it to the field of family therapy, making it 'nearly universal' (Winek, 2010, p. 89). The genogram or family tree provides a pictorial representation of three generations of the family across the family life cycle. It displays the age of family members, places where they live, occupations, changes, and alliances in the family. The genogram can be completed with the family in the session or the professional can use it as a planning or supervision tool outside the session.

Lowe (2004) has developed this model to include resources that each family member has and looks at what he terms 'contexts of competencies' – that is, interests of each family member or areas that they are getting on well in (work, sport and hobbies) – rather than focusing solely on the presenting problem. For example, the professional should include talents, hobbies and interests each member in the family has as well as information on moves, changes and difficulties they have experienced. This leads to a more strengths-based rather than problem-saturated conversation with the family and in particular the person who has been identified as having a problem.

In my experience, constructing the genogram with the family often brings to light experiences or situations that may never be discovered by direct questioning alone. It is also a useful therapeutic tool, as everyone – including children and young people – can become involved. Gaps in information and patterns in the family across generations can come to light and be discussed in a less invasive way. By mapping information on a genogram, Hills (2013) sees it as a key piece in family work that enables both practitioner and family get a clear picture of the overall family situation (**Figure 7.4**).

Figure 7.4: A Genogram of Zoe's Family

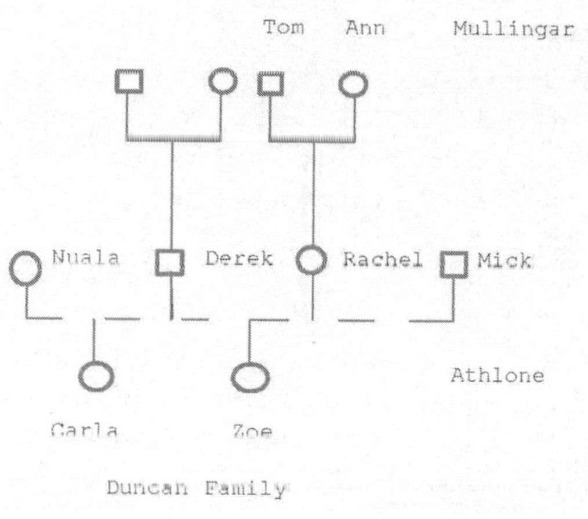

Family therapists often encourage people to look beyond their family system to the wider system. Outside agencies and relationships are explored in the hope of bringing change to the family situation. This may include the legal, health or political systems. The practitioner using a systemic lens does well to remember that they may not need to do everything and that they should enlist the help of extended family members, community leaders and other professionals in offering family support.

In the course of the work according to Geldard *et al* (2014), family therapy asks each member of the family to look at how their own ideas, perceptions and behaviours may be impacting on other members of the family. In a family session, new ways of communicating are explored. This may include listening to other perspectives from different family members and negotiating with each other more effectively. Adolescents and their parents may find this difficult and the therapy emphasises rights and responsibilities on both sides – for example, for the teenager to have more freedom means they need to show they can be trusted with this responsibility. Family members are asked to reflect on their thoughts and behaviours in order for them to see how they may be contributing to how the entire family is functioning. It is hoped that family members, with the support of the professional, will put forward solutions that are suitable for their family. The following case example illustrates how some systemic ideas and techniques can aid the practitioner when engaged with a family who are in transition.

Case Example: The Duncan Family

Referral Information

Zoe (14) lives with her mother, Rachel (32), who is a single parent. Rachel has a new boyfriend, Mick (28). Zoe recently has been physically aggressive towards her mother and is described by Rachel as 'having a violent temper'. Her school is not experiencing any displays of aggression but notes that Zoe is quiet and spends a lot of time on her own. They have recently moved to a new house, having previously lived with the maternal grandparents, Ann and Tom, who now live 30 miles away from them. Zoe says she does not like Mick. She has always been very close to her mother. She sees her father, Derek (35), infrequently. He has a partner, Nuala (30), and they have recently had a new baby girl, Carla, who is 4 months old. Based on the referral information, a genogram can be constructed by the practitioner (**Figure 7.4**). Of course, more information (like occupations, other relatives) will be included in the genogram after meeting with the family.

Intervention

It is possible to work with Zoe on her own through use of individual therapy. However, a family therapy approach might be more useful as it looks at changes, relationships, and dynamics between family members. The fact that Zoe has reached adolescence also may bring up some parenting dilemmas for Rachel, coupled with changes in the family system recently.

A systemic perspective encourages us to look at the following aspects:

- **Transitions and changes in the family:** There is a new relationship between Mick and her mother. They have moved house, which has meant that she no longer lives with her grandparents. We could hypothesise that, given her mother's age when Zoe was born, they may have lived with Zoe's grandparents since she was a baby and Zoe may be very attached to them. They now live 30 miles away so she may see them infrequently. This is another loss she has experienced recently;

- **The family as a system made up of subsystems:** Zoe and Rachel have been a subsystem up until now and her grandparents have been part of the family system. When Rachel and Mick started a relationship, this meant that they were now in a couple subsystem, with Zoe now on the periphery. The closeness between mother and daughter is being challenged by the arrival of Mick to the family system and Zoe may be reacting against this;
- **The function of the symptoms/behaviour (hypotheses):** Zoe's difficult behaviour may cause tension between Rachel and Mick. As it is a new relationship, Zoe at some level may hope that her behaviour will make Mick leave and she will be close to her mother again. Zoe's relationship with her father seems to be a distant or disengaged one. If Rachel cannot deal with the behaviour that Zoe is presenting with, perhaps she will have to contact Derek for help in dealing with Zoe, bringing him back into the family system;
- **The stage the family are at in the family life cycle:** Zoe has reached adolescence and she may be trying to construct her own identity separate to that of her mother and grandparents. She may now be more curious about her father in terms of her own ideas about her own identity. She is also likely to have some conflict with her mother as Rachel sets down boundaries and she begins to test these. If Mick has taken on a father role, she may be reacting against this as she may not respect his authority as a father figure. Also perhaps her grandparents have been in quasi-parental roles and Rachel is getting used to being the main parent of a teenager without their input (hypothesis).

The transition from childhood to adolescence usually brings some challenges to both parents and young people. However, in Zoe's family, this stage is further complicated as there have been a lot of other changes. Most recently, the birth of Carla may have had an impact on Zoe and she may hope her behaviour will re-engage her father with her.

Some Themes to Explore in the Therapeutic Process

Using some of the ideas discussed earlier, like the stage the family is at, the idea of subsystems in the family, as well as alliances between certain family members, it would be very useful to have some family sessions to discuss the changes they have experienced over the last few months. Zoe, in particular, needs an opportunity to voice her feelings and the hope would be that, as she does this in a therapeutic space, it will cut down on her need to show her feelings through aggression towards her mother. Family therapy, in contrast to individual therapy, gives the other family members a chance to hear how she is feeling while she also listens to how they respond to her.

The configuration of who attends the sessions might vary with different combinations attending at different times – for example, Rachel and Derek, Derek and Zoe or the entire family together.

In terms of therapeutic techniques, a genogram might be a non-invasive and non-threatening way of eliciting information on the changes in the family over the past few years. The different perspectives of each member in how they view these changes can be explored by constructing the genogram in collaboration with the family in a session.

Family sessions also would give some information on closeness or distance between different family members. Alliances between members or lack of relationship between others can be observed. The worker can ask questions of mother or father like 'Who is Zoe closest to?' (a circular question) to look at relationships and ascertain alliances/distance between family members. The hypothesis about Zoe and Rachel being a subsystem with Mick and Derek on the periphery could be tested.

The stage the family are at in terms of the family life cycle could be explored. Zoe is now a teenager and Rachel must alter her parenting style to allow Zoe to develop her independence while also making sure she is protecting her and keeping her safe. The role the grandparents have played in the parenting of Zoe could be explored. Similarly, it would be interesting to see if Mick is acting in a parental role and whether Zoe is reacting to this. Zoe's relationship with her father Derek could be discussed, particularly given the arrival of Carla. Also Derek's parenting style when Zoe is with him could also be looked at. It would be important to look at Rachel's own view of herself as a parent and how she feels she is dealing with a teenager who has undergone lots of transitions. She may need some encouragement and guidance as she takes on this phase of parenting.

The work ultimately would focus on supporting all members to adapt to the recent changes they all have gone through – marital breakdown, the birth of a new baby, new relationships, a new home and adolescence in a functional way. A positive outcome for Zoe and her family would be better communication between her and her mother, her and her father and her and Mick. Her parents, Rachel and Derek, would be empowered as parents of an adolescent. Zoe would be given the chance to begin to individuate from the family, in particular her mother, and take on the adolescent role with an interest in peer relationships rather than being so preoccupied with the family situation.

Conclusion

Dealing with the teenage stage can be a challenging but interesting time for parents, practitioners and the young person themselves. An understanding of what is happening at this stage of development and how the young person needs to begin the process of de-individuation from their parents is helpful. Some common dilemmas that parents and practitioners need to deal with were discussed through the lens of a systemic perspective. The usefulness of a systemic/family therapy approach was illuminated through the use of a case example with particular reference to systemic ideas and techniques. It is intended that these ideas may inform parents and practitioners navigate the changes that adolescence may bring, while strengthening relationships between adults and young people.

References

Bateson, G. (1972). *Steps to an Ecology of Mind: Mind and Nature*, New York: Ballantine Books.

Burnham, J. (1986). *Family Therapy*, London: Routledge.

Carr, A. (2014). 'The Evidence Base for Family Therapy and Systemic Interventions for Child-focused Problems', *Journal of Family Therapy*, Vol.36, Issue 2, pp.107-51.

Carter, E. and McGoldrick, M. (1980). The *Family Life Cycle: A Framework for Family Therapy*, New York: Gardner Press.

Comer, R. and Gould, E. (2011). *Psychology Around Us*, Hoboken, NJ: Wiley.

Coogan, D. (2012). 'Marking the Boundaries – When Troublesome Becomes Abusive and Children Cross a Line in Family Violence', *Feedback: Journal of the Family Therapy Association of Ireland*, Summer, pp.74-86.

Crane, R.D. (2014). 'The Cost-effectiveness of Family Therapy: A Progress Report', lecture to *First European Conference on Systemic Research in Therapy, Education and Organisational Development*, Heidelberg, Germany, 6-8 March.

Crane, R.D. and Christenson, J.D. (2014). 'A Summary Report of Cost-effectiveness: Recognizing the Value of Family Therapy in Health Care' in Hodgson, J., Lamson, A., Mendenhall, T. and Crane, R.D. (eds.), *Medical Family Therapy: Advanced Applications*, New York: Springer.

Dallos, R. and Draper, R. (2010). *An Introduction to Family Therapy: Systemic Theory and Practice*, third edition, Maidenhead: Open University Press.

Erikson, E. (1985). *Childhood and Society*, New York: W. & W. Norton.

Geldard, K., Geldard, D. and Yin Foo, R. (2014). *Counselling Children*, London: Sage.

Hills, J. (2013). *Introduction to Systemic and Family Therapy*, Basingstoke: Palgrave Macmillan.

Liddle, H.A. (2010). 'Multidimensional Family Therapy: A Science-based Treatment System', *Australian and New Zealand Journal of Family Therapy,* Vol.31, pp.133-48.

Lowe, R. (2004). *Family Therapy: A Constructive Framework,* London: Sage.

McGoldrick, M. and Gerson, R. (1985). *Genograms in Family Assessment,* New York: Basic Books.

Minuchin, S. (1974). *Families and Family Therapy,* London: Routledge.

Minuchin, S., Montalvo, B., Guerney, B.G., Rosman, B.L. and Schumer, H. (1967). *Families of the Slums: An Exploration of Their Structure and Treatment,* New York: Basic Books.

National Association of Principals and Deputy Principals (2014). 'Report Shows Sharp Increase in Cyberbullying over Past Year', *The Irish Times,* 27 April.

Palazzoli, M.S., Boscolo, L., Ceechin, G. and Prata, G. (1980). 'Hypothesizing – Circularity – Neutrality: Three Guidelines for the Conductor of the Session', *Family Process,* Vol.19, No.1, pp.3-12.

Satir, V. (n.d.). Retrieved 8 May 2014 from www.brainyquote.com / quotes / keywords / adolescent.html.

White, M. and Epston, D. (1990). *Narrative Means to Therapeutic Ends,* New York: Norton.

Winek, J.L. (2010). Systemic *Family Therapy,* London: Sage.

8: "There's an App for That!" – Parenting in a Digital Age

Tom Farrelly

> *The children now love luxury; they have bad manners, contempt for authority; they allow disrespect for elders and love chatter in place of exercise. Children now are tyrants, not the servants of their households. They no longer rise when elders enter the room. They contradict their parents, chatter before company, gobble up dainties at the table, cross their legs, and tyrannize their teachers.* (Socrates, 470/469 BC – 399 BC)

Parenting has always been, and continues to be, one of the most demanding (and rewarding) roles that people can be presented with. Each successive generation brings with it its own unique challenges, with each generation considering that it has to face a greater degree of difficulty than their predecessors. However, at the risk of overstating the case for the present era, the rate of change, levels of opportunity and risk presented by modern information communications technology (ICT) does provide a context for parenting that has never previously existed. In writing this piece, I am mindful that readers of this book come from different backgrounds in terms of interest in and knowledge of ICT and consequently the chapter begins with a brief explanation of the various terms associated with the digital world. Notwithstanding this explanation of terms section, I am very mindful that various software and hardware platforms can and do become outdated and thus I do not want to become too fixated on the technicalities themselves. Essentially, it is the issues raised by these technologies and how they impact on parenting that are the central focus of this chapter.

Terms Explained

As stated previously, I am mindful that the digital landscape is dynamic and consequently some of the current brand names and platforms may well grow, become obsolete or morph into something else. These limitations withstanding, even if you regard yourself as something of a technophobe, as a 21st century parent it is important that you have at least some degree of familiarity and understanding of the digital landscape that your child inhabits and interacts with. With apologies in advance to those possessing a more in-depth knowledge, this section is merely intended to provide a brief overview and explanation of various elements of the aforementioned digital landscape. So:

- The **World Wide Web** (www) or simply the 'web' is the set of protocols and hypertext language that were developed primarily by Sir Tim Berners Lee[1] that enabled the advancement of the user-friendly point and click Internet interface with which we have all become so familiar;
- **Web 2.0** is the term used to describe the development of the web that allowed the transformation of static Internet pages into a format whereby people could actively contribute to content and work collaboratively;
- Weblogs, or as they are more commonly called **'blogs'**, in effect are a development of the online diary. Postings by the author (blogger) are arranged in a chronological order. These postings can be in text form but additionally they may have audio, images and video elements. One of the most well-known microblogging sites (where the number of allowable characters is restricted) is **Twitter.com**.
- **Social media** is perhaps the most well-known aspects of Internet usage at the current time. It is the overarching term used to describe a variety of technologies that facilitate a range of activities (Kaplan and Haenlein, 2010), such as social networking (for example, Facebook), posting of blogs (for example, WordPress.com), playing online virtual world games (for example, World of Warcraft) and the sharing of video content (for example, YouTube). However, in reality, the lines of division between the categories are increasingly blurred as to whether a site is a social network, a blog and/or content sharing community such as Tumblr.

This very short list is intended only to provide the briefest of introductions to what is an increasingly diverse and complex area with a bewildering array of technologies. The best advice is to keep yourself as informed as possible. In fact, when it comes to parenting and using the

1 If you would like to see what the first webpage looked like, the European Organisation for Nuclear Research (CERN) has recreated a 1992 version of the very first website at **http://info.cern.ch/hypertext/WWW/TheProject.html**.

2 A private members bill (sponsored by Deputy Robert Troy), the *Cyberbullying Bill,*

Internet and mobile phones, there is no shortage of advice and resources. In fact, that may be part of the problem – information overload leading to confusion, bewilderment and in the end just avoiding the issue. As a way of starting this journey, you might wish to consider the approach that the UK's Parenting in a Digital Age Programme uses as a starting point.

The Parenting in a Digital Age Programme

Parenting in the Digital Age (PitDA) is an initiative by the Parent Zone in the UK that aims to 'help parents apply their parenting skills to the online world' (www.pitda.co.uk). While there are of course numerous useful and effective programmes across the world, I particularly like PitDA's systematic approach where it poses three fundamental questions that all parents should ask:

- WHO are your children talking to online?
- WHAT are they doing online?
- WHERE are they going online?

First, it is important to understand why it is important WHO your children are talking to. In the 'real' world, of course you are interested in who your children comes into contact with. Not everyone your children come into contact with will have their best interest at heart. In the online environment, where we do not see people, it is even more important as people may not always be who they seem to be. The tales of older men using social media sites to contact and groom younger boys and girls is sadly all too familiar, such as the case of 'a wheelchair-bound paedophile [who] posed as a former Disney On Ice skater to groom a 12 year old girl *via* Facebook before raping her' (*Daily Mail*, 2011). And while stories such as this are deeply disturbing, they represent only one end of the spectrum of concern with regard to 'who' they are talking to online. However, in many cases, the young person or child may not be the victim, they may be the person causing the distress and hurt to other young people. As we shall discuss in the next section, social media sites can become the vehicle for cyberbullying, sometimes with tragic results.

The second of the three questions is concerned with WHAT is your child doing online? This is a serious matter, as what they do may:

- Be illegal, like some downloads or hacking into someone else's account;
- Involve spending money, gambling or getting involved in online scams;

- Experience or get involved in bullying or harassing another person online;
- Create, upload and share images, video or other content that is inappropriate or even illegal (Parent Zone, 2014).

While children and young adults may have the online access to a whole range of goods and services, they may not possess the maturity or capability or financial resources to purchase these goods and services. A survey by VoucherCodes.co.uk found that 'over a fifth of children know how to use their parents' credit card details to buy things online ... even children of primary school age know how to use their parents' plastic – as many as one in 20 of those aged between 5 and 10' (Straus, 2014). Even where an adult has given a child permission to use their credit card, misunderstanding the terms and conditions of online use can result in a massive bill as the following case reported by Louise McBride in the *Irish Independent* illustrates. In 2013, the European Consumer Centre (ECC) Ireland took up the case of a man who had been presented with a bill for €4,075 from an online social media website after he had agreed to a charge of €15.32 on his credit card in order for his grandson to play an online game. Unbeknownst to the young man, every time he 'bought' game credits, he was racking up his grandfather's credit card bill at such a rate that the sum of €4,075 was accumulated in only one week. Although, the figure was subsequently reduced by €2,730, the man was still left with a substantial bill of €1,345 to pay (McBride, 2013).

Another matter of concern with regard to WHAT your child is doing online relates to the illegal downloading (online piracy) of music, games and movies. While the sheer scale of downloading (particularly music) may make the practice appear to be 'normal', it needs to be acknowledged that illegal downloading is theft to the same extent as if the person went into a shop and physically stole a CD or DVD. Companies are able to track individual subscriber's IP addresses and persistent offenders may find themselves in breach of their Internet provision contracts and have their connections removed and in certain circumstances may be prosecuted. Your child's response may be something like 'sure everyone does it'; as a responsible adult, that line of defence might be a little harder to use in court.

Cyberbullying

Arguably in terms of the digital world, one of the dominant concerns of parents and an area that attracts a lot of media attention is that of cyberbullying. 'While bullying predates the Internet, the phenomenon of cyberbullying … has attracted widespread public concern and is perceived as one of the most damaging risks that young people can encounter during the course of their Internet use' (O'Neill and Dinh, 2013, p.1). Although all forms of bullying are hurtful and damaging, Beale and Hall (2007, p.9) argue that 'it is the secretive nature of electronic bullying that helps to make it so insidious. A tormentor can get into a victim's home, harassing him or her while parents sit comfortably in the next room'.

So what exactly do we mean by the term cyberbullying? In a strictly legal sense, as of late 2014, there is no specific law[2] on the Irish statute books that specifically defines and prohibits cyberbullying. Depending on the specific circumstances, a number of sections of the *Non-Fatal Offences Against the Person Act, 1997*, may have application in instances of cyberbullying and the offending person(s) can be held accountable under the law for any relevant offence(s). Additionally, there are a number of other pieces of legislation which, again depending on the specific circumstances, can be used.[3]

While there is no exact definition of cyberbullying, the definition offered by the children's charity Barnardo's offers a very useful starting point where it is defined as: 'An aggressive intentional act carried out by a group or individual using electronic forms of contact, repeatedly over time against a victim who cannot easily defend himself or herself'. Sherrie M. Gordon, author of *Using Technology: A How-to Guide*, has categorised five types of cyberbullying, which are summarised in **Table 8.1**.

There is no doubt that high profile tragic cases of adolescent deaths, such as that of Phoebe Prince, where cyberbullying was implicated as a contributory cause, has certainly created a sense of fear and even panic amongst many parents. While not wishing to cause undue concern, this fear of the effects of cyberbullying is not unfounded. In 2011, the ISPCC (www.ispcc.ie) published the findings from the National Children's Consultation report, which highlighted some worrying trends with regard to Internet safety. The survey of more than 18,000 young people reported that '26% of respondents from secondary schools said they or someone they knew had been bullied and 22% of respondents from the

2 A private members bill (sponsored by Deputy Robert Troy), the *Cyberbullying Bill*, was presented before the Dáil in November 2013.

3 The *Post Office Amendment Act, 1951*, as amended. See Schedule 4 of the *Postal and Telecommunications Services (Amendment) Act, 1983*, s. 7 of the *Postal and Telecommunications Services (Amendment) Act, 1999* and Regulation 4(8) of Statutory Instrument 306/2003. The *Communications Regulation (Amendment) Act, 2007*, which substitutes a new section 13 for the former s.13 in the 1951 Act.

primary group said that they or someone they knew had experienced bullying' (X-Ray Data, 2014).

Table 8.1: Five Types of Cyberbullying

Type	Description
Harassing someone	Using text messaging, instant messaging and email to harass, threaten or embarrass the target. Posting rumours, threats or embarrassing information on social networking sites such as Facebook and Twitter.
Impersonating someone	Developing a screen name that is similar to the victim's screen name and then posting rude or hurtful remarks while pretending to be the victim.
Using photographs	Taking nude or degrading pictures of the victim in a locker room, a bathroom or dressing room without his or her permission. Sending mass emails or text messages that include nude or degrading photos of the victim. This behaviour is often called 'sexting'.
Creating websites, blogs, polls and more	Developing a website with information that is humiliating, embarrassing or insulting for the victim. Posting the victim's personal information and pictures on a website, which puts the victim in danger of being contacted by predators.
Participating in 'happy-slapping'	Using a camera phone to videotape a bullying incident, which may include one or more kids slapping, hitting, kicking or punching the victim.

Source: Gordon (2014).

In attempting to tackle cyberbullying, one of the issues that has been highlighted is that victims are often reluctant to report such incidents for fear 'that adults will take away their mobile phone, computer and/or Internet access' (Department of Education and Skills, 2013, p.38). This issue is certainly borne out in the ISPCC report (ISPCC, 2011), which found that, of those respondents who reported being bullied or knowing someone who had been bullied, 'fewer than 10% of them had told anyone other than friends about it' (ISPCC, 2011, p.3). This point is crucial to understanding the role that parents and other supportive adults can play in tackling cyberbullying. The Garda National Crime Prevention Unit (An Garda Síochána, 2012) has produced a crime prevention sheet, *Personal Safety – Online Harassment*, in which it advises that 'as a parent you know your child better than anyone. You are best placed to identify and deal with any incidences of cyberbullying they may encounter.

Children who have been bullied will have difficulty in overcoming this problem alone and will need your reassurance and encouragement in tackling it'. The sheet goes onto advise that there are some ways to minimise the risk of online harassment, including:

- **Don't reply** to messages that harass or annoy you;
- **Keep the message**. You don't have to read it, but keep it;
- **Report problems** to the people who are able to do something about it;
- **Parents** should ensure that children do not give away personal information online (An Garda Síochána, 2012).

It may not be the most pleasant realisation, but some parents do need to consider that their child actually may be the bully instead of the victim. In this case, the advice is to 'avoid hurting someone's feelings by emails or other forms of electronic communication' – specifically:

- Respect other people's online rights;
- Avoid insulting someone;
- If someone insults you, be calm;
- Avoid 'crashing' discussion groups or fora;
- Respect the privacy of other people online;
- Be responsible online (An Garda Síochána, 2012).

While cyberbullying and online harassment is a serious issue, there are number of other issues that also demand consideration.

Privacy and Ethical Issues

When one thinks about it, social networking sites (SNS) are an ingenious concept. Unlike a TV or radio station that has to produce or at least source content in order to attract an audience, with SNS the audience are both consumers and producers of content. The users themselves generate the content and in turn generate their own audience – an audience that advertisers are willing to pay handsomely for in order to gain access. Every day, millions of photographs and thousands of hours of video are uploaded onto SNS. For young people who have grown up in a digital world, this level of sharing and engagement has become commonplace and natural and often is entered into with little thought or regard for their own or others' privacy. However, 'social networking inevitably becomes a privacy issue because the exposure of large volumes of highly personal information is intrinsic to this media format' (Athique, 2013, p.223).

The problem with this high level of sharing is that there may be a whole raft of unintended and unanticipated consequences, either/or for those who produced the content and/or those who were featured in and/or viewed the content. This level of sharing has become so commonplace and accepted within modern society that frequently 'we do so without pause for thought as to the legal and social consequences of such sharing, either for ourselves or for others' (O'Dell, 2014). In the past, inappropriate acts that may have resulted in little more than mild embarrassment the next day can now leave a digital footprint that may come back to haunt a person and result in unforeseen negative outcomes.

Sources of Advice and Help

When researching this chapter, I came across a number of sources from the late 2000s that advised parents to consider limiting their child's Internet use to high-traffic areas of the house where the child would not be alone. While that advice may have been applicable when the majority of us accessed the Internet from a desktop PC in the living room, the massive growth in mobile access to the Internet makes this suggestion seem almost quaint.

There is a plethora of advice sites: some of them are government-funded, others run by voluntary agencies and some funded by commercial enterprises. Below is a list of some sources of information and guidance available. This should not be taken as an endorsement of any one site or organisation but it is I believe a useful resource to help you to identify some good sources of information and advice, particularly if you have little knowledge of the area. However, this list comes with the *caveat* that site addresses sometime change and links can be broken (note, where I have indicated a long web address, you may find it quicker to simply enter search terms such as the organisation name). Useful sites include:

- **Irish Internet Hotline:** The service provides an anonymous facility for the public to report suspected illegal content encountered on the Internet, in a secure and confidential way (www.hotline.ie);
- **Office for Internet Safety:** The OIS has primary responsibility for the development and promotion of strategic actions to promote the highest possible levels of Internet safety, particularly in relation to combating child pornography (www.internetsafety.ie/website/ois/oisweb.nsf/page/safety-en);
- **Irish Cellular Industry Association's Parents' Guide to Mobile Phones:** The ICIA is an alliance of the mobile operators – Meteor Mobile Communications, Three (including O2) and Vodafone – and

focuses on consumer-related issues and seeks to build media and public credibility on behalf of the mobile industry in Ireland (www.icia.ie/IBEC/BA.nsf/vPages/Business_Sectors~Telecommunications_and_Internet_Federation~mobile-phones--a-parents-guide-to-safe-and-sensible-use-16-12-2008/$file/Mobile%20Parents%20Guide.pdf);

- **Webwise:** The Irish Internet Safety Awareness Centre, which is co-funded by the Department of Education and Skills and the EU Safer Internet Programme (www.webwise.ie);
- **MakeITsecure:** An all-Ireland website dedicated to Internet security and sponsored by the Department of Communications, Energy and Natural Resources, the Northern Ireland Department of Finance and a number of key software companies including Microsoft, British Telecom, eircom and Vodafone (www.makeitsecure.org/en/index.html).

Regardless of how useful these sites and organisations are, if you suspect or know of any actions or activities that are illegal and/or threatening, the best advice is to contact the police and let them advise you, and where appropriate let them handle the matter.

Guidelines for Behaviour

Given the sheer scale and complexity of the digital world it is very difficult to provide an absolute set of guidelines that will protect Internet users and children in particular in every situation. Nonetheless, there are some excellent resources (both national and international) that have been devised and disseminated and which, if applied, can certainly help children and adults to enjoy and use the Internet with a greater degree of safety.

At the risk of promoting one set of guidelines over another, one particularly useful Irish guide is *Internet Safety Advice: Top 10 Tips for Parents* (Webwise, 2014). The table below is an abridged version of the guide, the full version of which is available on the website.

Admittedly, any set of general guidelines needs to be treated with some degree of caution. Clearly, judgement needs to be exercised, depending on the age and capabilities of the child. However, I particularly like this guideline because it treats children and young people with respect. Its starting point is not premised on fear, negativity or a top-down finger-wagging approach. Rather, it starts from a position that acknowledges that children and young people are naturally inquisitive and, given the opportunity, they will explore their environment regardless of whether that environment is real or virtual. If children and young people are not given support and guidance, they may find themselves in inappropriate, if not downright dangerous, online situations.

Table 8.2: Top 10 Tips for Parents

General Tip	Details
Discover the Internet together	Be the one to introduce your child to the Internet. For both parent and child, it is an advantage to discover the Internet together. Try to find web sites that are exciting and fun so that together you achieve a positive attitude to Internet exploration. This could make it easier to share both positive and negative experiences in the future.
Agree with your child rules for Internet use in your home	Try to reach an agreement with your child on the guidelines that apply to Internet use in your household. Here are some tips to get started: • Discuss when and for how long it is acceptable for your child to use the Internet; • Agree how to treat personal information (name, address, telephone, e-mail); • Discuss how to behave towards others when gaming, chatting, e-mailing or messaging; • Agree what type of sites and activities are OK or not OK in your family.
Encourage your child to be careful when disclosing personal information	It is important to be aware that many web pages made for children ask them for personal information in order to access personalised content. Being conscious of when and where it is all right to reveal personal information is vital. A simple rule for younger children could be that the child should not give out name, phone number or photo without your approval.
Talk about the risks associated with meeting online 'friends' in person	Adults should understand that the Internet could be a positive meeting place for children, where they can get to know other young people and make new friends. However, for safety and to avoid unpleasant experiences, it is important that children do not meet strangers they have met online without being accompanied by an adult, friends or others they trust.
Teach your child about evaluating information and being critically aware of information found online	Most children use the Internet to improve and develop knowledge in relation to schoolwork and personal interests. Children should be aware that not all information found online is correct, accurate or relevant.

General Tip	Details
Don't be too critical towards your child's exploration of the Internet	Most children use the Internet to improve and develop knowledge in relation to schoolwork and personal interests. Children should be aware that not all information found online is correct, accurate or relevant. Educate children on how to verify information they find by comparing it to alternative sources on the same topic. Show them trusted sites they can use to compare information.
Report online material you may consider illegal to the appropriate authorities	It is vital that we all take responsibility for the Web and report matters that we believe could be illegal. By doing this, we can help to prevent illegal activities online, such as child-pornography or attempts to lure children *via* chat, mail or messaging.
Encourage respect for others; stamp out cyberbullying	There is an informal code of conduct for the Internet. As in everyday life, there are informal ethical rules for how to behave when relating to other people on the Internet.
Let your children show you what they like to do online	To be able to guide your child with regard to Internet use, it is important to understand how children use the Internet and know what they like to do online. Let your child show you which websites they like visiting and what they do there.
Remember that the positive aspects of the Internet outweigh the negatives	The Internet is an excellent educational and recreational resource for children. There are millions of age-appropriate sites for younger children. Encourage your children to use such sites and to avoid registering for sites and services with adult content and behaviours.

However, especially for younger children who lack the necessary maturity and awareness to safely negotiate the digital world, there are a number of resources that can help to create and maintain a safer environment. One of most effective ways to control access to the Internet is to use filtering software that attempts to block access to specified Internet sites that have illegal or inappropriate content. 'There are two categories of filtering systems: software packages that you install and manage on your computer and filtering services that may be offered as service option by your Internet Service Provider' (Irish Internet Hotline, 2014). Internet settings that limit the type of sites that can be visited also can be set on mobile devices such as smartphones and tablets. While the use of filtering software and the use of Internet access settings serve a very useful purpose, a word of caution also required. For example, the effectiveness of any protective software depends on how up-to-date the software is maintained, as many harmful sites try to adapt and keep one step ahead of filtering software. Parents need to be mindful that out-of-date software may be providing only a limited degree of protection. Additionally, filtering will work only on those devices that have been configured as such. There is, however, no way of knowing what your child is doing if they access the Internet on other people's devices. This is not to imply that parents should not use parental control settings and software; they can be very useful but the danger of relying solely on such strategies is that, as your children get older and more technically savvy, such controls may have limited effectiveness.

Parents as Role Models

Thus far, we have looked at how parents can advise their child to safely navigate the digital landscape of the 21st century. While this type of protection and advice is very important, it is equally important to acknowledge that the problems with safe and appropriate Internet use may not always lie outside the home. Perhaps some parents may need to consider how their own online (including mobile/smart phone) activity might impact on the home environment.

Admittedly, while stories of the South Korean couple who were arrested for starving their three-month-old daughter to death while they spent hours playing a computer game that involved raising a virtual character of a young girl (Tran, 2010) are at the extreme end of online addiction, there is growing evidence that many parents/guardians are engaging in the same activity that parents are encouraged to monitor and prevent in children. John Bingham of the *Telegraph* newspaper remarked that 'those who order their offspring to switch off televisions, computers or mobile phones because they fear they are becoming addicted might need to take a long hard look at their own screen habits' (Bingham, 2014). In his article, he went onto to cite the findings from a study carried out on behalf of the New Forest National Park Authority by the research agency Opinion Matters, which found that almost 70% of children thought that their parents spent too much time on their mobile phone, iPad or other similar devices (Bingham, 2014).

In another study, a team of researchers from Boston Medical Center (Radesky *et al*, 2014) visited 15 fast food restaurants and observed the interactions between family members. In the study, 40 of the 55 caregivers were secretly observed to be preoccupied with their mobile devices at some stage during the meal, with almost one-third of the parents continuously occupied throughout the meal. A leading child psychologist and parenting expert, Dr Vicki Panaccione, notes that, while social media can help connect people from around the world, it also can act as a barrier to those who we should be closest to, our immediate family members. We have had the 'helicopter parent' and the 'tiger mom' and now we have the 'distracted parent'. Panaccione (2012) goes onto to say that 'distracted parenting appears to be on the rise. And with it, a rise in child injuries and even deaths!'. Admittedly, deaths and serious injuries may be extreme examples, but parents do need to consider whether they are allowing themselves to be distracted when they should be paying more attention to their young child instead of looking at their friend's latest posting.

Aside from the phenomenon of 'distracted parents', another issue that children may have to contend with is that of 'oversharenting'. This is the term used to describe parents who too post much information about their children online. While you may think that posting the image of your baby having a bath or dressed up in a costume is very cute, there are those have reservations about such actions. Given that many children now have a digital footprint based on their parent's actions, 'what happens in 10 or 15 years when a child inherits a Facebook page already full of embarrassing baby photos?', asks Eliana Dockterman (2013).

Conclusion

As previously discussed, there are a number of software tools and protocols that can be used to help protect and safeguard children. However, as was also noted, these arrangements have a limited capability particularly as children get older. What is needed is a 'toolkit', if you will, that children and young people can carry around with them and can use regardless of whether they are accessing the digital world at home, in a friend's house or simply on the move with a portable device. This 'toolkit' is simply a combination of those practices, habits, relationships and beliefs that inform and shape the young person's ability to navigate the digital world. At the heart of this toolkit are the qualities of parenting that have little to do with modern technology. These qualities are about instilling confidence, respect for self and others and trust. No amount of hi-tech gadgets can take the place of a parent or supportive adult who the child or young person feels that they can confide in and not be judged. No software package will stop a person being nasty to someone else if they see nothing wrong with what they are doing. And you yourself may need to consider how your own online habits might impact on your parenting – be careful that your behaviour does not convey a 'do as I say but not do as I do' message. In short, parenting in the digital age is different and yet it is the same. I chose the Socrates quote deliberately to show that for all the technological advances things haven't really changed all that much; at the heart of digital parenting is parenting, pure and simple. Yes, you do need to keep yourself informed but there is a limit as to what can be expected of you. The sources of advice that I have indicated are a good way to inform yourself but the best starting point is one that starts with the quality of relationships that you develop with your child.

References

An Garda Síochána (2012). *Crime Prevention Information Sheet: Personal Safety - Online Harassment*, available from www.garda.ie/Documents/User/CP%20Info%20Sheet%20-%20Online%20Harassment-2012-11-12.pdf, accessed 12 August 2014.

Athique, A. (2013). *Digital Media and Society: An Introduction*, Cambridge: Polity Press.

Beale, A. and Hall, K. (2007). 'Cyberbullying: What School Administrators (and Parents) Can Do', *Clearing House*, Vol.81, No.1, pp.8-12.

Bingham, J. (2014). 'Screen Addict Parents Accused of Hypocrisy by their Children', *Telegraph*, 22 July, available from www.telegraph.co.uk/technology/news/10981242/Screen-addict-parents-accused-of-hypocrisy-by-their-children.html, accessed 12 August 2014.

Daily Mail (2011). 'Girl, 12, raped by man she met on Facebook who pretended to be 13 year old disabled in Disney accident', 23 May, available from www.dailymail.co.uk/news/article-1389994/Girl-12-raped-man-met-Facebook-pretended-13 year old-disabled-Disney-accident.html#ixzz36PUhJLH1, accessed 14 July 2014.

Department of Education & Skills (2013). *Action Plan on Bullying Report of the Anti-Bullying Working Group to the Minister for Education and Skills*, available from www.education.ie/en/Publications/Education-Reports/Action-Plan-On-Bullying-2013.pdf, accessed 6 August 2014.

Dockterman, E. (2013). *Should Parents Post Pictures of Their Kids on Facebook?*, *TIME* Online, available from healthland.time.com/2013/09/06/should-parents-post-pictures-of-their-kids-on-facebook/, accessed 13 August 2014.

Gordon, M.S. (2014). *Five Types of Cyberbullying*, available from http://bullying.about.com/od/Cyberbullying/a/5-Types-Of-Cyberbullying.htm, accessed 12 July 2014.

Irish Internet Hotline (2014). *Filtering Software*, available from www.hotline.ie/filteringsoftware.php, accessed 26 August 2014.

ISPCC (2011). *This Will Come Back and Bite Us in the Butt: Children and the Internet*, available from www.ispcc.ie/file/4/12_0/NCC+report+-+Children+and+the+Internet.pdf, accessed 20 August 2014.

Kaplan, A.M. and Haenlein, M. (2010). 'Users of the World, Unite! The Challenges and Opportunities of Social Media', *Business Horizons*, Vol.53, No.1, pp.59-68.

McBride, L. (2013). 'Clicking up €20,000 in online gaming charges is child's play', *Irish Independent*, 1 September, available from www.independent.ie/business/

personal-finance/clicking-up-20000-in-online-gaming-charges-is-childs-play-29542331.html#sthash.Pzt7vgOw.dpuf, accessed 4 July 2014.

O'Dell, E. (2014). *Cyberethics & Cyberlaw – Sharing is Caring?*, available from www.tcd.ie/trinitylongroomhub/events/details/2014-04-14cyber_ethics.php, accessed 2 July 2014.

O'Neill, B. and Dinh, T. (2013). *Cyberbullying among 9-16 year olds in Ireland*, Digital Childhoods Working Paper Series (No.5), Dublin: Dublin Institute of Technology.

Panaccione, V. (2012). *Distracted Parenting*, available from http://parentingtodayskids.com/ article/distracted-parenting/, accessed 30 June 2014.

Parent Zone (2014). *Why is WHAT important?*, available from www.pitda.co.uk/what, accessed 30 June 2014.

Radesky, S.J., Kistin, J.C., Zuckerman, B., Nitzberg, K., Gross, J., Kaplan-Sanoff, M., Augustyn, M. and Silverstein, M. (2014). 'Patterns of Mobile Device Use by Caregivers and Children during Meals in Fast Food Restaurants', *Paediatrics*,Vol.133, No.4, pp.e842-e849, available from http://pediatrics.aappublications.org/content/early/2014/03/05/peds.2013-3703.full.pdf+html, accessed 12 August 2014.

Straus, R.R. (2014). *Watch out for the shock bills! A fifth of children know how to use their parents' credit card details to buy things online*, available from www.thisismoney.co.uk/money/bills/article-2568393/A-fifth-children-know-use-parents-credit-card-online.html, accessed 12 July 2014.

Tran, M. (2010). 'Girl starved to death while parents raised virtual child in online game', *The Guardian*, 5 March 2010, available from www.theguardian.com/world/2010/mar/05/korean-girl-starved-online-game, accessed 23 August 2014.

Webwise (2014). *Internet Safety Advice: Top 10 Tips for Parents*, available from www.webwise.ie/2014/parents/advice-top-10-tips-for-parents/, accessed 18 August 2014.

X-Ray Data (2014). *Cyberbullying Statistics and Laws in Ireland*, available from: www.xraydata.com/cyberbullying-statistics-and-laws-in-ireland/, accessed 18 August 2014.

9: Legal Gaps Impacting on Children of Lesbian, Gay and Bisexual Parents in Ireland[4]

Sandra Irwin Gowran

Introduction

This chapter will provide an overview of key legal and social issues for lesbian, gay and bisexual parents of children in Ireland. The section outlines how the face of the modern Irish family has changed in recent years and, within this, how lesbian and gay-headed families have become more visible. The chapter also deals with how lesbian and gay couples form families together and the significant legal issues they experience in trying to ensure legal security for their children.

The Status of Children and their Rights

Over the past two decades, a kaleidoscope of revelations, inquiries, and events have focused public discourse on how children are viewed and treated within Irish society and on the rights that children enjoy under the Irish *Constitution* and internationally under human rights conventions. Over this period, the status of children has changed from them being viewed as possessions of their parents to being respected as individuals in their own right with concomitant human rights. Some critical milestones along the way include:

- Ireland's signing of the United Nations *Convention on the Rights of the Child* in 1992;

4 This chapter does not purport to represent the issues experienced by trans parents, who often encounter additional societal and legal barriers as a consequence of their trans identity. However, it should be noted that many parents who are trans have become parents through a previous heterosexual relationship and, as a result, have a legal status as a biological parent.

- The establishment in 2011 of a Government Department with responsibility for children and overseen by a full Government Minister;
- The passing of a referendum to amend the *Constitution of Ireland* in order to expressly include children's rights (Government of Ireland, 2012), although the result of the referendum is currently the subject of a legal challenge;
- The establishment of Tusla, the Child and Family Agency in 2014. This resulted from the most comprehensive reform of child protection, early intervention and family support services undertaken in the state. Tusla was established against the background of multiple inquiries that resulted in the publication of a number of reports cataloguing decades of societal and state neglect of the care and support of children (Independent Child Death Review Group, 2012; Roscommon Child Care Inquiry, 2010; Commission to Inquire into Child Abuse, 2009; Shannon, 2007, 2008, 2009, 2010, 2011, 2013).

Alongside these developments, a sharper picture has emerged of the Irish family. While the family form of a married mother and father with children continues to be the most common form of family, other types of families increasingly are being recognised. So while the Irish *Constitution* only recognises one form of family, that of the family based on marriage, the *Child and Family Agency Act, 2013* (Government of Ireland, 2013a) defines family in much broader terms recognising the richness of blended and extended family forms:

> 'family' means spouse, parent, grandparent, step-parent, child (including a step-child), grandchild, brother, sister, half-brother, half-sister, and any other person who, in the opinion of the Agency, has a *bona fide* interest in the child. The term 'spouse' in turn is defined as 'each person of a couple in relation to the other'. 'Couple' is then defined as including a married couple, civil partners and cohabitants, both same-sex and opposite sex (Government of Ireland, 2013a).

The legislation cited above in effect recognises the diversity of family forms revealed in the most recent *Census*, carried out in 2011, in which for census purposes, family is defined as 'a couple with one or more children, a couple without children or a lone parent with one or more children' (Central Statistics Office, 2012a). Notable figures on different family forms include:

- 215,300 families are headed by lone parents with children (Central Statistics Office, 2012b);
- 44% of parents have never been married (Central Statistics Office, 2012b);
- The census recorded 49,005 households of cohabitating couples with children under the age of 15 years (Central Statistics Office, 2012a);
- The number of children living in cohabitating households is rapidly increasing, rising by 41% between 2006 and 2011 (Central Statistics Office, 2012a).

This data indicates that a significant number of children may be living in households with step-parents or with their biological parents' cohabiting partners. This has been confirmed also by the *Growing Up in Ireland* survey, which indicates that 14% of the infants sampled are living with lone parents and that 24% of those lone parents with one child are living with the child's grandparent(s) (Williams *et al*, 2010).

The 2011 *Census* recorded an almost doubling of lesbian, gay and bisexual (LGB) couples living together since the previous *Census* in 2006 (Central Statistics Office, 2012b). Arguably, the increase can be attributed in part to the increasing confidence of lesbian and gay people in recording their relationship in the *Census*, as well as to an actual increase in the number of lesbian and gay couples *per se* and follows a similar pattern to increases in previous censuses.[5] *Census 2011* recorded 230 LGB couples with children, the vast majority of these being female couples (Central Statistics Office, 2012b).

Family Formation

The past 20 years has been a period of unparalleled progress for lesbian and gay people in Ireland. A whole set of factors, including comprehensive equality legislation, has led to an increasingly open society where more and more lesbian, gay and bisexual people and lesbian and gay couples can live their lives openly, supported and acknowledged by family, friends, neighbours, work colleagues and by the wider community.

In this context, an increasing number of lesbian and gay couples, women in particular, are also parenting children, again, very often with the support of family, friends, schools and the wider community.

5 The 93% increase in *Census 2011* to 4,042 cohabiting same-sex couples mirrors the scale of increases across previous censuses: 156 same-sex cohabiting couples were counted in 1996; 1,300 couples in 2002 and 2,090 couples in 2006.

There are a number of pathways that lesbian and gay people may take to becoming parents; the particular pathway chosen often depends on personal circumstances and available avenues and can include the following:

- **Children from a previous relationship:** A common scenario is where one partner, who was previously in a married or unmarried heterosexual relationship, brings children from that marriage or unmarried relationship creating a step-family situation similar to other, heterosexual step-family arrangements. In many cases, the biological parents may have joint or shared parenting arrangements that involve both the biological parents and, in practice, also involve the new same-sex partner;
- **Conception by means of assisted reproduction:** This is more frequently used by female couples, one or other, or both, of whom conceive with the assistance of a professional fertility service or privately with the assistance of a 'known' donor. In the latter situation, there are varying degrees of involvement of the 'known' donor as father to resulting child/children; from no involvement at one end to shared parenting arrangements with the father (and possibly his partner) at the other. Shared parenting arrangements are not always without difficulty, as documented in the ruling by the Supreme Court on a case that centred on a dispute over one such agreement between a lesbian couple and a gay man (Supreme Court, 2009). The ruling granted access to the father, but denied him custody;
- **Adoption by one of the partners:** There is no prohibition in Ireland related to sexual orientation or gender identity that would prevent an individual from applying to become an adoptive parent. However, a lesbian or gay couple, even if they are in a civil partnership, are not permitted to jointly adopt a child or be considered as joint adoptive parents. Irish law states that a couple may only adopt jointly if they are married to each other (Government of Ireland, 2010a, Section 33). However, there is a current proposal before the Oireachtas that would change this situation and allow lesbian and gay couples to be considered jointly for adoption (Department of Justice and Equality, 2014);
- **Foster parents:** Although lesbian and gay couples are not entitled to jointly adopt a child, many foster children on behalf of the state. The report of the Government's Working Group on Domestic Partnership (2006) noted that lesbian and gay couples who are fostering children

form a small but significant group in terms of the overall numbers of same-sex couples parenting children;

- **Surrogacy:** Though practically and legally more complex, it is possible for a couple to enter into a surrogacy arrangement, whereby a third party agrees to carry a child on the couple's behalf. The complexity around surrogacy arrangements is illustrated in the report of the Commission on Assisted Human Reproduction (2005), which recommended legal recognition of surrogacy arrangements, provided certain strict conditions are met (see **Figure 9.1**).

Figure 9.1: Excerpt from the *Report of the Commission on Assisted Human Reproduction*

Donor Programmes and Surrogacy

The involvement of third parties as donors of gametes/embryos to assist infertile people to conceive raises a range of ethical, legal and social issues. All necessary steps must be taken in the selection of donors so as to ensure that donated sperm/ova are free from the risk of transmitting disease.

Appropriate counselling should be provided for all donors as a pre-requisite of informed consent but, in general, donors should not be allowed to lay down conditions for the use of their gametes nor should they be paid for donations. Children born through donated gametes should be entitled to know the identity of their genetic parents. Parental rights and responsibilities should be conferred on the recipient(s) of donations rather than on the donor(s).

The Commission gave lengthy consideration to the arguments for and against surrogacy and concluded, with one member dissenting, that surrogacy should be permitted subject to regulation. The majority of the Commission also considered that the child born through surrogacy should be presumed to be the child of the commissioning couple (Commission on Assisted Human Reproduction, 2005; p.*xiii*).

Legal Progress in Ireland

There has been considerable progress in legal protections for lesbian, gay and bisexual people in Ireland since the decriminalisation of homosexuality in 1993; **Table 9.1** outlines the key legislative and policy changes that have provided much needed protections for lesbian, gay and bisexual people.

Table 9.1: Key Legislative and Policy Milestones for LGB People in Ireland

Year	Legislation/Policy
1993	Equality-based reform that abolished old criminal laws on homosexuality. Equal age of consent established. *Unfair Dismissals Act* was updated to protect LGB workers.
1998	LGB employees are protected in all aspects of employment and recruitment in *Employment Equality Act*.
2000 & 2004	Protection for lesbian, gay and bisexual people in the provision of goods and services in *Equal Status Act*.
2006	Working Group on Domestic Partnership (2005) identifies civil marriage as the only equality option for lesbian and gay couples. The Working Group also recommended that lesbian and gay couples should be eligible for consideration to adopt any child who is eligible for adoption. An All Party Oireachtas Committee on the *Constitution* states that civil marriage for lesbian and gay couples would require a constitutional amendment and that legislation could provide a broad range of marriage-like rights and responsibilities. The *Parental Leave (Amendment) Act, 2006* (Government of Ireland, 2006) extended *force majeure* leave to lesbian and gay couples and allowed 'relevant parents' to take parental leave. The term 'relevant parent' brings a broad range of persons who actively parent within the scope of the legislation. The term now includes long-term foster parents, partners to the natural parent of a child where the natural parent may be divorced or separated and has formed a new relationship through remarriage or otherwise and other persons *in loco parentis*. Although not defined, '*in loco parentis*' applies to a person who is not a biological or adoptive parent and is involved in parenting a child (Department of Finance, 2006).
2010	Civil partnership legislation is passed by the Oireachtas with widespread political support. The *Civil Partnerships and Certain Rights and Obligations of Cohabitants Act, 2010* (Government of Ireland, 2010b) passed in the Dáil with the support of all parties and in the Seanad by a vote of 48 votes to 4 (Seanad Éireann, 2010). Legislation is passed under the *Social Welfare Act, 2010*, which treats civil partners the same as married couples in all social welfare provisions (Government of Ireland, 2010c). The Law Reform Commission published a report on legal aspects of family relationships that recommended the extension of guardianship to civil partners (Law Reform Commission, 2010, pp.41).

Year	Legislation/Policy
2011	The *Finance (No.3) Act, 2011* was passed, which treats civil partners the same as married couples in all taxation issues (Government of Ireland, 2011). Citizenship laws are amended to allow the civil partners of Irish citizens to acquire citizenship on the same basis as spouses of Irish citizens.
2013	The Constitutional Convention recommended that the *Constitution* should be changed to allow same-sex couples access to civil marriage. The Convention also recommended that, in the event of changed arrangements in relation to marriage, the State should enact laws regarding parentage and guardianship (Convention on the Constitution, 2013).This would ensure that lesbian and gay couples who are parenting together would be recognised as the legal parents of the children they parent with concomitant legal responsibilities and rights. In November, the Government agreed to accept the recommendations of the Constitutional Convention and hold a referendum in 2015 on providing access to civil marriage for lesbian and gay couples.

Social and Legal Issues Experienced by LGB Parents

In Ireland, significant legal progress has been achieved and currently there is legislation pending that would provide for guardianship and custody rights for children of lesbian and gay parents (Department of Justice and Equality, 2014). Nonetheless, as it stands, until legislation is enacted, there is still no legal framework to safeguard LGB-headed families.

The position for legal reform is further strengthened under the *European Convention on Human Rights*, to which Ireland is a party, under which states must respect the family life of all persons (Council of Europe, 1953). 'Family life' for this purpose includes relationships between people of the same gender and families comprising LGB people/same-gender couples and their children. It is unlawful, under the *Convention*, to discriminate against a person in relation to his or her family life on the basis of his or sexual orientation or gender identity. For instance, a biological parent cannot be denied custody of or access to a child on the basis of the parent's sexual orientation. Likewise, while under the *Convention*, there is no right to adopt, but where a state permits individuals to adopt, it cannot treat LGB applicants any differently from their heterosexual counterparts. Similarly, the *Convention* requires that, outside the context of marriage, same-gender and opposite-gender cohabitants must be treated the same.

Civil partnership and related legislation provides a strong legal framework analogous to marriage for same-sex couples but it does not recognise children being parented by same-sex couples who are civil partnered.

Issues that Can Arise for Children and Parents

The lack of legal recognition for LGB parents and the resulting implications for both children and parents have been highlighted as far back as 2006 in a report by a Government Working Group on Domestic Partnership (otherwise known as the 'Colley Report') (Working Group on Domestic Partnership, 2006). In particular, two legal obstacles were noted:

- The first is that, since joint adoption is restricted to married couples, lesbian and gay couples who have children cannot provide those children with the protection this legal relationship ensures. The negative implications of this for children being parented by a lesbian or gay couple are apparent in situations where adoption would be the most appropriate mechanism for investing both partners with legal rights and responsibilities. For example, the Colley report notes that lesbian and gay couples who have jointly fostered a child and who subsequently become eligible to apply for adoption have to make an arbitrary decision as to which partner will apply for adoption and who will relinquish any legal connections to the child. Thus the child, who had two foster parents, is only entitled to one legal parent.
- The second key legal obstacle is that, under current legislation, a non-biological parent may only apply for guardianship of a child they are parenting upon the death of an existing guardian or in other exceptional circumstances. This means that, although a lesbian or gay couple might jointly and equally parent a child from birth, there is no mechanism to allow the non-biological parent to take on any of the rights and responsibilities attached to the parental role.

These limitations pose many problems for LGB parents and their children – for example:

- Children are excluded from the protection and legal obligations of their non-biological parent towards them in terms of inheritance, maintenance and other benefits;
- In the event of the dissolution of a relationship or in the event of the death of the legal parent, the child / children can be separated from

their second parent, who has no legal connection to their child / children but who may have co-parented the child / children from birth. Equally, the child could be separated from the extended family of their non-biological parent – for example, *de facto* grandparents may have played a significant role in the life of the child but they have no legal link or connection to their *de facto* grandchild;

- Further day-to-day difficulties arise because the second parent has no legal connection with their child – for example, the non-biological parent may not be able to sign a consent form for medical treatment in the event of the other parent being incapacitated or unavailable. Similar issues arise in relation to registering a child for school and barriers to travel arising from non-recognition of the second parent.

These issues are experienced also by opposite-sex step-parents who have taken on a parenting role – where there is no provision for them to make an application for guardianship or for the biological parent or parents of a child to confer guardianship on them. The Law Reform Commission highlighted these issues in a report on *Legal Aspects of Family Relationships* (Law Reform Commission, 2010). The Commission also noted that there are couples who adopt the child in order to ensure that both parents are guardians but that this is not satisfactory as it requires the biological parent to adopt his or her own child and it severs all legal connection between the other biological parent and the child.

This clearly applies to lesbian and gay couples and the children they are parenting in a number of the scenarios outlined earlier (for example, where children have been brought to the relationship from a previous heterosexual relationship). However, a critical difference is that same-sex couples cannot jointly adopt even where this might best suit the circumstances and, in particular, be in the best interests of the child.

The Working Group on Domestic Partnership recommended in this respect that 'Given that the welfare of the child is paramount, in principle, same-sex couples who are married or in a full civil partnership should be eligible for consideration to adopt any child who is eligible for adoption' (2006, p.50).

Implications of the Omission of Children in Civil Partnership Legislation in Ireland

The provisions within civil partnership and related legislation are very extensive and, in most respects, replicate the obligations and entitlements that are conferred by law on married couples. However, insofar as children are concerned, civil partnership makes very little change in the current legal situation of children living with same-sex partners.

Table 9.2: Differences between Children Whose Parents are Married or in a Civil Partnership

Children within Marriage	Children within Civil Partnership
Biological or adoptive parent(s) have full rights and obligations in respect of child.	Biological or adoptive parent has full rights and obligations in respect of child.
Spouses are joint and equal guardians of children if they are both parents of the children.	Only biological or adoptive parent is guardian.
Step-parents can be obliged to maintain spouse's children if the step-parent accepts the child as a child of the family knowing he or she is not the biological parent of the child.	Civil partner of parent is not obliged to maintain child.
Step-parent cannot seek guardianship or custody (but can be made guardian on death of parent or removal of guardian).	Civil partner of parent cannot seek guardianship or custody (but can be made guardian on death of parent or removal of guardian).
Step-parent can seek access, if in a parental role.	Civil partner of parent can seek access, if in a parental role.
Step-parent not obliged to provide for spouse's child in will.	Civil partner of parent not obliged to provide for child in will.
Step-parent treated as a parent for purpose of gift and inheritance tax.	Civil partner treated as parent for purpose of gift and inheritance tax.
Couple can jointly adopt.	Couple cannot jointly adopt.

Source: Irish Council for Civil Liberties and Gay and Lesbian Equality Network (GLEN), 2012.

While a child has full rights in respect of a person who is his or her biological parent, the current law does not provide the child with any substantial rights in respect of the civil partner of the child's biological parent, who may have been involved in the planning for the child and the child's subsequent parenting since birth. For example:

- The child will not be able to seek maintenance from the non-biological parent in the event of a breakdown of the relationship between the parents;
- The child will have no rights of succession if the civil partner of the biological parent dies;

- Civil partnership does not recognise the interests of children in respect of the shared home of the civil partners;
- Unlike divorce, dissolution of civil partnership can be granted without regard to the interests of dependent children. If the court makes a maintenance order or any other order following dissolution of a civil partnership, it must take into account any obligation that either civil partner has to their *own* biological or adopted children. This does not extend to the child of a civil partner;
- The non-biological parent cannot ordinarily seek guardianship or custody of the child while all the child's other guardians are still alive;
- Civil partners may not adopt a child jointly, though, as is currently the case, either partner may adopt as an individual.

Exclusions such as these are not in the best interests and welfare of the children concerned, whose physical, psychological and emotional needs are best met by continuity and stability in their family relationships. There are significant differences and implications for children whose parents are unable to access civil marriage. **Table 9.2** sets out some of the most significant of these differences and limitations.

Children's Development by Family Type

For decades, researchers have been comparing the development of children with gay and lesbian parents and children of heterosexual parents. These studies have found no significant developmental differences between the two groups of children in their intelligence, psychological adjustment, social adjustment, popularity with friends, development of social sex role identity or development of sexual orientation (American Academy of Paediatrics, 1994; American Psychiatric Association, 2005; American Psychological Association, 2008; Australian Psychological Society, 2010; Cooper and Cates, 2006; Canadian Psychological Association, 2003; Patterson, 1992).

It is important that professionals working with gay and lesbian parent families and those involved in the assessment of LGB adults as potential foster or adoptive parents are aware of the very significant body of research evidence that demonstrates that LGB people are just as capable of being good parents as heterosexual people and that their children are just as likely to be healthy and well-adjusted. Below is a summary of the research on same-sex parents.

Table 9.3: A Summary of Research on Same-Sex Parenting

Parenting Issue 1: The Impact of Gay Parenting on Children's Development
The sexual orientation of parents does not affect: > The psychological well-being of children; > The social development of children; > The cognitive development of children. *Research references:* Tasker (2005); MacCallum and Golombok (2004); Wainright *et al* (2004); Golombok *et al* (2003); Fulcher *et al* (2003); Vanfraussen *et al* (2002); Chan *et al* (1998a); Chan *et al* (1998b); Patterson *et al* (1998); Brewaeys *et al* (1997); Flaks *et al* (1995); Tasker and Golombok (1995); Patterson (1994); Patterson (1992); Huggins (1989); Green *et al* (1986); Golombok *et al* (1983); Hotvedt and Mandel (1982); Kirkpatrick *et al* (1981).
Parenting Issue 2: The Quality of Parenting
The parenting skills of lesbian and gay parents are at least as good as those of heterosexual parents. The sexual orientation of parents does not affect the quality of their relationships with their children. Parent's mental health does not differ based on their sexual orientation. The quality of the couple relationship between the parents does not differ based on sexual orientation. *Research references:* Bos *et al* (2004); MacCallum and Golombok (2004); Golombok *et al* (2003); Perrin (2002); Chan *et al* (1998a); Flaks *et al* (1995); Tasker and Golombok (1995); Patterson (1992); Green *et al* (1986); Golombok *et al* (1983); Brewaeys *et al* (1997); Golombok *et al* (1997); Bigner and Jacobsen (1992); Bigner and Bozett (1990); Bigner and Jacobsen (1989).
Parenting Issue 3: Impact on Children's Gender and Sexual Development
Parent's sexual orientation: > Has no impact on children's gender identity; > Does not determine the sexual orientation of their children. *Research references:* MacCallum and Golombok (2004); Patterson and Chan (2004); Golombok *et al* (2003); Perrin (2002); Stacey and Biblarz (2001); Lamb (1999); Russell (1999); Golombok and Tasker (1996); Brewaeys *et al* (1997); Bailey *et al* (1995); Tasker and Golombok (1995); Patterson (1994); Green *et al* (1986); Golombok *et al* (1983); Kirkpatrick *et al* (1981); and Hoeffer (1981).

Source: Irish Council for Civil Liberties and Gay and Lesbian Equality Network (GLEN), 2011.

Current Legislative Proposals on Family Relationships

The *Children and Family Relationships Bill* (Department of Justice and Equality, 2014) that is currently before the Oireachtas, if enacted, will modernise Irish family law and take into account the many different family and parenting structures that exist in modern Ireland. The *Bill* will provide much needed legal security for the children of LGB parents. The intended consequences for LGB parents were outlined in a Department of Justice briefing paper on the *Bill,* key sections of which are:

- The Bill is intended to:
  - Allow civil partners, step-parents, those co-habiting with the biological or adoptive parent and those acting *in loco parentis* for a specified period to apply for guardianship of a child;
  - Establish that the best interests of the child are the paramount consideration in decisions on custody, guardianship and access and set out additional guidance for the court as to what constitutes the best interests test;
  - Set out how parentage is to be assigned in cases of assisted reproduction and surrogacy, enabling men and women to apply for declarations of parentage where children have been born to them through the use of their own genetic material or otherwise (Department of Justice, 2013).

If passed, the children and family relationships legislation will ensure that all children have access to the same protections and legal relationships to the people who are parenting them. A further issue is in the constitutional protection afforded to families based on marriage.

Extending access to civil marriage to lesbian and gay couples will ensure that the children of lesbian and gay parents enjoy the same constitutional protection and status as children of heterosexual married parents. Citizens in Ireland will vote in a referendum in 2015 to extend the right of civil marriage to lesbian, gay and bisexual couples. If passed, this will send a profoundly positive message to the children of LGB parents that their family is of equal value and status in society to others.

Conclusion

There is no doubt that parenting styles in Ireland have changed in recent decades. For the most part, these changes have been child-centred; childhood and children now enjoy a much better status in Irish society and in law. Families, however, continue to be created in all shapes and sizes as they always have; men and women will continue to come together to create families in the future, most of them within the legal and constitutional protections of marriage. LGB parents will continue also to have children together. With the new legislation, Irish family law will be brought into the 21st century and the best interests of all children assured. The children of LGB parents now and in the future deserve nothing less than the full protection and security of the Irish state.

References

American Academy of Paediatrics (1994). 'Children of Gay or Lesbian Parents', *Paediatrics in Review*, Vol.15, pp.354-58.

American Psychiatric Association (2005). *Support of Legal Recognition of Same-sex Civil Marriage*, Arlington, VA: American Psychiatric Association.

American Psychological Association (2008). *Lesbian and Gay Parenting*, Washington, DC: American Psychological Association.

Australian Psychological Society (2010). *Sexual Orientation and Homosexuality*, Melbourne: Australian Psychological Society.

Bailey, M., Bobrow, D., Wolfe, M. and Mikach, S. (1995). 'Sexual Orientation of Adult Sons of Gay Fathers', *Developmental Psychology*, Vol.31, pp.124-29.

Bigner, J.J. and Bozett, F.W. (1990). 'Parenting by Gay Fathers' in Bozett, F.W. and Sussman, M.B. (eds.), *Homosexuality and Family Relations*, New York: Harrington Park Press.

Bigner, J.J. and Jacobsen, R.B. (1989). 'Parenting Behaviours of Homosexual and Heterosexual Fathers', *Journal of Homosexuality*, Vol.18, No.1&2, pp.173-86.

Bigner, J.J. and Jacobsen, R.B. (1992). 'Adult Responses to Child Behaviour and Attitudes toward Fathering: Gay and Non-gay Fathers', *Journal of Homosexuality*, Vol.23, No.3, pp.99-112.

Bos, H.M.W., Van Balen, F. and Van Den Boom, D.C. (2004). 'Experience of Parenthood, Couple Relationship, Social Support and Childrearing Goals in Planned Lesbian Mother Families', *Journal of Child Psychology and Psychiatry*, Vol.45, No.4, pp.755-64.

Brewaeys, A., Ponjaert, I., Van Hall, E.V. and Golombok, S. (1997). 'Donor Insemination: Child Development and Family Functioning in Lesbian Mother Families', *Human Reproduction*, Vol.12, No.6, pp.1349-59.

Canadian Psychological Association (2003). *Position Statement on Gay and Lesbian Parenting*, available at www.cpa.ca/documents/GayParenting-CPA.pdf, accessed 12 August 2014.

Central Statistics Office (2012a). *Census 2011: Profile 5: Households and Families*, Dublin: Government Publications.

Central Statistics Office (2012b). *This is Ireland: Highlights from Census 2011, Part I*, Dublin: Government Publications.

Chan, R.W., Brooks, R.C., Raboy, B. and Patterson, C.J. (1998b). 'Division of Labour among Lesbian and Heterosexual Parents: Associations with Children's Adjustment', *Journal of Psychology*, Vol.12, No.3, pp.402-19.

Chan, R.W., Raboy, B. and Patterson, C.J. (1998a). 'Psychological Adjustment among Children Conceived *via* Donor Insemination by Lesbian and Heterosexual Mothers', *Child Development*, Vol.69, No.2, pp.443-57.

Commission on Assisted Human Reproduction (2005). *Report of the Commission on Assisted Human Reproduction*, available at www.lenus.ie/hse/bitstream/10147/46684/1/1740.pdf, accessed 12 August 2014.

Commission to Inquire into Child Abuse (2009). *Final Report*, Dublin: Government Publications.

Convention on the Constitution (2013). *Third Report of the Convention on the Constitution: Amending the Constitution to Provide for Same-sex Marriage*, Dublin: Government Publications.

Cooper, L. and Cates, P. (2006). *Too High A Price: The Case Against Restricting Gay Parenting*, second edition, New York: American Civil Liberties Union Foundation, available at www.aclu.org/files/images/asset_upload_file480_27496.pdf, accessed 12 August 2014.

Council of Europe (1953). *European Convention on Human Rights*, Strasbourg: European Court of Human Rights, available at www.echr.coe.int/Documents/Convention_ENG.pdf, accessed 12 August 2014.

Department of Finance (2006). *Amendments to Parental Leave Legislation: Amendments to Parental Leave Legislation*, reference No: E109/84/06, 1 June, available at http://circulars.gov.ie/pdf/letter/finance/2006/1.pdf, accessed 3 September 2014.

Department of Justice and Equality (2013). *Children and Family Relationships Bill: Briefing Paper*, available at www.justice.ie/en/JELR/Children%20and%20Family%20Relationships%20Bill%202013%20141113.pdf/Files/Children%20and%20Family%20Relationships%20Bill%202013%20141113.pdf, accessed 12 August 2014.

Department of Justice and Equality (2014). *General Scheme of Children and Family Relationships Bill (2014)*, available at www.justice.ie/en/JELR/General%20Scheme%20of%20a%20Children%20and%20Family%20Relationships%20Bill.pdf/Files/General%20Scheme%20of%20a%20Children%20and%20Family%20Relationships%20Bill.pdf, accessed 4 September 2014.

Flaks, D.K., Ficher, I., Masterpasqua, F. and Joseph, G. (1995). 'Lesbians Choosing Motherhood: A Comparative Study of Lesbian and Heterosexual Parents and Their Children', *Developmental Psychology*, Vol.31, No.1, pp.105-14.

Fulcher, M., Chan, R.W., Raboy, B. and Patterson, C.J. (2003). 'Contact with Grandparents among Children Conceived *via* Donor Insemination by Lesbian and Heterosexual Mothers', *Parenting: Science and Practice*, Vol.2, No.1, pp.61-76.

Golombok, S. and Tasker, F. (1996). 'Do Parents Influence the Sexual Orientation of Their Children? Findings from a Longitudinal Study of Lesbian Families', *Developmental Psychology*, Vol.32, No.1, pp.3-11.

Golombok, S., Perry, B., Burston, A., Murray, C., Mooney-Somers, J., Stevens, M. and Golding, J. (2003). 'Children with Lesbian Parents: A Community Study', *Development Psychology*, Vol.39, No.1, pp.20-33.

Golombok, S., Spencer, A. and Rutter, M. (1983). 'Children in Lesbian and Single-parent Households: Psychosexual and Psychiatric Appraisal', *Child Psychology and Psychiatry*, Vol.24, No.4, pp.551-69.

Golombok, S., Tasker, S. and Murray, C. (1997). 'Children Raised in Fatherless Families from Infancy: Family Relationships and the Socio-emotional Development of Children of Lesbian and Single Heterosexual Mothers', *Journal of Child Psychology and Psychiatry*, Vol.38, No.7, pp.783-91.

Government of Ireland (1993). *Unfair Dismissals Act*, Dublin: Government Publications.

Government of Ireland (1998). *Employment Equality Act*, Dublin: Government Publications.

Government of Ireland (2000). *Equal Status Act*, Dublin: Government Publications.

Government of Ireland (2004). *Equal Status Act*, Dublin: Government Publications.

Government of Ireland (2006). *Parental Leave Act*, Dublin: Government Publications.

Government of Ireland (2010a). *Adoption Act*, Dublin: Government Publications.

Government of Ireland (2010b). *Civil Partnership and Certain Rights of Cohabitants Act*, Dublin: Government Publications.

Government of Ireland (2010c). *Social Welfare Act*, Dublin: Government Publications.

Government of Ireland (2011). *Finance (No. 3) Act*, Dublin: Government Publications.

Government of Ireland (2012). *Thirty-first Amendment of the Constitution (Children) Bill*, Dublin: Government Publications.

Government of Ireland (2013). *Child and Family Agency Act*, Dublin: Government Publications.

Green, R., Barclay Mandel, J., Hotvedt, M., Gray, J. and Smith, L. (1986). 'Lesbian Mothers and Their Children: A Comparison with Solo Parent Heterosexual Mothers and Their Children', Archives of *Sexual Behaviour*, Vol.15, No.2, pp.167-84.

Hoeffer, B. (1981). 'Children's Acquisition of Sex-role Behaviour in Lesbian-mother Families', *American Journal of Orthopsychiatry*, Vol.51, No.3, pp.537-644.

Hotvedt, M. and Barclay Mandel, J. (1982). 'Children of Lesbian Mothers' in Paul, W., Weinrich, J., Gonsiorek, J. and Hotvedt, M. (eds.), *Homosexuality: Social, Psychological, and Biological* Issues, Beverly Hills, CA: Sage.

Huggins, S.L. (1989). 'A Comparative Study of Self-esteem of Adolescent Children of Divorced Lesbian Mothers and Divorced Heterosexual Mothers', *Journal of Homosexuality*, Vol.18, No.1&2, pp.123-35.

Independent Child Death Review Group (2012). *Report of the Independent Child Death Review Group*, Dublin: Government Publications, available at www.dcya.gov.ie/documents/publications/Report_ICDRG.pdf, accessed 3 September 2014.

Irish Association of Social Workers and Gay and Lesbian Equality Network (GLEN) (2010). *Lesbian, Gay and Bisexual People: A Guide to Good Practice*, Dublin: Irish Association of Social Workers and Gay and Lesbian Equality Network, available at www.glen.ie/attachments/IASW_LGB_Mental_ Health_Guide.pdf, accessed 12 August 2014.

Irish Council of Civil Liberties and Gay and Lesbian Equality Network (GLEN) (2012). *Know Your Rights: The Rights and Obligations of Civil Partners and Other Same-Sex Couples*. Dublin: Irish Council of Civil Liberties and Gay and Lesbian Equality Network.

Kirkpatrick, M., Smith, C. and Roy, R. (1981). 'Lesbian Mothers and Their Children: A Comparative Survey', *American Journal of Orthopsychiatry*, Vol.51, No.3, pp.545-51.

Lamb, M.E. (1999). 'Parental Behaviour, Family Processes and Child Development in Non-traditional and Traditionally Understudied Families' in Lamb, M.E. (ed.), *Parenting and Child Development in Non-traditional Families*, Mahwah, NJ: Lawrence Erlbaum Associates Publishers.

Law Reform Commission (2010). *Legal Aspects of Family Relationships* (LRC 101-2010), available at www.lawreform.ie/_fileupload/Reports/ r101Family(1).pdf, accessed 12 August 2014.

MacCallum, F. and Golombok, S. (2004). 'Children Raised in Fatherless Families from Infancy: A Follow-up of Children of Lesbian and Single Heterosexual Mothers at Early Adolescence', *Journal of Child Psychology and Psychiatry*, Vol.45, No.8, pp.1407-19.

Patterson, C. (1994). 'Children of the Lesbian Baby Boom: Behavioural Adjustment, Self-concepts and Sex-role Identity' in Green, B. and Herek, G. (eds.) *Contemporary Perspective on Lesbian and Gay Psychology: Theory, Research and Application*, Thousand Oaks, CA: Sage.

Patterson, C. and Chan, R. (2004). 'Gay Fathers' in Lamb, M. (ed.), *The Role of the Father in Child Development*, New York: John Wiley.

Patterson, C., Hurt, S. and Mason, C. (1998). 'Families of the Lesbian Baby Boom: Children's Contacts with Grandparents and Other Adults', *American Journal of Orthopsychiatry*, Vol.68, No.3, pp.390-99.

Patterson, J.C. (1992). 'Children of Lesbian and Gay Parents', *Child Development*, Vol.63, pp.1025-42.

Perrin, E.C. (2002). 'Technical Report: Co-parent or Second-parent Adoption by Same-sex Parents', *Pediatrics*, Vol.109, No.2, pp.341-44.

Roscommon Child Care Inquiry (2010). *Report of the Inquiry Team to the Health Service Executive*, available at www.tusla.ie/uploads/content/ Publication_RoscommonChildCareCase.pdf, accessed 3 September 2014.

Russell, G. (1999). 'Primary Caregiving Fathers' in Lamb, M.E. (ed.) *Parenting and Child Development in Non-traditional Families*, Mahwah, NJ: Lawrence Erlbaum Associates Publishers.

Seanad Éireann (2010). *Civil Partnership and Certain Rights and Obligations of Cohabitants Bill, 2009: Report and Final Stages*, Vol.204, No.3, available at http://debates.oireachtas.ie/seanad/2010/07/08/00009.asp, accessed 3 September 2014.

Shannon, G. (2007). *Report of the Special Rapporteur on Child Protection: A Report Submitted to the Oireachtas*, available at www.dcya.gov.ie/documents/ child_welfare_protection/Report_of_Special_Rapporteur_on_Child_Protection _Geoffrey_Shannon.PDF, accessed 3 September 2014.

Shannon, G. (2008). *Second Report of the Special Rapporteur on Child Protection: A Report Submitted to the Oireachtas*, available at www.dcya.gov.ie/documents/ publications/Geoffrey_Shannon_2nd_Report_191208.pdf, accessed 3 September 2014.

Shannon, G. (2009). *Third Report of the Special Rapporteur on Child Protection: A Report Submitted to the Oireachtas*, available at www.dcya.gov.ie/documents/

publications/Child_PRotection_Rapporteur_Report.pdf, accessed 3 September 2014.

Shannon, G. (2010). *Fourth Report of the Special Rapporteur on Child Protection: A Report Submitted to the Oireachtas*, available at www.dcya.gov.ie/documents/publications/Rapporteur-Report-2010.pdf, accessed 3 September 2014.

Shannon, G. (2011). *Fifth Report of the Special Rapporteur on Child Protection: A Report Submitted to the Oireachtas*, available at www.dcya.gov.ie/documents/publications/5RapporteurRepChildProtection.pdf, accessed 3 September 2014.

Shannon, G. (2013). *Sixth Annual Report of the Special Rapporteur on Child Protection: A Report Submitted to the Oireachtas*, available at www.dcya.gov.ie/documents/Publications/SixthRapporrteurReport.pdf, accessed 3 September 2014.

Stacey, J. and Biblarz, T.J. (2001). '(How) Does the Sexual Orientation of Parents Matter?', *American Sociological Review*, Vol.66, pp159-83.

Supreme Court (2009). *JMcD v PL and BM*, IESC 81, available at www.supremecourt.ie/Judgments.nsf/1b0757edc371032e802572ea0061450e/ce14854be09476c880257688003a0313?OpenDocument.

Tasker, F. (2005). 'Lesbian Mothers, Gay Fathers and Their Children: A Review', *Journal of Developmental & Behavioural Pediatrics*, Vol.26, No.3, pp.224-40.

Tasker, F. and Golombok, S. (1995). 'Adults Raised as Children in Lesbian Families', *American Journal of Orthopsychiatry*, Vol.65, No.2, pp.203-15.

Vanfraussen, K., Ponjaert-Kristoffresen, I. and Brewaeys, A. (2002). 'What Does It Mean for Youngsters to Grow Up in a Lesbian Family Created by means of Donor Insemination?', *Journal of Reproductive and Infant Psychology*, Vol.20, No.4, pp.237-52.

Wainright, J.L., Russell, S.T. and Patterson, C.J. (2004). 'Psychosocial Adjustment, School Outcomes and Romantic Relationships of Adolescence', *Child Development*, Vol.75, No.6, pp.1886-98.

Williams, J., Greene, S., McNally, S., Murray, A. and Quail, A. (2010). *Growing Up in Ireland: National Longitudinal Study: The Infants and their Families*, Dublin: Government Publications.

Working Group on Domestic Partnership (2006). *Options Paper*, the 'Colley report', Dublin: Government Publications, available at www.justice.ie/en/JELR/OptionsPaper.pdf/Files/OptionsPaper.pdf, accessed 12 August 2014.

10: Parenting Alone in Contemporary Ireland[6]

Rosemary Crosse and Michelle Millar

Introduction

18% of Irish children live with a lone parent, of whom 16% are lone mothers and this is the second most common family type in Ireland (Lunn and Fahey, 2011, p.56). The OECD (2011) reported that Ireland has the second highest rate of lone parent families in the OECD at 24.3%, compared to the average of 14.9%. An individual who parents alone is someone who is raising their children alone and can be single (never married), divorced, separated or widowed. A stereotypical view of a lone parent in Ireland is often one of young girls pushing buggies in urban wastelands (O'Brien, 2000); however, we will see that lone parent families are not a homogenous group. Rather this family form is varied and their numbers are growing. Between the 1981 and 2011 *Censuses*, the number of one-parent families grew from 29,658 (7.2% of all families) to 215,300, one in four of all families with children (Central Statistics Office, 1982, 2012a).

The following overview of the Irish lone parent profile emphasises the diversity of this group. In addition, a summary of historical and current policy responses to those parenting alone in Ireland draws attention to the fact that no allowances are made for such diversity. The reality of parenting alone, the existence of barriers to entering the labour market, societal views on lone parents, as well as current supports and services available to those parenting alone will be addressed here in an effort to shed light on the true reality of what parenting alone in contemporary Ireland really means.

---

6 Many thanks to Kate Hall for her assistance in presenting the *Census* data on lone parents.

The evidence presented in this chapter highlights the fact that lone parent families experience different challenges, rewards and are in need of different supports.

Lone Parent Profile in Ireland

An examination of the current profile of lone parents in Ireland will help to demonstrate significant differences between groups of lone parents, as well as differences between mothers and fathers who parent alone. Marital status and age profiles of both parents and children, in addition to differing levels of socio-economic status, reveal real diversity in this subset of the population.

Marital Status

Table 10.1: Marital Status of Lone Parents in Census 2011

Status	All Lone Parents	Males	Females
Single	86,866 (40.3%)	4,744 (5.5%)	82,122 (94.5%)
Married	9,026 (4.2%)	2,253 (25%)	6,773 (75%)
Separated	42,863 (19.9%)	6,704 (15.6%)	36,159 (84.4%)
Divorced	23,339 (19.8%)	3,521 (15.1%)	19,818 (84.9%)
Widowed	53,221 (24.7%)	11,809 (22.2%)	41,412 (77.7%)
Total	215,315	29,031 (13.5%)	186,284 (86.5%)

Source: Adapted from Central Statistics Office (2012b).

Table 10.1 displays significant differences in the marital status of all lone parents. Those differences are particularly evident between lone mothers and fathers. Just over 40% of all lone parents have never been married, 94.5% of whom are female, with the remaining 5.5% being male lone fathers who have never married. The number of widowed lone parents amount to a quarter of the total group (24.7%), with the largest group of lone fathers being part of that category (22.2%). 19.9% of all lone parents are separated, with an additional 19.8% of the total group being divorced. The legal introduction of divorce in 1997 initiated a new pathway into becoming a lone parent; the number of divorced people in Ireland increased by 150% from 35,059 in 2002 (the first *Census* after divorce was introduced) to 87,770 in 2011. However, the rate of marital breakdown in Ireland remains low at 9.7% of all marriages (Central Statistics Office, 2012a).

Age Groups of Lone Parents

Table 10.2 shows the age group of lone mothers and the number of children they have. Across all ages, more than half (56.9%) of all lone mothers have only one child, with only 15.4% of them having three or more children. Indeed, women aged 35 to 49 are the largest group of women with three children or more, with 25.3% of women falling into this category.

Table 10.2: Age Group of Lone Mothers in *Census 2011*

Age Group	Total	1 child	2 children	3 or more children
15 to 19	1,491 (0.8%)	1,414 (94.8%)	69 (4.6%)	8 (0.5%)
20 to 34	54,422 (29.2%)	33,474 (61.5%)	14,517 (26.7%)	6,431 (11.8%)
35 to 49	65,262 (35%)	26,703 (40.9%)	22,058 (33.8%)	16,501 (25.3%)
50 to 64	36,344 (19.5%)	21,339 (58.7%)	10,327 (28.4%)	4,658 (12.8%)
65+	28,785 (15.5%)	23,109 (80.3%)	4,598 (16%)	1,078 (3.7%)
Total	186,284	106,039 (56.9%)	51,569 (27.7%)	28,676 (15.4%)

Source: Adapted from Central Statistics Office (2012b).

In some instances, figures are similar for lone fathers, with 64.5% of them having only one child and 11.2% having three or more children. Men aged 35 to 49 are also the largest group that have three or more children. However, from **Table 10.3**, we can see that lone fathers are on average considerably older, with 65% aged 50 and over, whereas **Table 10.2** shows that 35% of lone mothers are in this age category.

Table 10.3: Age Group of Lone Fathers in *Census 2011*

Age Group	Total	1 child	2 children	3 or more children
15 to 19	39 (0.1%)	35 (89.7%)	3 (7.7%)	2 (2.6%)
20 to 34	2,150 (7.4%)	1,562 (72.7%)	443 (20.6%)	145 (6.7%)
35 to 49	8,113 (27.9%)	4,265 (52.6%)	2,404 (29.6%)	1,444 (17.8%)
50 to 64	10,860 (37.4%)	6,610 (6.9%)	2,880 (26.5%)	1,370 (12.6%)
65+	7,869 (27.1%)	6,254 (79.5%)	1,286 (16.3%)	329 (4.2%)
Total	29,031	18,726 (64.5%)	7,016 (24.2%)	3,289 (11.3%)

Source: Adapted from Central Statistics Office (2012b).

Lone Parents by Age of Youngest Child

In 2011, nine out of 10 lone parents were women and this ratio has persisted from 2001 to 2011; the number of women living as lone parents increased by 29.2% from 103,200 to 133,300 during that period (Central Statistics Office, 2012c).

Table 10.4 shows that the age of the youngest child was under 5 for 48% of lone parent mothers, while for 5% of lone fathers the age of the youngest child was over 15 years. Once again, this highlights the differing profile of lone parent mothers and fathers (Central Statistics Office, 2012b).

Table 10.4: Lone Parents by Age of Youngest Child in *Census 2011*

	000's		
Age of youngest child	Men	Women	% Women
0 to 4	2.7	48.1	94.7%
5 to 9	2.2	34.8	94.1%
10 to 14	4.2	29.6	87.6%
15 to 19	5.0	20.9	90.4%
Total	14.1	133.3	90.4

Source: Central Statistics Office (2012b).

Social Status of Lone Parents

Lone parents are generally a disadvantaged group in comparison to married parents; they have lower levels of education, are more likely to be situated in the lower manual social class and have higher unemployment rates.

Table 10.5: Social Class of Lone Parents in *Census 2011*

Status	All Lone Parents	Males	Females
Professional worker	5,103 (2.4%)	1,331 (26.1%)	3,772 (73.9%)
Managerial and technical	34,719 (16.1%)	5,226 (15.1%)	29,493 (84.9%)
Non-manual	42,594 (19.8%)	2,917 (6.8%)	39,677 (93.2%)
Skilled manual	23,145 (10.7%)	7,384 (31.9%)	15,761 (68.1%)
Semi-skilled	25,321 (11.8%)	3,921 (15.5%)	21,400 (84.5%)
Unskilled	10,240 (4.8%)	1,983 (19.4%)	8,257 (8.6%)
Others gainfully occupied and unknown	71,054 (33%)	5,541 (7.8%)	65,513 (92.2%)
Other	3,139 (1.5%)	728 (23.3%)	2,411 (76.8%)
Total	215,315	29,031 (13.5%)	186,284 (86.5%)

Source: Adapted from Central Statistics Office (2012b).

Table 10.5 shows that only 2.4% of all lone parents maintain a professional worker status.

Economic Status of Lone Parents

Table 10.6 shows the principal economic status of lone parents. Of lone parents in total, 42.5% are in paid employment compared to 69.3% for heads of two-parent households, 21.9% are homemakers and 14.4% are unemployed – for couples, the unemployed figure is 11.8% (see Central Statistics Office 2012c for comparative figures).

Table 10.6: Principal Economic Status of Lone Parents in *Census 2011*

Status	All Lone Parents	Males	Females
Person at work	91,583 (42.5%)	12,444 (13.6%)	79,139 (86.4%)
Unemployed, looking for first regular job	1,686 (0.8%)	117 (6.9%)	1,569 (93.1%)
Unemployed, having lost a job	29,242 (13.6%)	4,776 (16.3%)	24,466 (83.7%)
Student or pupil	6,593 (3.1%)	306 (4.6%)	6,287 (95.4%)
Looking after home/family	47,243 (21.9%)	1,359 (2.9%)	45,884 (97.1%)
Retired	25,113 (11.7%)	7,469 (29.7%)	17,644 (70.3%)
Unable to work due to illness	9,882 (4.6%)	1,758 (17.8%)	8,124 (82.2%)
Others not in labour force	834 (0.4%)	74 (8.9%)	760 (91.1%)
Not stated	3,139 (1.5%)	728 (23.2%)	2,411 (76.8%)
All persons 15 or over	212,716		

Source: Adapted from Central Statistics Office (2012b).

Impact of Socio-Economic Status

Fahey and Keilthy (2013), using data on 9 year old children and their families drawn from the *Growing Up in Ireland* survey, examined the direct impact of socio-economic status combined with the mother's age at first birth on the risk of continuous lone parenthood. They found that the dominant influence on the risk of continuous lone parenthood is early start family formation. Those who had their first child in their teens were 14 times more likely to be continuous lone parents when compared to those whose first birth occurred during the age of 26 to 29 (Fahey and Keilthy, 2013). Their analysis found that mothers with low educational levels have their first child more than three years younger than mothers with a high level of education. Furthermore, if these mothers were in economically strained households at 16, they are likely to have their first child an additional year younger (Fahey and Keilthy, 2013, p.14).

Lone Parent Poverty

Those parenting alone and their children are the biggest group at risk of living in poverty in Ireland and have been for some time. Fahey and Keilthy (2013) highlight the 'sharp' change that has taken place when characterising high poverty family types in Ireland. Forty years ago, the typical poor family in Ireland was comprised of two parents with a large number of children; today, the poor family is typically a small one-parent family. In 2012, 16.5% of all Irish households and 29.1% of lone parent households were at risk of living in poverty (Central Statistics Office, 2013). In 2005, 16.3% of Irish children lived in poverty compared to the OECD average of 12.7%. However, 74.9% of children in single parent households where the parent was not working were living in poverty; this fell to 24% when the parent was in paid employment. This compares to the poverty rate of 1.9% for those children living with both parents where both are working (OECD, 2011, p.41). Explanations for such high levels of poverty in lone parent households tend to centre on the fact that so many of these households have no adult in paid employment. Given the fact that lone parents tend to have lower levels of educational attainment, those that are attached to the labour market tend to work in low skill areas with consequent low pay (Watson *et al*, 2011), with high childcare costs being a significant barrier to progression according to (Richardson, 2012). Barriers to employment and training will be discussed in more detail later in the chapter.

Historical and Current Policy Responses to Parenting Alone

From an historical perspective, we must differentiate between those lone parents who had never been married and those who had been married and subsequently became lone parents either through desertion or widowhood. It was only in 1990 that state income support no longer differentiated between married and never married lone parents. This was primarily due to the fact that their paths into lone parenthood differed and were regarded as in need of different solutions by the State.

Under the *Poor Laws* from 1838 until the early 1900s, any parent in need of relief was obliged to enter the workhouse system. As Luddy (2011) explains, from the beginnings of this system unmarried mothers and their children were regarded as a problem, due to the high levels of infant mortality and numbers of illegitimate children in the workhouses. There was also concern that these 'sexually immoral women' (particularly those unmarried mothers with more than one child) and their children would be a bad example to other members of the workhouse. Indeed, those women deemed 'repeat offenders' often were placed in lunatic asylums deemed as possessing a mental deficiency or Magdalene laundries in an attempt to control their behaviour and prevent subsequent pregnancies. In the Irish Free State, the workhouses became county homes and there was a move by the state and Church to place unmarried mothers in religious-run mother and baby homes. These became synonymous as institutions designed to reform the moral nature of the unmarried mother through penitence and obedience and ensure that county homes would be the refuge of the 'respectable poor' (Luddy, 2011).

The first income support for lone parents introduced was the Widow's and Orphan's Pension in 1935, which provided support for widows to care for their children at home. However, for unmarried mothers, the policy of institutionalisation continued up until the 1970s. In keeping with the wider feminist movement in Ireland and extensive social change, state support was extended in 1970 to deserted wives with the introduction of an allowance (Deserted Wife's Allowance) in 1970 and benefit in 1973. Receiving the payment was far from straightforward, as there was an onus on the woman to prove that she had been deserted. In 1974, a Prisoner's Wife's Allowance based on the Deserted Wife's Allowance was introduced, followed by the Deserted Husband's Allowance in 1989. The latter was a landmark development in Irish social policy, as it acknowledged the role of men in caring for children in a society that had traditionally viewed this as the domain of women.

In 1973, the means-tested Unmarried Mother's Allowance was introduced. This was a ground-breaking acknowledgment by the state that single pregnant women were unable to economically bring up their children on their own and that institutionalisation was no longer an appropriate policy response. Kennedy described this move as 'like stepping onto a new planet', making the unmarried mother a 'visible recognised member of Irish society' (2001, p.219). In 1990, all assistance payments were combined into the Lone Parent's Allowance (LPA). There was no longer differentiation based on marital status or gender and the allowance was available to those parenting alone with dependent children up to the age of 18 (21 if in full-time education). Those in receipt of the LPA were prohibited from cohabiting and the payment was means-tested. The renaming of this welfare payment was significant, as it removed prejudicial terms such as 'deserted' and 'unmarried' from the social welfare code and desertion no longer had to be proven. In 1997, the name of the benefit was changed to the One Parent Family Payment

(OPFP), once again reflecting a societal shift in the discourse around those parenting alone.

For years, the assumption that underpinned welfare payments to those parenting alone was that recipients were not connected to the labour market (McCashin, 2004, p.181). This reflected the dominance of the male breadwinner model in the Irish, and indeed many other European countries', social policy paradigm (Lewis, 2006). An earnings disregard was introduced in 1994, as part of a pro-employment strategy that incentivised paid employment and OPFP recipients were permitted to engage with the labour market should they wish to (Millar *et al*, 2011). In 2006, the Department of Social and Family Affairs proposed the introduction of more stringent, compulsory activation proposals for recipients by replacing the OPFP with a Parental Allowance until the youngest child reaches seven, at which time the parent would take up employment, education or training.

The dual concerns of poverty rates amongst one-parent families and civil service disquiet about the amount of exchequer funds being spent on the payment prompted the drafting of the proposals (Millar *et al*, 2007, pp.122-24). Within this policy discourse, there is an underlying assumption that paid work ultimately will lead to social inclusion for lone parents and their child(ren) as it will facilitate in removing them from poverty. Furthermore, it is shaped by the notion of 'helping individuals to help themselves' through their (re-)integration into the labour force (Millar *et al*, 2011). Whilst an activation policy has been the focus of policy debates since 2006, it was only introduced in 2013 as a condition of the Troika bailout of Ireland in terms of savings to be made in social welfare spending and wider reform of social welfare (Millar and Crosse, 2014).

These changes meant that the age threshold of the youngest child be reduced from 18 to seven over a phased period of years; those recipients who no longer qualified for the OPFP would instead claim Jobseeker's Allowance (JA) and must be genuinely seeking work. In July 2013, more than 2,500 OPFP recipients were moved to the JA and, come July 2015, all those in receipt of the OPFP with a youngest child aged over seven will be moved to JA.

However, in acknowledgment of the difficulties such a radical change in social welfare arrangements will have for recipients, the Department of Social Protection has introduced a JA Transitional Arrangement. At present, those with children aged under 14 will be exempt from having to be available for and genuinely seeking full-time employment. Under this JA Transitional Arrangement, individuals will be obliged to engage with the Department of Social Protection's activation services. **Table 10.7** shows that, in 2010, almost 98% of the individuals in receipt of the OPFP were women. There is an underlying assumption that this activation process is the solution to tackle the levels of poverty experienced by those parenting alone and their children. However, this solution is not as straightforward as some would suggest, as there are many barriers preventing lone parents from taking up paid employment.

Table 10.7: Recipients of One Parent Family Payment by age in 2010

	Number		
Age Group	Men	Women	% Women
24 and under	28	13,159	99.8%
25 to 49	1,638	72,358	97.8%
50+	490	4,653	90.5%
Total	2,156	90,170	97.7%

Source: Central Statistics Office (2012c).

Barriers to Employment/Training

The impact of high childcare costs has been repeatedly acknowledged as an issue of concern for those parenting alone returning to paid employment (Hayes *et al*, 2005). The link between unemployment and childcare cost is particularly prevalent for lone mothers; the unemployment rate for lone mothers according to recent Central Statistics Office figures is 24.8%, compared to 12% of mothers in couples (Central Statistics Office, 2012c). Across the OECD, the average cost of childcare is 18% of the average wage and 12% of a family's net income for those families where both parents earn 100% of the average industrial wage (OECD, 2011, pp.165-7). Ireland spends nearly 30% of net family income (for dual earner families) on childcare (OECD, 2010), and this figure is much higher for lone parent families at over 50% (Immervoll and Barber, 2006). Due to the limited and costly options of childcare services available, reliance on informal, free sources of childcare is a common feature of family life in Ireland and particularly for lone parent families (Millar *et al*, 2007). The EU Commission's *Country Specific Recommendations for Ireland 2014* is the most recent report to highlight the need for quality affordable childcare for lone parents, the lack of which has contributed to a growing risk of poverty or social exclusion of children in Ireland and exacerbates the issue of the unequal labour market participation of women (European Commission, 2014).

Millar *et al* (2007) used a multi-method strategy to research the past and current level of engagement of those parenting alone in the labour market in Galway City and County, which included participants' experiences of this process. The findings suggest that the aspiration of many participants to engage in education, training and employment was to achieve their goals and improve the financial circumstances of themselves and their families.

However, it is also clear from the research that this desire is a tempered or conditional one. Any process that results in education, training and/or employment must take account of a number of barriers identified by the participants. Chief among these is the concern the participants expressed about caring for their children. The parents involved in the research very much viewed themselves, first and foremost, as primary carers for their children. Moreover, current social welfare policy for those parenting alone creates a division between those mothers who are in a relationship and those who are not and removes the choice of lone parents caring for their children full-time (Millar and Crosse, 2014).

Structural barriers to employment in the main consisted of a lack of flexible employment options that would facilitate the caring role of the participants; the availability of such options usually, according to the women, pertained to low skill areas with consequent low pay (Millar *et al*, 2007). There is no legal right to work part-time in Ireland; indeed part-time work and flexible working arrangements such as flexi hours, job sharing and working from home are at the discretion of the employer and vary greatly. In relation to the labour market attachment of lone mothers, Watson's analysis of 2006 *Census* figures show that lone mothers are more likely than their married counterparts to be in paid employment and suggest that:

> … what we may be seeing for this group of mothers is the impact of reduced choice. In the absence of a partner to share the earning burden, mothers are less free to choose to devote their time to caring for their family. Lone mothers who would prefer to remain outside the labour force to care for children are likely to find they are unable to afford this option' (Watson *et al*, 2011,p.46).

Difficulties surrounding organisational logistics and financial barriers, such as loss of secondary benefits like rent supplement and medical cards for example, as well as individual, personal and structural barriers were identified by the participants as issues that made it challenging for them to return to or remain in employment, education or training (Millar *et al*, 2007).

Recent 'activation' policies neglect the nuances of lone parent family life and fail to recognise the dual burden carried by Irish people who are parenting alone. If labour market activation policies are intended to increase social inclusion *via* paid employment to facilitate a removal from poverty, and, if such policies are shaped by the notion of helping individuals to help themselves through (re-)integration into the labour market (Millar *et al*, 2011), then account needs to be taken of the needs of all lone parents.

Reality of Parenting Alone

It is not just employment and education participation that present difficulties for those parenting alone. Being a lone parent encompasses a multitude of challenges that have to be coped with on a daily basis: difficulties in making ends meet, stigma, all-inclusive responsibility for the family unit, as well as negotiating relationships with the other parent, are all reflective of the challenges faced by those parenting alone.

As we have seen earlier in the chapter, in 2012, 29.1% of lone parent households were at risk of living in poverty (Central Statistics Office, 2013), and while percentages are telling, the reality of making ends meet for those parenting alone is something that cannot be quantified by percentages. Managing on extremely tight budgets means that, for many providing basic necessities such as food, heating and clothing is difficult, with very little left to pay for any forms of social activities enjoyed by other families, leading in many cases to the social exclusion of both parents and children (Millar *et al*, 2007).

The additional burden of housing causes significant problems and stress to a number of lone parents on low income. Substantial waiting lists for social housing means that many one-parent families are trapped in the rent supplement scheme. According to statistics from the Department of Social Protection, 13,032 lone parent families were in receipt of rent supplement in 2013 (Department of Social Protection, 2013). In many cases where rent caps are not in line with actual rent costs, this leads to rents being supplemented from already stretched incomes. This situation is set to continue due to the absence of appropriate social housing.

Efforts to meet the financial demands of raising children often result in additional financial burdens in the form of debt incurrence (Millar *et al*, 2007; Crosse, forthcoming). In situations of separation and divorce, debts incurred throughout marriages, as well as those incurred as a consequence of separation, place huge additional financial pressure on this group of lone parents. Lack of consistency and, in some cases, non-payment of child maintenance increase the financial burden on lone parents, not just those involved in cases of separation and divorce (Crosse, forthcoming). but across all groups (Millar *et al*, 2007).

In addition to dealing with financial difficulties, the challenges of parenting alone are numerous: dealing with worries, making decisions, as well as maintaining care of the family unit and everything that entails in terms of being solely responsible (in many cases) for the day-to-day care of children. Such challenges are more intense for those who do not have access to reliable support networks, which have often been cited as having a moderating effect on levels of stress experienced by those parenting alone (Millar *et al*, 2007; Millar *et al*, 2011; Millar and Crosse, 2014; Crosse, forthcoming).

Negotiating, facilitating and encouraging relationships between non-resident parents and children is another challenge often faced by those parenting alone. Problems pertaining to unreliability and irregularity of access visits by non-resident parents, as well as unequal roles in care, financial provision, decision-making and discipline are all issues that lone parents must manage to some extent through the course of their daily lives.

Societal Views on Lone Parents

Kitty Holland wrote in *The Irish Times* that Irish society 'reserves a particularly special disdain for single mothers' (Holland, 2014). She refers to the recent increase in commentary around Ireland's history in the treatment of unmarried mothers, where state and church together sought to punish women for their sin of falling pregnant outside of marriage and succeeded in stigmatising them and their children as being unfit to participate in civil society. Testament to this was the prevalence of mother and baby homes within the state and recent allegations of despicable conditions and treatment of women and children within those homes (Holland, 2014).

Whilst the issue of morality has changed, with 34% all births in Ireland occurring outside of marriage (Central Statistics Office,. 2012a), the discourse surrounding the drain that lone parents place on resources has certainly not disappeared and is experienced by the parents themselves (Millar *et al*, 2007), as well as being the primary motivator in social welfare policy in relation to this group. Recent debates on lone mothers raise the question whether societal views on mothers parenting alone have progressed in subsequent years. The collapse of the so-called 'Celtic Tiger' in 2008 and consequent austerity measures has seen a development of a process of scapegoating to justify post-boom cuts according to Monaghan *et al* (2013), with single mothers being a significant target for vilification.

This view of lone mothers as parasitic has seen a massive upsurge in recent times with debate over the removal of OPFP at fever pitch (Browne, 2012; Holland, 2014; Millar, 2009). Print media, as well as radio broadcasts, have been obsessed with public reaction to lone mother families. All sorts of justifications were posited for cuts in relation to social welfare, not least was the reputed immorality and irresponsibility of lone mothers. This proliferation of promiscuous women 'who do not accept their responsibilities' is creating 'a new lifestyle of welfare economy' that is 'morally and socially wrong', according to a view that was advanced in the Dáil by Fine Gael TD Derek Keating (see Browne, 2012). Former Bank of Ireland chief executive Mike Soden stated in an interview in the *Irish Examiner* that, if people choose the single parent family life, they have to be responsible for themselves and not depend on the state. He added that he found it 'aggravating' that single mothers who had 'not just one, but two or three children' expected state support (Millar, 2009). What we are seeing in the current day is a continuation of negative stereotypical perceptions of lone parents as having multiple children in order to increase their social welfare payments, despite the availability of data and statistics, presented at the beginning of this chapter, which suggest otherwise. The consequences of such views are far reaching: a recent survey conducted by One Family found that 78% of respondents experienced shame because of their family type, highlighting how 'stigma directed towards people parenting on their own outside of the "traditional" family unit remains a thing of the present' (One Family, 2014a).

Family Support

Given the extent of the demands on lone parents, it is pertinent to look at current supports available to those parenting alone in Ireland. McCroskey and Meezan (1998) view family-centred services as being divided into three separate types that are designed to serve families in different ways:

- **Basic social services:** Primarily encompassing child care, health care and income support, we have added housing and education in this category;
- **Family support programmes:** Providing a wide variety of services to counteract stresses, link families together and offer needed assistance;
- **Family preservation services:** Targeting families that are facing threats to family functioning and stability (McCroskey and Meezan, 1998).

The basic social services currently available to lone parents include:

- **Housing:**
  - Rent Supplement;
  - Mortgage Interest Supplement;
  - Local Authority Housing Assistance Payment (HAP): To be rolled out in 2015, allowing recipients to return to work and maintain some assistance towards housing costs.
- **Early childhood education and care (ECCE):**
  - Free preschool year;
  - Community Childcare Subvention Programme (CCS): Disadvantaged parents and parents in training, education or low paid employment can avail of childcare at reduced rates. The childcare is provided by community-based (not-for-profit) childcare services – but there are limited places;
  - City and County Childcare Committees (CCCs): Provide information to parents on local childcare facilities and information on parent networks.
- **Educational supports for lone parents:**
  - Back to Education Allowance: This scheme can enable a lone parent to go back to approved second or third level education to study on a full-time basis, without loss of secondary benefits; however, new claims for rent allowance on this payment will not be accepted AND/OR
  - Student Grant Scheme: Administers financial support for higher education – means-tested and dependent on a number of factors.
- **Social welfare payments for one-parent families:**
  - One Parent Family Payment (OPFP): A payment for men and women under 66 who are bringing children up without the support of a partner – it is means-tested. All OPFP for children over the age of 7 years will cease in July 2015. All claimants will be

transferred to Jobseeker's Allowance. Earnings Disregard is the amount of money you are allowed to earn while claiming OPFP; to be reduced to €90 a week by 2016;
  - Family Income Supplement (FIS): A weekly tax-free payment available to employees with children, giving extra financial support to people on low pay;
  - Supplementary Welfare Allowance: Provides a basic weekly allowance to eligible people who have little or no income.
  - Exceptional and Urgent Needs Payment: A single payment to help meet essential, once-off, exceptional expenditure.
- **Widows and widowers:**
  - Widows, widowers or surviving civil partner's contributory or non-contributory pension;
  - Widowed or surviving civil partner's bereavement grant.
- **Health:**
  - Medical cards;
  - GP visit cards;
  - Primary care, mental health and hospital services (see Crosse, forthcoming).

Table 10.8: Family Support and Family Preservation Services Aimed at Those Parenting Alone

Family Support	Family Preservation
Advocacy Income supports Healthcare Childcare Family-centred work policies Parent education Development-enhancing education Recreation Family planning services School-linked health and social services Information and referral services	Family support centres Family resource programmes Home-visiting programmes Counselling services Parent aide services Support groups Services for single parents Family mediation services

Curry (2011) states that, as the role of state services has increased, so too has that of the voluntary sector. In fact, many 'essential services are provided by voluntary organisations and the role of the sector in delivering social services, combating poverty and in community development is growing' (Lacey, 1998). It is predominately organisations affiliated with the community and voluntary sector that provide a substantial amount of the specific types of services required by lone parent families. The following is an overview of some of the services provided by community and voluntary groups:

- **Barnardo's:** Provides family support services, where the individual needs of each child and family are considered;
- **Citizens Information:** A voluntary network that provides comprehensive information on public services and on the entitlements of citizens in Ireland;
- **Community Women's Resource Centres:** Provide a range of services for individual women, for women's groups and for the community;
- **Free Legal Advice Centres (FLAC):** Offer basic, free legal services to the public, in the form of information and advice. Usually attached to local citizen information centres;
- **One Family:** Offers a range of supports to all members of one parent families, as well as to professionals working with those parenting alone;
- **Open:** Represents the diversity of interests of lone parents and their children;
- **Rainbows:** Operates a peer support programme to assist children and young people who have experienced a painful family transition such as death, separation or divorce;
- **St Vincent de Paul (SVP):** Tackles poverty in all its forms through the provision of practical assistance to those in need;
- **Women's Aid:** Provides support and information to women and their children who are being physically, emotionally or sexually abused.

Even though the provision of social services in Ireland has increased and has developed to take account of a multitude of needs, it has always suffered from '*ad hoc* solutions, resulting in the bureaucratic equivalent of a national patchwork quilt; it may cover the country, but it is miles from being a coherent design', according to Fitzgerald (2014).

On 1 January 2014, the Child and Family Agency was re-launched as Tusla. It encompasses a number of services pertaining to the family; its vision is to remove fragmentation between all services and provide leadership to all organisations and agencies that provide services to children, young people and families (Tusla, 2014). However, this vision of reduced fragmentation and leadership does not address the serious gaps that exist in the area of lone parent provision. One Family states that the

Department of Social Protection has put one-parent families in the frontline of austerity and the back of the queue for recovery due to the lack of development of joined-up policies and supports. Cuts to OPFP (such as those previously outlined) without supports have resulted in what feels like a sustained attack on one-parent families (One Family, 2014b).

Issues of choice, childcare, as well as practical support in terms of information, advice and assistance in areas pertaining to benefits, entitlements, negotiating the welfare system, education, training and employment are all areas where gaps in services have been highlighted (Millar *et al*, 2007). Furthermore, there needs to be more flexibility in the operating systems of such institutions in terms of altering the existing 'one type fits all' practice. Issues around qualifying for and maintaining housing and welfare support, as well as a lack of communication between services are all areas that need to be improved (Crosse, forthcoming).

In addition, changes to the maintenance system within the family courts also have been highlighted as an area that requires alteration. This would address some of the financial issues experienced by many lone parents – for example, having set parameters in terms of amounts awarded, removing the need for judicial discretion and enforcement of orders already made (which needs to include some form of ensuring payment of any arrears). Making non-resident parents responsible for providing for their children, as well as taking the onus of reasonability to pursue maintenance from resident parents, are all issues that require urgent attention (Crosse, forthcoming).

More empathy from representatives of social institutions is crucial in facilitating the progression of those parenting alone. In conjunction with the need for empathic institutions is the view that a more personalised form of support is needed for parents in this situation. As we have already seen, the experience of parenting alone can create huge stress and anxiety. Access to a more personalised type of support would be extremely helpful, a need for both one-on-one support from social institutions, as well as some form of group support where interaction with people in similar situations is facilitated (Millar *et al*, 2007; Crosse, forthcoming) have been highlighted as areas requiring improvement.

Conclusion

The challenges faced by those parenting alone are both multidimensional and different, depending on individual circumstances. As previously stated, lone parents in Ireland are not a homogenous group and although some challenges may be similar, they also can be diverse and this diversity needs to be acknowledged both at a societal and policy level. What also needs to be acknowledged is the multifaceted nature of the daily lives of lone parents; far from being women 'who do not accept their responsibilities', the people who parent alone have done exactly that. The challenges they face highlight how the responsibilities of lone parents are all encompassing. They involve fulfilling every day obligations such as safeguarding children's physical and emotional needs, facilitating other parent relationships, as well as maintaining financial responsibility for households – all of which is often accomplished alone without the support of a partner or in many cases a support network to shoulder some of the burden.

Overall, those parenting alone often supersede role expectations in terms of care and/or financial provision, but difficulty arises when they also have to take on the other parent role, which has been the case for many. The crux of the whole issue of responsibility lies in the implementation of policies that maintain inequalities within the sphere of the family by ensuring one parent is responsible for all aspects of a household and these policies are being executed in such a way that makes it impossible for all such roles to be fulfilled. An appreciation of the challenges faced by those parenting alone, both personal and structural, must be incorporated not only into any process that aims to facilitate employment/training opportunities but also into the national consciousness for lone parents to successfully progress.

References

Browne, C. (2012). 'Facts about lone parents rubbish claims they abuse welfare system', *Irish Examiner*, 19 December, available at www.irishexaminer.com/viewpoints/columnists/colette-browne/facts-about-lone-parents-rubbish-claims-they-abuse-welfare-system-217380.html, accessed 8 July 2014.

Central Statistics Office (1982). *Census of Population of Ireland 1981, Vol.3*, Dublin: Government Publications.

Central Statistics Office (2012a). *Census of Population is Ireland 2011, Profile 5: Households and Families*, Dublin: Government Publications.

Central Statistics Office (2012b). *Census 2011 Statistics on Lone Parent Families*, Dublin: Government Publications, available online at www.oneparent.ie/CSO-Statistics-On-Lone-Parent-Families-2011.pdf.

Central Statistics Office (2012c). *Women and Men in Ireland 2011*, Dublin: Government Publications.

Central Statistics Office (2013). E*U-SILC Living in Ireland Survey*, Government Publications.

Crosse, R. (forthcoming). *Irish Mothers' Experiences of Marital Dissolution and their Perspectives on Support Services*, Galway: National University of Ireland Galway.

Curry, J. (2011). *Irish Social Services*, Dublin: Institute of Public Administration.

Department of Social Protection (2013). *Statistical Information on Social Welfare Services*, available at www.welfare.ie/en/downloads/Social-Stats-AR-2013.pdf, accessed 10 July 2014.

European Commission (2014). *Council Recommendation: On Ireland's 2014 National Reform Programme and Delivering a Council Opinion on Ireland's 2014 Stability Programme*, No. SWD (2014) 408 final, Brussels: European Commission.

Fahey, A. and Keilthy, P. (2013). *Absent Fathers, Absent Siblings: Two Sides of Lone Parenthood for Children*, UCD Geary Institute Discussion Paper: Geary WP2013/03, Dublin: University College Dublin.

Fitzgerald, F. (2014). *Check Against Delivery*, Department of Children and Youth Affairs, available at http://dcya.gov.ie/viewdoc.asp?Docid=3088&CatID=12&mn=&StartDate=1+January+2014, accessed 25 July 2014.

Hayes, N., Bradley, S. and Newman, C. (2005). *An Accessible Childcare Model*, Dublin: National Women's Council of Ireland.

Holland, K. (2014). 'Why Ireland is not a welcoming place for single parents', *The Irish Times*, 27 June, available at www.irishtimes.com/news/social-affairs/why-ireland-is-not-a-welcoming-place-for-single-parents-1.1846542?page=1, accessed 8 July 2014.

Immervoll, H. and Barber, D. (2006). *Can Parents Afford to Work? Childcare Costs, Tax-Benefit Policies and Work Incentives*, Discussion Paper No.1932, Bonn: IZA (Institute for the Study of Labour).

Kennedy, F. (2001). *Cottage to Crèche: Family Change in Ireland*, Dublin: Institute of Public Administration.

Lacey, B. (1998). *Towards a White Paper on Supporting Voluntary Activity: Poverty Today*, Dublin: Combat Poverty Agency.

Lewis, J. (2006). *Children, Changing Families and Welfare States*, Cheltenham: Edward Elgar.

Luddy, M. (2011). 'Unmarried Mothers in Ireland, 1880-1973', *Women's History Review*, Vol.20, No.1, pp.109-26.

Lunn, P. and Fahey, T. (2011). *Households and Family Structures in Ireland: A Detailed Statistical Analysis of Census 2006*, Dublin: Family Support Agency and The Economic and Social Research Institute.

McCashin, A. (2004). *Social Security in Ireland*, Dublin: Gill and Macmillan.

McCroskey, J. and Meezan, W. (1998). 'Family-Centered Services: Approaches and Effectiveness', *The Future of Children*, Vol.8, pp.54-71.

Millar, M. and Crosse, R. (2014). 'Irish Work/Family Policies: An Emerging Paradox', in Readdick, C. (ed.), *Irish Families and Globalization: Conversations about Belonging and Identity across Space and Time*, Groves Monographs on Marriage and Family Vol.3, Ann Arbor, MI: University of Michigan Press.

Millar, M., Coen, L., Bradley, C. and Rau, H. (2011). '"Doing the Job as a Parent": Parenting Alone, Work, and Family Policy in Ireland', *Journal of Family Issues*, Vol.33, pp.29-51.

Millar, M., Coen, L., Rau, H., Donegan, M., Canavan, J. and Bradley, C. (2007). *Towards a Better Future: Research on Labour Market Needs and Social Exclusion of*

One Parent Families in Galway City and County, Galway: The One Parent Family Research Steering Group.

Millar, S. (2009). 'Lone parent remark sparks outrage', *Irish Examiner*, 18 September, available at www.irishexaminer.com/ireland/lone-parent-remark-sparks-outrage-101212.html, accessed 15 July 2014.

Monaghan, L., O'Flynn, M. and Power, M.J. (2013). *Scapegoating in Post 'Celtic Tiger' Ireland: Framing Blame in Crisis Times*, University of Limerick Department of Sociology Working Paper Series, No. WP2013-06, Limerick: University of Limerick.

O'Brien, B. (2000). 'Review of single-parent payment avoids issues', *The Irish Times*, 9 September.

OECD (2010). *Gender Brief*: Paris: OECD Publishing.

OECD (2011). *Doing Better for Families*, Paris: OECD Publishing.

One Family (2014a). *Lone Parents and Shame*, available at www.onefamily.ie/wp-content/uploads/One-Family-Survey-Results-June-2014_Shame.pdf, accessed 30 July 2014.

One Family (2014b). *A July of Fear and Insecurity for over 9,000 Lone Parents*, press release, 3 July, available at www.onefamily.ie/press-releases/a-july-of-fear-and-insecurity-for-over-9000-lone-parents/, accessed 30 July 2014.

Richardson, L. (2012). 'Can Parents Afford to Work? An Update', paper presented at the *European Population Conference*, Stockholm, June.

Tusla (2014). *About Us*, available at www.tusla.ie/about, accessed 28 July 2014.

Watson, D., Lunn, P., Quinn, E. and Russell, H. (2011). *Multiple Disadvantage in Ireland: An Equality Analysis of Census 2006*, Dublin: Equality Authority and Economic and Social Research Institute.

11: Parents with Intellectual Disability

Anna Moore Asgharian

Introduction

Parents with intellectual disability are a heterogeneous group, each parent with their own individual experience of life and their own strengths and challenges. They share a common vulnerability and the experiences they encounter provide an insight into our society and our treatment of each other. The aim of this chapter is to present this area of specialism; this will be done by way of reviewing the literature and by introducing case studies based upon the real experiences of the author. We will consider the characteristics of the population and the issues they face at an individual and a system level. We will look at the challenges this group face as they partake in one of the most 'ordinary' and accepted life choices that we as human beings have: that of rearing our children.

The population of parents with intellectual disability is recognised in the literature as being largely 'invisible' (Whitman *et al*, 1986). This is due to the fact that estimates vary, caused by variations in definitions of intellectual disability, and because many parents may not be known to services (McGaw and Sturmey, 1993). International studies reveal that more people with intellectual disability are becoming parents (Booth and Booth, 1993; Dowdney and Skuse, 1993; Tymchuk and Feldman, 1991). However, this group face an increased risk of having their children removed (Booth, 2000). It also shows that, for those parents reliant upon services, a lack of provision is a key factor in influencing court decisions regarding placement of children (Tarleton *et al*, 2006).

What is Intellectual Disability?

Intellectual disability is defined as a developmental disorder which constitutes a deficit in intellectual and adaptive functioning that is first evident in childhood (American Psychiatric Association, 2013). The spectrum of needs of people with intellectual disability ranges from those with a profound level, who need constant care and may not be able to communicate, to those at the mild level who can function independently but with some degree of social supports. Research has shown that most parents with intellectual disability are functioning in this mild to borderline range (International Association for the Scientific Study of Intellectual and Developmental Disabilities, 2008). Many individuals are functioning in society without access to services. It is only when they become parents and, due to the increased responsibilities and pressures they reach crisis point where concerns about child protection bring them to the attention of services (Morris, 2003; Young and Hawkins, 2006).

People with intellectual disability have difficulty with all round learning, affecting their understanding and expression of language, their memory and their ability to problem-solve. They may have difficulty dealing with novel or abstract situations, as they find it difficult to generalise their learning from one situation to another. Difficulties with adaptive functioning refer to the skills we need to live an independent life. These include social skills, such as being aware of rules and customs, detecting the motivations of others, and practical life skills like cooking, dressing, time-keeping and occupational skills. Intellectual disability is a lifelong condition. It can affect a person's ability to function in most areas of everyday life to varying degrees.

Challenges of Parenting with Intellectual Disability

In a recent survey conducted by the National Disability Authority in Ireland, members of the public were asked whether they thought people with intellectual disability should have the same rights as others to be parents: only 38% agreed (National Disability Authority, 2011). The main reason cited was concern about the child's emotional well-being. Comparable attitudes have been documented internationally and are referred to in the literature as the 'unhelpful presumption' (Whitman and Accardo, 1990). This is the belief that neglect and abuse of children is inevitable when parents have an intellectual disability. Conversely, however, researchers agree that there is little relationship between measured intelligence and parental competence (Whitman and Accardo, 1990) except when it falls below the range of 55 to 60 IQ points (Dowdney and Skuse, 1993).

Tymchuk and Andron (1994) found that, when there are parental capacity concerns with this group, their children are most at risk of 'unintentional neglect,' as the parents do not know how to perform childcare tasks. In addition, McGaw and Newman (2005) state that it is rare for mothers with intellectual disability to deliberately harm their children and, when abuse does occur, it is most often by a person known to the mother.

Parents with intellectual disability may be at greater risk of experiencing life challenges known as 'social factors' (Gath, 1988). Social factors can be a challenge for any parent and include issues such as low social economic status, unemployment, social isolation and exclusion. In addition, however, parents with intellectual disability also may have been more likely to have experienced poor parenting role models and childhood experiences, difficult relationship histories and increased psychological distress (Dowdney and Skuse, 1993; Gath, 1988; McGaw and Newman, 2005; Whitman and Accardo, 1990). Challenging early experiences impact on their relationships with others and their ability to cope with raising children (Dowdney and Skuse, 1993; Gath, 1988; McGaw and Newman, 2005). Parental skills need to evolve as the infant develops. In addition, having more children can lead to increased pressure in terms of providing for them and catering to their differing developmental needs.

Children

Feldman *et al* (1985) showed that there is a higher prevalence of developmental delay and medical problems in children whose parents have intellectual disability and that this is associated with inadequate early stimulation. Keltner *et al* (1999) found that children are vulnerable to delays with cognition and language. In general, however, the evidence is that most of the children of parents with intellectual disability will grow to be brighter than their parents.

Case study: Tony and Michelle

This couple was referred to the clinical psychologist in the health service. Both Tony and Michelle were recognised to have learning needs at school age, but neither had been in contact with services as adults. It was only when they became parents and their children were showing signs of possible developmental delay and neglect that they once again were seen by services.

Concerns were expressed about the development of Tony and Michelle's two daughters by nursery teachers and the primary care nurse. The children were aged 3 and 4 years; they were said to be small in size and to have delayed motor development. Both girls were experiencing language delay and were said to have difficulties getting along with peers.

Tony, the girls' father, had been raised in the care system since the age of 2 years. With developmental delay detected in childhood, Tony had attended a school for children with special needs. His disability was in the mild range. Michelle, their mother, had been raised at home. She had a difficult childhood, whereby she experienced neglect and emotional abuse. Michelle was less able than her partner; her disability was in the moderate range.

Over the assessment period, the extent of the problems the family were experiencing began to emerge. Tony's provision of care was disorganised: he would remember to feed the girls but only if he felt hungry himself and they were with him. When he got his money, he could spend it all with no plan of how his family would cope financially for the rest of the week. Tony loved his daughters, he would hug them and sing to them, but Tony lived in the moment. He often would become distracted and go out with friends, leaving Michelle to cope on her own. Neither parent had a supportive social network to help them with caring for their daughters. They were unemployed and the house they lived in was disorganised and unclean.

Motherhood was Michelle's lifelong ambition; the role gave her enormous pride. Michelle, however, could be challenged by periods of anxiety and depression; she could often find it difficult to get out of bed and face the morning routine. Michelle was overwhelmed on a daily basis by trying to meet the needs of her two daughters and was petrified of having them taken away.

When working with a family such as Tony and Michelle's, practitioners need to hold in mind the needs of the parents and the children at the same time. The aim can be to find ways of supporting the parents so that they can provide their best caregiving to the child. For Tony and Michelle, this initially consisted of practical supports such as help with building in a routine to a child's life and with nutritional advice and organising the household. Tony and Michelle, however, needed a lot more support in terms of understanding and responding to the needs of their children as they developed. They needed 24-hour supports from social care workers and a decision had to be made whether this was practical and in the best interests of the children. In Ireland, the needs of the child always come first (Department of Children and Youth Affairs, 2011) and the purpose of the assessment is to work out whether parents can be supported in such a way as to meet the needs of the child.

Theories of Parenting

Winnicott (1953) introduced the concept of the 'good enough mother'. He presented the idea that, when the baby is first born, it is given undivided and devoted attention by the mother. As the child develops, however, the mother responds to its needs less predictably. As a result, the child learns to cope with her failure to be perfect. This was seen as a preferable way for a mother to be as it prepares the child for the real world.

The importance of the quality of parenting will determine how the child develops emotionally and socially. So, what defines 'good enough parenting'? Budd *et al* (2011, p.64) state: 'Parenting is essential to human life, yet so basic it defies easy description'. Types of parenting can be subject to critique depending upon many variables including education, culture, age and socio-economic background. There is, therefore, no agreed concept of parenting and no specific definition of what is 'good enough'. Professionals are left to consider what is good enough in terms of the effect the parenting has upon the child. For parents who have intellectual disability, a standard of 'minimal parenting capacity' is particularly relevant. The basis of this approach, as described by Budd (2001), is that it is important not to compare the relative abilities of caregivers, but to consider the minimum standard of acceptable parenting that is sufficient to protect the safety and well-being of the child.

What Do We Know About Parents with Intellectual Disability in Ireland?

There is a large body of international literature informing us about the characteristics and needs of this group of parents. In Ireland, however, there is a paucity of such publications. Of the work that is available, Sheerin *et al* (2013) found similar themes to the international context. They interviewed a self-selecting sample of four women with intellectual disability about their interactions with Children and Family Services in the Republic of Ireland. The women spoke of their feelings of isolation and their fear of losing their children. Using a qualitative descriptive design, the themes they found were that the responses of professionals and services were inadequate and ubiquitous. They concluded that this had a disempowering effect on the women.

Other published sources from Ireland include newspaper articles and testimonials from practitioners. Holland (2011) quoted a lobby group from Inclusion Ireland in *The Irish Times*, stating that the state is removing children from parents who have mild intellectual disabilities 'with little or no effort made to support these people as parents'. It said that, in the majority of cases, the health service was successful in having care orders granted when the parent or parents had intellectual disabilities. This statement reveals some of the challenges for this vulnerable group of parents in Ireland. However, it appears that such outcomes are not unique to parents with intellectual disabilities. O'Mahony *et al* (2012) looked at the outcomes for **all** parents who went to court with regards to the custody of their children and found that the overwhelming majority of children ultimately are placed into the care of the state.

In 2013, a literature review was conducted through University College Dublin, comparing the countries of Ireland, England and Australia as regards lessons of best practice in social work. After exploring the interplay between parental rights and disability in the Irish child protection system, the literature review concluded that there is a 'likelihood that parents with intellectual disabilities may be treated unfavourably in the Irish court system' (McLaughlin, 2013, p.51). In the previous year, an oral presentation was made at the 2012 IASSID World Congress in Canada describing working with parents with intellectual disability in Ireland and how, although the issues encountered for parents can be similar to other Western countries (for example, low social economic status and lack of support) as there are no specialist services, there is a greater requirement for the advocacy and understanding of the needs of this vulnerable group (Moore Asgharian, 2012).

Although this group share similar challenges to those in other countries, Ireland has its own unique history and it is important to be cognisant of this in order to understand how the legacies of the past affect this group today. Ireland's history of denying vulnerable people responsibility and freedom is documented by Kelly (2005), who records the experiences of mothers who were pregnant outside marriage, and, who as a result of the prevailing social climate dominated by the church and conservative state, were pressured to relinquish their children for adoption. Brennan (2013) documents how the national public asylum system was developed in the 19th century and how the institutions were a significant feature of Irish communities set up as a way of managing the social problems in society.

Disability Legislation

In today's Ireland, as we move on from the past and the doctrinaire of the Catholic Church, many institutions have closed, couples may live together before getting married, and a minority of well-functioning people with intellectual disability have access to paid employment. However, in the present day, the signs of Ireland's history are still evident. Hunt (2012) spoke in the press about a woman who has intellectual disability and for who 'not only is it socially unacceptable for [her] to have sex with her boyfriend, it is a crime. And if she gets married, she is not legally protected against rape'. This is a referral to section 5 of the *Sexual Offences Act, 1993* (Government of Ireland, 1993). Under this Act, it is currently an offence to have sexual intercourse with a person with an intellectual disability unless it is within a marriage. There is no recognition that people with disability can engage in consensual sexual activity and in loving sexual relationships. There is no protection from sexual abuse within a marriage, as there is no provision for consent. Without this, a person with intellectual disability is not protected by the law should they be sexually abused within a marriage as they are deemed incapable of consent.

Another example of historical legacy is the *Lunacy Regulations Act, 1871*. This allows for a person to be made a 'Ward of Court', whereby all the decisions about their lives are made by a judge. Still in operation, this act may come into play when a person has difficulty making financial decisions and, if they are made a Ward of Court, it will affect their whole life in terms of their medical, marriage and travel choices.

What is being proposed to replace these Acts are the *Assisted Decision-making (Capacity) Bill, 2013* and the *Criminal Law (Sexual Offences) (Amendment) Bill, 2014* (Government of Ireland, 2013, 2014). The proposed *Assisted Decision-making Bill* will affect the legal basis for how we decide whether someone has the 'capacity' to make a decision, and how someone is supported to make a decision if this is deemed necessary. It also will provide a new system to replace the current Ward of Court system allowing people with disabilities (who are able) to make decisions about their own lives and to be supported as needed. The *Criminal Law Bill* proposes to eliminate discrimination against people with disabilities and to ensure that they have the same freedoms to consent to sexual activity as other people.

Status *versus* Functional Assessment

The overall aim for Irish law is to move away from a 'status-based' assessment of capacity (where an individual is given the 'status' of lacking capacity) to a 'functional-based' assessment. The status approach deems that it is the *person* who does or does not have the capacity to make decisions, or, who is 'mentally impaired' and thus incapable of consenting to sexual activity. The functional approach in contrast is task-specific. This means that a person's capacity to make decisions will need to be looked at on an item-by-item basis. Competency is attached to the decision-making process, and not to the person. In relation to the *Assisted Decision-Making Bill,* Inclusion Ireland has stated: 'it represents a paradigm shift in how people with an intellectual disability… are to be viewed' (Connolly, 2013).

Advocacy and the *In Camera* Ruling

Another development is in the advocacy arena, where there is a move forward in recognition of the need for people with disabilities to have a voice and to protect their rights. In 2011, the National Advocacy Service for People with Disabilities (2012) set up independent, representative advocacy services across the country. These services have been used for parents with intellectual disability to gain support and advocacy for when they appear in court – for example, for the purpose of making access arrangements to see their children. In addition, there has been a recent change to the *in camera* ruling, whereby now there will be an option for family court cases to be covered by the media thus contributing to a greater level of transparency. These changes could have very important implications for parents with intellectual disability, particularly when child protection cases come to court.

Parental Capacity Assessments in Ireland

Typically, a parenting capacity assessment is sought following on from a new awareness of child protection or parental capacity concerns. Different presenting issues in families call for different types of assessments, which vary in size and content. Assessments also may vary, depending upon the professional background of the assessor, the service resources and remit and the specific requirements of the case. Nationally, assessors are usually social workers or clinical psychologists. Referrals can be made from a variety of sources, including primary care, education and child protection services, or through the court system.

A psychological assessment of parental capacity may involve the following stages:[7]

- **Stage 1: Referral enquiry:** Establishing whether the service and/or assessor are suitable to meet the needs of the assessment. This can be a two-way process between the referrer and the assessor. They need to consider the type of skills and experience required as well as the time frame for the report;
- **Stage 2: Referral questions:** The referral questions need to be accepted by the assessor. This will provide a remit for the assessment. These questions may need negotiation between the referrer and the assessor. If a guardian *ad litem* is involved, they may wish to contribute to this process;
- **Stage 3: Background reading and planning:** The assessor familiarises themselves with the background to the case. They plan out who to interview and what type of assessment tests and tools may be needed. They schedule dates to see the clients and professionals to be interviewed;
- **Stage 4: Gaining consent and explaining confidentiality:** It is good practice to explain to the client the nature of the assessment, how long it may last and who will receive the report. If the case goes to court, all information may be divulged;
- **Stage 5: Interview:** The interviews are conducted, including use of any questionnaires or assessment tools;
- **Stage 6: Report writing:** The report is written up;
- **Stage 7: Client feedback:** Where possible, the main findings of the assessment are fed back to the client. This may involve verbal feedback and/or time to go through the report;
- **Stage 8: Report dissemination:** The report is disseminated to persons as agreed in stage 4. This may include the referrer, the relevant legal professionals and the parent themselves. Meetings may be needed in order to make planning decisions based upon the findings of the report.

Case Study: Sharon

The following case study will be used as a way of illustrating how, when working with vulnerable parents, the assessor needs to keep the needs of the child at the foremost of one's mind whilst developing an empathy

7 This procedure was developed by the author, Dr Anna Moore Asgharian, for the purpose of undertaking parenting capacity assessments.

and understanding of how the parent can provide care. In this case, it was crucial that Sharon understood that it was the psychologist's role to provide an objective assessment that focused on helping her reach her potential rather than finding fault. Background information provided insights into Sharon's life experiences, but what was key in this situation was the point where the psychologist reflected upon their own emotional reaction to the client's presentation.

This case was referred to a clinical psychologist in the health service by a social worker. The parent was presenting as withdrawn and concerns were expressed about how she would care for her baby. Sharon had been known to Child Protection Services previously in relation to her older daughter who, at the age of 4 years, sustained an injury from being scalded with hot water. The ensuing investigation took a long time and the child was removed from Sharon's care on a care order. When the case was eventually heard in court, the scald was found to have been an accident and the child was returned to Sharon's care.

Sharon had struggled through her school age years, both academically and socially. Prior to leaving primary school, she was assessed by an educational psychologist and was found to have cognitive function in the range of mild intellectual disability. Sharon left school aged 16 with no exams. She had done a work experience placement but never held down any formal type of employment. Sharon lived at home and had a few relationships with different men until she met her current partner. Her current partner was considerably older than her, he did not have any type of disability and he held down a job as a manual labourer. When she became pregnant with this man, she moved in with him. She was 25 years of age; her older child was aged six and from an earlier relationship, and her youngest child aged four months.

In clinical interview with the psychologist, Sharon was asked questions about her family upbringing and her life today living with her partner. Sharon presented as exceptionally quiet, there were long silences after each question. Sharon eventually might give a monosyllabic response; she showed no emotion on her face. If Sharon's partner were present, she would look towards him to answer.

Sharon admitted no symptoms of low mood or depression. She did not disclose symptoms of anxiety. During one interview with her partner present, he blurted out his frustration, saying "do you want the kid to stay with us or not?". Sharon did not show any response to this question.

The partner's emotional outburst was helpful to the psychologist as it brought to the fore what a difficult situation this was. The increased awareness of this frustration gave unexpected clarity as to how much

Sharon's inexpressive and unemotional presentation would mean grave concerns as regards her parental capacity. Sharon's presentation needed to be fully understood and she needed to be afforded the opportunity to show herself in a better light.

With re-energised focus, the psychologist used a slow and patient approach with Sharon. While looking at her strengths and skills, the aim was to increase her confidence and to help her feel more comfortable. Less time was spent on direct questioning and more time was spent being with her and her children. Gradually, over time, Sharon's presentation began to transform as she became more relaxed in the company of the psychologist and gained confidence in the assessment process. Ultimately, Sharon began to talk more and to show expressions on her face. She then was able to volunteer information that was helpful to the assessment process.

Sharon's early presentation was explained by the fact that the whole interview process petrified her. Due to her previous experiences, she understood the serious nature and the possible ramifications of her performance in these interviews. Yet, due to her learning problems and her lack of confidence generally, she could not use words to argue or defend her case. She had been stunned: a rabbit caught in the headlights, immobilised by fear. Although this formulation of Sharon's presentation was hypothesised early into the assessment, it was important for the validity of the assessment that Sharon be allowed the time to reveal a different self.

The Role of Attachment Theory

The concept of attachment refers to the emotional relationships we have with other people. The most important tenet of attachment theory is that an infant needs to develop a relationship with at least one primary caregiver. This provides a secure base for learning about the self and the environment. The early relationship affects the child's emotional development and the way the brain develops, it is seen as providing the foundation for future relationships. Sensitive and competent caregiving is an important predictor of a child's social and emotional development. When caregiving is insensitive or abusive, or if it is disrupted, there is an increased risk to the child of psychopathology such as anxiety, depression, post-traumatic stress, substance use and psychosis (Mueller *et al*, 2010).

Bowlby (1988) identified the attachment behaviour of the child as being an innate survival instinct, so that when the infant has any discomfort such as hunger or pain, their attachment system becomes activated and, through their behaviour, they seek protection. Howe (2005, p.30) writes about how 'children develop strategies that help them adapt to their parent's caregiving style in order to increase parental availability and willingness to respond'.

Attachment theory can be particularly useful when attempting to understand and explain the parent's style of caregiving and the behavioural response of the child. This can be particularly important for informing parental capacity assessments and any therapeutic supports that may be required. The case of Sarah shows how important information regarding caregiving can be inferred by assessing the behaviour of the child. This not only informs about the quality of the caregiving, but also about the needs of the child.

Case Study: Sarah

Sarah's mother was referred to intellectual disability services for a parental capacity assessment. The assessment that followed was a joint piece of work by the clinical psychologist and the social worker. Sarah is aged two and a half. She spends half her week with her mother and half her week with her foster mother. In addition to an assessment of Sarah's mother's parental capacity, the referring social workers in Child Protection Services wanted to know how the 'shared care' model was affecting Sarah.

Sarah's mother had a mild intellectual disability, which was detected when she was in school. This young woman had experienced a history of domestic violence and rejection. She now suffers with depression and anxiety. Growing up, she did not have the opportunity to develop a secure attachment bond with a primary caregiver.

There are various types of attachment assessment summarised by Prior and Glaser (2006). What is described here are two home setting visits that reveal naturalistic observations of interactions. This observational piece is described from the author's viewpoint using a narrative style; the purpose is to capture the story in order to gain a qualitative understanding of how Sarah gets her needs met. Sarah was observed on different occasions with her mother and her foster mother. The observation method proved useful as, when coupled with the parental capacity assessment, it provided insightful information. There is a contrast in Sarah's attachment style in the two settings. Her behaviour is interpreted in terms of attachment theory.

> It's Monday, Sarah is at home with her mom. She is clean and dressed appropriately. As her mother makes some food, Sarah stays close. When her mom asks her if she is hungry, Sarah looks away. She has little or no expression.
>
> All around Sarah, the house is disorganised and cold. It's a rural setting, there are cows in the field. The fire is lit but no warmth emanates. The *Jeremy Kyle Show* blares from the television. Sarah picks up a story book. She holds it out to me. I begin to read to her, she shows interest briefly but then she backs away, over to her mother. Sarah trips on the floor. She whimpers to herself half-heartedly.

Sarah appears confused; she stays close to her mother but does not respond when addressed. Sarah appears aimless and irritable; she is detached, almost despairing. She does not seem able to concentrate and she has no will to play.

Sarah's presentation appears disorganised, she wishes for safety but she does not know whether to approach or to avoid her mother. Sarah's mother has difficulty interpreting Sarah's behaviour and feelings. When Sarah gets upset, her mother does not know how to cope. Sarah does not feel safe. She experiences her mother as frightened.

> It's Thursday, Sarah is at her foster placement. As the front door is opened by the foster mother, Sarah is seen standing beside her. Her hair is neat; she is wearing a hair clip with a flower on it. Sarah stays back as we enter the lounge; she is holding a plastic toy animal. Sarah stays close to her foster mother, she looks at us warily as we talk the adult talk.
>
> After a minute or so, Sarah's attention is taken by the array of plastic toy animals next to her. She gets what looks like a toy washing machine. She puts one of the animals inside and presses a button. Red lights come on and a whirring sound is heard. Sarah smiles with delight; she claps her hands together, she looks to her foster mom then she looks over to us. Sarah proceeds to play her game again with a different animal. Gradually, she includes us in the play, using the social opportunity to have fun.

Sarah stays close to her caregiver at first when the strangers enter. She uses her as a safe base from which to explore. Sarah appears to be relaxed and playful. She is able to concentrate and to enjoy what she is doing.

Within a few minutes, Sarah wants to extend the play to share it with others.

Sarah has a more secure attachment style in this setting. This is a response to the foster carer's more consistent caregiving. Sarah feels safe with the foster carer. If she were to get upset in this environment, she knows she would be provided with comfort that is sensitive to her needs.

What Support Do Families Need?

The best predictor of parental competence for this group of parents is the quality and frequency of social and practical support they have access to. Research evidence shows that parents can learn to apply new knowledge and maintain new skills (Feldman, 1994). The types of programmes that have been identified for use with parents with intellectual disability include skill-focused behavioural teaching strategies such as modelling, practice, feedback, praise and tangible reinforcement (Feldman, 1994). Feldman found that interventions were likely to be more successful when taught individually and broken down into small steps. Other types of interventions have included self-directed learning (Feldman and Case, 1999), home-based safety interventions (Llewellyn *et al,* 2003) and developing supportive peer relationships (McGaw *et al,* 2002). Studies indicate that a range of home-based and family centre programmes is needed to improve the chances of generalising learning. In relation to the long-term effects of such types of training, McGaw and Newman (2005) state that longer and more intense training increases the chances of maintenance. The success of such training will be influenced by a number of factors, including the maternal interest to learn, their involvement with the child, as well as the location and nature of the training, and ongoing support (Downey and Skuse, 1993).

In relation to attachment disorders, Larson *et al* (2011) found that people with mild/moderate intellectual disability show the same range of attachment styles as the general population. Furthermore, Granqvist *et al* (2014) found that, of mothers with intellectual disability, a substantial proportion of their children had secure attachment styles and only a small minority had insecure attachment styles. It was only when the women had experience of severe maltreatment that the children were more likely to have a disorganised attachment style. Intellectual disability was not found to be the cause of an attachment disorder. This research finding has important practical implications for both assessments and interventions targeting parents with intellectual disability.

Conclusions

This overview of literature and case study exploration has introduced some of the complexities of working with parents with intellectual disability. It shows how on an international scale, this group faces discrimination and challenges within the system. In order to work towards alleviating this situation, the Special Interest Group on Parents and Parenting with Intellectual Disability emphasises the need for efforts to be made internationally in order to gather together and generate knowledge from research findings in order to inform policy and practice (International Association for the Scientific Study of Intellectual Disability, 2008).

In Ireland, more research is needed in order to paint a more defined picture of the needs of this group. In addition to the proposed legislative changes, what is needed is to create good practice guidelines for practitioners. The newly-established Tusla states that its parenting support strategy is to 'ensure that there are appropriate supports and services available to parents within their community and that these services are accessible and friendly' (Tusla, 2014). In order to achieve this goal for parents with intellectual disability, we need to safeguard against discrimination through an increased professional awareness of individual parental needs with clear and fair assessment procedures and the availability of appropriate supports and training.

References

American Psychiatric Association. (2013). *Diagnostic and Statistical Manual of Mental Disorders*, fifth edition, Arlington, VA: American Psychiatric Publishing.

Booth, T. (2000). 'Parents with Learning Difficulties, Child Protection and the Courts', *Representing Children*, Vol.13, pp.175-88.

Booth, T. and Booth, W. (1993). 'Parenting with Learning Difficulties: Lessons from Practitioners', *British Journal of Social Work*, Vol.23, pp.459-80.

Bowlby, J. (1988). *Attachment and Loss, Vol.3: Loss, Sadness and Depression*, London: Pimlico.

Brennan, D. (ed.) (2013). *Irish Insanity: 1800-2000*, New York: Routledge.

Budd, K.S. (2001). 'Assessing Parenting Competence in Child Protection Cases: A Clinical Practice Model', *Clinical Child and Family Psychology Review*, Vol.4, pp.1-18.

Budd, K.S., Clark, J. and Connell, M.A. (2011). *Evaluation of Parenting Capacity in Child Protection*, Oxford: Oxford University Press.

Connolly, P. (2013). *Inclusion Ireland Welcomes Long Awaited Assisted Decision-Making (Capacity) Bill – Lunacy Act 1871 Finally Replaced*, retrieved on 24 July 2014 from www.inclusionireland.ie/content/media/1062/inclusion-ireland-welcomes-long-awaited-assisted-decision-making-capacity-bill.

Department of Children and Youth Affairs (2011). *Children First: The National Guidance for the Protection and Welfare of Children*, Dublin: Government Publications.

Dowdney, L. and Skuse, D. (1993). 'Parenting Provided by Adults with Mental Retardation', *Journal of Child Psychology and Psychiatry*, Vol.34, No.1, pp.25-47.

Feldman, M., Case, L., Towns, F. and Betel, J. (1985). 'Parent Education Project I: Development and Nurturance of Children of Mentally Retarded Parents', *American Journal of Mental Retard Deficiency*, Vol.90, pp.253-58.

Feldman, M.A. (1994). 'Parenting Education for Parents with Intellectual Disabilities: A Review of Outcome Studies', *Research in Developmental Disabilities*, Vol.15, pp.299-332.

Feldman, M.A. and Case, L. (1999). 'Teaching Child-Care and Safety Skills to Parents with Intellectual Disabilities Through Self-Learning', *Journal of Intellectual and Developmental Disability*, Vol.24, No.1, pp.27-44.

Gath, A. (1988). 'Mentally Handicapped People as Parents. Is Mental Retardation a Bar to Adequate Parenting?', *Journal of Child Psychology and Psychiatry*, Vol.29, pp.739-44.

Government of Ireland (1871). *Lunacy Regulations (Ireland) Act*, available from www.irishstatutebook.ie/1871/en/act/pub/0022/print.html.

Government of Ireland (1993). *Criminal Law (Sexual Offenses) Act, 1993*, retrieved 9 September 2014 from www.irishstatutebook.ie/1993/en/act/pub/0020/index.html.

Government of Ireland (2013). *Assisted Decision-Making (Capacity) Bill, 2013*, retrieved on 9 September 2014 from www.oireachtas.ie/viewdoc.asp?DocID=24147&&CatID=59.

Government of Ireland (2014). *Criminal Law (Sexual Offences) (Amendment) Bill, 2014*, retrieved 9 September 2014 from www.oireachtas.ie/viewdoc.asp?DocID=26090&&CatID=59.

Granqvist, P., Forslund, T., Springer, L., Fransson, M. and Lindberg, L. (2014). 'Mothers with Intellectual Disability, Their Experiences of Maltreatment and Their Children's Attachment Representations: A Small Group Matched Comparison Study', *Attachment and Human Development*, Vol.16, pp.417-36.

Holland, K. (2011). 'Disabled parents' children removed with no support', *The Irish Times*, 1 June, retrieved 20 August 2014 from www.irishtimes.com/newspaper/ireland/2011/0601/1224298206233.html.

Howe, D. (2005). *Child Abuse and Neglect: Attachment, Development and Intervention*, Basingstoke: Palgrave Macmillan.

Hunt, C. (2012). 'Time every citizen had right to a sex life', *Sunday Independent*, 21 October, retrieved 30 July 2014 from www.independent.ie/opinion/analysis/carol-hunt-time-every-citizen-had-right-to-a-sex-life-3266225.html.

International Association for the Scientific Study of Intellectual Disability (2008). 'Parents Labelled with Intellectual Disability: Position of the International Association for the Scientific Study of Intellectual Disability (IASSID) Special Interest Research Group (SIRG) on Parents and Parenting with Intellectual Disabilities', *Journal of Applied Research in Intellectual Disabilities*, Vol.21, No.4, pp.296-307.

Kelly, R. (2005). *Motherhood Silenced: The Experiences of Natural Mothers on Adoption Reunion*, Dublin: The Liffey Press.

Keltner, B., Wise, L. and Taylor, G. (1999). 'Mothers with Intellectual Limitations and Their 2 Year Old Children's Developmental Outcomes', *Journal of Intellectual and Developmental Disabilities*, Vol.24, No.1, pp.45-57.

Larson, F.V., Alim, A., Tsakanikos, E. (2011). 'Attachment Style and Mental Health in Adults With Intellectual Disability: Self Reports and Reports By Carers', *Advances in Mental Health and Intellectual Disabilities*, Vol.5, No.3, pp.23.

Llewellyn, G., McConnell, D., Honey, A., Mayes R. and Russco, D. (2003). 'Promoting Health and Home Safety for Children of Parents with Intellectual Disability: A Randomised Controlled Trial', *Research in Developmental Disabilities*, Vol.24, pp.405-31.

McGaw, S. and Newman, T. (2005). *What Works For Parents With Learning Disabilities?*, Ilford: Barnardo's.

McGaw, S. and Sturmey, P. (1993). 'Identifying the Needs of Parents With Learning Disabilities: A Review', *Child Abuse Review*, Vol.2, pp.101-17.

McGaw, S., Ball, K. and Clarke, A. (2002). 'The Effect of Group Intervention on the Relationships of Parents with Intellectual Disabilities', *Journal of Applied Research in Intellectual Disabilities*, Vol.15, pp.354-66.

McLaughlin, S. (2013). *Parents with Intellectual Disabilities and the Child Protection System: International Lessons of Best Practice from Ireland, England and Australia*, University College Dublin, in part fulfilment of the degree of Master of Social Science (Social Work) in the College of Human Sciences.

Moore Asgharian, A. (2012). 'Working with Parents with ID in Ireland: From Individuals to Systems', presentation at *International Association for the Scientific Study of Intellectual and Developmental Disabilities (IASSID) World Congress*, Halifax, Canada, 9 to 14 July.

Morris, J. (2003). *The Right Support: Report of the Task Force on Supporting Disabled Adults in their Parenting Role*, York: Joseph Rowntree Foundation.

Mueller, S., Maheu, F., Dozier, M., Peloso, E., Mandell, D., Leibenluft, E., Pine, D. and Ernst, M. (2010). 'Early-Life Stress is Associated With Impairment in Cognitive Control in Adolescence: An FMRI study', *Neuropsychologia*, Vol.48, pp.3037-44.

National Advocacy Service for People with Disabilities (2012). *Annual Report*, retrieved on 13 January 2015 from www.citizensinformationboard.ie/publications/advocacy/advocacy_index.html.

National Disability Authority (2011). *A National Survey of Public Attitudes to Disability in Ireland*, Dublin: National Disability Authority.

O'Mahony, C., Shore, C., Burns, K. and Parkes, A. (2012). 'Child Care Proceedings in the District Court: What Do We Really Know?', *Irish Journal of Family Law*, Vol.15, No.2, pp.1-14.

Prior, V. and Glaser D. (2006). *Understanding Attachment and Attachment Disorders: Theory Evidence and Practice*, London: Jessica Kingsley Publishers.

Sheerin, F.K., Keenan, P.M. and Lawler, D. (2013). 'Mothers with Intellectual Disabilities: Interactions with Children and Family Services In Ireland', *British Journal of Learning Disabilities*, Vol.41, pp.189-96.

Tarleton, B., Ward, L. and Howarth, J. (2006). *Finding the Right Support? A Review of Issues and Positive Practice in Supporting Parents with Learning Difficulties And Their Children*, London: The Baring Foundation.

Tusla (2014). 'Parenting Information: How Will the Child and Family Agency Support Parents?', retrieved 24 October 2014 from www.tusla.ie/services/family-community-support/parenting-information/.

Tymchuk, A.J. and Andron, L. (1994). 'Rationale, Approaches, Results and Resource Implications of Programmes to Enhance Parenting Skills of People With Learning Disabilities' in Craft, A. (ed.), *Practice Issues and Sexuality and Learning Disabilities*, London: Routledge.

Tymchuk, A.J. and Feldman, M.A. (1991). 'Parents with Mental Retardation and Their Children: A Review of Research Relevant to Professional Practice', *Canadian Psychology (Psychologie Canadienne)*, Vol.32, pp.486-96.

Whitman, B. and Accardo, P.J. (1990). *When a Parent is Mentally Retarded*, Baltimore, MD: Brookes Publishing Co.

Whitman, B., Graves, B. and Accardo, P.J. (1986). 'The Mentally Retarded Parent in the Community: An Epidemiological Study', *Developmental Medicine and Child Neurology Supplement*, Vol.53, p.18.

Winnicott, D.W. (1953). 'Transitional Objects and Transitional Phenomena: A Study of the First Not-Me Possession', *International Journal of Psychoanalysis*, Vol.34, No.2, pp.89-97.

Young, S. and Hawkins T. (2006). 'Special Parenting and the Combined Skills Model', *Journal of Applied Research in Intellectual Disabilities*, Vol.19, pp.346-55.

12: Grandchildcare: Grandparents and Childcare in Ireland

Michelle Share and Liz Kerrins

It is not something I ever thought I would be doing, but in the end I offered to help with their childcare because they have such a big mortgage like so many young people now. ('Joan', grandmother, cited in Condon, 2013)

Granny, she's always looking after like everybody, like, all the children and everything. Because like, it's like everyone, like this is the house, the whole family like always comes here, it's like the heart of the family. And Granny, like, she's always, always looking after kids and that and I think she really enjoys it, you know having the little kids around and stuff. ('Emma O'Brien', granddaughter aged 17, cited in Murphy, 2009, p.61)

Introduction

Grandparenting always has been an important part of parenting but, given the focus on the nuclear family unit, often has been neglected. In contemporary Ireland, as in many other countries, changes in work patterns, family structure, state policy and the health and well-being of older people have stimulated greater interest in the experience of grandparenthood. An important part of this is the role of grandparents as providers of diverse forms of care to their grandchildren.

This chapter outlines some key aspects of grandparent childcare, or *grandchildcare*, based on research in comparable countries and recent Irish data. It argues that grandparent childcare is an important issue and offers some definitions, theories and typologies. It examines available data on the extent of grandparent childcare in Ireland and what we know of the social characteristics of those – children, parents and grandparents – involved. It explores the factors that influence grandparent childcare and the impact of caregiving on grandparents' health and well-being. It looks to the future of grandparent childcare in a society that is both ageing and globalising.

The Changing Global Context

Social, economic and demographic shifts have resulted in a greater emphasis on intergenerational aspects of parenting and the role of grandparents in supporting families. As a consequence, there has been growing international research on grandparenting, focused on three areas:

- Grandparents' demographic and personal characteristics;
- Behavioural and psychological aspects of grandparenthood;
- The outcomes of grandparenting for children, parents, grandparents and other family members (Bates and Taylor, 2013).

In addition, researchers have examined the economic impact of grandparenting. The field of grandparenting studies is eclectic. It spans – but is not limited to – the disciplines of psychology, sociology, anthropology, economics, social policy, health and medicine, and gerontology. Studies of grandparenthood can help us to better understand intergenerational family relations and changing patterns of parenting.

As grandparenthood is a universal phenomenon, transnational research can show how it is understood across varied cultural contexts. For example, traditional filial culture in Confucian societies such as China and Korea positions grandparents as elders to be respected and cared for by their children, but this is changing with increasing Westernisation, urbanisation and modernisation (Lo and Liu, 2009; Chen *et al*, 2011; Lee and Bauer, 2013). In the United States, changes in family forms and economic pressures have seen new roles for grandparents, especially in female-headed Black and Hispanic populations (Posadas and Vidal-Fernandez, 2012).

Grandparenting childcare support is an important issue for migrant families across the world (Wall and Sao Jose, 2004). With increased global labour mobility and new communications technologies (also impacting significantly on Irish society), transnational grandparenting is a phenomenon that needs to be considered, including the extent to which grandparents use new technologies and visits to Ireland to develop their relationships with their grandchildren.

In Ireland, historical changes in the workforce also have altered family ties. Up to the 1960s, male agricultural workers and farm families dominated the workforce; 'stem households' were then common, in which grandparents, parents and grandchildren cohabited. Alternatively, children sometimes left the parental home to live with their grandparents for reasons associated with large family size or education (Gray *et al*, 2013). Such multigenerational households diminished in significance, though did not disappear, with the rise of suburban nuclear families.

A consistent increase in Irish women's labour force participation has pushed the issue of childcare up the agenda. As in other Western societies, Ireland has seen a range of childcare options emerge, including formal day care (crèches and childcare centres), and various forms of 'informal' care, such as unregistered childminders, *au pairs*, and family. Care of children by their grandparents always has been an important aspect of childcare, with implications for children, parents and the grandparents themselves. Yet in Ireland, this has been a neglected issue in research and public policy (Share and Kerrins, 2009). It can be argued that the willingness of many grandparents to support their children and grandchildren has been invisible and taken for granted.

Why is Grandparent Childcare an Important Issue?

Europe is an ageing society. Even if the percentage of the population aged over 65 years in the Republic of Ireland is the lowest of all 27 EU countries (European Commission, 2011, p.18), Irish society is also ageing. The number of those in this age group is due to increase from 535,716 in 2011 to 769,484 in 2021 (Barrett *et al*, 2011), partly due to greater longevity and better health and well-being amongst older people.

Today's Irish grandparents have a longer life expectancy than their own parents and grandparents and are in better health. This generation of Irish children is thus more likely than their predecessors to know their grandparents into their own adulthood and grandparents will have a longer relationship with their grandchildren: we know from the Irish longitudinal study of children *Growing Up in Ireland* that, at age 3, the great majority of Irish children are already in regular contact with their grandparents (Williams *et al*, 2013). There are also more people with living parents, who also have dependent children and grandchildren: the so-called 'sandwich generation' (McGarrigle and Kenny, 2013). Such changes in demography and family structure have increased the social significance of grandparenthood as a life stage (Murphy, 2009).

The issue of grandchildcare reflects changing relationships among parents, children and grandchildren. Gray *et al* (2013) analysed Irish longitudinal data and found that the balance of power has shifted over time: in the past, grandparents had more control over the lives of their grandchildren and their own adult children. Today, grandparent-parent-grandchild relationships may be characterised in terms of interdependence, as each generation balances its own autonomy and needs. Challenges may arise for grandparents as their own children seek their support with childcare, while this middle-generation also seeks to protect the autonomy of the nuclear family.

Grandparent support in the care of very young children can have important influences on child development. Babysitting on a parents' night out means direct grandparental interaction with the child or children and an indirect influence that supports the parental relationship; this might be expected to positively affect parental interactions with the child (Quail *et al*, 2011). Such care is also important for children and parents in periods following divorce or separation (Hetherington, 2003; Hogan *et al*, 2003).

Grandchildcare is significant from the point of view of economics and livelihoods. For lone parents, grandparents who provide childcare enable parents' access to employment and training (Sandfort and Hill, 1996). In the United States, a connection has been demonstrated between grandparents' childcare responsibilities and their own attachment to the paid labour force (Posadas and Vidal-Fernandez, 2012). Overall, grandparent care reduces the societal cost of providing childcare: in the UK, it has been estimated that grandparental care and educational support for grandchildren is valued at £8bn (*c.* €10bn) *per annum* (Family and Childcare Trust, Grandparents Plus and Save the Children, 2014).

What Is 'Grandparent Childcare'?

Social researchers need to operationalise a concept such as 'grandparent childcare' to provide a concrete, objective basis for the phenomenon to be measured. While it might seem straightforward, the concept of grandparent childcare is difficult to pin down, owing to considerable variation in how it is defined in different studies (Condon *et al*, 2013). It even can be difficult – especially given the increasing diversity of family forms – to define the term 'grandparent'.

In 2013, a private member's bill was proposed in the Dáil to amend Irish child guardianship law. An aim of the new law was to support grandparents in their desire to continue their relationships with their grandchildren in the event of parental marriage breakdown. The *Bill* contains what would be the first Irish legal definition of 'grandparent':

> 'Grandparent', in relation to a child, means a grandparent, whether of the whole blood, half blood or by affinity, and includes the spouse of any such person, a parent of a child's adoptive parent and an adoptive parent of a child's parent (Government of Ireland, 2013).

Interestingly this definition reflects a broader understanding of the family than can be found in the Irish *Constitution*.

Even if we can agree on the definition of 'grandparent', variations in the concept of 'care' also make for complexities (**Table 12.1**).

Table 12.1: Definitions of 'Grandparent Childcare' in Research

Definition	Research study	Country
Childcare arrangements most often and next most often for youngest (under 6 years) and second youngest child (under 12 years) when parent is at work.	Fine-Davis *et al* (2002)	European study: Ireland, Italy, Denmark and France
Grandparents providing regular informal childcare for their grandchildren when parents are away from home for work or other activities.	European Social Survey (round 2, 2008)	European study: 23 countries, including Ireland
In the last two years, grandparents (or spouse/ partner) spending at least one hour per week taking care of grandchild(ren)/great-grandchild(ren) who live outside grandparents' household.	TILDA	Ireland
Is your baby minded by someone else, other than you or your resident spouse/partner, on a regular basis each week?	GUI (9 months, wave 1)	Ireland
Is child being minded by someone other than parent or resident spouse/partner for eight hours or more per week during the day?	GUI (9 month olds at age 3, wave 2)	Ireland
Time when grandparents are responsible for the care and wellbeing of grandchildren, usually in the absence of a parent. In some cases, a grandparent may be undertaking the tasks of grandchildcare alongside a parent. This is different to 'seeing' grandchildren, which is characterised by social time without caregiving responsibilities, often in the company of parents.	Horsfall and Dempsey (2013)	Australia

A study[8] of first-time grandparents in Australia (Condon *et al*, 2013) differentiates between 'grandparent childcare' and 'grandparent contact'. The former is when the parent leaves the child to be looked after by the grandparent, who is then responsible for the care of the child. The latter refers to time the grandparent has in face-to-face contact with the child: this may mean 'care without responsibility' – for example, when a grandparent comes to visit.

What is needed, but is seldom found in research on grandparent childcare, is detail on the *tasks* grandparents perform in the care of grandchildren. Studies that examine grandparent childcare often describe it in terms of time spent on care without any specificity on the type of care involved (Hank and Buber, 2007; Ferguson *et al*, 2008). But, as Duffy (2011, p.138) points out in another context, 'care work is a mix of human relationship, skilled intervention, and plain hard work'. It is a complex set of activities.

Theories and Typologies of Grandparent Childcare

To better understand grandparent childcare, it is useful to think of *theories* that attempt to explain the phenomenon, and of *typologies* that seek to categorise it. Theory is important as it can guide research methods, analysis and interpretation of results, as well as future research and practice. It allows us to make sense of the phenomenon under investigation (Fine and Fincham, 2013). A typology can help us to understand the range of relationships involved and can describe the quantity and the nature of the care.

Theories

Theories on grandparenting are situated within the broad realm of family theories (Fine and Fincham, 2013). There is no dominant theoretical approach to grandparenting: a broad diversity of explanatory frameworks is evident. Bates and Taylor (2013, p.51) have noted that scholarly research on grandparenting has 'tended to borrow a concept from this theory and a concept from that theory and plugged them in where they seemed to fit best', while much work in the area does not make any overt use of theory. This diversity, Bates and Taylor suggest,

8 Australian longitudinal study of 430 first-time grandparents. The grandparents were recruited *via* pregnant mothers who were attending antenatal clinics at an Adelaide public hospital. The grandparents were interviewed when their grandchild was born, and followed up at 6, 12, 24 and 36 months.

reflects the wide range of disciplines, topics and international research in the field of grandparenting studies.

Key grandparenting theories relevant to an understanding of grandparents as childcarers include intergenerational solidarity theories; intergenerational transfer theory; ambivalence theory and identity and role theory:

- *Intergenerational solidarity* points to intergenerational support between family members, where adult children care for their parents and grandparents care for their grandchildren (O'Dwyer *et al*, 2012);
- *Intergenerational transfers* are defined as the transfer of time or money across generations: for example, from parents to their own parents and to their children. Non-financial help, such as grandparent childcare, can also be a form of intergenerational transfer;
- The *political economy of grandparenting* points to how the experience of grandparenting is shaped by inequalities, including those of class, gender and ethnicity. It is part of a 'critical gerontology' approach[9] that also embraces feminist perspectives on ageing (Walker and Foster, 2014);
- Grandparenting research has revealed *ambivalence* in such intergenerational relationships and exchanges. There may be contradictions and tensions for grandparents in terms of the roles that they play. For example, grandparents may be happy to help their own child with childcare but glad to be able to return the children to their parents. They may also have conflicting feelings about being grandparents. Grandparents may be called on for support, but expected not to 'interfere' in childrearing (Arber and Timonen, 2012);
- Grandparenting research that uses *identity theory and role theory* is concerned with the meanings grandparents ascribe to their role through their familial interaction, such as 'historian', 'benefactor' or 'nurturer' (Kornhaber, 1996). Grandparent roles may overlap with other family roles – for example, where grandparents are caring for both their own children and their grandchildren; perhaps their own parents as well. Studies that use role theory show that the grandparent role is not fixed, but is multi-dimensional and changes over time according to family needs (Kruk, 1994).

---

9 Critical gerontology goes beyond 'objective' scientific approaches to critique societies' assumptions about ageing to analyse how these influence the process and experiences of ageing.

Typologies

Researchers have developed a number of typologies of grandparent care, based on varied aspects of motivation, commitment and task orientation. These help to describe the phenomenon in more structured ways. For example, Goodfellow and Laverty (2003) categorise grandparent carers as follows:

- **Avid carers:** Those whose lives revolve around their grandchildren;
- **Flexible carers:** Those who are concerned with family but also prioritise their own personal time;
- **Selective carers:** Those whose grandchildren are an important part of their lives but who do not want to be defined simply as grandparents;
- **Hesitant carers:** Those who did not anticipate caring for their grandchildren.

Vandell *et al* (2003) divide grandparent care into extended full-time, extended part-time, sporadic and no routine care. Arthur *et al* (2003) describe grandparenting childcare in terms of three broad models:

- Grandmothers who regularly look after their children;
- Those who look after their grandchildren frequently but in a more informal and *ad hoc* way;
- Those whose role in childcare is less frequent but more formal and pre-planned.

The model adopted by grandparents, or with specific grandchildren, may be explained by factors such as the need for help, the financial need for a mother to work, lack of alternative childcare arrangements, as well as the availability and location of the grandmother and her physical capacity to help. A key element was the preference attached by grandmother and mother or father to the grandmother undertaking the childcare over alternative arrangements (Arthur *et al*, 2003).

Herlofsen and Hagsted (2012) categorise grandparent childcare in terms of its broader function as 'mother saver' or 'family saver'. This is related to the context of state support for childcare: where women's employment is not strongly supported by public childcare, grandparent childcare works as a 'mother saver'; where there is stronger support for public childcare and an emphasis on work-life balance, grandparents fulfil a 'family saver' role in terms of the provision of extra support.

The Extent of Grandchildcare

We do not know how many people in Ireland are grandparents. The national census does not ask whether people are grandparents nor whether they provide childcare to grandchildren. Moreover, parents are not asked whether their children receive grandchildcare. Thus we must rely on large-scale surveys, such as *Growing Up in Ireland* and *TILDA* (**Figure 12.1**) to reveal the extent of the practice.

Figure 12.1: Irish Longitudinal Studies on Childhood and Ageing

Growing Up in Ireland [GUI] is a national study of children that started in 2007. It is funded by the Irish Government and undertaken by the Economic and Social Research Institute and Trinity College Dublin. It is a 'longitudinal' study of children: this means the research will take place over a number of years. It examines the health, development and well-being of two groups of children – 8,500 9 year olds and 11,000 9 month olds – on a number of occasions at important periods throughout their childhood. By studying a representative sample of children over a period of time, it is possible to identify the key factors that most encourage or undermine their development.

The Irish Longitudinal Study on Ageing [TILDA] is a large-scale, nationally-representative, longitudinal study on ageing in Ireland that started in 2009. It researches the lives, health and quality of life of 8,500 people who are over 50 years old. It is funded by the Government, Irish Life and Atlantic Philanthropies, and undertaken by Trinity College Dublin.

Though it has proven difficult to measure, a number of studies do indicate the prevalence of grandparent childcare in Ireland. The data examines the issue from three perspectives: the child's, the parents' (usually mothers'), and the grandparents'.

European Social Survey data (Jappens and Van Bavel, 2012) indicates that Ireland is similar to other EU countries such as The Netherlands, Portugal, Germany, Great Britain, Spain and Finland, in that from a quarter to a third of employed mothers use grandparents as their main source of childcare. In Ireland, it is difficult to generate comparative data, as different studies use different measures and definitions, and there are many confounding factors (such as age and number of children, full and part-time work, and so on).

Fine-Davis *et al* (2002) reported that 17% of employed mothers in Ireland used grandparents as the main source of care for their youngest child. A decade later, the *GUI* study (**Table 12.2**) indicates that 12% of children at 9 months of age (mothers employed or not) are looked after by grandparents. For those families who make use of non-parental childcare, grandparent care is the most popular (at 32% of families), followed by crèche/childcare centre (27%) and childminder/*au pair*/nanny (20%) (McGinnity *et al*, 2013, p.57). As children get older, the use of grandparent care declines: in the *GUI* study, by the time the 9 month olds were 3 years of age, 9% were being cared for by their grandparents, compared to 12% at age 9 months.

Table 12.2: Extent of Grandparent Childcare in Ireland (longitudinal studies)

Growing Up in Ireland			
Data wave	Year data collected	Age of study children	% children regularly cared for by grandparent
1 (a)	2008	9 months	12.4
2 (b)	2012	3 years	9
The Irish Longitudinal Study on Ageing			
Data wave	Year data collected	Age of study adults	% adults regularly caring for grandchildren
1 (c)	2009-2010	50+	47
2 (d)	2012	50+	35

Sources: (a) McGinnity *et al* (2013, p.57); (b) Williams *et al* (2013, p.59); (c) Barrett *et al* (2011, p.47); (d) McCrory *et al* (2014, p176).

A rather different picture emerges when questions about care of grandchildren are asked of the carers themselves. In the *TILDA* study, Irish people aged 50 years and over were asked about their involvement in care of grandchildren: 35% reported that they 'took care' of their grandchildren for at least one hour a week (McCrory *et al*, 2014, p.176).

We cannot say that there is a contradiction between the two sets of data: rather, different perspectives and definitions are at play. Also, in the absence of census data, there is considerable variation in the scope and focus of the survey data that is available. More work is required to clarify what is happening in Ireland in relation to grandparent care.

Characteristics of Grandchildcare

Notwithstanding the variations in the available data, we can say something of the characteristics of grandchildcare in Ireland.

Cost

According to *GUI*, only a third of relatives engaged in childcare (of 9 month old babies) were paid (McGinnity *et al*, 2013). Of paid carers, grandparents were the least expensive, with the most frequent cost being €49 or less per week, compared with €91 to €100 for home-based care and €151 to €200 for centre-based care (McNally *et al*, 2014, p.7). The lower cost of grandparent care may reflect that, on average, they provide fewer hours and fewer days of childcare when compared with other childcare types: an average of 21.5 hours/3.3 days per week, compared to 28.4 hours/4 days for centre-based care (McNally *et al*, 2014, p.6).

The Jigsaw of Care

Some families use grandchildcare as their main source of childcare, while others integrate it within a jigsaw of childcare that includes formal and informal models. The *GUI* study found that 13% of 9 month olds were in multiple childcare settings during the week. By the time these children were 3 years of age, this had decreased to 7% (McGinnity *et al*, 2013), suggesting a greater dependence on more formal arrangements.

Grandparental Care and Support

GUI asked parents about the frequency and types of weekly support that their own parents provided to their families when the children were 9 month olds (**Table 12.3**). Some of these could be included as types of grandchildcare, though the *GUI* questions were not couched in that context.

Table 12.3: Frequency and Types of Support provided by Grandparents in Ireland

	Frequency (%)		
Type of support	Never	Sometimes	Often
Babysit	19	48	33
Have baby to stay overnight	62	32	6
Take baby out	46	30	24
Buy toys or clothes for baby	4	81	15
Help parent around the house	56	26	18
Help parent out financially	71	26	3

Source: Quail et al (2011).

A picture of complex intergenerational transfers is evident in *TILDA*, reminding us that grandchildcare is about more than working mothers. Financial transfers reported in that study (Barrett *et al*, 2011, pp.45-47) were much more likely to go in the direction of parent to adult children (and grandchildren, where present). The prevalence of grandchildcare (35%, as indicated above) may be augmented by other forms of support to adult children such as doing shopping and household chores.

PROFILE OF GRANDCHILDCARERS IN IRELAND

Gender and Age

Mothers' care of their children is generally supported by other women. As with other forms of care, grandchildcare is a gendered endeavour, though it is difficult to find Irish data to support this contention. The TILDA study has reported on the caring activities of women in the 'sandwich generation', but has not provided similar data on men's caring responsibilities.

These women are caring for family members in the generations above and below them. In a sample of 3,196 women aged 50 to 69, with both a living parent and children, over a third provided care for both generations. For grandchildcare, this proportion increased with age: 23% aged 50 to 54 years helped 'look after' grandchildren while 69% of 65 to 69 year-olds did so (McGarrigle and Kenny, 2013). Women aged 50 to 69 years with living parents and with grandchildren looked after the latter for on average 34 hours per month. 'Sandwich generation' women who cared for their parents were found to be more likely to be supporting their children financially and non-financially, including providing childcare (McGarrigle and Kenny, 2013). The proportion of older grandparents (75 years +) providing childcare is lower than their younger counterparts (McCrory *et al*, 2014): this suggests reduced ability to care, or perhaps that the grandchildren are now older and no longer require care.

There is as yet no Irish social research that specifically investigates the roles and relationships of grandfathers. There is some international evidence on the role of grandfathers in childcare, much of it from the US (Wilton and Davey, 2006). In the US, although more grandmothers (54%) provide childcare, grandfathers (38%) also make a significant contribution (Ochiltree, 2006). The childcaring that grandfathers undertake is often in the company of a spouse (Wheelock and Jones, 2002) and such engagement for many grandfathers may be their first experience of participation in childrearing.

Location

Pioneering Irish qualitative research by Lundström (2001) indicated that the majority of grandparents live within 15km of grandchildren and, on average, saw them at least once a week. The *GUI* and *TILDA* reports provide further evidence of such proximal relationships. *GUI* found that having grandparents living close by predicted grandparent childcare use: having a crèche close by the grandchild's home did not reduce grandparent childcare (McNally *et al*, 2014). In the *TILDA* study, 74% of older people lived in close proximity to their children (Barrett *et al*, 2011, p.49), presumably giving them easy access to their grandchildren.

Ethnicity and Country of Origin

Ireland has become an increasingly multicultural and globalised society. The 2011 *Census* reveals 69,531 couples with children and 17,620 lone parents with children in the country as having 'non-Irish' nationality (Central Statistics Office, 2012, p.43). Through *GUI*, we are beginning to get an insight into grandparenting amongst such families. One-third of 9 month olds had at least one 'non-Irish' parent, further classified as either being from the Republic of Ireland, UK, EU-13, EU accession states, Africa, Asia, or 'other' (Röder *et al*, 2014, p.12). Of the infants in regular non-parental care, 42% were cared for by a relative, primarily grandparents (79%) (Röder *et al*, 2014, pp.67-68). Regardless of the parents' nationality, grandchildcare dominated relative care (**Figure 12.1**).

Figure 12.2: Family Relative Providers of Childcare to GUI 9 month old Infants according to Household Nationality

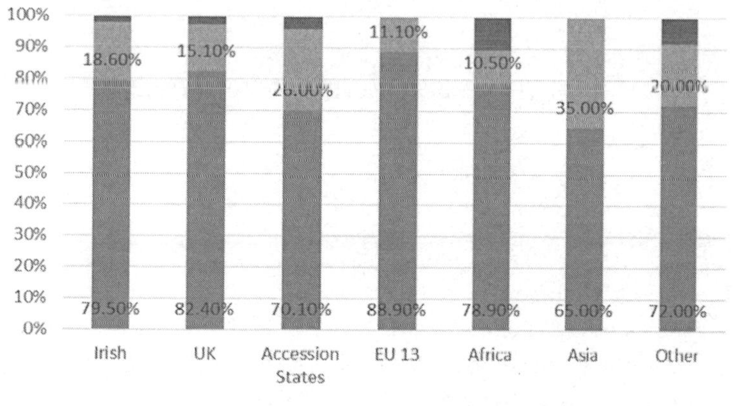

Source: Röder *et al* (2014, p.68).

As shown in **Figure 12.2**, the lowest use of grandparents as relative childcare was amongst households where one or both parents were from Asia (65%), followed by the EU accession states (70%) and Africa (79%). The proportion was higher where one of both parents was from an EU-13 state (89%), while the figure for Irish-born parents was 80%. It should be borne in mind when interpreting this data that the majority of 'non-Irish' households had at least one parent from the UK (10.7%), followed by EU accession states (6.7%), with the remainder from the other categories.

Research (Wall and Sao Jose, 2004) undertaken in other EU states indicates that grandparent childcare acts as an important social support for first and second generation immigrant families who have been able to bring a grandparent to the new host country, and so is an important element in helping families cope with their care responsibilities. However, *GUI* indicates that 22.7% of the 9 month olds did not have grandparents living in Ireland. Households where one or both parents were born in an African country were the least likely to have grandparents living in Ireland (52%), followed by Asian families (42.2%) and EU accession states (39.5%). While *GUI* does not include information on the grandparent support provided to these children, it does provide data on the 2,569 new Irish families with infants with Irish-resident grandparents. Of these infants, 96% had clothes or toys bought for them at least every three months by grandparents, but where one or both parents were from Africa (28.8%) or Asia (18.3%), this was less likely to happen. Irish and UK households were most likely to have grandparents babysit and take the infants for overnight stays, with African and Asian grandparents the least likely.

There is much more to be known about those Irish children with grandparents who reside in other countries. There is a need to understand how the use of digital technologies, such as Skype, support grandparent/grandchild relationships (King-O'Riain, 2014).

Factors Influencing Grandparent Childcare in Ireland

Parental Age, Income and Education

According to *GUI*, income, education and age are the most relevant parental factors in childcare use (McNally *et al*, 2014). These variables are strongly associated with grandparent childcare. Families with lower incomes were significantly more likely to use grandparent childcare for their 9 month old infant. Those with higher levels of formal education were more likely to choose group care. Parents with lower secondary,

Leaving Certificate, or non-degree education were significantly more likely than those with a degree to use grandparent childcare. In regards to age, parents under 30 years old were most likely to use grandparent childcare, with those aged 35 or over significantly less likely to do so.

The Impact of Grandparent Childcare on Health and Well-being

Impact on Families

There is no direct evidence of the impact of grandchildcare in Ireland. In *GUI*, the majority (72%) of parents of 9 months olds felt that they got enough help / support from family and friends (which may have included grandparents) and 6% stated that they did not need any help (Quail *et al*, 2011). But 10% said that they did not get enough help and 5% said they got no help at all, with the latter response more prominent from mothers with larger families. Research by Doyle *et al* (2010) on the role of grandparent support and care in cases of marriage or relationship breakdown in the 'middle generation' suggests that it can '[act] as [a] bridge across the formally dissolved family lines [and] is frequently the lynchpin to successful transition to life after divorce or separation both for their adult children and grandchildren' (Doyle *et al*, 2010, p.596).

Impact on Grandchildren

Qualitative interviews with 122 9 year olds as part of the *GUI* study (Harris, 2011) suggest that children have close relationships with their grandparents. For some children living in close proximity, their grandparents were an everyday feature of their lives. When Murphy (2009, pp.79-80) interviewed children specifically about their relationship with their grandparents, she found it difficult to elicit information, suggesting that this 'lack of communication and perceived lack of interest in talking about [grandparents] is reflected in previous work on intergenerational relations that show how the youngest generation place the least value on the importance of three generations'. Murphy suggests that this may be an outcome of how children communicate about social arrangements, rather than any lack of quality in the relationship. There is clearly scope for further research in this area.

Impact on Grandparents

Grandparent childcare brings with it a number of health, social and emotional costs and benefits for grandparents. Around 20% of the Irish grandparents interviewed for Lundström's (2001) research found it tiring

– a finding echoed in Australian grandparent research (Goodfellow and Laverty, 2003; Ochiltree, 2006). Yet a US study of 12,872 grandparents reported that the provision of childcare by grandparents does not impact negatively on their physical and mental well-being. Where there are health problems, these are due to prior characteristics. Evidence was found of benefits to grandmothers who provided 200 to 500 hours care per year for their grandchildren: these included having fewer functional problems, a greater likelihood of taking exercise and a decline in depressive symptoms (Hughes *et al*, 2007).

In Ireland, *TILDA* suggests that increased social participation in social activities and relationships (and this may include grandchildcare) is associated with improved life expectancy, better self-rated health and higher quality of life for older people. Self-rated quality of life was found to be higher amongst those caring for their children and grandchildren than those not (McCrory *et al*, 2014). In a study of parents of teenage daughters with children (Hurley, 2012), it was found that most grandparents said that they enjoyed caring for their grandchild, but that it was physically and psychologically demanding and often socially limiting. As most of the grandparents lived in the same home as their child and grandchild, there were tensions when it came to conflict over childcare responsibilities, ground rules, and trying not to get involved in how their daughter raised her child.

O'Dwyer *et al* (2012, p.225) describe the 'structural fragility' of modern families, where family members, including grandparents, can experience confusion about their family roles following separation or divorce. Grandparents and their adult children continue to retain norms of non-interference and obligation: grandparents then adopt a strategy of being tactful about the separation/divorce process, avoid painful conversations, and indicate their capacity for non-judgmental support. But reduced contact with grandchildren can induce feelings of extreme loss and powerlessness, impacting on grandparents' psychological well-being.

Overall, the research in Ireland as elsewhere indicates the continuing importance of grandparent/grandchild relationships.

Conclusion

This chapter identified the prevalence of grandparent childcare in Ireland, outlined and analysed some of its key aspects and characteristics in contemporary Irish families, and explored certain factors influencing the extent of grandchildcare, using recent research and Irish data. It also evaluated definitions of grandchildcare and offered theories to explain the phenomenon and typologies to categorise it.

Grandparents are increasingly important as support to families in Ireland in their need for childcare. Grandchildcare is the most common form of childcare in Ireland for 9 month old infants, with 12% of children experiencing it, though this figure reduces as children get older and move into more formal childcare arrangements. Some families continue to use a mix of formal childcare and grandchildcare. Between a third and a half of Irish people aged over 50 provide some level of grandchildcare.

Historically, grandchildcarers in Ireland have been 'mother savers', as they provided childcare in an era of little or no state childcare support for women in the workforce. With public investment has come a substantial increase in childcare places, but many families still rely on informal care, such as grandchildcare, as group care is very expensive and may not meet parents' needs and preferences. Grandchildcare can also be a parental preference. Kinship caring relationships are based on trust, mutuality and reciprocity, differing from other forms of childcare either in the formal or informal sectors. Intergenerational support is a feature of modern family life.

There are many social, economic and demographic factors that influence grandchildcare in Ireland: the child's age and number of siblings; mothers' employment rates; childcare costs and options; family proximity to grandparents; parental age, income and education; family type; grandparent life expectancy; and grandparent health and age. Some of these will have a considerable impact on the extent and nature of grandchildcare in the future, particularly older people's longevity and health, birth rates, women's employment, and changes to the retirement age.

Irish society is ageing as older people experience greater longevity and better health and well-being. Older people generally indicate a good quality of life and health, and positivity about ageing. This generation of Irish children is more likely than their predecessors to know their grandparents into their adulthood and grandparents will have a longer relationship with their grandchildren. Grandchildcare is thus more of an option than previously. Grandparents may be avid or flexible grandchildcarers, or they may be selective or even hesitant, not wanting to be defined simply by their grandparenting role, and may be busy in their social networks and activities.

Women with children are central to the Irish workforce. Government policy will continue to define the number of childcare places available, their location, cost, and quality. The availability of such childcare options will influence the extent of grandchildcare. The availability of grandparents to take on caring duties will be influenced by Ireland's age of retirement from employment. Grandparents tend to increase their grandchildcare role from age 65 years, but pushing out the retirement age may result in a decline in grandparents' ability to provide childcare to their grandchildren. As with all aspects of parenting in Ireland, the future of grandchildcare is likely to be complex and contested.

References

Arber, S. and Timonen, V. (2012). 'Grandparenting in the 21st Century: New Directions' in Arber, S. and Timonen, V. (eds.), *Contemporary Grandparenting: Changing Family Relationships in Global Contexts*, Bristol: Policy Press.

Arthur, S., Snape, D. and Dench, G. (2003). *The Moral Economy of Grandparenting*, London: National Centre for Social Research.

Barrett, A., Savva, G., Timonen, V. and Kenny, R. (2011). *Fifty Plus in Ireland 2011 – First Results from the Irish Longitudinal Study on Ageing* (TILDA), Dublin: Trinity College Dublin.

Bates, J. and Taylor, A. (2013). 'Taking Stock of Theory in Grandparent Studies' in Fine, M. and Fincham, F. (eds.), *Handbook of Family Theories: A Content-based Approach*, London: Routledge.

Central Statistics Office (2012). *Census 2011: Profile 6: Migration and Diversity*, Dublin: Government Publications.

Chen, F., Liu, G. and Mair, C. (2011). 'Intergenerational Ties in the Context: Grandparents Caring for Grandchildren in China', *Social Forces*, Vol.90, No.2, pp.571-94.

Condon, D. (2013). 'A New Role for Grandparents?', *Irish Health.com*, 24 July, available at www.irishhealth.com/article.html?id=22404, accessed 26 July 2014.

Condon, J., Corkindale, C., Luszcz, M. and Gamble, E. (2013). 'The Australian First-time Grandparents Study: Time Spent with the Grandchild and Its Predictors', *Australasian Journal of Ageing*, Vol.32, No.1, pp.21-27.

Doyle, M., O'Dwyer, C. and Timonen, V. (2010). 'How Can You Just Cut Off a Whole Side of the Family and Say "Move On"?' The Reshaping of Paternal Grandparent-grandchild Relationships following Divorce or Separation in the Middle Generation', *Family Relations*, Vol.59, No.5, pp.587-98.

Duffy, M. (2011). *Making Care Count: A Century of Gender, Race and Paid Care Work*, New Brunswick, NJ: Rutgers University Press.

European Commission (2011). *Active Ageing and Solidarity between Generations: A Statistical Portrait of the European Union 2012*, Luxembourg: European Commission.

European Social Survey (2008). *European Social Survey Round 2: ESS-2 2004 Documentation Report, Edition 3.1*, Bergen: European Social Survey Data Archive, Norwegian Social Science Data Services.

Family and Childcare Trust, Grandparents Plus and Save the Children (2014). *Time to Care: Generation Generosity under Pressure*, available at www.familyandchildcaretrust.org/time-to-care, accessed 26 July 2014.

Ferguson, E., Maughan, B. and Golding, J. (2008). 'Which Children Receive Grandparental Care and What Effect Does It Have?', *Journal of Child Psychology and Psychiatry*, Vol.49, No.2, pp.161-69.

Fine-Davis, M., Fagnani, J., Giovannini, D., Højgard, L. and Clarke, H. (2002). *Fathers and Mothers: Dilemmas of the Work-life Balance: A Comparative Study in Four European Countries*, Dordrecht: Kluwer Publishers.

Fine, M. and Fincham, F. (2013). *Handbook of Family Theories: A Content-based Approach*, London: Routledge.

Goodfellow, J. and Laverty, J. (2003). 'Grandparents Supporting Working Families: Satisfaction and Choice in the Provision of Child Care', *Family Matters*, Vol.66, pp.14-19, available at www.aifs.gov.au/institute/pubs/ fm2003/fm66/jg.pdf, accessed 14 September 2008.

Government of Ireland (2013). *Rights of Grandparents Bill, 2013,* Dublin: Government Publications.

Gray, J., Geraghty, R. and Ralph, D. (2013). 'Young Grandchildren and Their Grandparents: A Secondary Analysis of Continuity and Change across Four Birth Cohorts', *Families, Relationships and Societies*, Vol.2, No.2, pp.289-98.

Hank, K. and Buber, I. (2007). *Grandparents Caring for their Grandchildren: Findings from the 2004 Survey of Health Ageing and Retirement in Europe*, Munich: Mannheim Research Institute for the Economics of Aging.

Harris, E., Doyle, E. and Greene, S. (2011). *Growing Up in Ireland: The Findings of the Qualitative Study with the 9 year olds and Their Parents,* Dublin: Government Publications.

Herlofsen, K. and Hagestad, G. (2012). 'Transformations in the Role of Grandparents across Welfare States' in Arber, S. and Timonen, V. (eds.), *Contemporary Grandparenting: Changing Family Relationships in Global Contexts*, Bristol: Policy Press.

Hetherington, E. (2003). 'Social Support and the Adjustment of Children in Divorced and Remarried Families', *Childhood*, Vol.10, No.2, pp.217-36.

Hogan, D., Halpenny, A. and Greene, S. (2003). 'Change and Continuity after Parental Separation: Children's Experiences of Family Transitions in Ireland', *Childhood*, Vol.10, No.2, pp.163-80.

Horsfall, B. and Dempsey, D. (2013). 'Grandparents Doing Gender: Experiences of Grandmothers and Grandfathers Caring for Grandchildren in Australia', *Journal of Sociology*, doi: 10.1177/1440783313498945, accessed 12 April 2014.

Hughes, M., Waite, L., LaPierre, T. and Luo, Y. (2007). 'All in the Family: The Impact of Caring for Grandchildren on Grandparents' Health', *Journal of Gerontology: Social Sciences*, Vol.62B, No.2, S108-S119.

Hurley, P. (2012). *Grandparents before Time: Exploring the Needs and Experiences of Parents Whose Children become Teenage Parents,* adapted and condensed version of a dissertation presented for a MA in Health Promotion and University College Cork, unpublished, available at http://tpsp.ie/cork.PAGE13.html, accessed 23 June 2014.

Jappens, M. and Van Bavel, J. (2012). 'Regional Family Forms and Childcare in Europe', *Demographic Research*, Vol.27, No.4, pp.85-120.

King-O'Riain, R. (2014). 'Transconnective Space, Emotions and Skype: The Transnational Emotional Practices of Mixed International Couples in the

Republic of Ireland' in Benski, T. and Fisher, E. (eds.), *Internet and Emotions*, London: Taylor and Francis/Routledge.

Kornhaber, A. (1996). *Contemporary Grandparenting*, Thousand Oaks, CA: Sage.

Kruk, E. (1994). 'Grandparent Visitation Disputes: Multigenerational Approaches to Family Mediation', *Mediation Quarterly*, Vol.12, No.1, 37-53.

Lee. J. and Bauer, J. (2013). 'Motivations for Providing and Utilizing Childcare by Grandmothers in South Korea', *Journal of Marriage and Family*, Vol.75, No.2, pp.381-402.

Lo, M. and Liu, Y. (2009). 'Quality of Life among Older Grandparent Caregivers: A Pilot Study', *Journal of Advanced Nursing*, Vol.65, No.7, pp.1475-84.

Lundström, F. (2001). *Grandparenthood in Modern Ireland*, Dublin: Government Publications.

McCrory, C., Leahy, S. and McGarrigle, C. (2014). 'What Factors are Associated with Change in Older People's Quality of Life' in Nolan, A., O'Regan, C., Dooley, C., Wallace, D., Hever, A., Cronin, H., Hudson, E. Kenny, R.A. (eds.), *The Over 50s in a Changing Ireland: Economic Circumstances, Health and Well-being*, Dublin: Trinity College Dublin.

McGarrigle, C. and Kenny, R.A. (2013). *Profile of the Sandwich Generation and Intergenerational Transfers in Ireland*, Dublin: The Irish Longitudinal Study on Ageing.

McGinnity, F., Murray, A. and McNally, S. (2013). *Mothers' Return to Work and Childcare Choices for Infants in Ireland*, Dublin: Government Publications.

McNally, S., Share, M. and Murray, A. (2014). 'Prevalence and Predictors of Grandparent Childcare in Ireland: Findings from a Nationally Representative Sample of Infants and Their Families', *Child Care in Practice*, Vol.20, No.2, pp.182-93.

Murphy, F. (2009). *An Exploration of Grandparenting in Contemporary Ireland*, unpublished thesis, Waterford Institute of Technology, available at http://repository.wit.ie/id/eprint/1390, accessed 27 February 2014.

O'Dwyer, C., Doyle, M., Moore, E. and Timonen, V. (2012). '"We Have All Moved On": How Grandparents Cope with Their Adult Child's Relationship Breakdown', *Families, Relationships and Societies*, Vol.1, No.2, pp.223-41.

Ochiltree, G. (2006). 'The Changing Role of Grandparents' in Commonwealth of Australia (ed.), *AFRC Briefing, No. 2*, Melbourne: Australian Institute of Family Studies.

Posadas, J. and Vidal-Fernandez, M. (2012). *Grandparents' Childcare and Female Labor Force Participation*, IZA Discussion Paper No.6398, Berlin: IZA (Institute for the Study of Labor).

Quail, A., Murray, A. and Williams, J. (2011). *Support from Grandparents to Families with Infants*, ESRI Research Bulletin 2011/01/04, available at www.esri.ie/UserFiles/publications/RB20110101/RB20110104.pdf, accessed 23 June 2014.

Röder, A., Ward, M., Frese, C. and Sánchez, E. (2014). *New Irish Families: A Profile of Second Generation Children and Their Families*, Dublin: Trinity College Dublin.

Sandfort, J. and Hill, M. (1996). 'Assisting Young, Unmarried Mothers to Become Self-sufficient: The Effects of Different Types of Early Economic Support', *Journal of Marriage and Family*, Vol.58, No.2, pp.311-26.

Share, M. and Kerrins, L. (2009). 'The Role of Grandparents in Childcare in Ireland', *Irish Journal of Applied Social Studies*, Vol.9, No.1, pp.33-48.

Vandell, D.L, McCartney, K., Tresch Owen, M., Booth, C. and Clarke-Stewart, A. (2003). 'Variations in Childcare by Grandparents during the First Three Years', *Journal of Marriage and Family*, Vol.65, No.2, pp.375-81.

Walker, A. and Foster, L. (eds.) (2014). *The Political Economy of Ageing and Later Life: Critical Perspectives*, Cheltenham: Edward Elgar.

Wall, K. and Sao Jose, J. (2004). 'Managing Work and Care: A Difficult Challenge for Immigrant Families', *Social Policy & Administration*, Vol.38, No.6, pp.591-621.

Wheelock, J. and Jones, K. (2002). 'Grandparents are the Next Best Thing: Informal Childcare for Working Parents in Urban Britain', *Journal of Social Policy*, Vol.31, No.3, pp.441-63.

Williams, J., Murray, A., McCrory, C. and McNally, S. (2013). *Development from Birth to Three Years – Infant Cohort*, Dublin: Government Publications.

Wilton, V. and Davey, J. (2006). *Grandfathers: Their Changing Roles and Contribution*, Blue Skies Report No. 3/06, Wellington: The Families Commission.

13: FATHERS AND PARENTING

Colin Shaw, Maria Lohan and Noel Richardson

INTRODUCTION

The aim of this chapter is to present a contextual and empirical account of men as fathers in Ireland, along with an analysis of recent, relevant developments in policies and laws. Much of parenting of a child occurs in the home. Consequently, how couples inhabit the home greatly influences how their children experience childhood and, in many ways, the story of fatherhood in Ireland is the product of the on-going changes in the domestic sphere. Whether men are driving these changes, embracing or resisting them will provide the substance of much of this chapter. The first section presents basic demographic figures and trends based on census data to answer the questions: who are the fathers, what type of families do they live in and how involved are they in childcare? The second section presents recent research on contemporary fatherhood, both international and, where possible, national. The next section explores the policies and legal measures that affect fathers, their duties and their rights in the home and at work, while the final section will discuss the historical legacy of fatherhood that is particular to Ireland. The conclusion will draw together these threads and ask what might be the future of fatherhood in Ireland, its challenges and possible successes.

WHO ARE THE FATHERS?

Fathers Today: Fewer and Older

As a recent study of fatherhood in the UK demonstrated, presenting a definitive picture of a parenting relationship that has overlapping legal, social, biological, and personal meanings is a complex task.[10] An exhaustive taxonomy of father-child relationships quickly becomes

10 Lee's (2008) study of the *British Household Panel Survey* documented 73 different 'paternal careers' in a sample of 2,183 men.

fragmented as family circumstances and individual life stories can give rise to a myriad of possible configurations. Consequently, fatherhood is often presented with a number of prefixes (step, separated, incarcerated, teenage, etc.) that try to capture specific aspects of the relationship. As it is beyond the scope of this chapter to explore the complexities of many of the types of fatherhood, our starting point will be the basic demographics of fatherhood in Ireland, the family types they live in and an insight into what constitutes their involvement with their children.

Establishing the demographics of fatherhood is, in itself, a complex task. Fatherhood can have biological and social aspects (step, foster, or adoptive) and standard census data can only give a partial picture of how many men are actually 'fathers'. Indeed, male fertility rates (the number of men who have fathered a child during their lifetime) are not published by official figures. Whereas female fertility rates are systematically recorded, the identity (and, therefore, the number) of men 'giving birth' to children was not obligatorily (until recently) registered,[11] meaning that figures for men must be 'inferred' from those provided for women (Greene and Biddlecom, 2000). Despite this, it can be estimated that 80% of men living in Ireland today will become fathers during their lifetimes.

Interestingly, this number is falling; extrapolating further from figures recorded for women, the proportion of men who father children has been falling since the 1940s; 85% of women born in 1945 have had one or more children during their lives, whereas this drops to 80.7% for women born in 1960. Again, official statistics do not record the age of fathers at the birth of their first child. However, based on Central Statistics Office and OECD statistics for women, it can be estimated that the average age for men to become fathers is 32 years old, an increase of 6.5 years since 1980. This trend mirrors that of women's age at the birth of their first child (currently 29 years old) (Central Statistics Office, 2012, OECD, 2011).

Trends in Childlessness

An OECD report, *Doing Better for Families* (2011), highlighted current trends in childlessness in Ireland, leading to newspaper headlines announcing a 'childless generation' and 'Irish women have the third highest rate of childlessness in the developed world' (*Irish Independent*, 2014). Childlessness is an issue more often considered in association with women's lives than men's, since decisions on birth control and pregnancy

11 The *Civil Registration (Amendment) Bill, 2014*, Section 6, provides that where the mother of the child attends alone, she must provide (except in exceptional circumstances) information as to the father's name and contact details.

fall primarily to the female partner (Dykstra and Keizer, 2009) and consequently, research has often neglected men's role in fertility decisions (Marsiglio *et al*, 2013). However, in countries such as Ireland where Catholic-inspired 'pronatalist' attitudes still prevail, the social impact of permanent childlessness, whether involuntary or by choice, for both men and women can be significant. A recent cross-national study exploring how childlessness was experienced by both sexes, highlighted that, in pronatalist countries, 'women suffer more stigma than men for remaining child-free since women's (not men's) traditional familial roles are to rear children' (Tanaka and Johnson, 2014). However, the study also found that:

> … child-free male respondents are unhappier and less satisfied with their lives than are child-free female respondents [and further concluded that] Perhaps males are more heavily stigmatised than their wives for failing to produce an heir (Tanaka and Johnson, 2014, p.17).

Similarly, a UK-based in-depth qualitative study also found that 'not only do some childless men indicate a desire for parenthood comparable to childless women, but (…) they may also suffer similar or higher levels of depression and isolation as a consequence' (Hadley, 2009). More generally, it has been acknowledged that men have been marginalised in research on infertility and that measuring levels of grief due to childlessness between men and women is only one element of the increasingly common contemporary experience of involuntary childlessness amongst men (Culley *et al*, 2013).

More Family Types and Fewer Children

Changes in marriage rates, family size, and the timing of births have also altered the landscape of family life in Ireland (Kennedy, 2001). Although the decline has slowed in recent years, the number of children per family has fallen steeply in Ireland over the past decades. In 1991, families had on average two children, falling to 1.8 in 1996, 1.6 in 2002 and remaining level at 1.4 from 2006 to 2011. In addition, while the marriage rate has fallen over the past 40 years, the 'traditional' married couple with children still remains dominant in Irish society; in 1980, less than 5% of children were born outside marriage while, by 2011, this number had risen to just over 30% (Central Statistics Office, 2012). However, the decline in 'marital' births has not translated into a proportional rise in cohabitation; the vast majority of non-marital births are to single-parent families. Cohabiting (unmarried) couples account for only 7% of all families with children, with the remaining 23% of families being made up of predominantly female-headed single-parent households (Central Statistics Office, 2012). Married couples tend to have more children than cohabiting and lone parent couples. Consequently, the distribution of children within family types is slightly different, with 75% living with two married parents, 18% with a lone parent and 6% with cohabiting parents.

Single Fathers

Few areas of family life illustrate the gendered nature of childcare than the phenomenon of single parenthood in Ireland. Census figures show that single parenthood has stabilised in recent years with around one in 10 of all households being headed by a one parent (Central Statistics Office, 2012). The proportion of male-headed one-parent families is also stable at around one in eight of all such families. Several reports on single fatherhood in Ireland have pointed out that this group is relatively invisible and often excluded from discussions on the family (Murphy *et al*, 2008). As discussed below, the legal implications of being an unmarried parent are very different for men and women, with men having no rights of guardianship of their own children born outside of marriage. Consequently, many fathers raising their children alone either cannot or do not avail of benefits designed to support one-parent families. Figures from the Department of Social and Family Affairs show that, although women account for 87% of single-parent families, they are in receipt of 97.7% of One Parent Family Payments (OPFP). This 'invisibility' was commented on by a report compiled by the Department of Social and Family Affairs in 2004:

> Vulnerable men in Ireland are in most respects invisible as fathers, rarely even warranting a mention in the plethora of debate about vulnerable families, be it in relation to lone parents, 'unmarried mothers', marital breakdown, balancing work and family responsibilities, and so on. The only real capacity in which some 'vulnerable' fathers are acknowledged in families is as violent, abusive, 'dangerous men' (Ferguson and Hogan, 2004, p.2).

What Do Irish Fathers Do?

In many ways, the developments in family and society, in Ireland as elsewhere, reflects the changes in women's lives. With regard to, amongst other areas, education, childcare, paid employment, political and social rights, changes in how women live their lives in turn have transformed how children, men and women experience family life. Legal measures to redress the inequalities experienced by women in the workplace have narrowed the gender gap in terms of the pay and conditions for women. However, while legal means can address 'public' practices, they are less effective in changing how attitudes to how women's 'private' or family lives are arranged. Becoming a parent is still the largest impediment to women's equality, largely because women take on the vast majority of the consequent duties of raising children (Astone *et al*, 2010; O'Brien and Shemilt, 2003). This means that, even where men and women are treated equally in the workplace, gaps in employment due to maternity leave, the prevalence of part-time work for mothers and the combined effects of working at home and performing at work mean that the so-called 'motherhood penalty' is alive and well in Ireland in the 21st century (Hays, 1996). Indeed, the 'could do better' verdict that falls at the end of most reports on fatherhood is largely a consequence of what has been called men's lagged or stalled adaption to these changes. Simply put, men have not stepped into the gap created by women's new role outside the home and, for working women, shared labour *in the home* is a far-off goal (Brannen *et al*, 2004).

The Irish national time-use survey reported how men and women spend their time, highlighting the gendered nature of how 'unpaid' (domestic) tasks are shared (McGinnity *et al*, 2005). Based on diary entries collected from a representative sample of Irish adults, the report show that 15% of all men reported doing some childcare during the week, rising to 17% at weekends. This compared to, respectively, 31% and 29% of all women. This imbalance is not 'corrected' by the intensity of the activities reported, with men spending an average of 31 minutes supervising and caring for children during the week, rising to 51 at the weekend. By comparison, women spent on average 150 minutes doing the same activities on weekdays, and 157 minutes at weekends. Women out-perform men in terms of childcare (and, to a lesser extent, other forms of domestic labour, such as cooking) and by a factor of almost 4:1.

Some of this disparity is accounted for by inequalities in employment status; the principal economic status of more than a quarter of all women aged over 15 in Ireland (487,800 women or 26%) is 'looking after home/family' according to the Central Statistics Office (2013). This means that, by virtue of their place of primary activity, women are more available to carry out such tasks. Nevertheless, while approaching parity in *paid* work, women's burden in the *home* has not changed, leading the authors of the 2005 report to conclude: 'there is a substantial difference in the gender division of gainful work and domestic work' (McGinnity *et al*, 2005, p.29).

Fathers and Parenting Culture

In recent years, the impact on children's and parents' well-being of 'intensive parenting' – a highly demanding, child-centred approach to childrearing, which is both a time- and emotionally-intensive enterprise – has become the subject of much debate (Lee *et al*, 2010). Features of intensive parenting include the perceived need for continuous parental control, and anxieties over decisions made for a child that may determine their future, thereby heightening the pressure to make the right choices (Shirani *et al*, 2012). Some authors have suggested that this phenomenon is better described as 'intensive mothering', as men are less likely to be exposed to sometimes conflicting 'expert advice' directed at mothers, especially during the peri-natal period.

A report by the Office of the Minister for Children and Youth Affairs into parenting styles and discipline published in 2010 provides some insight into gender similarities on matters of parental responsibilities in Ireland (Halpenny *et al*, 2010). Notably, the study did not identify any significant differences in parental values or attitudes to discipline between fathers and mothers. The report found that a 'striking proportion of parents (84%) indicated that there was greater pressure on contemporary parents when compared with 20 years ago' (Halpenny *et al*, 2010, p.44). The report also found that this pressure was felt equally by mothers and fathers:

> Parents' self-reports on the impact of a variety of pressures on the parenting role suggest that most of these parents experience a great deal of pressure in their everyday parenting activities. This pressure does not appear to be clearly related to the age or number of children being parented, and is experienced more or less equally by mothers and fathers (Halpenny *et al*, 2010, p.46).

Analysing Fatherhood

'Could Do Better'

The contemporary debate surrounding men and parenting today is essentially a discussion of how men adequately contribute to the well-being of their children. The traditional social contract where fathers provided the financial support (by working outside the home) and mothers provided the affective support for their families (at home) is no longer considered an adequate or indeed sustainable arrangement; men had stunted home lives, women had stunted economic opportunities

(Francis, 2007). However, the corollary of the economic expansion of women's lives would suggest that there be an equivalent expansion of men's domestic lives. As reported in the previous section, for many authors, this has not happened (Gershuny *et al*, 1994; Gerson, 2004; Sayer *et al*, 2004).

Not surprisingly, readers of studies on fatherhood, of which there are many, quickly become accustomed to their seemingly inevitable conclusions that can best be summed up as: 'Fathers: could do better'. Whether the issue of paternal involvement is framed in terms of gender equality, child development or the men's own well-being, men are consistently seen to let down their female partners, their children and indeed themselves when it comes to fulfilling their role as fathers. Dozens of international and national reports speak of the persistent gap between (a) the contemporary ideal that suggests that the relationship between a father and a child should be permanent and meaningful, even in the event of family separation; (b) the reality of two-parent families where the mother carries out the majority of the caring duties; and (c) the rise of predominantly female-headed, one-parent families where the children often have fragmented contact with their biological father (Dermott, 2008; Doucet, 2009; Miller, 2011). Consequently, the metaphor of 'fatherhood in crisis' dominates much of the scholarly and media discussion of contemporary fathers (see Hobson, 2002, for an overview).

As noted above, Ireland, like many other Western nations, is also experiencing the transformation of fatherhood and family life with co-existing ideals of the nurturing, involved father, the persistence of gender inequality and the rise of predominantly female-headed lone parent families. So while fewer Irish men live with their children than a generation ago, the expectation is that, regardless of whether fathers live together or separately from their children, they should be more involved with them than their own fathers were, especially where it comes to their emotional lives and general well-being. Changing the structural bias (especially the organisation of workplace) inherent in the way parents can organise work and family commitments may go some way to providing opportunities to fathers to become more fully engaged with their children, but what other factors affect men's commitment to family life?

Parent Number Two

Research has shown that men are less secure in their identity as fathers than women are in their role as mothers. Put simply, men need more encouragement to become involved with their children, whereas the mother-child bond requires less outside support for it to develop (Bolte,

2001). This difference may be accounted for by the greater value placed on the mother-child relationship culturally, as well as the far greater amount of time mothers actually spend with their new-born child. This underlines the importance of father-child relationship in early infancy. Fathers sometimes can take a back seat when it comes to a baby's first days and months, preferring to take on the role of 'parent number two' and to support the mother in her role as primary carer and nurturer (Jordan, 1990; Deeney *et al*, 2012). Men can more easily see their involvement as appropriate once the child can engage with outdoor physical play and activities and it is not uncommon to refer to a father 'babysitting' his own children (Wilson and Prior, 2010). Data collected by the Australian Bureau of Statistics has shown that full-time employed fathers spend an average of 7% of their time with children alone and 74% in the company of their spouse (Craig, 2002).

However, the experience of sole responsibility has been found to be very important for fathers in developing confidence and competence in childcare. It is also important for children, by altering their perception of fathers as parents in their own right rather than mothers' helpers (Coltrane, 2000). Although necessarily taxing, perhaps for both parties, fathers caring for their babies alone can positively affect the level of mutual attachment (Lamb and Lewis, 2004). By contrast, the impact of low or no-father involvement is seen in a range of negative outcomes in children's health and education (Pleck and Masciadrelli, 2004). For example, low involvement by fathers in a child's education has a very strong negative impact on their achievement, stronger indeed than contact with the police, income levels, family make-up, social class, housing and even the child's personality. This is particularly marked for father-son involvement (Blanden and Britain, 2006).

Men's Well-being and Fatherhood

The interest in father-child relationships often emphasises the benefits to the child. However, research has shown that fatherhood can present strong health benefits for the man. Naturally, simply being a father provides no insurance against ill-health, but cohabiting fathers with children, a Swedish study showed, are less likely to suffer from forms of addiction or to die from injury than childless men (Ringbäck Weitoft *et al*, 2004). Other studies describe how the early stages of childcare can be a danger zone for men's psychological well-being, with expectant and new fathers reporting higher levels of stress, feelings of isolation and higher rates of depression than childless men of the same age. Overall, men describe the advent of fatherhood as a process of maturing, increased consciousness of the importance of relationships, new empathic abilities and better self-confidence (Plantin *et al*, 2011). A possible explanation for this is that children give additional structure and meaning to their lives and provide positive mental and physical cues (talking, reading, playing), as well as increased opportunities to socialise with other adults, thereby strengthening social integration and social support (Ringbäck Weitoft *et al*, 2004; Bartlett, 2004). At the very least, becoming a father presents men with improved, if not voluntary, opportunities to connect with health and social services.

It is not all good news, however; some men, after becoming fathers, report that the number and quality of their social relations diminishes as does time spent in socialising (Bost *et al*, 2002). The findings are different for mothers; the same study found that a mother's close relationship to the child during infancy and early childhood often positively influences social contact with others but that the effect can weaken over time as the child becomes more independent. However, the headline message for men is that taking time off work and spending it with their infant children is very important for all concerned; a close relationship to young children increases both the child's and the parent's emotional well-being.

Fatherhood Policies

These contradictory cultural and societal shifts are being met with 'pull and push' responses through government policies based on a momentum of growing evidence of the importance of fathers' involvement in children's lives. Pull policies, best exemplified by Swedish pro-fatherhood initiatives, aim to foster men's involvement with their children and include the extension of parental leave (that can be taken by men or women) as an alternative to maternity leave, the presumption in family law that both parents share custody of their children equally after parents separate, and the inclusion of men in the design of social and health programmes aimed at children. Push policies, such as those widely practiced in the USA and more recently in the UK, take a more punitive approach to ensure that fathers, through so-called liable relative determination orders, continue to provide financially for their children when couples separate. As discussed below, Irish policies on fatherhood arguably have been more of the pull variety with fewer measures designed to promote fatherhood involvement rolled out recently (see Rush, 2009 for a detailed discussion).

Fathers-to-be

There is perhaps no single area more important to generating a fuller engagement of fathers in the lives of children than in maternity services. While the obstetric and midwifery professions have shown greater willingness to accommodate men in ante-natal education, ante-natal health appointments and at the birth of the baby, available research suggests further small improvements could reduce fathers' feelings of being an 'outsider' or mere 'bystander' within the maternity services as well as in neo-natal services (Kaila-Behm and Vehviläinen-Julkunen, 2000; Locock and Alexander, 2006; Deeney *et al*, 2012.). Such small improvements, identified in this research, include directly addressing fathers' questions and concerns in relation to parenthood; up-skilling fathers in infant care, addressing fathers' health needs in preparing to be a father and in the post-partum period – for example, it may be the perfect time to help fathers to give up smoking, contributing to their own health and that of their children (Oliffe *et al*, 2010). Whilst the biological aspects of caring for women and the unborn infant arguably will always be foremost, if midwifery, in particular, is to remain relevant as the main conduit of health services to expectant parents and in preparing parents for birth, assisting in the inclusion of fathers will certainly be increasingly necessary and useful to the broader aims of midwifery care.

Young Fatherhood

Rates of teenage pregnancy in Ireland, although high by comparison with the rest of Europe, have been falling consistently over recent decades. Nevertheless, the Crisis Pregnancy Programme reports that, in 2011, there were 1,720 births to teenagers and 443 abortions to women under 20 giving Irish addresses in UK clinics (Crisis Pregnancy Programme, 2012). It is increasingly apparent to researchers, practitioners, parents and others who work with youth that targeting young men is an important, yet sorely neglected part of addressing teenage pregnancy (Lohan *et al*, 2011). Boys are currently much less likely to receive education in relation to pregnancy prevention in schools and research from Ireland and the US both suggest that parents are far more likely to have discussed sex and pregnancy with their daughters than with their sons (Aventin and Lohan, 2013a; Hyde *et al*, 2010). Nevertheless, an unintended pregnancy also can be an immense crisis in a young adolescent male's life, leaving him unsure about how to make decisions about the pregnancy (for an overview, see Lohan *et al*, 2010). Recognising this need, the Health Services Executive Crisis Pregnancy Programme, together with the

Department of Education and Science, recently sponsored an initiative to deliver a targeted educational intervention to teenage men aimed at raising their intentions to avoid an unintended teenage pregnancy. This research informed intervention entitled, *If I were Jack* (Aventin and Lohan, 2013b), is being rolled out to second level schools in Ireland to both boys and girls as part of relationship and sexuality education. The longer term effectiveness of this educational approach also will be evaluated (Lohan *et al*, 2014).

Further concerted efforts are required to help young fathers assume fatherhood responsibilities. In their research work with young, vulnerable fathers, Ferguson and Hogan (2004, p.20) referred to 'the astonishing lack of social supports for fathers in Ireland', particularly in relation to 'in need' fathers who, they argued, were essentially ignored by health and social services providers. They recommended that there was an onus on all agencies that work with children and families to develop more explicit father-inclusive policies and practices. Teenage and young fathers, in particular, can frequently become marginalised around the birth of their baby and in the post-natal period, especially in cases where they or their partners are under the legal age of sexual consent (age 17 years) (Bunting and McAuley, 2004; Quinton *et al*, 2002). Most young mothers want their child to have a positive relationship with the father, so failing to integrate young fathers into the maternity services is usually ignoring both the young mothers' and fathers' wishes (Fisher, 2007). Although teenage fathers can become isolated as a result of not residing with their partner, recent studies have shown that adolescent fathers can be 're-integrated' into fathering roles. For example, the Millennium Cohort Study found that 21% of non-resident fathers (many of them young) who had some level of contact with their 9 to 10 month old infants were in more frequent (and sometimes daily contact) when their child was aged 3 (Dex and Ward, 2007).

Separated Fathers

A father who is not married to the mother of his children does not have automatic guardianship rights to those children. As divorce and separation are increasingly part of life for families in Ireland, the effects of this legal principle are being contested and debated in the courts and society more widely. The role of fathers after separation is the subject of two recent reports from Northern Ireland and Ireland (Sneddon, 2014; Office of the Minister for Children and Youth Affairs, 2011). Each report emphasises the importance of sustaining the father-child relationship in the interest of both parties; fathers can suffer psychologically in the event of prolonged separation from their children. Also, child outcomes, be they academic, behavioural and general well-being also are affected by an involuntary lack of contact with father. The conclusions of both reports highlight how the legal context and court practices provide opportunities to minimise family conflict and mitigate the adverse impacts on all family members.

Grandfatherhood

Research into grandfathers is an especially neglected area, despite the general observation that being a grandparent of either gender can be an extremely rewarding experience. Grandfathers often are overwhelmingly positive and sometimes ecstatic about their relationship with their young grandchild and how being a grandparent has changed their life for the better (Bates and Taylor, 2012). One study on grandparenthood described how it can be a vital relationship for older adults to maintain ties with family and wider society (Kivett, 1985). A UK survey reported that over half of respondents (55%) said that being a grandparent contributed 'enormously' to their quality of life and a third (31%) said it contributed 'a lot'. Only 4% said it contributed 'not at all' (Clarke and Roberts, 2003). However, an American study showed that the emotional benefits of grandparenting may not be matched by physical well-being; grandparents with the role of caregivers were significantly more likely to report lower satisfaction with health (Minkler and Fuller-Thomson, 1999). New legislation will facilitate grandparental access to their grandchildren after family break-up by introducing a legal definition:

> A grandparent in relation to a child means a grandparent whether of whole/half blood or by affinity and includes the spouse of such person, a parent of a child's adopted parent and an adoptive parent of a child's parent (Government of Ireland, 2013).

Working Fathers

Reconciling Work with Fatherhood

Central to the 'Fathers: could do better' debate (see earlier) is the presentation of incriminating *versus* mitigating factors in terms of how men reconcile work with fatherhood. In a historical context, paid work has occupied a central focus in men's lives, and traditional masculine values in Ireland have tended to centre on the hard-working man and the 'good-provider' role (Hearn *et al*, 2002). Whilst there have been significant changes to more traditional gendered work practices, this, as highlighted earlier, has not been reciprocated in terms of a reconfiguration of men's roles as carers or in terms of domestic labour (Astone *et al*, 2010; McGinnity *et al*, 2005; Fine-Davis and Clarke, 2002). Men continue to spend longer hours than women in paid employment. For example, in 2013, almost three-quarters (72.1%) of all those who worked 40 hours or more a week were men, with 44.1% of married men working for 40 or more hours per week compared with 16.8% of married women (Central Statistics Office, 2013).

In a survey of family-friendly/work-life balance policies and practices in Ireland, Drew *et al* (2003) reported concern not just with long working hours having become the norm in Irish society, but that working such hours was increasingly seen as the hallmark and price of career progression into managerial grades. The same report highlighted gender differences in work-life balance arrangements. Whilst reduced working hours (in the form of part-time working and job-sharing) was a predominantly female working pattern, men tended to prefer flexible full-time working and working from home. There was also the suggestion of a 'penalty clause' in relation to the uptake of part-time working/job-sharing, in that employees may have perceived that their career prospects would be compromised. The report also noted that the complexities of balancing the notion of 'new fatherhood' with factors such as inflexible work demands, the harsh reality of economic necessity for many men and disapproval or ridicule from other men, are often overlooked (Drew *et al*, 2003). Indeed, Ferguson (2001) cites the negative attitudes of employers and colleagues as the biggest barrier to creating family-friendly workplaces and as a reason why so few fathers in Ireland avail of parental leave. The report on the national consultation process on families and family life (Daly, 2004) also notes that successfully implementing family-friendly, work-life balance arrangements goes beyond HR policy and practice and in effect implies implementing a programme of cultural change and challenging the way work is done within an organisation.

Clearly therefore, policies that are designed to improve work-life balance must be carefully thought through, so as not to penalise (even if unintentionally) workers who avail of such options in their attempt to reconcile paid work with caring and other responsibilities. It is also imperative as Drew *et al* note:

> ... to avoid a twin track in which men are in the fast lane involving continuous and often excessive hours in full-time employment,

partly from home, and women in the slow lane working/seeking reduced hours and/or opting for career breaks (Drew *et al*, 2003, p.130).

The Invisibility of Fathers

Despite repeated calls from various advocacy, research and policy groups for increased statutory/financial support for fathers, fathers remain largely invisible in terms of any such supports. While the provision of maternity leave in Ireland now exceeds the minimum EU requirement, there is no statutory entitlement to paternity leave outside of the Civil Service (which provides three days paid leave on the birth or adoption of a child). By contrast, statutory paternity leave with full pay has become the norm in many other European countries – for example, Norway (four weeks), France (two weeks consecutive paternity leave) and Denmark (14 days). In Finland, there is a statutory entitlement to 18 weeks paternity leave, paid at 65% of salary. Feldman *et al* (2004) reported that the taking of longer paternity leave was associated with higher paternal preoccupation with infant, more marital support, and higher 'family salience'.

Currently, fathers in Ireland are entitled only to unpaid parental leave (up to 18 weeks off work in respect of children aged up to 8 years of age). While many countries (for example, Sweden, France, Luxemburg, Norway, Austria, Belgium and Italy) pay a flat rate to employees when taking parental leave, parental leave in Ireland remains largely unpaid. It is worth noting that, in Sweden, parental leave has long been seen as a family entitlement, with the current provision of a 'use it or lose it' incentive for fathers (60 days paid at approximately 77% of father's salary up to a certain ceiling). The most recent European-wide study carried out on behalf of the European Commission (Eurobarometer, 2004) found that, whilst 75% of fathers knew of their right to parental leave, only 16% had taken it up or intended to take it up. The principal factors in the report that deterred Irish fathers from staying at home were:

- Financial reasons, with 18% saying they could not afford to and 42% citing insufficient financial compensation;
- Lack of information (34%);
- Concerns about their careers, with 31% saying their careers would be affected and 20% not wanting their careers to be interrupted.

Brandth and Kvande (2002) conclude that the introduction of paid paternity leave in Scandinavian countries has been instrumental in changing employers' views on fathering, creating an accepting corporate atmosphere toward parenting, and increasing fathers' participation in childcare and family life. It also should be stressed that the experience from Scandinavia highlights two other important lessons; that men can change when there is appropriate institutionalised support and a wider cultural change; and that women too benefit in terms of a shift towards equality of gender relations. As Holter notes:

> The Nordic 'experiment' has shown that the majority of men can change their practice when circumstances are favourable … When reforms or support policies are well-designed and targeted towards an on-going cultural process of change, men's active support for gender-equal status increases (Holter, 2003, p.126).

Pointing towards Policy and Legislative Change for Fathers

Significant gaps remain at both a policy and practice level in terms of simultaneously supporting and enabling fathers to be more available as 'fathers' and combatting what remains a 'persistent gender division of gainful work *versus* domestic work' (McGinnity *et al*, 2005, p.29). Efforts to encourage and support men towards more family-friendly, work-life balance work practices need to be grounded in more fundamental cultural and institutional change. Consideration also needs to be given to the provision of paternity leave and to the increased uptake of existing parental leave by fathers as part of a wider gender-relations approach to equality in the workplace, and to child-care and domestic labour within the home. In calling for more 'gender-competent father-inclusive policies and practices', Ireland's *National Men's Health Policy* states that the promotion of active fatherhood needs to be seen by policy-makers and practitioners as a form of social inclusion, from the moment of pregnancy awareness, through to the early months and years of the child's life (Department of Health and Children, 2009, p.54). Both the Fatherhood Engagement Research Project (Government of South Australia, 2010) and The Fatherhood Quality Mark[12] (UK) provide worthwhile examples of best practice in terms of supporting men to reconcile their role as fathers with their work and of developing more father-inclusive policies and practices in Ireland in the future.

---

12 For further information, see www.fatherhoodinstitute.org/2007/the-fatherhood-quality-mark-a-new-badge-of-excellence-for-working-with-fathers/.

Fatherhood and the Legacy of the Past

In addition to these policy responses, the wider debate on fatherhood in Ireland often is framed in starkly contradictory terms. Recent high profile activism for social justice for fathers emphasises how society often prioritises mothers as the 'natural' carers of children. As discussed above, Irish family law only provides unmarried mothers with automatic rights to guardianship of their children while fathers, even if they cohabit with the mother and children, need to apply for guardianship through a court order and gain the consent of the mother. This arrangement can mean that, in the event of unmarried parents separating, the father is not in a position to oppose or consent to his children leaving the county, undergoing medical procedures or being adopted. Similarly contentious issues exist for men in gaining access to their children following separation from their spouse or partner.

Furthermore, in Ireland, the historical context of this 'illegitimacy' of the father with regard to his children born outside of marriage is often seen in a different light; this lack of legal responsibility also provided men with the opportunity to escape parental rights and duties, a practice that ultimately gave rise to the establishment of institutions such as the mother and baby homes and Magdalene laundries. As this issue hit the headlines in recent years, the legacy of social attitudes to illegitimacy was being played out in media and government investigations into these homes and laundries. The inequality of disgrace and hardship experienced by women and men conceiving a child outside of marriage is an uncomfortable backdrop upon which fatherhood activists must make their bid for a new gender equality. Consequently, calls for parental rights of guardianship to be extended to unmarried fathers frequently are seen as controversial, as these calls do not always acknowledge that the currently situation is not, arguably, the result of a feminist campaign against men but, more accurately, the legacy of patriarchy that once allowed men to avoid the very rights they seek today.

Conclusion

Fatherhood is in vogue. Celebrities such as Colin Farrell, Brad Pitt and Simon Cowell are keen to tell the world how fatherhood is 'their greatest role' (*International Business Times*, 2014). *The Irish Times* newspaper ran a weekly column on stay-at-home fatherhood for seven years (2006 to 2013) and the same newspaper frequently has published John Waters', and others', views on fathers' rights. The portrayal of men as 'activists' in their commitment to fatherhood often is contradicted by other stories of men shirking their parental responsibilities, either by leaving their partners to raise their children alone, or failing to pay maintenance thereby forcing the state to 'step in' and provide financial support (*Irish Examiner*, 2014).

Obviously, much of what constitutes the social reality of fathering falls between the image of the doe-eyed father gazing at his infant and the figure of the 'feckless, absent father'. Fatherhood, for most men, is a profoundly meaningful bond that, perhaps because it is familiar, routine and permanent, goes largely unquestioned.

References

Astone, N.M., Dariotis, J.K., Sonenstein, F.L., Pleck, J.H. and Hynes, K. (2010). 'Men's Work Efforts and the Transition to Fatherhood', *Journal of Family and Economic Issues*, Vol.31, No.1, pp.3-13.

Aventin, Á. and Lohan, M. (2013a). 'You're Wha…? Including Young Men in Reproductive Planning', *The Practicing Midwife*, Vol.16, No.7, pp.21-23.

Aventin, Á. and Lohan, M. (2013b). 'I'm All Right, Jack', *Every Child Journal*, Vol.3, No.5, pp.38-43.

Bartlett, E. (2004). 'The Effects of Fatherhood on the Health of Men: A Review of the Literature', *Journal of Men's Health and Gender*, Vol.1, No.2-3, pp.159-69.

Bates, J.S. and Taylor, A.C. (2012). 'Grandfather Involvement and Aging Men's Mental Health', *American Journal of Men's Health*, Vol.6, No.3, pp.229-39.

Blanden, J. and Britain, G. (2006). *Bucking the Trend: What Enables Those Who Are Disadvantaged in Childhood to Succeed Later in Life?*, Department for Work and Pensions Working Paper No.31, retrieved from http://dera.ioe.ac.uk/7729/1/WP31.pdf.

Bolte, C. (2001). *On Father's Ground: A Portrait of Projects to Support and Promote Fathering*, Montréal: Université du Québec à Montréal, GRAVE-ARDEC.

Bost, K.K., Cox, M.J., Burchinal, M.R. and Payne, C. (2002). 'Structural and Supportive Changes in Couples' Family and Friendship Networks across the Transition to Parenthood', *Journal of Marriage and Family*, Vol.64, No.2, pp.517-31.

Brandth, B. and Kvande, E. (2002). 'Reflexive Fathers: Negotiating Parental Leave and Working Life', *Gender, Work and Organization*, No.9, p.186-203.

Brannen, J., Moss, P. and Mooney, A. (2004). *Working and Caring over the 20th Century: Change and Continuity in Four-generation Families*, Basingstoke: Palgrave Macmillan.

Bunting, L. and McAuley, C. (2004). 'Research Review: Teenage Pregnancy and Parenthood: The Role of Fathers', *Child & Family Social Work*, Vol.9, No.3, pp.207-15.

Central Statistics Office (2012). *This is Ireland: Highlights From Census 2011*, Cork: Central Statistics Office.

Central Statistics Office (2013). *Women and Men in Ireland*, Cork: Central Statistics Office.

Clarke, L. and Roberts, C. (2003). *Grandparenthood: Its Meaning and Its Contribution to Older People's Lives*, Sheffield: Growing Older Programme.

Coltrane, S. (2000). 'Research on Household Labor: Modeling and Measuring the Social Embeddedness of Routine Family Work', *Journal of Marriage and Family*, Vol.62 (November), pp.1208-33.

Craig, L. (2002). *Caring Differently: A Time-use Analysis of the Type and Social Context of Childcare Performed by Fathers and Mothers*, Sydney: University of New South Wales Social Policy Research Centre.

Crisis Pregnancy Programme (2012). *Research on Teenage Sexuality*, retrieved from www.crisispregnancy.ie/publications/research-into-practice-on-teenage-sexuality/.

Culley, L., Hudson, N. and Lohan, M. (2013). 'Where Are All the Men? The Marginalization of Men in Social Scientific Research on Infertility', *Reproductive Biomedicine Online*, Vol.27, No.3, pp.225-35.

Daly, M. (2004). *Families and Family Life in Ireland: Challenges for the Future*, Dublin: Department of Social and Family Affairs.

Deeney, K., Lohan, M., Spence, D. and Parkes, J. (2012). 'Experiences of Fathering a Baby Admitted to Neonatal Intensive Care: A Critical Gender Analysis', *Social Science & Medicine*, Vol.75, No.6, pp.1106-13.

Department of Health and Children (2008). *National Men's Health Policy 2008-2013. Working with Men in Ireland to Achieve Optimum Health and Well-being*, Dublin: Government Publications.

Dermott, E. (2008). *Intimate Fatherhood: A Sociological Analysis*, London: Routledge.

Dex, S. and Ward, K. (2007). *Parental Care and Employment in Early Childhood*, Abergavenny: Fatherhood Institute, retrieved from www.fatherhoodinstitute.org/uploads/publications/257.pdf.

Doucet, A. (2009). 'Gender Equality and Gender Differences: Parenting, Habitus and Embodiment', 2008 Porter lecture, *Canadian Review of Sociology/Revue Canadienne de Sociologie*, Vol.46, No.2, pp.103–21.

Drew, E., Humphreys, P. and Murphy, C. (2003). *Off the Treadmill: Achieving Work-life Balance*, Dublin: Department of Enterprise, Trade and Employment, National Framework Committee for Work-Life Balance Policies.

Dykstra, P. and Keizer, R. (2009). 'The Well-being of Childless Men and Fathers in Mid-life', *Ageing and Society*, Vol.29, No.8, p.1227.

Eurobarometer (2004). *European's Attitudes to Parental Leave*, Brussels: EU Directorate of General Employment and Social Affairs.

Feldman, R., Sussman, A. and Zigler, E. (2004). 'Parental Leave and Work Adaptation at the Transition to Parenthood: Individual, Marital and Social Correlates', *Journal of Applied Developmental Psychology*, Vol.25, No.4, pp.459-79.

Ferguson, H. (2001). 'Men and Masculinities in Late-modern Ireland' in Pease, B. and Pringle, K. (eds.), *A Man's World? Changing Men's Practices in a Globalised World*, London: Zed Books.

Ferguson, H. and Hogan, F. (2004). *Strengthening Families through Fathers: Developing Policy and Practice in relation to Vulnerable Fathers and Their Families*, Waterford: Waterford Institute of Technology Centre for Social and Family Research.

Fine-Davis, M. and Clark, H. (2002). 'Ireland and Cross-National Comparisons' in Fine-Davis, M., Fagnani, J., Giovannini, D., Højgard, L. and Clarke, H. (eds.), *Fathers and Mothers: Dilemmas of the Work-life Balance: A Comparative Study in Four European Countries*, Dordrecht: Kluwer Publishers.

Fisher, D. (2007). *Including New Fathers: A Guide for Maternity Professionals*, Abergavenny: The Fatherhood Institute, retrieved from www.fatherhoodinstitute.org/uploads/publications/246.pdf.

Francis, M. (2007). 'A Flight from Commitment? Domesticity, Adventure and the Masculine Imaginary in Britain after the Second World War', *Gender & History*, Vol.19, No.1, pp.163-85.

Gershuny, J., Godwin, M. and Jones, S. (1994). 'The Domestic Labour Revolution: A Process of Lagged Adaptation?' in Anderson, M., Bechhofer, F. and Gershuny, J. (eds.), *The Social and Political Economy of the Household*, Oxford: Oxford University Press.

Gerson, K. (2004). 'Understanding Work and Family through a Gender Lens', *Community, Work & Family*, Vol.7, No.2, pp.163-78.

Government of Ireland (2013). *Rights of Grandparents Bill*, Dublin: Government Publications.

Government of South Australia (2010). *Fatherhood Engagement Research Project Report 2009-2010*, available at www.decd.sa.gov.au/docs/documents/1/FatherhoodEngagementRepor.pdf.

Greene, M.E. and Biddlecom, A.E. (2000). 'Absent and Problematic Men: Demographic Accounts of Male Reproductive Roles', *Population and Development Review*, Vol.26, No.1, pp.81-115.

Hadley, R. (2009). *Navigating in an Uncharted World: How Does the Desire for Fatherhood Affect Men?*, unpublished MSc thesis, University of Manchester.

Halpenny, A.M., Nixon, E. and Watson, D. (2010). *Parents' Perspectives on Parenting Styles and Disciplining Children*, Dublin: Office of the Minister for Children and Youth Affairs.

Hays, S. (1996). *The Cultural Contradictions of Motherhood*, New Haven, CT: Yale University Press.

Hearn, J., Pringle, K., Müller, U., Oleksy, E., Lattu, E., Tallberg, T. and Olsvik, E. (2002). 'Critical Studies on Men in Ten European Countries (3) The State of Law and Policy', *Men and Masculinities*, Vol.5, No.2, pp.192-217.

Hobson, B. (2002). *Making Men into Fathers: Men, Masculinities and the Social Politics of Fatherhood*, Cambridge: Cambridge University Press.

Holter, O.G. (2003). *Can Men Do It? Men and Gender Equality – The Nordic Experience*, TemaNord series, Kobenhavn: Nordic Council of Ministers.

Hyde, A., Carney, M., Drennan, J., Butler, M., Lohan, M. and Howlett, E. (2010). 'The Silent Treatment: Parents' Narratives of Sexuality Education with Young People', *Culture, Health & Sexuality*, Vol.12, No.4, pp.359-71.

International Business Times (2014). 'Father's Day 2014: Celebrity Dads from Brad Pitt to David Beckham share their thoughts on fatherhood', 13 June.

Irish Examiner (2014). 'One in ten liable parents in maintenance cases can't be traced', 13 March.

Irish Independent (2014). 'One in five women still childless in their 40s', 25 April.

Jordan, P. (1990). 'Laboring for Relevance: Expectant and New Fatherhood', *Nursing Research*, Vol.9, No.1, pp.11-16.

Kaila-Behm, A. and Vehviläinen-Julkunen, K. (2000). 'Ways of Being a Father: How First-time Fathers and Public Health Nurses Perceive Men as Fathers', *International Journal of Nursing*, Vol.37, No.3, pp.199-205.

Kennedy, F. (2001). *Cottage to Crèche: Family Change in Ireland*, Dublin: Institute of Public Administration.

Kivett, V.R. (1985). 'Grandfathers and Grandchildren: Patterns of Association, Helping and Psychological Closeness', *Family Relations*, Vol.34, No.3, pp.565-71.

Lamb, M.E. and Lewis, C. (2004). 'The Development and Significance of Father-child Relationships in Two-parent Families' in Lamb, M.E. (ed.), *The Role of the Father in Child Development*, Hoboken, NJ: Wiley.

Lee, E., Macvarish, J. and Bristow, J. (2010). 'Editorial: Risk, Health and Parenting Culture', *Health, Risk and Society*, Vol.12, No.4, pp.293-300.

Lee, K. (2008). *Fragmenting Fatherhoods? Fathers, Fathering and Family Diversity*, unpublished PhD thesis, London: City University

Locock, L. and Alexander, J. (2006). 'Just a Bystander'? Men's Place in the Process of Fetal Screening and Diagnosis', *Social Science & Medicine*, Vol.62, No.6, pp.1349-59.

Lohan, M., Aventin, A., McGuire, L., Clarke, M., Linden, M. and McDaid, L. (2014 in press). 'Feasibility Trial of a Film-based Educational Intervention for Increasing Boys' and Girls' Intentions to Avoid Teenage Pregnancy: Study Protocol', *International Journal of Educational Research*.

Lohan, M., Cruise, S., O'Halloran, P., Alderdice, F. and Hyde, A. (2010). 'Adolescent Men's Attitudes in relation to Pregnancy and Pregnancy Outcomes: A Systematic Review of the Literature from 1980–2009', *Journal of Adolescent Health*, Vol.47, No.4, pp.327-45.

Lohan, M., Cruise, S., O'Halloran, P., Alderdice, F. and Hyde, A. (2011). 'Adolescent Men's Attitudes and Decision-making in relation to an Unplanned Pregnancy: Responses to an Interactive Video Drama', *Social Science & Medicine*, Vol.72, No.9, pp.1507-14.

Marsiglio, W., Lohan, M. and Culley, L. (2013). 'Framing Men's Experience in the Procreative Realm', *Journal of Family Issues*, Vol.34, No.8, pp.1011.

McGinnity, F., Russell, H., Williams, J. and Blackwell, S. (2005). *Time-use in Ireland 2005: Survey Report*, Dublin: Economic and Social Research Institute.

Miller, T. (2011). *Making Sense of Fatherhood: Gender, Caring and Work*, Cambridge: Cambridge University Press.

Minkler, M. and Fuller-Thomson, E. (1999). 'The Health of Grandparents Raising Grandchildren: Results of a National Study', *American Journal of Public Health*, Vol.89, No.9, pp.1384.

Murphy, C., Keilthy, P. and Caffery, L. (2008). *Lone Parents and Employment: What are the Real Issues?*, Dublin: OneFamily.

O'Brien, M. and Shemilt, I. (2003). *Working Fathers: Earning and Caring*, Manchester: Equal Opportunities Commission.

OECD (2011). *Doing Better for Families*, Paris: OECD Publishing.

Office of the Minister for Children and Youth Affairs (2011). *Post-Separation Parenting: A Study of Separation and Divorce Agreements made in the Family Law Circuit Courts of Ireland and Their Implications for Parent-child Contact and Family Lives*, Dublin: Department of Health and Children.

Oliffe, J.L., Bottorff, J.L., Johnson, J.L., Kelly, M.T. and LeBeau, K. (2010). 'Fathers: Locating Smoking and Masculinity in the Postpartum', *Qualitative Health Research*, Vol.20, No.3, pp.330-39.

Plantin, L., Olukoya, A.A. and Ny, P. (2011). 'Positive Health Outcomes of Fathers' Involvement in Pregnancy and Childbirth Paternal Support: A Scope Study Literature Review', *Fathering: A Journal of Theory, Research, and Practice about Men as Fathers*, Vol.9, No.1, pp.87-102.

Pleck, J.H. and Masciadrelli, B.P. (2004). 'Paternal Involvement by US Residential Fathers: Levels, Sources and Consequences' in Lamb, M.E. (ed.), *The Role of the Father in Child Development*, fourth edition, Hoboken, NJ: John Wiley & Sons.

Quinton, D., Pollock, S. and Golding, J. (2002). *Report to the ERSC: The Transition to Fatherhood in Young Men*, Bristol: University of Bristol.

Ringbäck Weitoft, G., Burström, B. and Rosén, M. (2004). 'Premature Mortality among Lone Fathers and Childless Men', *Social Science & Medicine*, Vol.59, No.7, pp.1449-59.

Rush, M. (2009). *The Two Worlds of Father Politics in the Republic of Ireland: The Scandinavian Model or the United States Model?*, UCD School of Applied Social Science Working Paper Series, Dublin: University College Dublin.

Sayer, L.C., Bianchi, S.M. and Robinson, J.P. (2004). 'Are Parents Investing Less in Children? Trends in Mothers' and Fathers' Time with Children', *American Journal of Sociology*, Vol.110, No.1, pp.1-43. doi:10.1086/386270

Shirani, F., Henwood, K. and Coltart, C. (2012). 'Meeting the Challenges of Intensive Parenting Culture: Gender, Risk Management and the Moral Parent', *Sociology*, Vol,46, No.1, pp.25-40. doi:10.1177/0038038511416169

Sneddon, H. (2014). *Report: Fathers, Separation and Co-Parenting*, Belfast: Workers Educational Association.

Tanaka, K. and Johnson, N.E. (2014). 'Childlessness and Mental Well-being in a Global Context', *Journal of Family Issues*, (March). doi:10.1177/0192513X14526393

Wilson, K. and Prior, M. (2010). 'Father Involvement: The Importance of Paternal Solo Care', *Early Child Development and Care*, Vol.180, No.10, pp.1391-1405.

14: Working on Parenting

Edel Lawlor

My Personal Journey into Parenting Support Work

Travelling back from holiday recently, I boarded an aeroplane with my children. An hour into the flight, the adults in the family in front me continued to drink and, in their minds, get into the holiday mode. The family were a mixture of grandparents, parents and children. I could not help but notice the different experiences of children. While I settled my little girl and made sure she was comfortable and could sleep with my arms wrapped around her, I met with the eyes of a child of similar age; she watched me and smiled. The little girl, dressed in a little summer dress, all ready for her family holiday, tried to get comfortable to sleep. She eventually laid her head on the hard steel handrest and fell asleep.

Sometimes, we can see something and it stays in our minds like an imprint. When invited to contribute to a chapter in this book about parenting, this is the first thing that springs to mind, this image and the stark differences in parenting and child well being. The question what makes one parent aware of the child's comfort and security while another remains disconnected to the child's needs and world.

I have worked with children and parents for many years now. Understanding the differences in parenting approaches has been central to my understanding of how the experiences of parents during their own childhood impacts so dramatically upon their understanding of their role as a parent and their understanding of childhood. My own experience of motherhood has enabled me to really connect with other parents because I can empathise and understand the struggles of parenting. Every parent has dark days. I often say to parents the perfect parent is the dangerous parent and all you need to be is good enough.

My journey began while I was working with children in a women's refuge. The experiences of the children I was privileged to work with shaped my understanding of children and gave me the passion to pursue a career in play therapy. My profession is play therapy; I also have a degree in social care, sand tray therapy and therapeutic art and I find the combination of these fields has given me excellent insight into the dynamics that affect both children and parents. I believe that therapy is an essential tool for healing and development for adults and children alike and that, as a professional, understanding the dynamics between the psychological and social aspects of people's lives is a valuable resource when working with families.

During my journey in the refuge, I was granted the knowledge and understandings of the effects of domestic violence on children. Through play, children expressed the circumstances they had witnessed and were able to explore in a safe environment what had happened. I also witnessed how parents would try to hide their worries and upset from children and how this disempowered children or left them confused. For example, I remember one child asking his mother if she was crying and she replied that she was fine and was not crying. This answer created doubt in the child's mind and taught him/her that they also should not cry or express their feelings. The experience of domestic violence is frightening for children and I noticed how play was very beneficial and therapeutic. However, because children are hypersensitive and alert during periods in the refuge, healing can occur when children are safe and free from witnessing domestic violence. As suggested by Sullivan and Bybee (1999), it can be difficult to cope with the behaviour of children who have witnessed or lived with domestic violence.

Working with children in the refuge raised my own awareness that parents needed support around their daily struggles, so that they were more capable of supporting their child through difficult times. To do this requires honesty and truth because, when a child tries to understand what is happening in the absence of truth, they can imagine the situation to be different than it really is and suffer more. Taking the above example, if the mother had responded with age-appropriate honesty, the child would have been able to process the mother's sadness and his world would have been more real and true. The parent responds to the child believing that this is the best approach, to try and hide and cover up what the child is actually part of. There was a golden opportunity for this parent to express their feelings and let the child know that she is an adult and can manage her sadness, which teaches the child that it is OK to express their feelings and that they do not have to become the caregiver. Despite the confusion that it causes children in their own cognitive processing of the violence, it is common for a mother to try to hide the difficulty. As stated by Radford and Hestor:

> Shielding children from the abuse by trying to manage the abuser's behaviour, or preventing the children from witnessing or overhearing the violence, were strategies women very commonly used (2006, p.42).

I have seen extremes where young children try to become the parent themselves and forget their own needs in order to become the family caretaker. I have also seen cases where children miss their fathers or feel extreme anger towards their fathers but are unable to express their feelings through fear of upsetting mum. While I worked with women and children affected by domestic violence, I wish to acknowledge that men also may be victims of abuse. It was when I made these connections that I personally realised that there is so much work to be done with parents to enhance the well-being of children. Abrahams (1994) found that the experience of domestic violence created an emotional distance between the mother and her child. As such, the basics of connecting and re-establishing bonds became part of my work.

Key to the work with the children was nurturing. At very stressful times, parents can be distracted and find it difficult to nurture children and this nurturance became part of my practice because I began to realise the fundamental need for it. The importance of nurturing was to connect with the children's core selves and value them. I designed small programmes and implemented them as sessions with the children. These later became techniques and skills shared with parents to help them strengthen or re-establish attachment relationships.

I began studying and engaged in further training to look at ways to benefit and enhance coping skills for children. Research tells us that using play to build on imagination increases coping skills:

> … the value of pretending and of make-believe play seems less obvious … indeed, many parents are uncomfortable when they watch toddlers and preschoolers pushing blocks and toy figures around while talking to themselves … play is not just a feature of growth *en route* to the emergence of logical, orderly thought. Rather it is an intrinsically adaptive feature of our human condition … we can sustain ourselves in periods of stress with the hope generated by imagined explorations (Singer *et al*, 1994, p.7).

Building on my training as a play therapist, I broadened out my knowledge base to train in parenting support and theraplay, which look at parents becoming aware of their own and the child's needs and can involve regression whereby the attachment relationship can be strengthened. I use these techniques to help parents connect with their child and to allow a child space to receive nurturance. In play, children can sometimes regress and act out infancy, they may want to be rocked and fed and held; this is a child searching to fulfil a need that may not have been met in infancy: 'theraplay treatment involves replicating as much as possible the pleasurable interactions that are an essential part of the healthy parent-infant relationship' (Jernberg and Booth, 2001, p.7).

Research tells us that, during the stages of attachment between parent and child, the infant relies wholly upon the caregiver for survival (Prior and Glaser, 2006). Nurturance and safety are highly significant to the development of healthy and secure attachments. It is possible to meet the physical needs of a child without establishing bonds through nurturance and security but unfortunately this hinders healthy psychological development (Cozolino, 2006). When children have experienced difficulties, it is possible to re-connect with an earlier time to re-establish secure attachment through regression techniques and thereby reconnect with a caring individual to prevent future difficulties.

For children who have experienced domestic violence, nurturance and self-esteem are particularly relevant. Nurturance and self-esteem are at risk in poor attachment relationship, but also when healthy attachment is affected by an increase in stress caused by abusive relationships and life events (Radford and Hestor, 2006). This illustrates how the combination of understanding both the parent's psychological capacity and how outside factors can affect the parent is important.

I carried on working with children and became driven to help as many children as I could. This was the beginning of another academic journey. I was drawn to specialise in the psychoanalytical models of play therapy and how the unconscious processes of the mind can impact upon the child without their being aware of these processes. So when working therapeutically with children, these unconscious or contained traumatic experiences were allowed to come to light; the child could then face the reality of their difficulty face on, which allowed for healing and moving on from difficulties instead of having their lives shadowed by trauma (Axline, 1964). Moving on from working at the refuge, I opened my own play therapy practice.

The need for such a service was apparent and I wanted to help children from all walks of life. I had seen the benefits of the work with children coming from a background in domestic violence and felt these benefits were valid for all children. Children visit the therapy centre for various reasons such as bereavement, trauma, attachment difficulties, behavioural difficulties, shyness, self-esteem, bullying and aggression to name a few.

Unfortunately, at times things happen that are beyond the control of families and, for this reason, children can need additional supports. Unlike adults, whose natural form of communication is talking, children's natural form of communication is play (Axline, 1947). I had a vision of creating a service where all children could be facilitated and supported. From my individual work with children, I began to put together workshops that could be delivered to groups of children, both boys and girls. I still use the programmes and deliver them at my practice and to schools and other agencies. The ethos of these workshops is to enhance children's self-esteem and reinforce the value of play and imagination.

Parenting Support

Many people forget to look at parental difficulties when they are supporting children presenting with difficulties. However, parental support is highly significant to this process as children need parents to help them to regulate their emotions. When parents are stressed, they may find it difficult to support their child. For parenting support workers, this is something that is fundamental to the work. At times, it is the professional's role to regulate the parent's emotions so that they can then learn to help regulate the child's emotions. Because of this, a parent support worker needs to be fully aware of themselves and their part in this process. In other words, they can do more damage if they are inexperienced or unaware of their own issues. For example, if a parent support worker reacts when a parent discloses information, it is likely to cause more anxiety to the parent because they can be highly sensitive to the support worker's response.

For the parent support worker, not having personal self-awareness may cause them, as a professional, to feel out of their depth while working with parents and this will cause both parent and professional to feel uncomfortable in the relationship. In my experience, parent support workers should have at least two years' supported practical training experience so that they see the person holistically as opposed to just the theoretical framework. As a professional, they also should be committed to personal development and therapy to develop their self-awareness. For parenting support to work, one needs to have the ability to form relationships with parents. Based upon the work of Carl Rogers, there are certain traits that enable the development of therapeutic relationships. Traits such as empathy, unconditional positive regard, genuineness and warmth create circumstances where trust can be built up and then change can occur:

> If I can provide a certain type of relationship, the other person will discover within himself the capacity to use that relationship for growth, and change and personal development will occur (Rogers, 1967, p.33).

Parents also can be dismissive of a support worker who may not have first-hand experience of parenting. This can undermine the support worker, who can be left feeling helpless and doubt themselves in their ability to support the family. This has been evident in my work training professionals to support parents and understand their parental struggles. I believe this is an area that needs further research and practice tools to help the support worker manage such circumstances.

I have worked with many parents and worked as a parent support worker in a resource centre alongside my own practice. I realised that parents sometimes needed the same support as the children I worked with. Parents also can be significantly affected if they have experienced trauma, attachment difficulties or if circumstances have an impact on their capacity to parent. As with children, parents needed an opportunity to express themselves and I found some of the techniques used in play therapy also were therapeutic for parents and could be applied to this work. The significant advantage in working with parents is the knock-on effect for children. When parents have been given the space and opportunity to express themselves through talking or creativity, they begin to understand how healing and beneficial it has been for them and take on board the knowledge and techniques involved to use with their children.

Durham (2006) proposes that communication is the foundation of successful work with both children and adults, fostering the use of imagination as a tool for self-discovery. In doing so, it is possible to open a pattern of communication that is supportive and empowering. Promoting positive and aware parenting has become a natural part of my work with families. When children come in to my centre for play therapy, I work with the parents first. I do this to gain the optimal picture of the family's life but also to give parents a space to work on their own struggles and challenges. This helps the parent to support their child while they are in the therapy process. It also provides the parent with support and guidance in relation to their own behaviour and how they express themselves.

From my practice, I began to notice how parenting struggles were widespread and could be generalised. Although parenting needs could be varied, fundamental themes such as guilt, anxiety, trauma and emotional and behavioural difficulties were becoming apparent. I have also worked with various professionals who are reluctant to look for support as they feel they should be capable and coping because they are teachers, social workers doctors, etc. For parents involved in professions such as medicine, education, social care and community services to name a few, seeking support can be highly shameful, as perceived by the individual. There is a general lack of acceptance that, for whatever reason, parents need support and this requirement is not unique to targeted groups. Gaining this insight into the needs of parents spurred me on to develop my own parenting workshop, Creative Parenting.

I noticed how many parents were connecting with the service for parenting support and began to realise that there was a demand for support. The residual nature of social policy means that parenting support is targeted and many parents do not fit into the remit to receive these targeted supports, despite requiring support. Other parents are reluctant to engage with the targeted services because they are regarded as highly stigmatising (Kavanagh, 2014).

It was my aim to develop a programme that provided a natural and unthreatening space for parents to come together and receive support and information. I also wanted to intertwine this programme with some of the therapeutic techniques that I use with children and in one-to-one parenting support sessions. In this respect, my parenting programme is unique. The Creative Parenting workshop has been received well by parents and, on evaluation, parents felt it was of significant benefit to them in relation to both their own feelings of self-worth and also empowering them to view things from their child's point of view.

Parenting Struggles

Parental behaviour often can influence children's behaviour. Research shows us how children mirror their parent's behaviour (Friedman, 1985). In light of this, parents are gently guided to see how their responses to their child can have an impact on the dynamics that are causing difficulties. When parents are shown the skills to combat or adapt their own behaviour, often the child's behaviour will follow and problems can be dealt with (Kumpfer and Alder, 2006). Through the use of experiential learning and role play, the parent is encouraged to enter the child's world and to view things as a child would. This often can be a very powerful experience for parents and can empower them to begin a journey to heal their own childhood difficulties, which may be holding them back in their parenting (Friedman, 1985).

In practice, when this is highlighted, there can be a sense of relief for parents as they realise that they can change their behaviour to support their child. There is often a 'light bulb moment' for parents in realising this fact.

Sometimes, parents do not like parenting and this is something I refer to as the 'dark days' of parenting. Although it can be common for this to happen, the parent may feel very ashamed of it, especially in a society where perfect parenting is accentuated through the media. This is compounded also by a sense that it is also shameful to look for support (Kavanagh, 2014). Through my work, I often come across this difficulty and have become aware of how society is not parent-friendly or realistic and this can cause feelings of failure for parents. To combat this, I look at the parents' strengths and encourage parents to carry on doing what is productive. Following on from this, I will try to suggest different ways of doing things that will enhance positive parenting and also may point out to parents skills that they could use with their child. This process is illustrated by the following example.

During a session with one parent and her child, there was a difficulty with attachment. I noticed how the child made simple non-verbal cues to the mother to connect physically and how the mother was oblivious to the child's cues. I pointed out to the mother basic child cues for connecting, such as the child laying their head on the mother's lap. Instead of correcting the child and sitting them upright, I showed the mother how the child was looking for connection and how to notice these cues and how to engage and connect. For instance, when the child put her head down, the child was looking for the mother to connect and it was a golden opportunity for the mother to nurture the child. By not connecting to the child, the mother was causing frustration for the child, which would result in behavioural patterns that would engage the mother but these were always negative exchanges. By showing the mother what had been missed, she was then more in tune to these cues and later found it easier to connect with the child through play. This simple example shows how subtle parenting support can be and how through giving parents knowledge and skills the child-parent relationship can be significantly enhanced.

There are many struggles in parenting and the dark days of parenting are one example that can be especially challenging for parents. Having someone they can talk to openly about this is very comforting and knowing that they are not alone in their feelings can really help parents. Other struggles can include sibling rivalry, crying, food, bedtime, homework, friendships, defiance, anger, tantrums and so on. The commonality in these struggles is conflict and unfortunately these become battles that both parent and child engage in. The bigger the problem is to the parent, the more frustration it will cause them and this will be transferred to the child. This means that the child will continue to respond to the parental stress because the parent is losing control and the child will follow suit. Circumstances such as these become a pattern and 'conflict rituals' in daily lives of families. As a parent support worker, it is important to understand that the majority of parents are doing a great job and need to be gently guided sometimes to form an understanding of why and how to adjust their own behaviour before they will be able to solve issues.

Working with parents and identifying things that could enable them to solve issues with their own behaviour can be very difficult because it has to be delivered to them in a way that does not blame them or cause guilt and shame. In this respect, parent support workers need to be creative in their approach and also very sensitive in how they communicate with parents.

Parental Anxiety and Guilt

Shyness and low self-esteem can worry many parents. In circumstances where a child witnesses a parent being unable to assert themselves or avoid situations where they feel uncomfortable, a child sometimes will learn these patterns of behaviour too. The role of the parent support worker here might be to work with the parent to encourage positive self-esteem and self-care so that the parent can pass along these skills to their child. When working with parents, we also need to be very aware and capable of referring them onto appropriate services such as mental health and social services. I have often found that, when working with children who are attending therapy, if their parents are also in therapy or receiving support from other agencies, this can be extremely beneficial for the whole family. Parents and professionals can spend a lot of time and resources in helping children and trying to change children's behaviour but, in my opinion, there are many times when the whole family needs to be helped as a whole and a 'support scaffolding' created around them.

It is important to acknowledge the role of guilt in the parent psyche, especially in relation to support work. What can really help to alleviate feelings of guilt is having acceptance and not feeling isolated. A good example of this comes from a recent research study investigating my work (Kavanagh, 2014). In this research, an observation was made about parents and guilt. The observation found that anxiety around parenting and worries about anything happening to children were universal among the group, yet manifested in several different ways. The diversity of issues parents experience include illness, bullying, road traffic accidents, choking and child care facilities. Despite the variations in these issues, the common thread for parents was that the levels of stress, anxiety and guilt were unanimous and experienced by all parents present.

When discussing such fears during a Creative Parenting workshop, I often will discuss guilt with parents and guide them to understand how feelings of guilt also can be a manifestation of their fears and a sense of not being good enough. Providing parents with a space to discuss their fears and guilt can be very therapeutic because parents may feel very ashamed of their feelings, which feeds into their guilt. It is important to try to help parents acknowledge their guilt and how it can affect their parenting. I do this by using therapeutic techniques with parents, by naming their fears and guilt and asking them to pick a symbol for it or to draw a picture. Other mediums that can be used to acknowledge guilt are through clay, art and sand tray work, which can help parents move on.

Guilt and anxiety are very significant for parents and often are compounded by the media. In this respect, parents may need reassurance and techniques to enable them to deal with their anxiety in order to de-escalate such emotions and to avoid transferring them to their child. When this anxiety is transferred to the child, it reduces their capacity for normal functioning as illustrated by the following example.

I have worked with children showing signs of obsessive compulsive disorder and have noticed that the behaviours are mirrored in the parent. In one particular case, a little girl had rubbed away the skin on her hands to get rid of germs and dirt. This meant that the child was constantly concerned about touching anything in the therapy room and the severity of the anxiety was quite overwhelming. In this case, the family had to rework a new pattern of behaviour for everyone in the family into their household and had to be referred to mental health services. The child continued play therapy alongside a multidisciplinary engagement with the mental health service. This approach is referred to as support scaffolding.

Difficulties such as anxiety manifest in different ways and the above example shows how the need for cleanliness and eradication of germs has caused detrimental effects for one family. Unfortunately, this is not unique, and to a degree has been exacerbated by messages in advertising and media. Suicide, child abduction and violence are other examples of a group of parental fears that are more and more evident in my practice.

In my work, I try to foster a sense of being 'good enough' (Winnicott, 1953), for parents who for one reason or another suffer guilt that becomes manifested in anxiety. In this way, I concentrate on what they have done well and try to reassure parents that they are doing a good job. This is known as the strengths perspective (Canavan *et al*, 2000). For parents whose anxiety and fears have impacted more severely on the child, work has to be done first with the parent before therapy can begin with the child. This is due to the fact that children will revert to old patterns if the underlying problem has not been dealt with.

Parenting Diversity

Parenting struggles are common and, for some parents, there are additional challenges. Those studying the fields of social care, psychology, child care and many other courses will be somewhat familiar with some of the challenges faced by parents and children when there is a learning difficulty, autism, disability or medical difficulty. As a professional, I have journeyed with many parents and children where, alongside the daily challenges, they are faced with further difficulties. Such difficulties can make parenting much more challenging, especially when there is a lack of understanding or awareness generally within our society. As this chapter will reach individuals learning about parenting, I would like to name issues such as selective mutism, gender identity, hyperlexia, foreign adoption and the many medical disorders I have encountered. My reason for doing so is to acknowledge that rare problems may not be easily identified and that practitioners should have an open and curious mind to ensure they really explore possibilities for families so that timely and appropriate support is sourced for families at the earliest opportunity.

A large number of children and parents I have worked with have experienced trauma in their lives. When we think of trauma, we think of one-off events such as fires or wars. However, trauma is far more common than this and often can co-exist with an underlying issue such as a rare medical condition.

Trauma

Trauma can affect the lives of many children and it is not uncommon for trauma to be present alongside other difficulties. Trauma is highly complex, and often can be mistaken for a different problem leading to misdiagnosis (Thomas and Johnson, 2005). Trauma has far-reaching psychological consequences and either can cause a behavioural difficulty or phobic and anxious responses. In this respect, trauma can be widespread for children and parents for a variety of reasons without being obvious or acknowledged. Brown *et al* suggest that children diagnosed with ADHD have higher exposure to trauma and that 'Providers may focus on ADHD as the primary diagnosis and overlook the possible presence of a trauma history which may impact treatment' (Brown *et al*, 2014).

Also, in some cases of foreign adoption, parents can be unaware of the possible trauma a child has experienced before adoption and this trauma can result in highly challenging circumstances for parenting and family well-being.

To illustrate the subtleties of trauma, consider the example of a foreign adoption. In my experience, the trauma children have been exposed to in their young lives is not initially obvious, but is played out in therapy through subconscious and sensory memory process. I use this example to provide students at my workshops with an insight into the possible reality of the work that they may encounter in their future careers.

Foreign Adoption

Recently, I have been seeing more cases of parenting difficulties around foreign adoption. In one such case, a child may have experienced extreme trauma and neglect during their infancy and this can cause problems for children during early and mid-childhood, in forming relationships with both adoptive parents and peers. In later childhood, these problems can be exasperated by puberty. The difficulty with foreign adoption is that the child's history can be clouded and the orphanages are not regulated by Irish standards or legislation. Therefore, I am concerned that orphanages may have fabricated the child's history and have not given a true representation of their role as caregiver during the initial attachment stage for fear of being criticised. Is it possible that a caregiver will be able to deliver optimum care for a number of small infants at one time and meet all the children's needs? In my work, fear and anxiety fostered by institutionalisation is apparent in children's behaviour and also triggered by their sensory memory. For instance, one child I worked with would stand very still but flap their arms trying to regulate their anxiety if a toy fell to the ground or there was a loud noise. This may have been a stress response to earlier experiences.

Children from foreign adoption cases may have missed out on simple early interaction in their infancy. In some cases, this means that they are unable to read facial expression and at times do not understand simple expressions like happiness and sadness. Their own facial expression can be blank and hard to read. This can be very challenging for adoptive parents and peers alike. For parents, they can find it hard to communicate with the child and often are perturbed by this phenomenon, which can unfortunately hinder the formation of attachment bonds between child and caregiver, further compounding the previous trauma for the child.

Parents can find these circumstances incredibly difficult, which is understandable because their expectations have been undermined. For parents, they feel like they are doing something good and that they will be providing a child with the opportunity to have a better life and also may have been longing to become a parent. When faced with a completely different reality, it is only natural that parents would be confused and disillusioned. Parent support workers should be aware of some of these unusual dynamics because the occurrence of such difficulties is increasing.

Working with parents and children is a privilege. I have been honoured to work in this professional area and to witness some of the most powerful transformations in the lives of families. I will endeavour to carry on working with parents and children to make a difference to the lives of families who are for their own reasons in need of support.

The Kilflynn Enchanted Fairy Festival Back to Basics

To conclude this chapter about working with parents and children, I wanted to acknowledge and celebrate the importance of childhood and memories. Recently, I came together with other businesses and the community members in the local village where my centre is located to put on a fairy festival. The Kilflynn fairy festival was an extension to the fairy workshops and camps that I have developed over the years. I wanted to use the techniques and ideas to create a day for families to reconnect to imagination and fun.

I am very fortunate as I have been given training and tutorage by many wonderful teachers. I have found that having a background in both psychotherapy and social care has really enabled me to see a bigger picture. The fairy festival was a simple idea, based on the fact that children are spending less time playing outside and using their imaginations. The festival became a real vehicle to foster social capital within the locality and a great example of the power and achievement that can be made when people come together. 'Social capital represents a major resource, which can play a key role in contributing to positive outcomes for children, their families and the communities in which they live' (O'Doherty, 2007, p.5).

The festival consisted of a parade where an ancient map would be released, plotting out the invisible houses of the fairies and elves. For one day only, the magical houses could be viewed as the fairies had decided to make their homes visible to all the children that believed. The local people pulled together and volunteers worked tirelessly for six weeks to make the festival come to life. From fairies, elves, knights and escaped wolves being chased across the countryside, to the peace in the meadow where magicians, percussionists and free activities were available to children, the whole village came to life to celebrate family life and bringing children back to the basics of adventuring and exploring the countryside with their families.

The beauty of the festival was also that there was no hard sell. The activities were free, so parents were not put under pressure to spend money. Families were invited to bring picnics and seating facilities were available. The volunteers on the day were all experienced in working with children and families, so there was a great atmosphere in the village. Volunteers had devised characters and stories and so were able to tell children stories about their characters and this added to the magic of the day. The success of the festival was due to the commitment and dedication of the members of the festival organising committee, the use of imagination, the happiest cows in Ireland and believing it would work.

It is my hope that the festival will be a success for many years to come. As with many of those simple ideas I have tried throughout the years, it can sometimes be the simplest idea that has the most profound effect on people's lives. Bringing things back to basics can produce real results and I am very grateful for being able to facilitate such events.

Looking at parent support and family well-being I am reminded of the Canadian redwood tree whereby 'Diversity is crucial to the redwood forest; every plant, tree, and even fallen logs, play a crucial role … These trees have shallow root systems that extend over 100 feet from the base, intertwining with the roots of other redwoods. This increases their stability during strong winds and floods' (www.parks.ca). As with a strong community, when a storm comes, they hold each other up. The trees are connected and support one another. When a new sapling grows, it simply connects to the roots of those trees beside it as it becomes one with the overall life force. I believe we can learn many lessons from the nature that surrounds us and I believe that, with the potential to join together and become a unified collective, we are capable of achieving support scaffolding around our parents naturally and when needed.

References

Abrahams, C. (1994). *The Hidden Victims – Children and Domestic Violence,* London: NCH Action for Children.

Axline, V. (1947). *Play Therapy,* New York: Ballantine Books.

Axline, V. (1964). *Dibs in Search of Self,* New York: Ballantine Books.

Brown, N., Brown, S., German, M., Belamarich, P. and Briggs, R. (2014). *Associations between Adverse Childhood Experiences and ADHD: Analysis of the 2011 National Survey of Children's Health,* New York: The Children's Hospital at Montefiore.

Canavan, J., Dolan, P. and Pinkerton, J. (2000). *Family Support: Direction from Diversity,* London: Jessica Kingsley Publishers.

Cozolino, L. (2006). *The Neuroscience of Human Relationships: Attachment and the Developing Social Brain,* New York and London: W. & W. Norton.

Durham, C. (2006). *Chasing Ideas: The Fun of Freeing your Child's Imagination,* London: Jessica Kingsley Publishers.

Friedman, E. (1985). *Generation to Generation: Family Processes in Church and Synagogue,* New York: The Guildford Press.

Jernberg, A. and Booth, P. (2001). *Theraplay: Helping Parents and Children Build Better Relationships through Attachment-based Play,* San Francisco: Jossey Bass.

Kavanagh, J. (ed.) (2014). *Advancing Creative Parenting: Advancing a New Model of Parenting Support Appropriate for The South West Region,* Tralee: Institute of Technology Tralee.

Kumpfer, K. and Alder, S. (2006). 'Dissemination of Research-based Family Interventions for the Prevention of Substance Abuse' in Sloboda, Z. and Bukoski, W.J. (eds.), *Handbook of Drug Abuse Prevention,* New York: Springer.

O'Doherty, C. (2007). *A New Agenda for Family Support: Providing Services that Create Social Capital,* Dublin: Blackhall Publishing.

Prior, V. and Glaser, D. (2006). *Understanding Attachment and Attachment Disorders: Theory, Evidence and Practice,* London: Jessica Kingsley Publishers.

Radford, L. and Hester, M. (2006). *Mothering through Domestic Violence,* London: Jessica Kingsley Publishers.

Rogers, C. (1967). *A Therapist's View of Psychotherapy: On Becoming A Person,* London: Constable and Robinson.

Singer, M., Anglin, T., Song, L. and Lunghofer, L. (1994). 'Adolescents' Exposure to Violence and Associated Symptoms of Psychological Trauma', *Journal of the Medical Association,* Vol.273, pp.477-82.

Sullivan, C. and Bybee, D. (1999). 'Reducing Violence Using Community-based Advocacy for Women with Abusive Partners', *Journal of Consulting and Clinical Psychology,* Vol.67, pp.43-53.

Thomas, B. and Johnson, P. (2005). *Empowering Children Through Art and Expression: Culturally Sensitive Ways of Healing Trauma and Grief,* London: Jessica Kingsley Publishers.

Winnicott, D.W. (1953). 'Clinical Varieties of Transference', *International Journal of Psycho-Analysis*, Vol.37, p.386.

15: Advancing Parenting – A New Perspective on Parenting Support

Jennifer Kavanagh

Introduction

This chapter is based on a research study that was undertaken to examine current parenting support provision and which identified flaws in current parenting support practice. During the research process, a model of best practice in parenting support was constructed, as a response to counteract the flaws that were identified in the research study.

This chapter will look at the definition of parenting, why parents need support, how the current system that is in place supports parents and will finish by presenting a new model of best practice that can be used to support parents in modern Irish society.

Defining Parenting

Traditionally, parenting is defined as 'the process of rearing a child until adulthood' (Wilson, 2000). Maslow expanded upon this by identifying the requirement for parents to fulfil the basic needs or requirements of the child – for instance, unconditional love, a safe home, nutrition, and nurture being the most basic needs (Maslow, 1943). Daniel *et al* (2011) add that parenting also is supporting a child to develop through key stages to hit the same developmental advancement as is considered to be in line with those of the average of their peer group.

However, in reality, the concept of parenting is so much more than this simple definition. At its best, parenting is the evolution and development of a relationship between an adult and a child (not necessarily a biological parent). Parenting is a journey concerning the care, positive reinforcement of behaviour and holistic development of a child by engaging in the parenting process. A parent responds to a comprehensive range of needs as a child moves through childhood and adolescence into adulthood (Daniel *et al*, 2011). A parent is taking part in the child's life journey and likewise the child takes part in the parent's journey: the experience of one directly affects the other.

> Parenting is fundamental to the survival and success of the human race. Everyone who has ever lived has had parents and most adults in the world become parents (Luster and Okagaki, 2005, p.*ix*).

Parenting is a complex web, weaving a multitude of determinants together that impact on one another and then upon an individual's capacity to parent. These are described by McKeown (2011) as 'direct' and 'indirect' causal determinants on the well-being of parents, which then indirectly impact upon the well-being of the child. Factors include cyclical parenting, psychological limitations on parental capacity and sociological structural limitations (such as poverty, work-life balance and lack of support) on parenting. The functions of both psychology and sociology have a compounding effect on one another and parenting across the spectrum of socio-economic status and have an impact on parenting capacity. The phenomenon of these intermingled factors is the ecological perspective:

> … the child's family and the environment in which they live influence one another in a constant process of reciprocal interaction. The ecological perspective links the well-being of parents and children to the characteristics of the environment that they inhabit (O'Doherty, 2013, p.279).

Parenting is something that affects everyone, whether we are parents ourselves or children. This means that our parenting and the capacity of our parents has far-reaching consequences for us all. What could be more important within modern Irish society? Yet, as a society, we belittle parenting and ignore its significance through policies that are not family-friendly. Parents and children are encouraged to compete with their peers to be the best. Parents and children are targeted above any other demographic profile by advertisers and dehumanised by our consumerist culture. Where can parents look for support to combat this rise in expectations to be perfect in modern Irish society?

Why Parents Need Support

Essentially, supporting parents is a fundamental approach used to protect the children in our society. I undertook a research study over a two year period (2012 to 2014), whereby I investigated and explored many dimensions of parenting and the complex factors that can impact upon parenting capacity.

The aim of the research was to provide a comprehensive knowledge of parenting theory and parental support programmes to the field. Through an analysis of programmes, the research followed on to construct a model of best practice in parenting support. Central to the research was the question of whether support for parents should remain a very residual and targeted response: for parents dealing with specific childhood behavioural challenges, for children who are seen as at risk or where child protection issues have been found. Put simply, can support for parents be a natural everyday value for all our parents and children? Is it possible that universal supports for parents can be facilitated as a natural early intervention that can prevent childhood behavioural problems from escalating and promote positive parenting and pro-social behaviour in general? Of course, it is acknowledged that not all challenges are totally preventable, but evidence has shown that parenting programmes have made significant progress in addressing challenges after they have escalated, so why not try using them as a preventative measure to improve the outcomes of all children?

The research objectives included:

1. To obtain a comprehensive knowledge of the topic, to include psychological and sociological theory.
2. To gain an understanding of the complexities involved in parenting and the risk and protective factors that the impact of good or weak parenting can have on the child.
3. To document this interwoven complex relationship and the impact it can have on parenting and children.
4. To gain knowledge and understanding of the parenting programmes available both nationally and internationally, why they have been created, which theories they use to inform their practice, have they be proven to be effective, how has this been measured and why?
5. To gain a comprehensive insight into the thoughts, beliefs, or attitudes of parents:
   i) What level of intensity of support is required by parents?
   ii) Would all parents like to have support available to them?
   iii) Where support is required are parents receiving adequate supports?

6. To gain a comprehensive insight into the thoughts, beliefs or attitude of professionals working to support parents.
   i) Is current provision adequate?
   ii) What are the gaps in the provision?
   iii) Should intervention remain targeted or become universal?
   iv) Do parenting programmes work and why?
   v) How can we move forward to get optimal effective outcomes for all families?
   vi) What is the best and most natural way of integrating parenting programmes universally?

A triangulation research methodology was used to gain the insights of both parents themselves and professionals working in the area and to ascertain whether participants held the same views across the board. As this was an iterative process, each method informed the next method sequentially. The research began using quantitative data collection in order to gain a broad sense of whether parents actually felt they required support and, if so, which topics or areas they felt support was necessary. The research then moved on to the stages of qualitative methodology. Parents were sourced and invited to participate through purposeful sampling and this enabled the researcher to gain a broad understanding of why and how parents felt they required support across socio-economic status. Lone parents, dual parents, high income parents, middle income parents, low income parents, parents in receipt of social welfare and parents with children with high level end needs were approached. Professionals working in the area of parenting support were then sourced and approached to find out whether they felt the current system was appropriate to support the needs of parents. The methods used in this research study were:

- Questionnaire;
- Participant observation of parenting programmes;
- Semi-structured interviews with five parents and nine professionals;
- Two focus group enquiries.

The results of the research study suggested that targeted parenting support has become obsolete and indicates that all parents and children should be entitled to the same supports regardless of socio-economic status. The research highlights the reality that parenting struggles are not unique to targeted groups. The absence of generic provision creates difficulties for parents who are not designated as disadvantaged. Parenting support should become a natural and valued daily activity, focusing on self-care and positivity in relationships, alongside a new universal gateway model of parenting support that will be described in detail in the following text. The research also addressed the development of a new universal system of support for all children within the educational environment. A culture of valuing childhood and parenting needs to be encouraged so that parenting is supported, and a higher functioning society can be created. As shown in **Figure 15.1**, when society gets behind parents, in improving circumstances for parents and children, individuals feedback in to a more positive society.

Figure 15.1: The Integrated Cycle of Valuing Parenting

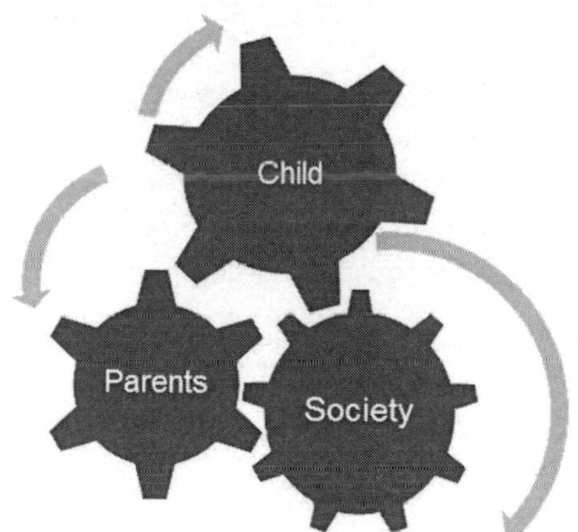

Source: Kavanagh (2014).

In this research, it is suggested that advancing the position of parenting within modern Irish society is possible using a new gateway model of parenting support that will make changes to the current system and improve outcomes for more families. How this gateway can be established will be dealt with later in the chapter. However, first I would like to identify and explain why parents require support, then I will discuss how the current system works, followed by how this system could be improved using the new gateway model of parenting support.

The Ecological Perspective on Parenting

Parents require support for a multitude of reasons. These can be defined as psychological and social factors that affect parenting capacity. By observing these factors independently, it is then possible to begin to piece these factors together and understand how factors converge. The consideration of these factors and how they are intertwined is referred to as the ecological perspective.

The psychological capacity of an individual parent may affect the future well-being of the child. This psychological capacity may be affected by:

- Parents' attachment style – which will have been shaped by their own experience of being parented;
- Social learning – how individuals have learned to behave through role modelling parental behaviours. Social learning also explains how tolerance of certain stimuli such as violence and addiction patterns can become normalised;
- Parenting style – which also will impact upon the child's understanding of morals – in other words, whether they learn to behave pro-socially due to an understanding of how their behaviour affects others (internalisation) or whether the behaviour is directed to avoiding punishment (externalisation).

Social factors can also influence the individual's life course. Social factors include:

- Social support;
- Poverty;
- Neighbourhoods;
- Lack of social capital;
- Family composition;
- Education;
- Exposure to violence and crime.

Depending upon the combination of both individual psychological capacity to parent and the social factors that affect the child's environment, these can lead to either resilience or vulnerability.

Risk and Protective Factors

Daniel *et al* (2011) have developed the resilience matrix shown in **Figure 15.2 to** illustrate how the dynamics of attachment style and other factors interrelate and how risk factors (adversity) and protective factors counteract each other. Secure attachment is a key protective factor that leads to resilience; insecure attachment is a risk factor that can lead to vulnerability.

Figure 15.2: The Resilience Matrix

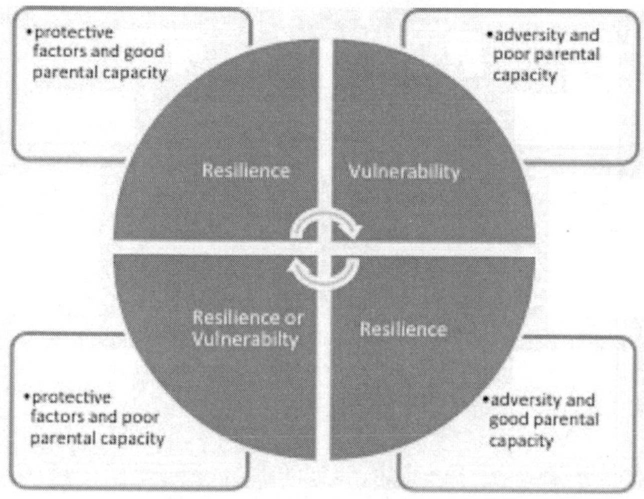

Source: Daniel *et al* (2011).

Daniel *et al* (2011) argue that a child living with positive attachment and experience of positive parenting in a neighbourhood experiencing poverty has the protective factor of good parenting and strong attachments and, as a result, the child is likely to be resilient and resilience leads to better outcomes. Conversely, a child living in poverty with parents with poor mental and or physical health, living in a disadvantaged environment is likely to fair less well, have less resilience and poor attachments. The outcomes for this second child are likely to be adverse (Daniel *et al*, 2011).

Table 15.1: Risk Factors

Type of risk	Actual risks
Family	Parental attitudes, family dysfunction and low social capital.
Educational	Poor academic attainment and early school leaving.
Psychological	Low self-esteem, poor bonding, neuroticism and impulsivity and behavioural problems (conduct disorder).
Attitudinal	Tolerance for deviance and norms of behaviour.
Behavioural	Lack of law abidance and deviant behaviour.
Emotional	Need for excitement and sensation-seeking.
Psychopathological	Stress, anxiety and depression.

Source: Canavan *et al* (2000, p.155).

Canavan *et al* (2000) identify risk factors by the type of risk and actual risk – for example, social structure is the type of risk, and the actual risk is low socio-economic status and disadvantaged neighbourhoods.

Risk factors co-exist with one another. Protective factors have to compete against such risks. Protective factors can be seen as direct opposites to the risk factors. For example, good parental attitude to education and positive encouragement towards achievement can combat educational risk. Moreover, good parental attitudes towards education also might combat psychological, emotional and behavioural risks. Other protective factors include positive attachment relationships to parents, good relationships with extended family, social support networks and social capital with the community, such as family support centres and community development projects.

THE DEVELOPMENT OF FAMILY AND PARENTING SUPPORT

Family support structures have been introduced incrementally in Ireland, recognising that the family is the best place for a child to grow up (Department of Children and Youth Affairs, 2004). The thinking behind family support is to increase protective factors and to minimise risk factors.

O'Doherty (2007) suggests that different types of family support can be beneficial for parents and children. These include formal, semi-formal and informal support.

Formal support is likely to be targeted and based on practical support: child care issues for instance, involvement with family support workers and parenting programmes.

Semi-formal support is a broad and universal categorisation. Typically, this can involve support that is low key and non-specific – for example, parents having somewhere they can go and talk to other parents and network within their community.

Informal support can be manifested as universal pursuits available to parents and children within their community, which, in turn, gives them a sense of value in themselves, such as GAA clubs and other sports communities.

> ... family well-being is promoted when the relationships between families and wider society is characterised by respect for the family as an asset ... all families benefit from being supported and esteemed by their immediate community and wider society ... family well-being is influenced by the interplay between children's

> developmental needs, parenting capacity and wider family and environmental factors. (O'Doherty, 2012, p.20)

A key source of formal support, suggested by Canavan *et al* (2000), is 'the importance of school'. Webster-Stratton (1984, 1989) and Webster-Stratton *et al* (2008) recognised the importance of school in the design of the Incredible Years Programme. In this programme, the focus is on home-school partnership in order to prevent and treat child behavioural problems and to reduce the risk factors associated with the ecology of parenting.

A school-based programme can reach more children in need without the introduction of formal services and also can be instrumental in decreasing the level of stigma associated with seeking help. A school-based programme also may facilitate a positive school experience, creating both a secure base and arena of comfort (Canavan *et al*, 2000). A further benefit is that a school-based programme can potentially break the links between risk factors by creating a turning point for the family as a developmental pathway (Webster-Stratton *et al*, 2001).

Dimensions of Parenting Support

This next section looks at how parents are supported and how programmes have been developed to facilitate and promote positive parenting practices.

Szapocznik, cited in Kumpfer and Alder (2006), found that there are four approaches across levels of intervention that are effective in reducing behavioural and emotional problems for children:

- Behaviour parent training (parental cognitive behaviour training);
- Family skills training (parenting and child skills and practice);
- Family therapy (structural/behavioural/functional therapy);
- In-home family support.

The approach used by family support interventions is dependent upon the echelon or level of support required.

Supporting parents is not a simple matter. It is clear that child and family support must be balanced against a whole host of considerations – for instance, environment, individual circumstance and levels of family functioning. My research took the view that there are six realms of family support. These are set out in the following table and adapted from the typologies used by Hardiker *et al* (1991), Gilligan (1995) and Sanders *et al* (2000).

Table 15.2: Levels of Support

Level of support	Examples	Experts' terms
Level 1: Universal/General – available to all families	Pre-natal classes, schools, post-partum services, vaccinations, child benefit and Government-funded preschool places	Developmental – Gilligan (1995) Universal – Sanders *et al* (2000) Universal – Hardiker (1991)
Level 2: Entitled – available to disadvantaged groups	Family resource centres, Springboard, HSE-run parenting programmes, KDYS, Jigsaw, St John of God, Brothers of Charity, KES, Enable	Compensatory – Gilligan (1995) Selective – Sanders *et al* (2000) Support/Therapeutic – Hardiker (1991)
Level 3: Targeted – at construed societal concerns – behavioural or criminality problems that have developed for individuals and families	Strengthening Families programme, social services, parenting programmes, mentoring, Gardaí diversion, KDYS programmes, Springboard	Compensatory – Gilligan (1995) Primary care – Sanders *et al* (2000) Specialist – Hardiker (1991)
Level 4: Therapeutic – established long-term concerns, intensive family therapy for a number of problems that require more intense intervention, seen as severe difficulties	Respite care, social services, family welfare conferences, residential care, Youthreach, juvenile liaison	Preventative – Gilligan (1995) Standard – Sanders *et al* (2000) Therapeutic – Hardiker (1991)
Level 5: Crisis – when family breakdown has become unavoidable, children have been removed from parental custody and the emphasis is on rehabilitation	Juvenile delinquency, advanced criminality, anti-social behaviour, rehabilitation, restorative justice. acute trauma	Preventative - Gilligan (1995) Adjunctive/Enhanced – Sanders *et al* (2000) Intensive – Hardiker (1991)
Private – available to those who can pay to receive support privately at the level of support they require	Many different difficulties	Not applicable

Source: Kavanagh (2014).

Services are likely to operate on more than one level of intervention and may be intertwined with other services. For instance, interventions at levels 3, 4 and 5 may deal with anti-social behaviour and criminal behaviour. Service delivery may depend upon the ecological perspective of the child's history and parental engagement with services. For example, intervention for anti-social behaviour applicable at level 3 indicates that the school, Gardaí and social workers are working with parents to challenge this behaviour. However, if parental engagement is low, criminality may become more severe, resulting in social workers, psychologists and juvenile liaison officers operating at levels 4 and 5 in a more intense intervention. It is argued by Sanders *et al* (2000, 2003) that a multi-level approach should be used in programme design to maximise effective use of services and to reach more individual families in a community.

Research Findings

The findings of my research support the wider use of universal programmes (Level 1) to act as a protective factor for families, to prevent a greater number of families using the higher level services. As suggested by both parents and professionals alike in interviews and focus groups, 'timely and appropriate support' in some cases would prevent family problems reaching crisis point. 'Everything is crisis-led, which means it won't be until something bad happens that families will get referred for help; the problem grows until it is unmanageable (professional participant).

Within Irish society there is an over-focus on targeted support. This was identified through my research as an approach that was viewed as detrimental for parents and children. While targeted support does reach vulnerable children and families, in the experience of professionals, it only does so when difficulties have been accelerated to a serious level of need. Universal and early interventions were found to be lacking and badly needed. As stated by one professional, 'it is exactly that which is missing: a universal programme – family support and HSE services are all appointed at higher levels – we are level 3 and 4 and it would be great to have a step down service that could be tapped in to as people come down the levels and certainly be used in general to prevent families going up the levels in the first place' (professional participant).

Current support provision is skewed towards parents within 'disadvantaged areas' or 'disadvantaged populations'. However, the process of identifying and labelling these areas and groups within them is again a reactive policy. This policy reinforces inequality, stigma and a cycle of disadvantage as outlined in **Figure 15.3**. This cycle of disadvantage feeds back in to itself, whereby positive outcomes may be experienced by only a small number of families. As stated by a professional participant, 'targeted interventions are still for the minority of families … but the majority of the population still need help. Without help, we are only going to increase the targeted percentages. We need to stop a temporary problem becoming a crisis by having somewhere to go for support when problems arise – it stands to reason' (professional participant).

Figure 15.3: A Categorical Cycle of Targeted Support

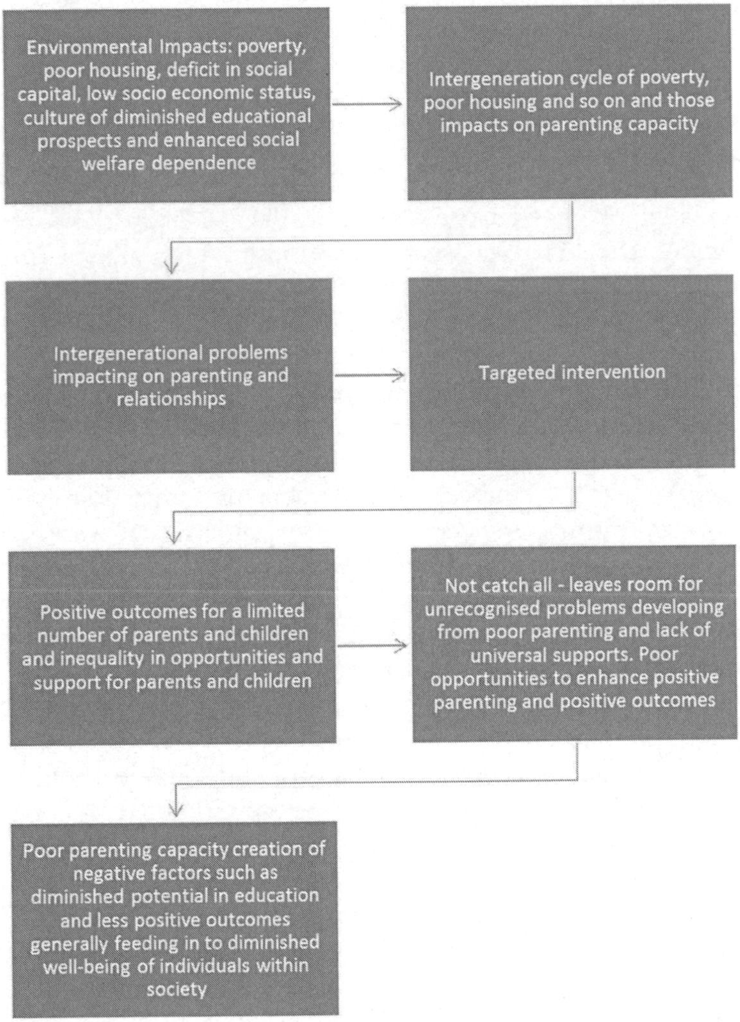

Environmental Impacts: poverty, poor housing, deficit in social capital, low socio economic status, culture of diminished educational prospects and enhanced social welfare dependence

→ Intergeneration cycle of poverty, poor housing and so on and those impacts on parenting capacity

→ Intergenerational problems impacting on parenting and relationships

→ Targeted intervention

→ Positive outcomes for a limited number of parents and children and inequality in opportunities and support for parents and children

→ Not catch all - leaves room for unrecognised problems developing from poor parenting and lack of universal supports. Poor opportunities to enhance positive parenting and positive outcomes

→ Poor parenting capacity creation of negative factors such as diminished potential in education and less positive outcomes generally feeding in to diminished well-being of individuals within society

Source: Kavanagh (2014).

The Establishment of a Universal System of Parenting Support

Throughout my research, the theme of universal parenting support was revisited. Parents feel that they need support during the whole parenting experience, in line with their child's stage of development. For professionals with expertise in parenting support, they recommended a universal system as an early intervention to decrease alienation and some of the difficulties they witnessed in many families, regardless of their socio-economic background. The message from the research is that all parents should be provided with support. This position is supported by research carried out by the Department of Children and Youth Affairs:

> Progressive universalism, help to all and extra help to those that need it most ... we insist that there is an unanswerable case for universal provision of high quality supports and services (2013, p.2).

The research also suggested that, alongside a universal support system, a positive charter for all children that allows for unique individual development should be put in place. This can be facilitated using the Incredible Years Programme (currently being implemented in many schools throughout the country, with training also offered for parents, the Incredible Years Programme works on three strands and encourages child, parent and teacher co-operation, as well as focusing on pro-social behaviour and positivity in relationships) in conjunction with therapeutic play skills, within all preschool and primary schools to encourage pro-social behaviours (and healing from family dysfunction for those that need it). This then should be replaced by a curriculum-based module in second level around personal development, self-care and healthy sexual relationships. Therapeutically-trained professionals should be made accessible to all schools. The assessment process that occurs when problems are flagged needs to be facilitated by a range of professionals with different expertise, so that all eventualities or possible problems are identified as early as possible.

The research indicated that many parents who are considered to be from the 'coping classes' – parents who are assumed to not require support due to their social status – seek support within schools. It is within schools that the representation of mainstream parents seeking support can be found. This highlights the limitations of current service provision whereby support is provided for targeted and disadvantaged populations. As expressed by one professional, 'what we are talking about here is bringing in one programme to enmesh the current programmes together rather than having a little bit of everything all over the place. You won't ever lose the targeted but you could reduce it and improve outcomes for more families' (professional participant).

Figure 15.4: A Categorical Cycle of Universal Support

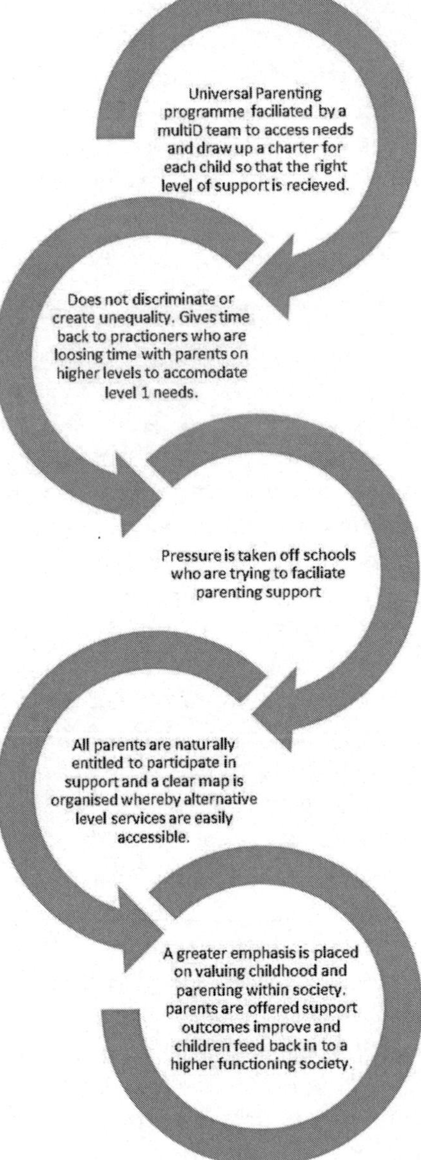

Source: Kavanagh (2014).

Currently, those working with disadvantaged school populations feel that the requirement for support is necessary, but also identify the need for support to be universal, leading to a catch-all scenario as illustrated in **Figure 15.4**.

A New Value Placed on Parenting

Parents and professionals alike identified the need for a higher value to be placed on parenting. This was an area where participants felt the culture within society needs to be encouraged to change in order to normalise more positive behaviours. A national campaign would be especially effective in projecting positive messages to all members of society that childhood needs to be valued and that all parents across the spectrum also should be valued and supported. This is a massive task, and needs to come from government level and filter down. As expressed by one parent, 'what do we want our society to look like and what do we want our children to be feeding into as a society. I want positivity and for them to receive positivity and I think that needs to be facilitated by both parents and society at large' (parent participant).

Fundamentally, a cultural shift requires society to value parenting; this shift should be clearly expressed in terms of implementing family friendly policies. As stated by one professional, 'it works both ways; if government and society doesn't value parents, parents don't value their parenting. As a society if we all valued parenting, it would filter down. Valuing both parents and childhood' (professional participant).

Policy also needs to challenge how a newly-developing two-tier structure around childhood and parenting is evolving, where targeted parents are seen as being in need and thus are stigmatised. Conversely, parents who may require support but are not viewed as in need are not entitled to help unless they seek help privately. This evolving structure in parenting support needs to be revised and a new model of parenting support put in its place that values every child and every parent regardless. 'If society values its children, it must cherish their parents' (Bowlby, cited in Sunderland, 2006, p.268).

Creating a Climate for Change

Professional and parent participants collectively expressed the view that government, community and individuals need to create a climate for change. These views were very solution-focused and participants shared ideas of how change could be achieved. Some felt that it starts at the individual level, where parents act as advocates for children, causing a catalyst for change through extensive lobbying to have children rights facilitated. Some professionals felt they themselves could act as a vehicle for change through their services, by working to improve the lives of as many children and parents as possible, which will remain a focus of their work. However, unanimously, participants agreed that change needs to come from Government level and filter down. As stated by the Expert Advisory Group, 'This must begin with leadership by Government and include all levels of service delivery, including national, regional and individual services' (Department of Children and Youth Affairs, 2013, p.25).

Government Investment

The view expressed from all participants was that the Government needs to take parenting and social concerns more seriously. Many of the participants have lost faith in the current system and fear it is failing both parents and children generally. Concern was expressed regarding the cuts to education. Schools are under tremendous pressure to provide academic, emotional and practical support for parents during a time when budget cuts have affected schools, particularly mainstream schools.

> The economic benefits of early intervention are clear and consistently demonstrated a return on investment. Spending on programmes that are high quality, based on effective interventions, and well-implemented can save significantly more then they cost over a number of years. (Department of Children and Youth Affairs, 2013, p.6)

The division between school communities has been exacerbated by current social policy, whereby disadvantaged schools are offered more funding and support despite the same requirements existing across society. As expressed by one professional, 'children are going hungry and it is not just the targeted children' (professional participant).

Participants discussed the impact of the cuts on local community projects and how these projects are suffering also as a result of the changes that have been introduced to community employment schemes. This point was highlighted several times during the research. Employment opportunities that benefit parents financially through these schemes have been hugely diminished. This has made people reluctant to take up community employment, which represents a substantial element of the community resource work force. It was felt by participants that the government needs to reinvest in community and family services, in part to deal with the social dislocation caused by the cuts as mentioned above.

Children's Rights

A universal system of parenting support is fundamental to child protection, ensuring that children's rights are upheld. At the time of writing (November 2012), the *Children's Rights Referendum* has been passed. As a society, we are yet to see what developments will occur as a result of the referendum. However, the professional participants expressed the view that they did not feel that the referendum went far enough to uphold the rights of children as set out by the United Nations *Convention on the Rights of the Child*, which Ireland signed in 1992.

Professionals expressed the view that each child should have a charter that outlined their individual needs and accounted for these throughout the child's life until adulthood. What was described by this professional was in line with the gateway of services model presented in the following section. In summary, each child born is provided with an assessment and, from that assessment, their needs are identified. This includes a mainstream charter for each child that may never require specialist services but is set up to ensure that they have a minimum standard of care all the way through. This is echoed in the *Convention on the Rights of the Child*, where it is recommended that states 'develop rights-based, co-ordinated, multi-sectoral strategies in order to ensure that children's best interests are always the starting point for service planning and provision' (Children's Rights Alliance, 2010).

An example that one professional provided to illustrate this point was that 'children don't have the freedom to go out and play because the infrastructure doesn't support this and that is just one example of how the current system is failing children' (professional participant).

Transitional Pathways – Increasing Social Capital for Young People

Highlighted by professional participants, the teenage years are a crucial time for young people and there is a transitional pathway that occurs in these teenage years. During this time, young people are forming their identity and it is a time when it can be crucial for young people to have protective factors in their lives. Some professionals working with families are able to catch young people during this time and act as a source of protective buffer. For example, if the young person has begun to feel lost, they can work therapeutically with the young person helping them work towards forming their identity and discovering what they might want to pursue in their future.

Yet not all young people on this transitional pathway are afforded the appropriate support at the right time and some can make bad decisions that can lead to detrimental outcomes, such as crime and juvenile delinquency. Professional participants suggested that targeting and only providing support for young people who are deviant causes confusion for other young people who maybe experiencing the same difficulties and who may question why someone who is causing trouble at school for instance is then being treated to a therapeutic work. This is explained in the following example expressed by one participant, 'we have a system at the moment that can be looked at as valuing bad behaviour … there are two distinct pathways but there is a pathway in the middle, a grey area along that pathway … you have kids who could go either way … if they are vulnerable and they see 'Johnnie' who commits crimes and leaves school early being given a whole load of opportunities and special treatment, what is to stop them from acting out, thinking they will get a better deal?' (professional participant).

In line with the charter for children suggested above, supports should be put in place for all young people, so that they are all afforded the same opportunities to increase their chances of developing social capital. This would reduce the incentive to act out or display problem behaviours because all young people would be entitled to support and opportunities. Furthermore, changes to the education system that provide opportunities for young people to experiment with ideas for their future career were deemed desirable.

> To be able to move between 'being at harbour' and to 'navigate' plays a key part in young people's lives, not only in terms of their well-being but also in the creation of new opportunities and identities … social capital helps us understand the social context within which youth transactions occur and how the agency of young people is bounded 'by the surrounding opportunity structure' (Boeck, 2009, p.95).

Media Campaigns

Both parents and professionals felt that the media has contributed to some of the current social problems. It was acknowledged that the media is not 100% responsible for problems such as recreating inequality. An example of a media problem was given as the 'immediate gratification factor', which was described by professionals as media advertising aimed at children and the creation of a sense of guilt for parents that their child is unloved or unacceptable if they do not provide these consumer goods. Fashions and fads, of course, have been part of society for many years; however, exposure to advertising is at a higher level than ever before, especially through television and Internet advertising.

In this current social climate, more so then ever before parents are faced with multitude of very real dilemmas and fears. These fears can be exasperated by the media: 'Simply reporting the facts can be enough to generate concern, anxiety or panic' (Cohen, 1973, p.16). With this in mind, it shows a requirement for the media to act more responsibly and to replace its consumerist agenda with a parent-friendly one. A suggested solution to this, as stated by participants, is a more positive attitude to parents, families and childhood in society generally. The vehicle and opportunity to do this is the through the media itself.

A New Model of Best Practice

The requirement of a gateway model for universal service was a recurring theme throughout the research. As stated by one parent: 'we definitely need a map of where to go for the differing needs and that map needs to be holistic to include all sorts of variants so that unique needs are covered. We can have general basic parenting skills – but also specifics … so first we need universal support, which then links to specific requirements' (parent participant).

Highlighted by both parents and professionals, the potential of this new gateway model for parenting support is the fact it will be of assistance in co-ordinating the services already in place and thereby reduce fragmentation, duplication of provision and enhance collaboration. This can be achieved by drawing upon the services that are already in place and immersing them into a new gateway model.

The participants in the research described a system where all parents were assessed and a logical clear pathway then was accessible, based upon individual needs. This also needs to allow for some categorisation within the levels so that all parents are receiving appropriate support initially. The reasoning behind this gateway is that parents receive support when it is required. This support is also preventative so that parents receive support – for example, on Level 1 – before a problem escalates to Level 3.

The creation of a new universal approach to Level 1 intervention will incorporate some of the current content already provided in basic parenting skills. All levels of intervention should be focused on nurturing parents, therapeutic approaches to parents and children and the use of creative techniques and outdoor pursuits to give families more opportunities at less cost.

Figure 15.5: A Gateway Model for a Universal Parenting Support System

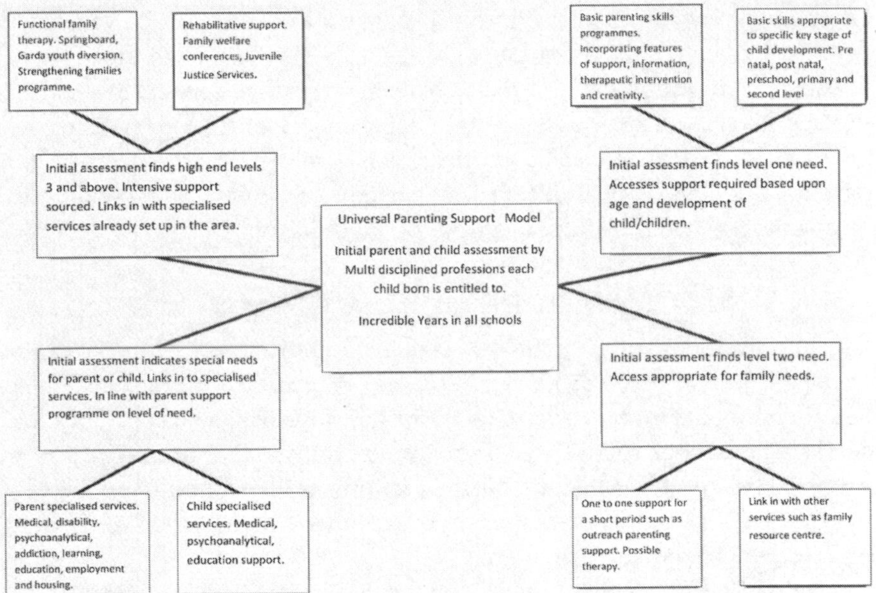

Source: Kavanagh (2014).

Levels of support are interlinked as shown in **Figure 15.6** below. Level 2 can step down to Level 1, while Level 4 can step down to Levels 3, 2 or 1. Special requirements are accessed and support is available within the levels depending upon need. These levels are explained in more depth in **Table 15.3**.

Table 15.3: Description of Levels

Level	Description
5: Crisis intervention	Parenting issues such as anger management and child behavioural problems. Intensive and long term support. The child may have been removed from parental custody, juvenile delinquency, crime and risk of self-harm.
4: Therapeutic intensive intervention	Where a problem has been established and other support has been ineffective, so more intensive positive parenting. Mediation before child is taken into care setting. Likely to have a multidisciplinary team.
3: Targeted intervention	Support for specific problems in specific areas. Problems in school, truancy, conduct problems. Parental neglect, substance abuse or anti-social behaviour.
2: Selective	Support available to disadvantaged groups – family resource centres, child care support, advice on childhood developmental challenges. Intervention for families in need, positive parenting to protect children against adversity in poor environment.
1: Universal	Support available to the mainstream population, health care, education, local community amenities, sports clubs. Pre natal care, mother and baby groups, breastfeeding groups. Early childcare, facilitated by government, available to all. Media-based positive parenting, raising awareness of parenting issues. De-stigmatising of parental stress and provision of information to all parents regardless of socio-economic status.
Special requirements work at all existing levels and are accessed on a needs basis	Support is available to all parents where a special individual circumstance is assessed, for instance a parent with a disability may require more specialised parenting support where basic skills have been adapted to suit the needs of the parent. Specialised support for parents with a child with a disability may require links to current services (such as Enable Ireland) to ensure optimal well-being for both parent and child.

Source: Kavanagh (2014).

Figure 15.6: Linkage between Levels of Support

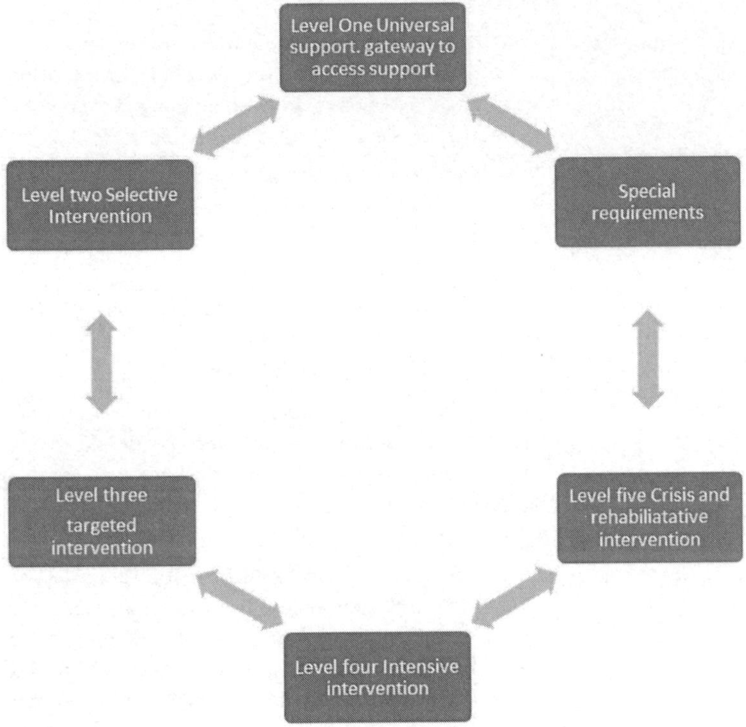

Source: Kavanagh (2014).

Alongside the universal parenting support model, a new approach to self-care and personal development should be brought into the educational curriculum as set out in **Figure 15.7**.

Figure 15.7: Universal School Intervention

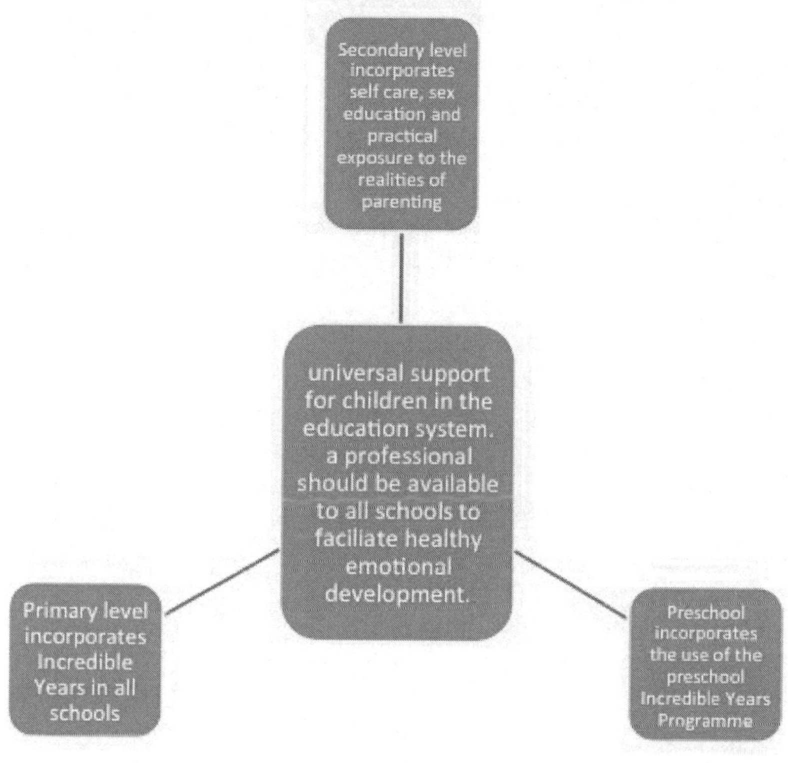

Source: Kavanagh (2014).

Nurturing Parents as Part of Parent Support

The collective opinion expressed by both parents and professionals was a requirement for parenting support to feature an element of nurturance and value for the parents themselves. Parents who had previous experience of parenting programmes felt programmes were too directive and patronising or that 'eyes were boring into your back as you enter the place'. For parents who had not attended parenting programmes, they choose not to because of the targeted element and also they had the impression programmes would be demeaning. 'The support that is out there is there for people who are doing bad. If there was a programme that you didn't feel that something was wrong with you, then I would definitely be interested because I have had some really bad times' (parent participant).

Many of the participants felt experiential learning, such as role plays, would be beneficial as they would provide practical experience.

Participants could be shown techniques in a way that could be practiced and used later in the home. The benefit of experiential learning is that it gives parents the opportunity to learn, reflect and use techniques as opposed to being given information. Experiential learning is especially important in parenting because it is easier to remember. Such techniques are used in programmes by providing DVD vignettes. However, role playing is thought to be more effective by professionals, who felt that DVD material was not culturally appropriate and that parents learn better through experiential learning.

Fatherhood

The theme of fatherhood was revisited throughout the research. Regardless of whether a father is within the household environment, it is clear that they have a significant role to play in childrearing (Utting, 2008). Fathers can be an immense emotional and practical support for their children, as role models, as mentors and guides. They can also provide stability and a secure base for the family (Biddulph, 2009).

In discussing the importance of fathers and parenting support, both parents and professionals expressed the requirement for support to be aimed at fathers and made more attractive to fathers. They suggested this could be done by including father-friendly activities in terms of the recreational side of the programme. This could be done in conjunction with services set up for men in order to facilitate parenting support.

Online Support

A suggestion made during the parent focus group was that online support could be made available to parents as part of a universal system, so that there is a forum to access support at any time, which would allow parents near-immediate support. This was a very valuable point, especially when parents are residing in rural areas. A system where general information is available online and there is a facility to contact a professional would be especially useful. Parents felt that online support could be used by many parents and that it should be incorporated into a universal system. With ever-increasing advances in technology, online support would be a logical and up-to-date vehicle for delivering basic support, which could be used alongside a programme where parents met a facilitator face-to-face. The professionals providing online or telephone support should be trained appropriately and have a background in the area of parenting/family support.

Co-facilitation, Background Training of Professionals and Collaboration of Services

The role of professionals will vary depending upon the level of support they deliver. For the initial assessment, there should be a wide variety of professionals involved, such as psychoanalytical, social care, medical and educational welfare. 'Strong leadership will help to ensure that in the delivery of services … there are clearly defined roles and responsibilities to give clarity about who does what, when and where, it will also help ensure cohesive structures through which the sector will be led' (Department of Children and Youth Affairs, 2013, p.25).

The professional participants viewed background to be a highly significant factor to consider when facilitating parenting programmes. Parents need to feel comfortable and at ease with facilitators and a professional linked into schools could aid the development of a profession of parenting support, which could begin by creating a role in schools.

The Importance of Schools

> Evidence reminds us of the wide scope for accomplishment of different kinds which schools can offer, even to children who are not high flyers. The key is for adults – teachers, parents and other professionals – to be alert to the value of school experience (Canavan *et al*, 2000, p.21).

The relationships between professional participants and the schools they have worked with was highly regarded by professionals. Parents also regard schools as a source of support and information. In relation to parenting support, schools should be a partner in a model of best practice. However, the responsibility of delivering parenting support should not be the role of school staff, as current workloads do not allow staff to do this. Through continued collaboration between schools and services, relationships and networks could be built to ensure the best interests of the child are always supported by the system as a whole.

Participants shared the view that the universal system of parenting support should exist alongside support in schools so that a professional person is affiliated to a particular school and can provide immediate support when required. This professional should be trained to work therapeutically with children and be specialised in parenting support. This should follow through to operate in second level and incorporate personal development, self-care, sexual education, lifespan development and preparation for parenting.

As a process in lifelong learning, parenting support could be brought in line with lifelong learning programmes and personal development, which would be based on a three-strand model that begins in early years and continues throughout life, starting from preschool using the Incredible Years Programme. This model is outlined in **Figure 15.8**.

Figure 15.8: A Pathway of Universal Support from Early Childhood to Parenthood

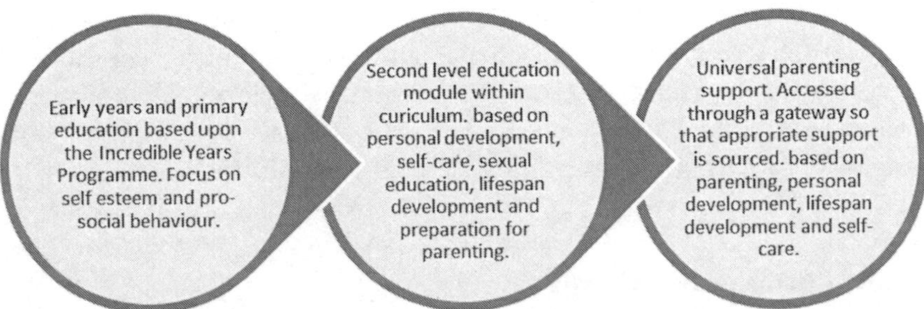

Source: Kavanagh (2014).

All participants emphasised the value of providing support for children within the education system, because the education system has everyday contact with children. The scheme outlined above was described by participants as an ideal way to ensure all children receive the same supports, regardless of socio-economic status. This support will lead naturally to a system of personal development and parenting support as young people become parents themselves. This model provides the opportunity for continuous social, emotional and personal development over a lifetime and is a long term-process that will eventually lead to a higher-functioning and more positive society in general.

Creation of a Higher-functioning Society

The creation of a model of best practice in advancing parenting support will have a positive impact upon society, whereby the focus is on positivity and reduced dysfunction within society. By creating a climate for change, it is possible that a child-friendly and family-friendly policy could be developed by implementing this model to benefit society on individual, community and wider society levels.

Taking into account that parenting is a social construct (meaning that how parenting is viewed within our society is created by the society itself), it would be crucial for society and social policy-makers to recognise that the current view of parenting and childhood has become obsolete and needs to be adapted in order for our society to progress in line with our European neighbours.

If society supports parenting through the mechanism of universal support and the use of more family-friendly media and advertising, then it is likely parents will feel more valued in their role and capacity to parenting will increase across the board. By increasing parenting capacity, family functioning will be enhanced. Improving circumstances for children within their family also will be complemented through experiencing support and personal development with the education system, so for children the outcomes are positive in multiple opportunities.

Conclusion

The current provision for parenting support is inconsistent, while parents require support for a multitude of reasons that have been described within this chapter. As such, a new model of parenting support is required. Based on my own research results, which takes into account the views of experienced professionals as well as parents, a new gateway model has been designed. This model incorporates the use of similar support system models placed within the education system to promote pro-social learning and positive self-care for children within our society. It is proposed that, if we view society itself as a large family, we can see the results of unhealthy attitudes and relationships developing throughout our society. Parenting support has the potential to deconstruct some of the current dynamics that reproduce an unhealthy society. Essentially, society begins with parents, so it should be seen as imperative that all parents and children receive nurturance and encouragement in order to improve the culture we are living in.

References

Biddulph, S. (2009). *Raising Boys: Why Boys are Different and How to Help Them Become Happy and Well-balanced Men*, London: HarperCollins.

Boeck, T. (2009). 'Social Capital and Young People' in Woods, J. and Hine, J. (eds.), *Work with Young People*, London: Sage.

Canavan, J., Dolan, P. and Pinkerton, J. (2000). *Family Support: Direction from Diversity*, London: Jessica Kingsley Publishers.

Children's Rights Alliance (2010). *United Nations Convention on The Rights of the Child; Introduction by the Children's Rights Alliance*, Dublin: Children's Rights Alliance.

Cohen, S. (1973). *Folk Devils and Moral Panics: The Creation of the Mods and Rockers*, St Albans: Paladin.

Daniel, B., Wassell, S. and Gilligan, R. (2011). *Child Development for Child Care and Protection Workers*, London: Jessica Kingsley Press.

Department of Children and Youth Affairs (2013). *Right From the Start: Report of the Expert Advisory Group on the Early Years Strategy*, Dublin: Government Publications.

Department of Health and Children (2004). *Children First: National Guidelines for the Protection and Welfare of Children*, Dublin: Government Publications.

Gilligan, R. (1995). 'Family Support and Child Welfare: Realising the Promise of the *Child Care Act, 1991'* in Ferguson, H. and Kenny, P.(eds.), *On Behalf of the Child: Professional Perspectives on the Child Care Act, 1991*, Dublin: A. and A. Farmar.

Hardiker, P., Exton, K. and Barker, M. (1991). *Policies and Practices in Prevention in Childcare*, Aldershot: Avebury.

Kavanagh, J. (2014). Master's research, pending publication.

Kumpfer, K. and Alder, S. (2006). 'Dissemination of Research-based Family Interventions for the Prevention of Substance Abuse' in Sloboda, Z. and Bukoski, W.J. (eds.), *Handbook of Drug Abuse Prevention*, New York: Springer.

Luster, T. and Okagaki, L. (2005). *Parenting: An Ecological Perspective*, Mahwah, NJ: Lawrence Erlbaum Associates Publishers.

Maslow, A. (1943). 'A Theory of Human Motivation', *Psychology Review*, Vol.50, No.4, pp.370-96.

McKeown, K. (2011). *Strategic Framework for Family Support within the Family and Community Services Resource Centre Programme*, Dublin: Family Support Agency Ireland.

O'Doherty, C. (2007). *A New Agenda for Family Support: Providing Services that Create Social Capital*, Dublin: Blackhall Publishing.

O'Doherty, C. (2012). 'Social Care and Family Support Work' in Lalor, K. and Share, P. (eds.), *Applied Social Care Reader*, Dublin: Gill and Macmillan.

Sanders, M., Markie-Dadds, C., Tully, L. and Bor, B. (2000). 'The Triple P Positive Parenting Program: A Comparison of Enhanced, Self-Directed Family Intervention for Parents of Children with Early Onset Conduct Problems', *Journal of Consulting and Clinical Psychology*, Vol.68, No.4, pp.624-40.

Sanders, M., Pidgeon, A., Gravestock, F., Connors, M., Brown, S. and Young, R. (2003). *Does Parental Attribution Retaining and Anger Management Enhance the Effects of the Triple P Positive Parenting Program with Parents at Risk of Child Maltreatment?*, Brisbane: Families International Publishing.

Sunderland, M. (2006). *The Science of Parenting*, London: DK Publishing.

Utting, D. (2008). Parenting Services: *Filling in the Gaps Assessing and Meeting the Need for Parenting Support Services*, London: Family and Parenting Institute.

Webster-Stratton, C. (1984). 'Randomised Trial of Two Parent Training Programs for Families with Conduct Disordered Children', *Journal of Consulting and Clinical Psychology*, Vol.52, No.4, pp.666-78.

Webster-Stratton, C. (1999). *How to Promote Children's Social and Emotional Competence*, London: Sage Publications.

Webster-Stratton, C., Reid, J. and Stoolmiller, M. (2008). 'Preventing Conduct Problems and Improving School Readiness: Evaluation of the Incredible Years teacher and Child Training Programs in High Risk Schools', *Journal of Child Psychology and Psychiatry*, Vol.49, No.5, pp.471-88.

Webster-Stratton, C., Reid, M. and Hammond, M. (2001). 'Preventing Conduct Problems, Promoting Social Competence: A Parent and Teacher Training Partnership in Head Start', *Journal of Clinical Child and Adolescent Psychology*, Vol.30, No.3, pp.283-302.

Wilson, J. (2000). *The Nurturing Parent Programmes*, Washington, DC: Department of Justice.

16: Parenting in a Multicultural Society: Migrants and Their Experiences of Parenting in Ireland

Gertrude Cotter and Olaniyi Kolawole

Introduction

In the last two decades, Ireland has been transformed into a culturally-diverse society as a result of net immigration of people from both European Union and non-European Union countries. According to the 2011 *Census* figures, 12% of the population of Ireland were non-Irish nationals in 2011 (Central Statistics Office, 2012). This chapter explores the concepts, meanings and realities of parenting for migrant parents now living in Ireland but who grew up in a different country. Parents may have moved by choice or through forced migration. They may or may not be married or in a partnership with a person born in Ireland.

The reflections in this chapter are based on one author's 20 years' experience of working with migrant parents, recent semi-structured interviews with 20 parents from around the world and the personal experiences of the other author of parenting in Ireland as a new country. Rather than cover a broad range of parenting themes, it attempts to distil and present the points that are more distinctively related to being a migrant parent in Ireland. The chapter asks what impact moving to a new country has made on their parenting skills, abilities, values, styles and beliefs?

In relation to migrants with families, research has revealed that migration leads to changes in family relations, with migrant families in most cases living in two cultures (Kwak, 2003; Vazsonyi *et al*, 2006). Migration experience has also been described as 'a highly disorganising' one (Maiter and George, 2003, p.426) and 'a disruptive process somewhat congruent with a crisis situation' (Shamai *et al*, 2002, p.23). The literature reveals that immigrant families are more likely to experience downward socio-economic status (Kwak, 2003; Roopnarine *et al*, 2006). It is of little surprise then that the parents interviewed for this chapter were very interested in talking about their experiences of parenting in Ireland. It is clear that this is a subject that interests parents and also that it should be of great interest to anyone concerned with the well-being of families and children growing up in Ireland.

Literature Review

The demographic changes that occurred in Ireland over the last two decades have resulted in researchers, policy-makers and service providers beginning to examine the impact of migration on the parenting styles and practices in Ireland. A recent report from Trinity College Dublin, *New Irish Families: A Profile of Second Generation Children and their Families* (Röder *et al*, 2014), presents the first results from the Irish Research Council-funded project, New Irish Families. This is one of the first studies in Ireland to focus on children born in Ireland to migrant parents, who now make up a large and growing proportion of families in the country. It includes valuable statistical information, such as the fact that one-in-four children born in Ireland in 2012 had a non-Irish born mother; 'mixed' couples with one parent from Ireland and one migrant parent are more frequent than couples made up of two migrants amongst the parents included in the study; there is now much greater diversity in terms of religion, linguistic, and ethnic and national background amongst young families in Ireland; Roman Catholicism is the most common religion, followed by other Christian denominations, Muslim and Protestant. More than half of households headed by at least one parent from an EU accession state did not speak English in the home (Röder *et al*, 2014).

The ISPCC report, *The All Ireland Programme for Immigrant Parents Research Phase Report*, also provides a comprehensive literature review and useful findings with a view to producing a training resource for migrant parents. Key findings here are that there is still a lack of information about living in Ireland, including aspects of Irish culture, services, and norms, and there are high levels of stress amongst migrant parents resulting from their migrant status, financial and other stresses being confounded by language barriers (ISPCC, 2008).

A study of immigration and schooling in Ireland (Devine, 2011) highlights the lack of adequate integration policies in Ireland and the consequent impact on the experiences of migrant children and parents in the new multi-ethnic schools in Ireland. It finds that parenting experiences of migrants are shaped by the pervasiveness of cultural racism in Ireland (Devine, 2005, 2011). The Irish 'intercultural'[13] integration policy has been highly criticised as being incoherent and not addressing the challenges faced by migrants in the area of employment and access to services in Ireland (Mac Einrí, 2006, 2007; Beirne and Jaichand, 2006; Russell *et al*, 2008; Boucher, 2008).

Several other research findings also reveal that racism shapes the everyday experiences of migrants in Ireland in relation to accessing social services, housing and employment (Garner, 2004; Lentin and McVeigh, 2006; Russell *et al*, 2010; Fanning, 2007, 2011).

The impact of the socio-economic position of migrant parents on parenting styles is well-documented in the academic literature (Belsky *et al*, 2006; Hutchings and Lane, 2005; Leseman and van Tuijl, 2001; Reid *et al*, 2001). The Trinity research report shows that, despite the higher educational qualifications of migrants in Ireland, migrants (especially from outside the old EU countries) were more likely to be found in the lower semi- and un-skilled social classes with lower household income and higher risk of poverty. This downward socio-economic status of migrant parents has been argued to impact negatively on the experiences of migrant parents in the area of parenting in Ireland. This is because when working-class children are compared with middle-class or upper-class children, it is found that working-class children are at a disadvantage especially in the area of educational resources and parental attention available to them (Röder *et al*, 2014).

While there are many negative and challenging outcomes from immigration (for example, racism, downward socio-economic status and increased intergenerational conflict between first generation migrants and their children who are born or brought up in another culture), the literature also recognises the variety of ways in which immigrant parents meet these difficulties positively in order to support their children's development and well-being (ISPCC, 2008).

Methodology

The methodology used to inform this chapter involved both a literature review and a series of interviews with 20 parents. Parents were asked a series of open-ended questions on a range of issues, such as parenting styles, child development and education, and the impact of migration,

---

13 'Interculturalism is fundamentally about creating the conditions for interaction, equality of opportunity, understanding and respect between all the communities in Ireland' (Department of Justice, Equality and Law Reform, 2005, p.38).

conflict, religion, culture, legal, social, economic factors on them as parents living in Ireland. All parents, except for two, grew up in a different country of origin than Ireland but they all are now parenting in Ireland. Two of the parents were Irish and married to a spouse who grew up in a different country. The interviews were with 10 men and 10 women. The countries of origin of the participants were Nigeria, Romania (one Romanian and two Romanian Roma), Kenya, Mexico, Ireland (married to non-Irish spouses), UK, Greece, Thailand, Poland, Zimbabwe, US, South Africa, Hungary, Iraq, Afghanistan, Pakistan, China and Ukraine.

Two of the parents were parenting alone; one parent was a wheelchair user, and one was from a same-sex partnership. Most parents were in their 20s, 30s and 40s, with three in their 50s, 60s and 70s. All but one parent had their children with them in Ireland at the time of interview and the children ranged in ages from new-borns to their 40s. Most of the parents interviewed had children between the ages of 4 and 13, with fewer having children in their teens or older. The parents were from across the socio-economic spectrum, with approximately one-third each in low, medium and high income, professional and educational backgrounds. The parents lived mostly in rural and urban areas of Cork, Dublin and Limerick with the majority living in Cork city and county. They were accessed through an initial snowballing approach, but were then stratified to ensure representation from the three different socio-economic groups and different parts of the world. In addition, an attempt was made to identify other variables such a parents with a disability, parenting alone and lesbian parenting.

While such a diverse group of people inevitably would present a wide range of views and opinions, what was perhaps surprising was how similar some views were about parenting in Ireland, both positive and negative. A number of key themes emerged, some of which showed clear patterns and issues that Ireland as a country might benefit from hearing in both a parenting and wider societal context.

Findings and Discussion

Education

Migrants' access to education and educational materials are key determinants for successful integration in their host societies. Both academic and non-academic research in the area of migration and parenting has identified education as one of the main primary services migrants accessed and interacted with in their new society (Bornstein and

Cote, 2004; Buki *et al*, 2003). Education has been closely linked with migrants' integration, especially for refugee families (Bridging Refugee Youth and Children's Services, 2007). In order to effectively access educational services and best support and advocate on behalf of their children, migrant parents require information regarding educational norms in their new country. The lack of information about how the educational systems operate in the new society can increase the stress level of migrants and negatively impact their parenting practices (ISPCC, 2008). This may ultimately put migrant children at risk of early educational failure (Van Tuijl *et al*, 2001).

One of the first factors mentioned by all parents in this survey was education. All of parents said they valued education 'very highly'. There were three quite stark discoveries in relation to education. First, every participant referred, in different ways, to what might generally be called 'civic education' in Ireland. There was much criticism of the lack of real engagement with international events and teaching about the Irish political system. The Greek participant said that she was not happy with the 'apathy' that results in Ireland as a result of this *lacuna* in the education system. Several people, particularly those from African countries, asked why the national anthem is not sung in schools in the morning. One Nigerian participant said she felt this would give a sense of belonging and pride in being Irish.

Second, almost all the parents referred to incidents of racism in the schools. One parent referred to incidents where the principal expressed 'patronising opinions' that he, the principal, was 'surprised' that this Zimbabwean man was articulate. The principal expressed the view that he was not like the 'other Africans'. The man made a complaint about this comment and the complaint was not treated with the importance the parent felt it should be. His conclusion was 'they think we came down from the trees'. The parent had come across this often. He saw it as 'cultural racism' and 'othering' based on ethnicity. Some try to be 'nice'; he said, "this is almost worse. They want to embrace us, the poor kids from Africa". This parent worried deeply for his children and felt he had to constantly prepare them to deal with such attitudes. He did so by talking and communicating all the time with his children so that they learned coping mechanisms to deal with attitudes like this. He said, "if Séan does something wrong, it is because he is Séan; if my son does it, it is because he is African". This finding reinforces earlier findings of specificities of Irish racism such as Ireland's discriminatory treatment of the Travellers and Roma people, the stigmatisation and marginalisation of asylum-seekers and pathologisation of migrants, especially of African origin as culturally inadmissible (Lentin and McVeigh, 2006; Garner, 2004; Lentin and Lentin, 2006).

Several parents referred to the education system as being monocultural and not prepared in a real and deeper way for the fact that there are now so many children from ethnic minorities living in Ireland. This is reflected in school books, attitudes, procedures, values and 'ways of doing things' that are not truly embracing diversity. One Afghan parent said, "we are OK if we do things the Irish way, we are tolerated, but they don't really want to hear about different ways of doing things and if they do, it feels like lip-service sometimes". This form of racism is described by Dwivedi (2002) in the context of cultural racism. He says that migrant groups who do not adjust their cultural customs can experience discrimination. He says 'the culture of minority ethnic parents is seen as deficient in social customs, manners, appropriate attitudes, etc. and holding them back. If they refuse to turn their back on their own culture, then any "discrimination" is their fault' (Dwivedi, 2002).

The parent who grew up in the UK gave very specific examples of how the history curriculum does not reflect accurately both UK and international history and politics. As a practicing Catholic who cared deeply about her religion, she also was critical of how religion is taught in Ireland. She felt that her children had not had anything like the quality of religious education she had had. "All they got", she said "was how to recite a few prayers in a meaningless way and how to answer the questions in the confirmation book".

Thirdly, it became very clear that, the higher the level of education of parents, the greater was their discontent with the education system in Ireland *vis-à-vis* the education in their own countries. Those who had lower levels of education in their own countries were generally 'very happy' with the education system in Ireland. One woman who grew up in rural Kenya said that she had had poor educational opportunities both in terms of quality and quantity but that the Irish system of education is 'very good quality, has excellent teachers and is fair'. Praise of teachers as a profession was evident with all but two interviewees. However, all but one (Nigerian woman) of those who had had high levels of educational opportunity in their own countries were highly critical of the education system in Ireland.

The criticisms related to three areas in particular. First, several parents referred to the lack of development of an attitude of 'assertive challenge'. Four parents (from South Africa, Mexico, the US and Iraq) felt that the Irish system encouraged a deference to 'the system' and a spirit of challenge was not welcomed within schools. For all four, this was a very important factor and one that disturbed them. One said that, even when his teenage son's friends came to visit at home, they "mumbled something to him" instead of confidently shaking hands and saying "Hello Mr ..." and engaging in mature conversation. He felt this related to the education system.

Second, there was some criticism of the education system still being about 'rote' learning and not focused on problem-solving. The parent from the US, himself an educationalist, was particularly critical.

Third, the issue of children being believed if they reported a racist incident was another cause of concern. Many parents gave specific examples of their child not being taken seriously. One child had experienced a group of school-mates continually saying "black people used to be slaves, we don't want to play with you" and another had two classmates say "I don't like black people". Parents did feel strongly that more cultural competency was required as well as stringent, anti-racism policies and procedures. Many also referred to the dilemma of being seen as 'aggressive' if they complained and they found it hard to support their children when teachers say things like "ah sure, that isn't racism, that is just children being children".

One Kenyan parent praised support she herself had received in the local primary school in a course called *How to Help Your Child with Their Homework*. She said this helped her personally but also enabled her to support her children in a way she felt would never have been possible in the past because in her area "girls were not allowed to go to school after about the age of 8". On the other hand, she and another parent had attended two 'parenting courses' aimed at asylum-seekers that they found "patronising in the extreme".

Most of the parents also were concerned about the cost of education, the cost of books, uniforms and school trips. There was significant disquiet about the school transport system, although not in all areas.

All aspects of educational difficulty were accentuated for those living in the Direct Provision (Asylum) system. It is not possible within the confines of this chapter to highlight the many issues facing asylum-seeking parents. These have been well-documented elsewhere (Veale and O'Connor, 2001; Fanning and Veale, 2004; Christie, 2006). However, the two parents living in Direct Provision were deeply worried about their children's education, the lack of choice over schools, the difficulties of studying in what they said were often "dangerous and noisy" environments and the lack of real concern by the schools, albeit a certain amount of "oh poor you mentality". The two parents involved were "scared" to speak out for fear of isolating their children even further and for fear of their legal cases being affected. "They don't really care, they pretend to, but they really do not know and they have a naive and almost childlike attitude" were the words of one parent. She said, "they haven't got a clue what we have been through and they see us as poor and uneducated people". However, once again, the praise for teachers was stronger than for school authorities and administrators. One parent said, "the teacher can see how bright X (her child) is".

The two parents from the Roma community were very happy with the education system and one admitted that at first he struggled with the notion of his daughter going to school. However, over the last 15 years, he had learned more about Ireland and he felt that the Irish education system was one of the best aspects of Irish society. It is one of the few places he said were we don't get "discriminated against and judged ... well not as much as in other things".

Economic and Legal Impact of Migration on Parenting

By and large, migrants have been found to experience downward socio-economic status as a result of loss of human capital when they migrate (Kwak, 2003; Capps *et al*, 2004). Covert and overt racism within the labour market limits their access to full employment opportunities (Gyoh, 2007). Most parents interviewed felt that one of the main impacts of migrating was the fact that they had to start new careers at an age when most parents their age would be more established in their careers. One Chinese man, who had worked in the public service in his country and married an Irish woman, claims he had a much easier quality of life at home, but had to "start from scratch" in Ireland and retrain. He felt that, as a parent at his age, he could not offer his children the kind of housing and extra-curricular benefits that he would have loved. Very much linked to this was the repeated emphasis by almost all interviewees on the lack of networks and contacts and consequent lack of knowledge of how things work in general and specifically in their career areas. One man put it well when he said "there are a lot of unwritten cultural expectations and we don't know about them". He said he could see this changing over time as his children grew up, and said that clearly the children make friends easier than he does. Nevertheless, he still feared his children will never fully feel they belong.

The issue of sub-standard housing and long waiting lists for council housing also was mentioned by several parents, who felt that their current accommodation was impacting on their children's ability to study and indeed to make friends from a wider range of economic backgrounds. Without exception, those on 'social welfare' felt embarrassed; they did not come from countries with a reliance on social welfare and they worried that their children would be called 'scroungers', which in fact one child had experienced. Again the TCD report also talks about housing concerns: 'Second generation children and their families are more likely to live in rented accommodation and apartments rather than houses, and have less access to gardens or other common spaces. The vast majority of immigrant families feel settled and part of their local communities, but less so than Irish families' (Röder *et al*, 2014).

For some, the uncertainty around ongoing legal residency in Ireland was a cause of great concern. Parents felt that the uncertainty about the future and associated stress impacted on them as parents because they "worried all the time" and this in turn impacted on their children "who are very tuned in to this". One referred to her child always trying to protect her and that she felt her child had no opportunity for a real childhood with these worries "hanging around all the time". This was particularly the case for the parents living in Direct Provision, where the parents felt that their children had never had an opportunity for a real family life, where their parents could make their own food, go to work and visit friends and extended families. Living on €19.10 a week meant a normal life was not possible on many levels.

Several also talked about the cost of travel, visiting family and bringing children to see their families. This was impossible for those on very low incomes and, even for middle and high-income earners, it was a strain, especially when more than one family member travelled. It also meant that it was difficult to go on holidays to other countries and to have family holidays together. Most were sending money to their families at home. The Greek parent was struggling very much, despite being on a relatively high income, because of the downturn in the economy in Greece.

Socio-Cultural Aspects of Migration on Parenting

Closely linked to the economic and legal factors was one issue that was expressed by every participant from all countries and across all classes. The loss of the extended family network has a significant impact on parenting for migrant families. All parents talked about how much they missed their families, how lonely this was, the emotional impact such separation had on children who no longer had aunts, uncles, grandparents, cousins and other close family ties. Many parents cried when they spoke of how their children were losing out in this respect. One said that the child's grandparents knew them through Skype, which is useful but "not the same thing". One family did say that they did not miss the claustrophobia of the family system in their country but they did feel the emotional loss. Not having the extended family network also had an economic impact because parents did not have siblings and grandparents to help with child-minding and other costs. One parent from Thailand spoke about how she missed her mother's support and "wise advice".

The impact of the loss of extended family is reflected also in the Trinity College Dublin report, which shows that 'Childcare is a major challenges for all parents ... but this is even more so for immigrant parents who less often have family living close by' (Röder *et al*, 2014).

Many spoke of the extra pressures and expectations on their children, both from society and from themselves. One Pakistani parent summed it up as follows: "sometimes it seems that she represents her entire country when she is out in the world or at school. If an Irish person does something, it doesn't feel like this is how 'Irish are'. If my child does it, it becomes 'this is how Pakistani people are'. This brings pressures all the time. Then I suppose I expect too much. I moved here for her to have a better life, I put pressure on her to do well at school. I expect too much maybe. I think a lot of migrants are like that". Most parents also worried "all the time" about their children being happy, not being different and being able to cope with difficult situations resulting from being from a non-dominant ethnicity.

Generally people were relatively positive about religion and the more visible aspects of culture, such as food and dress. Almost all said that they found it easy to practice their religion even though Ireland is largely a Catholic country. Some did feel that their children were singled out at school during religion time but this varied considerably and both schools and families came to different arrangements. There is no one answer but as one Irish parent said, "this doesn't have to be difficult if people just used commonsense. Obviously if your child is the only one not taking religious instruction, you just sit down with the family and work out what works best. Each school and family will be different". The parents noted that, when there were other children from different backgrounds, not necessarily migrant backgrounds but for instance children who did not follow a Catholic faith, it was easier for the child because then they were not "as obvious". The issue was more related to the child being singled out and different than to ethnicity *per se* but it was difficult to untangle the two. The parents who described themselves as "having a strong faith", regardless of religion, were less critical of being in a Catholic school than the parents who said they did not follow any faith practice. Those who did not want to bring their children up in any faith were angry that the school system is dominated by the Catholic Church and several found it difficult to understand why religion was not taught outside of the school system.

Some parents did not come from traditions where there were dress or eating codes that were very different from Irish customs. However, some people from African backgrounds liked to pass on these more visible customs to their children and did not find it difficult to do so. Some people did find Irish food bland in general and found that their children's friends were sometimes unaccustomed to different tastes. Those with a strong interest in the politics of migration and integration matters spoke of how organisers of public events trying to 'include' migrant communities often thought about dress and food and occasionally religion, but when it came to real reforms that would really improve the life of their families, this "lip-service" was just skin deep. Others welcomed this sense of inclusion and welcome and were grateful to Irish society for accepting them in this way. They felt that they would not like to be critical. One Kenyan woman said, "I should be grateful, not critical, for my life here".

The exception in relation to clothing were the Roma parents, who were clearly upset about recent Garda racial-profiling where Roma children were taken from their homes. This is something the Irish government apologised for but the events and other recent local incidents had instilled a certain fear and distrust and concern for the safety of their children. One woman who was expecting a baby and who accompanied the parent who was being interviewed, started to cry and said she was worried her child would be taken from her.

One over-riding point of agreement is that people felt their children were safe. Some parents did not take this for granted because they came from more violent and unstable environments. They felt that their teenagers were relatively safe meeting friends "in town" or after school in their houses. Another clear finding was the feeling that (a) there are not enough extra-curriculum activities for girls and those that are there are very expensive. For boys there are opportunities around sport. However (b) for boys not interested in sport, there was not enough choice of other affordable interesting activities. This was a widely and strongly-held view and one that surprised most parents.

There were certain very strong and often-mentioned issues that could be loosely categorised under what we might call "the specificity of Irish culture and mores". A significant majority spoke more critically of "other parents" at school than of the school itself. One woman said "it is sometimes very subtle but the worst is when it is subtle. I just know but can't explicitly say that some parents don't want their children to be with mine. Some also seem to think 'those poor African kids" and I don't think some organisations helping Africa and migrants help that either. The pictures of Africa can be crazy". The word "patronising" was used more than once, especially by people from Asian and African backgrounds.

Several parents also pointed to the class hierarchies in Ireland. One said "I automatically get put into the 'this is a Roma therefore lower class' category". This woman also said she was constantly asked if she needed help, which, while well-meaning, was "over-the-top". She did not feel that other parents were being constantly asked if they needed help. "Why do they keep asking this, why do they assume I need help all the time?" Another also spoke of the class issue, "the higher class get preferential treatment. It is 'hush hush' but everyone knows it. If you are the child of a doctor, Garda officer or nurse you are treated in one way, if you are the child of an immigrant you are treated another way. I want to give money to the school as a donation, so that they will think I am important and take my children and me more seriously. I am saving up for this. I want to buy respect for my children". These views seemed to reflect what can be termed a specifically Irish type of racism. The over-riding feeling is that this is a society which is paternalistic and many felt that they felt like they had to be "grateful". Several parents worried greatly about their children, some born in Ireland and some not, in the area of 'civic belonging'. This was a recurrent theme, raising the question of whether their children would ever fully feel this sense of belonging.

One parent was very positive about belonging and she felt that she and her children moved easily between Irish and Nigerian communities. She did not feel that there was a lot of real integration in society at large but she felt comfortable herself, as did her children, in moving between what she called "the two worlds". "I don't really know how I do it. I just go to events which are Nigerian and Irish and it seems to work for us. We feel very welcome in this (small rural) town". Most parents also felt that overall it was very good for their children to be exposed to a different and new culture so that they could see the world from different perspectives before making judgements.

Parenting Styles and Values

Parenting styles and values differed from one family to another. However, there were several factors that were mentioned repeatedly. First, many of those interviewed felt that one important cultural value they held was that of respect for elders and they did not feel that this was quite as strong in Ireland as in their countries, both in relation to care but also to listening to the wisdom of elders. That was a strong value they wanted to instil in their children. In one family we met, the youngest boy had to apologise to his older (10 year old) brother for shouting at him for taking his toy. Several also mentioned that they felt children were more included in their cultures. The parent from Mexico saw a big difference in this respect and felt that children could be valued more and included more. Several parents said that such a sense of inclusion and more respect for children might help with issues of mental health and suicide in Irish society.

There was not as much reference to intergenerational difficulties in this survey as there has been in other literature. This is possibly because many of the children in the families were under the age of 13. However, one parent from Afghanistan did say that he could see "worrying problems ahead" as his daughter grew up in this completely different society. He particularly referred to the role of girls and women in Irish society, which he admitted he "struggled with" because where he grew up woman and men had very different expectations. He did acknowledge that he himself needs to change his views but he felt his daughter was currently "changing her culture too quickly". A similar view was expressed by a member of the Roma population, who felt it was the role of men to take leadership roles. "It is OK for my daughter to go to school but I think men should be leaders".

The parents in this survey did not refer in detail to the issue of discipline and one or two said they were "researched to death on discipline". For the African parents, there was a definite concern that this was the only issue professionals often spoke about in relation to their parenting styles.

In terms of parenting styles in general, most parents felt that they did continue the traditions of parenting styles within their own families and rather than "become Irish", it was more a matter of adapting and using "commonsense" rather than completely changing how they "did things". One woman said that while "they (professionals) try to interfere with my private life, in the end your private life is your own when you close the door. Most families have a parenting style and it is not like all immigrants have the same style".

Gender also was discussed in other contexts. Some questioned the role of women in Irish society and mentioned incidents such as the death of Savita Halappanavar and the recent events surrounding a migrant asylum-seeker in Ireland who, wishing to have an abortion, was not allowed to travel to the UK and tried to take her own life. One parent called talked about these "medieval attitudes to women around reproductive rights". This parent from Greece worried about her child growing up in such an environment.

Other women did feel that their own attitudes to gender had changed and that this would impact on their parenting skills. One woman said, "I would not want my daughter to be treated the way I was growing up and Ireland does offer hope for her as a girl and as a woman. God bless Ireland".

The oldest interviewee quoted Maya Angelou, who, when talking about her life as a mother, asked 'Do your eyes light up when they enter the room'? If they do, this parent said, "they know you love them and that more than anything else is what I want my children to know".

Conclusion

The education of their children is of paramount importance to the migrant parents interviewed. While there is regard for teachers, there is discontent amongst some regarding being patronised, children not being believed regarding incidents of racism and a lack of civic education. Migrant parenting requires discussing coping skills to help deal with this 'othering' based on ethnicity. Parents worry that their children, even if born in Ireland, will never feel a full sense of belonging. There is also some concern about a lack of emphasis on assertiveness, critical thinking and problem-solving skills within the system.

Some parents are happy with the system and feel their children have better opportunities than they had. Useful locally-based interventions include courses run for parents about helping children with their homework, although some concern arises when parents feel patronised as in the case of parenting skills courses attended by two parents.

All of the issues raised above are accentuated for those living in the Direct Provision centres.

Being a migrant parent is affected by both legal and economic factors. Some parents are struggling financially, having had to retrain and work on a low salary. Low quality housing impacts on their children's ability to study and make friends from different economic backgrounds. This is linked to a lack of knowledge of Irish cultural norms, peer support and networks to support career progression and understanding of the jobs-market. Those in the asylum system or on social welfare are concerned they and their children are viewed as 'scroungers'. Even those on medium to high income levels struggle with the strains of remittances being sent home and the cost of visiting families. This stress is confounded in some cases by uncertainty about legal issues relating to residency status in Ireland.

With regard to socio-cultural considerations, one issue mentioned by all participants is the importance of extended family networks and the associated emotional, financial and practical supports to them as parents. In addition, parents often refer to the extra pressures they and society places on their children to almost 'represent' their country and to do well academically and otherwise. While generally religious and cultural practices relating to food and dress do not pose great concern, there is some concern regarding religion being taught in schools. However, most feel that they can maintain their own cultural values within their homes. Some refer to how they move between communities and cultural mores with pragmatism but others find it more difficult to integrate and to feel a sense of belonging.

While there was little criticism about the ability to follow visible cultural practices, there is some reference to this being tolerated but "real change and real integration" is not happening behind the veil of multicultural parties and events. In addition, members of the Roma community did not feel their dress code was respected.

On the positive side, people felt their children were safe but that there are not enough extra-curricular activities for girls and for boys not interested in sport. There were mixed feelings about the GAA, with praise and criticism in terms of their willingness to include migrant children in the GAA.

In what might be loosely called a reference to "Irish mores and norms", a number of interviewees spoke critically of "other parents" at school than of the school itself. The word "patronising" was used more than once, especially by people from Asian and African backgrounds. Several parents also pointed to class hierarchies in Ireland. Several parents worried greatly about whether their children will ever fully feel a sense of belonging, even if born in Ireland. On the other hand, some do feel that they can move between their own community and the 'Irish' community. This point is interesting, because there is a sense of different communities rather than one integrated community.

Parenting styles and values differ from one family to another. However factors such as respect for older people, inclusion and 'listening to' children in family life are highlighted as important values by many parents. Intergenerational issues are emerging for parents with teenage children in particular. Most parents do feel that they can continue their traditional parenting styles rather than "become Irish" but commonsense is required when there is a need to adapt to Irish norms.

On gender issues, some women in particular feel more liberated in Ireland than in their own country and are happy for their children to understand gender equality. However, some are worried about the treatment of women in relation to reproductive rights in Ireland.

The over-riding conclusion arising from this research is that we as a society, all of us together, need a more mature approach and debate on our mutual understandings about what is means to live in and parent in this country. We all need to reflect on the structures, values, attitudes and mores in this society and reflect and take action in a manner that respects the dignity and rights of all of us who live here together. The next generation need us to do so. As one Irish saying says, 'The future is not set, there is no fate but what we make for ourselves'. We need to listen. As the African proverb says, 'Not to know is bad, not to wish to know is worse'.

Recommendations

Education

- Schools and voluntary organisations should provide more detailed information about the education system, norms and values in Ireland;
- School authorities might consider anti-racism training for staff, particularly for those in positions of authority, to explore issues such as 'believing' children who experience racist incidents and to explore in a more mature manner questions of stereotyping, patronising attitudes and 'othering' in order to develop a culture of real inclusivity;
- The education system and society as a whole might consider discussing the issue of class within our education system and within our society. The media and public debates might explore the issues arising here and why migrants so clearly see a class system in this country that is hard to penetrate;
- Schools should consider enhancing pedagogy on 'civic engagement' and close examination of how national and international history and politics are approached in the classroom. The education system and society as a whole also might initiate debates on the issue of 'assertive challenge' and self-reflect on the perceptions raised here about deference to 'the system';
- Courses, workshops, trainings and education that supports migrant parents to support their children are welcome and should receive increased funding but the content and delivery should be carefully designed in consultation with migrant parents so as to avoid experiences of being patronised, particularly when it comes to how to raise children;

- The Direct Provision system should be abolished and individuals and families should be supported to find suitable employment, housing, autonomy and access to education;
- Schools should take into account the specific kinds of extra costs experienced by migrant families and address these issues in a sensitive and professional manner through appropriate policies and practices that are transparent and consistent across the school as a whole. Schools might explore why the issue of transport has been highlighted to a high degree here and perhaps ensure that migrant families have full information about services available.

Economic and Legal Recommendations

- Employers, employer bodies and those in positions of political influence, should be encouraged and supported to take a leadership role in combating racism in the workforce, including at recruitment stages;
- As a society, we need to understand the fact that many migrants experience downward mobility. Deeper research is needed by policy-makers and by academia on recognition of experience and qualifications from other countries. A mature public debate is required about the values of Irish society that lead to exclusion from the labour market of certain segments of society in proportionally much higher numbers;
- Those supporting migrants to access the labour market might consider creating spaces and opportunities to create peer-to-peer networks and 'buddying' programmes that actively welcome migrants with a view to understanding cultural expectations and *modus operandi*, particularly in relation to employment sectors such as the legal system, education, trades, industry, agriculture and so on;
- The Direct Provision system should be abolished, the legal system in relation to asylum should be radically changed and people should not be waiting in limbo for many years without the right to work, education and a normal life.

Socio-cultural Aspects of Migration on Parenting

- Those working with migrant populations might consider a deeper level of support and more creative approaches to the specific kinds of stresses associated with migrant life. For instance, are there models that could be explored to help to some extent with the loss of extended family and associated supports? Do some migrant parents need specific mentoring around experiences of low self-esteem arising from downward social mobility, poor housing and need to access social welfare? Are specific interventions required to support parents struggling to feel they belong but in particular to help them support their Irish and non-Irish children to understand that they do indeed belong? Can we examine structural issues within all aspects of public and private life that allow this to happen in our society as a whole?

- Specific interventions may be required in relations to groups within the migrant population who are particularly marginalised;
- The issue of religious education in schools is often debated in Ireland. Public consultations and media debates might consider including migrant voices where possible;
- While festivals and celebrations are very important, these need to be accompanied by real reform and political action on issues such as employment, racism and direct provision;
- The issues raised regarding extra-curricular activities for girls and boys have wider implications, which communities might wish to respond to pro-actively.

Parenting Styles and Values

- Parenting values and styles differ from one family to another but what we as a society can now do is listen to those who see this society with new eyes. Questions such as how we treat older people and children, how we deal with questions of sexuality, abortion and reproductive rights and what implications these have for everyone in this society and future generations are important discussion points on how we organise our society;
- The issue of intergenerational struggles within families is one that will require further attention in the years to come. Those working with migrant families might again consider creative approaches that will build the capacity of children and parents to understand, communicate and resolve differences around values and culture;
- While discipline is an issue for parents, those who support migrant parents should not always focus on this as the only or key issue when we speak of parenting styles.

References

Beirne, L. and Jaichand, V. (2006). *Breaking Down Barriers: Tackling Racism in Ireland at the Level of State and Its Institutions*, Dublin: Amnesty International.

Belsky, J., Bell, B., Bradley, R.H., Stallard, N. and Stewart-Brown, S.L. (2006). 'Socio-economic Risk, Parenting during the Preschool Years and Child Health age 6 years', *European Journal of Public Health*, Vol.17, No.5, pp.508-13.

Bornstein, M.H., and Cote, L.R. (2004). '"Who is Sitting Across from Me?" Immigrant Mothers' Knowledge of Parenting and Children's Development', *Pediatrics, Vol.114, No.5*, pp.e557-e564.

Boucher, G. (2008). 'Ireland's Lack of a Coherent Integration Policy', *Translocations*, Vol.3, No.1, pp.5-28.

Bridging Refugee Youth and Children's Services (2007). *Involving Refugee Parents in their Children's Education*, retrieved from www.brycs.org/documents/upload/brycs_spotspring2007-2.pdf.

Buki, L.P., Ma, T.-C., Strom, R.D. and Strom, S.K. (2003). 'Chinese Immigrant Mothers of Adolescents: Self-Perceptions of Acculturation Effects on Parenting', Cultural Diversity and Ethnic Minority Psychology, Vol.9, No.2, pp.127-40.

Capps, R., Hagan, J. and Rodriguez, N. (2004). 'Border Residents Manage the U.S. Immigration and Welfare Reforms' in Kretsedemas, P. and Aparicio, A. (eds.), *Immigrants, Welfare Reform, and the Poverty of Policy*, Westport, CT: Praeger.

Central Statistics Office (2012). *Census 2011: Profile 6: Migration and Diversity*, available at www.cso.ie/en/media/csoie/census/documents/census2011profile6/Profile,6,Migration,and,Diversity,entire,doc.pdf.

Christie, A. (2006). 'From Racial to Racist State: Questions for Social Professionals', *Irish Journal of Applied Social Studies*, Vol.7, No.2, p.4.

Department of Justice, Equality and Law Reform (2005). *Interculturalism is fundamentally about creating the conditions for interaction, equality of opportunity, understanding and respect between all the communities in Ireland*, press release, 27 January.

Devine, D. (2005). 'Welcome to the Celtic Tiger? Teacher Responses to Immigration and Increasing Ethnic Diversity in Irish Schools', *International Studies in Sociology of Education*, Vol.15, No.1, pp.49-70.

Devine, D. (2011). *Immigration and Schooling in the Republic of Ireland: Making a Difference?*, Manchester: Manchester University Press.

Doob, C.B. (2013). *Social Inequality and Social Stratification in US Society*, New York: Pearson.

Dwivedi, K.N. (ed.). (2002). *Meeting the Needs of Ethnic Minority Children –Including Refugee, Black and Mixed Parentage Children: A Handbook for Professionals*, London: Jessica Kingsley Publishers.

Fanning, B. (2011). *Immigration and Social Cohesion in the Republic of Ireland*, Manchester: Manchester University Press.

Fanning, B. (ed.) (2007). *Immigration and Social Change in the Republic of Ireland*, Manchester: Manchester University Press.

Fanning, B. and Veale, A. (2004). 'Child Poverty as Public Policy: Direct Provision and Asylum-seeker Children in the Republic of Ireland', *Child Care in Practice*, Vol.10, No.3, pp.241-251.

Garner, S. (2004). *Racism in the Irish Experience*, London: Pluto Press.

Gyoh, S. (2007). *Institutional Response to the Development Needs of African Community in Ireland: A Preliminary Report*, report to the Africa Centre AGM 2007.

Hutchings, J. and Lane, E. (2005). 'Parenting and the Development and Prevention of Child Mental Health Problems', *Current Opinion in Psychiatry*, Vol.18, pp.386-91.

ISPCC (2008). *The All Ireland Programme for Immigrant Parents Research Phase Report*, Dublin: ISPCC.

Kwak, K. (2003). 'Adolescents and Their Parents: A Review of Intergenerational Family Relations for Immigrant and Non-immigrant Families', *Human Development*, Vol.46, No.2-3, pp.115-36.

Lentin, A., and Lenţin, R. (eds.) (2006). *Race and State*, Cambridge: Cambridge Scholars Press.

Lentin, R. and McVeigh, R. (2006). *After Optimism: Ireland, Racism and Globalisation*, Dublin: Metro Eireann.

Leseman, P.P.M. and van Tuijl, C. (2001). 'Home Support for Bilingual Development of Turkish 4-6 year old Immigrant Children in the Netherlands: Efficacy of a Home-based Educational Programme', *Journal of Multilingual and Multicultural Development*, Vol.22, No.4, pp.309-24.

Mac Einrí, P. (2006). 'Migration in Ireland: A Changing Reality', *Social Policy in Ireland Principles Practice and Problems*, pp.357-84.

Mac Einrí, P. (2007). 'The Challenge of Migrant Integration in Ireland'. *Evidence from New Countries of Immigration*, Vol.9, No.1, pp.75-90.

Maiter, S. and George, U. (2003). 'Understanding Context and Culture in the Parenting Approaches of Immigrant South Asian Mothers', *Affilia*, Vol.18, No.4, pp.411-28.

Reid, M.J., Webster-Stratton, C. and Beauchaine, T.P. (2001). 'Parent Training in Head Start: A Comparison of Program Response Among African American, Asian American, Caucasian, and Hispanic Mothers', *Prevention Science*, Vol.2, No.4, pp.209-27.

Röder, A., Ward, M., Frese, C. and Sánchez, E. (2014). *New Irish Families: A Profile of Second Generation Children and their Families*, Dublin: Trinity College Dublin.

Roopnarine, J.L., Krishnakumar, A., Metindogan, A. and Evans, M. (2006). 'Links between Parenting Styles, Parent-child Academic Interaction, Parent-school Interaction, and Early Academic Skills and Social Behaviors in Young Children of English-speaking Caribbean Immigrants', *Early Childhood Research Quarterly*, Vol.21, No.2, pp.238-52.

Russell, H., McGinnity, F., Quinn, E. and King O'Riain, R. (2010). 'The Experience of Discrimination in Ireland: Evidence from Self-report Data' in Bond, L., McGinnity, F. and Russell, H. (eds.), *Making Equality Count: Irish and International Research Measuring Discrimination*, Dublin: The Liffey Press.

Russell, H., Quinn, E., King O'Riain, R. and McGinnity, F. (2008). *The Experience of Discrimination in Ireland: Analysis of the QNHS Equality Module*, part of the Equality Authority / ESRI Research Programme on Equality and Discrimination, Dublin: Equality Authority.

Shamai, S., Ilatov, Z., Psalti, A. and Deliyanni, K. (2002). 'Acculturation of Soviet Immigrant Parents in Israel and Greece', *International Journal of Sociology of the Family*, Vol.30, No.1, p.21-49.

Van Tuijl, C., Leseman, P.M., and Rispens, J. (2001). 'Efficacy of an Intensive Home-based Educational Intervention Programme for 4- to 6-year-old Ethnic Minority

Children in the Netherlands', *International Journal of Behavioral Development*, Vol.25, No.(2), pp.148-159.

Vazsonyi, A.T., Trejos-Castillo, E. and Huang, L. (2006). 'Are Developmental Processes Affected by Immigration? Family Processes, Internalizing Behaviors and Externalizing Behaviors', *Journal of Youth and Adolescence*, Vol.35, No.5, pp.795-809.

Veale, A. and O'Connor, D. (2001). *Beyond the Pale: Asylum-seeking Children and Social Exclusion in Ireland*, Dublin: Irish Refugee Council.

17: Foster Parenting

Declan Smith

Introduction

In 1999, our family comprised me, my wife and our four daughters aged 9, 10, 12 and 14. Within a year, due to a decision we had all agreed upon, our family composition would change and all our lives would never to be the same again. We had agreed to become a family that fosters. The objective of this chapter is to endeavour to provide the reader with an insight, albeit a very brief one, into fostering, as experienced by us since becoming a family that fosters almost 14 years ago. This chapter begins with a general introduction into fostering in Ireland, its objectives, the types of foster care that exists and the legal framework governing the placing of children in care. There is a brief look at some of the reasons as to why people decide to foster. A policy document, *National Standards for Foster Care*, published by the Department of Health and Children (2003) with the objective of providing 'useful and constructive guidelines to Health Boards and foster carers ... [regarding] ... quality of services is referred to on numerous occasions as 'National Standards'. Within this chapter, the terms 'placement disruption' and 'placement breakdown' are interchangeable, as are the terms 'foster carer' and 'foster parent'. The term 'family' is generally used to describe the family composition at that time and includes all our natural children and those children placed in our care at that time. Finally, the views expressed in this chapter are personal and, as such, might not be generalisable to other foster carers or foster care placements.

The History of Foster Care in Ireland

Throughout Irish history, there has been a tradition of 'fosterage'. Brehon law promoted the placement of sons, generally aged between 7 and 17, of clan leaders with each other, as it promoted peace and alliances between clans (Kelly, 1988). Similarly, it was accepted practice that parents often placed their children, girls as well as boys, with craftsmen and artists in the hope they might learn a trade or art. In a modern context, foster care is a diverse activity where children of different ages, cultures, backgrounds, and temperament with varying life experiences, are placed, most often with strangers. The objective is to endeavour to ensure the physical, emotional, educational and psychological needs of the placed child – needs that are not currently being met – will be satisfied, within a family home environment. The current care system in Ireland is based upon Article 20 (Appendix 2) of the United Nations *Convention on the Rights of the Child* (United Nations, 1990), whereby a child is only removed from a family home where it is in their best interests to do so. One of the primary objectives of foster care is to provide a child with a secure base from which a child feels confident enough to investigate and explore the world, thus promoting learning and development as a child becomes aware that there exists a safe environment to which they may return when stressed or anxious (Beek and Schofield, 2004).

The Numbers of Children in Care

In 2001, there were 5,517 children being cared for by the Irish state. By May 2014, this figure had increased to 6,517 (www.tusla.ie). Of these, 6,054 of these children are in foster care: 4,182 in general foster care – placed with carers who are largely strangers to the child yet who are generally selected based upon suitability to provide for the unique needs of that child – while 1,872 are in relative foster care – placed with relatives. These figures denote numbers of known children in care; however it is possible that this number is greater, as it does not take into consideration children who might be living with relatives or others in an unofficial capacity – for example, grandparents looking after a grandchild. While there appears to be a general perception that children generally enter the care system as a result of abuse, in Ireland the majority of children are in care for reasons such as parental mental health problems, stress, illness, poverty or addiction problems (Department of Health and Children, 2004).

Why Foster?

Research indicates that there are numerous reasons why a person might wish to become a foster carer. Altruism, or a concern for the welfare of others, without reward and often at a personal cost, is one such reason. Some foster because it increases their sense of self-esteem: others because they have had positive experiences of fostering in their own life, possibly having been fostered or been part of a family that fosters themselves. (Schofield *et al*, 2000). Some observers propose that foster carers look after the children of others' due to a 'sense of social obligation' (Chipungu and Bent-Goodley, 2004, p.83).

Another suggested reason that people decide to foster is to receive the foster care allowance that accompanies the child to assist in ensuring their needs are met (Sinclair *et al*, 2005), this being paid every two weeks by the Health Service Executive (HSE). On first glance, this allowance of €352 per child per week appears attractive; however, as all parents will attest, it can be expensive ensuring the most basic needs of the child such as food, shelter, clothing and education are met. In accordance with the *National Standards for Foster Care*, 'foster carers [should] provide a stimulating environment and opportunity for play and learning (Department of Health and Children, 2003, para 9.2, p.21).

Such opportunities may include sports, hobbies, computer games or alternate pursuits, at an age-appropriate level, all having additional associated costs. Obligatory school and religious occasions, such as First Communion, Confirmation or graduations, as well as family events, such as holidays and day trips, all can prove costly. There may be additional financial outlay associated with engaging alternative professional services that have been recommended to assist a foster child or members of a foster family to cope with the challenges arising from the placement. Other monetary expenses may include travelling to and from family visits with a foster child. In our experience, this allowance barely covers such physical costs without taking into consideration the emotional, psychological or time costs to the foster family. Since commencing fostering, we have yet to meet any foster carer who indicated that this was their motivation to foster. Similarly, given the many challenges that arise, almost daily, due to the nature of fostering, some of which will be outlined later in this chapter, we feel that if our motivation to foster had been based solely upon remuneration, we would have ceased to foster many years ago.

A Framework for Fostering

There are various forms of foster care placements in Ireland:

- **Short-term placements** are where a child is placed with a foster family for a number of days or at most a few weeks. Short-term placements are used in a variety of situations, including where parents are experiencing health problems, where there is abuse or neglect but where a child might return home;

- **Long-term placements** may evolve from short-term ones, where situations have not improved or it is not safe for a child to return to the family home, and could last years;
- **Emergency placements** are used when a child must be removed immediately from a dangerous environment;
- **Respite foster care** affords parents, including other foster parents, an opportunity for a break away from a stressful environment;
- **Specialist foster care placements** may be provided for children with special needs or behavioural difficulties where foster parents have received specialist training to assist in coping with additional associated challenges (Irish Foster Care Association, 2012).

In accordance with the *Child Care Act, 1991*, a child may enter foster care under the following orders:

- **Voluntary Care Order (section 4):** The parent has agreed to place a child in the care of the state until such time as they are capable of providing for the needs of the child;
- **Emergency Care Order (section 13):** A child may be removed from home where it appears there is imminent serious risk of harm to a child;
- **[Full] Care Order (section 18):** There is evidence of abuse or neglect and a child requires protection, so the child is removed from the family home, and responsibility for care lies with the State;
- **Interim Care Order (section 17):** Where an application for a care order has been made, a court may order a child removed from the family home and placed in the care of the state pending the outcome of this care order application (Government of Ireland, 1991).

Social Work Teams

All foster carers and foster children should have an individual dedicated social worker known as a link worker. In accordance with *National Standards*, a child or young person should be allocated this link worker as soon as it becomes known they will be entering into state care. Similarly, a link worker should be available to them for as long as they remain in care (Department of Health and Children, 2003, para 5.1, p.16).

The link worker's responsibilities include:

- Safety and welfare of the child in care;
- Placing a child with suitable foster carers;

- Visiting the child regularly in their placement;
- Arranging and maintaining contact with birth families, where it is in a child's best interest to do so;
- Ensuring specialist services, including psychology, speech and language therapy or occupational therapy services are available, if necessary, for the child in care.

The responsibilities of the foster family link worker include:

- Responding to initial queries and assessment of potential foster carers;
- Providing support for carers and their families;
- Organising training;
- Providing relevant information and advice regarding children coming into care;
- Ensuring counselling is available in the event of placement breakdown, if necessary.

Our Story

Why did we become foster carers? It's a question my wife and I have reflected upon regularly and there is no one reason that we can think of. This decision appears to have been due to circumstances in which we found ourselves at the time; a case of right place, right time. We both came from large families; my wife had 10 siblings, while my own family lagged a bit behind with only eight. At the time, we had four daughters aged 14, 12, 10 and 9. Our house was always a hive of activity, with the girls and their friends coming and going, and my wife provided lodgings for visiting foreign students on an *ad hoc* basis. In addition, we had recently relocated to an area of Ireland that is very popular as a holiday destination and, as such, had been inundated with visiting relatives and friends, especially during the summer holidays. One weekend, there were 21 people in our five-bedroomed house.

My wife came home from work one evening with an information leaflet regarding an open meeting being held locally, the purpose of which was to recruit potential foster carers in the area. This leaflet might as well have been trying to recruit astronauts to travel to Mars or promoting membership of a cult, such was my level of ignorance regarding fostering at this time. We attended the meeting, co-presented by members of the local social work team and foster carers, which was very informative and at the end we felt that it was something we could do. Our initial hope, which we both agreed upon, was that, if we could make a difference in even one child's life, for even a small time, then we would have done something beneficial. Following on from this meeting, we discussed the possibility of becoming foster carers with our daughters, who as one agreed to actively participate. However, I do think they all had images of looking after a cute little baby and all that goes with it. Thus began a new chapter in the life of our family.

From the start, we agreed there should be some basic 'house rules'. All children in the family home – birth and foster children – would be treated, insofar as possible, equally, by us, as parents. All would be encouraged to respect each other and negative talk about all birth families, ours included, discouraged. All family members were exhorted to treat others as they would like to be treated themselves. Similarly, the property and personal space of others was to be respected by all. If issues arose, rather than take matters into their own hands, children would be encouraged to discuss the matter with us. We were not that naïve to expect that these 'rules' would always be adhered to but did believe it was possible, in general, to promote such behaviours, starting with our own behaviour towards all children in the household. There have been times when conflict has arisen among the children in the home but such behaviour is not unusual in most families where siblings compete with each other, this being considered a natural phenomenon between family members that can assist in social development, promoting negotiation and interaction skills (Munn and Dunn, 1989).

We have always endeavoured to promote values and skills that we feel are important to all children and that will assist them in achieving independence, so that when the time comes for them to leave home and enter the world on their own, they are capable of looking after themselves.

Training

Initially, my perception was that, as an experienced parent, I automatically had acquired skills that were transferable to the role as foster parent and would not require much training. Not so! There is a major need for additional training, pre-placement (as well as throughout fostering), during which some of the additional challenges that fostering brings, many of which we would encounter personally later, are presented and discussed, with some coping strategies being introduced. Training bolsters competence and increases the self-confidence of foster parents (Cooley and Petren, 2011), creating among foster carers a perception of self-efficaciousness or a belief in one's own ability to cope with the challenges arising due to foster placements, thus reducing stress and anxiety and promoting placement stability (Oosterman, 2004, Morgan and Baron, 2011). The objective of the training was – and still is – to prepare prospective foster parents and their families for these challenges, insofar as possible. In our experience, the training did give us an insight into some of the challenges that could arise. The initial training took place over about a 10-week period. During this time, information and advice on fostering in general, on self-care, on establishing guidelines to promote privacy and respect within the home as well as numerous other pertinent subjects was given. Attendees were allocated various roles, such as a young person exhibiting challenging behaviour or a foster parent confronted by such a child, which they were to play while others observed the interactions and led discussions on these vignettes. These mini-dramas, and subsequent question and answer sessions, in my opinion, formed an important part of the training.

One of the greatest challenges we have experienced since becoming foster parents is being open to allegations, which can take many forms, too numerous to mention here, being made against us. Allegations against foster carers and their families are one of the primary de-motivators, possibly leading to placements ending or people quitting as foster carers (Farmer *et al*, 2004). Unlike the normal judicial process of being innocent until proven guilty, there may be a perception among carers that they are being judged guilty until proved innocent, as all allegations regarding foster carers and their families, founded or unfounded, should be investigated thoroughly. Only when an investigation is concluded, can the allegation be dismissed or further appropriate action taken. The training incorporated one evening dedicated to dealing with allegations and some of the subsequent challenges arising. The next week, when we resumed our training, three out of 10 potential fostering couples did not attend. They did not re-appear during the course of our training nor have I encountered them as foster carers over the last 14 years.

The Importance of Support Networks

Despite the best efforts of our trainers, drawn from a pool of experienced social workers and foster carers, over time we have, encountered situations that no training can prepare you for, some of which I will briefly discuss later in this chapter. When this happens, having a good support network is vital for both the fostering family and the foster child. Supports may be formal such as social work teams, allied professionals and foster care support groups such as Irish Foster Care Association (IFCA). Informal supports include families, friends, GPs, teachers and the community in general who interact with the fostering family and the foster child. While little research exists to support the hypothesis that increased levels of support promotes placement stability, the research does highlight that poor or inadequate support can negatively impact upon the placement success (Sinclair, 2005). There is also a link between placement stability and the levels of contact, face-to-face or telephone, between social workers and foster carers (Stone and Stone, 1983, cited in Strijker *et al*, 2008).

While it is recommended that all children in care and foster carers have separate, dedicated social workers, figures published in 2012 by the Department of Children and Youth Affairs indicate that this was not the case. Almost 92% of children in care and just over 83% of approved foster carers had link workers allocated to them (www.tusla.ie). Ó Cionnaith (2011) highlighted that, with a continuing embargo on employment in the HSE, more urgent cases are given priority over those perceived as less serious. Taking these facts into consideration, we have been extremely privileged in that we have always had a link worker as have the foster children placed with us. These professionals have endeavoured to make themselves available, sometimes at very short notice, when needed. Compared with other foster carers we are personally aware of, many of whom are in different HSE areas of responsibility, we have generally been included in decision-making for the children in our care. As the state is ultimately responsible for the care provision of foster children, many decisions can only be made by senior social workers, such as an area child care manager. Their permission must be sought to allow a foster child receive an immunisation injection, a filling in a tooth, to travel abroad or in the case of hospitalisation for a routine procedure such as having tonsils removed. This can be very frustrating for foster carers, as it may take time to ensure the correct paperwork is completed before the child can be facilitated and, in our experience, foster children have been refused routine non-invasive procedures due to incomplete paperwork.

For a placement to be successful, much depends upon the relationship that exists between the foster family and the social work team. Fostering, according to the *National Standards*, should be a professional partnership between foster carers and social care teams (Fisher *et al*, 2011), where the primary concern should relate to the well-being and needs of the foster child. It should be noted, however, that the success of foster care is generally based upon the human qualities of foster parents – empathy, unconditional positive regard and ability to attach – and should foster care be viewed as a profession, there is a possibility these qualities could be lost (Hollins and Larkin, 2011).

We feel that we are very fortunate to be viewed as being an integral part of a team and that we have forged an excellent trusting relationship with the social work team in our area. It is our opinion that this has been made possible due to the ethos that permeates all levels of the local area social work. We have been able to openly discuss issues we may have felt were important to us and our opinions were taken on board, although not always agreed with. Similarly where major challenges have arisen, we have been able to call upon link workers and team leaders for assistance. On a personal level, and in my role as Voluntary Support and Advocacy Officer with the IFCA, we have encountered other foster carers who have not been so fortunate.

First Experiences of Foster Care

Having successfully completed the training and subsequent screening process, including Garda vetting, we were contacted within about three weeks of completing the assessment process, to enquire whether we would be available to provide a placement for two young foreign-national children, aged 2 and 4. A family emergency had arisen and, as there was no other family present to look after the boys, it was necessary to place them in the care of the state, albeit on a short-term basis. These boys returned home as soon as the situation warranted it.

It was quite some time before another child was placed in our care, so much so that we began to question whether we had done something wrong in our first placement. When we discussed this with our link worker, it then became apparent that our original assessment form had been incorrectly completed. According to our files, we were only interested in fostering babies, yet we had stated were would be willing to look after children at least two or three years younger than our youngest daughter, 9 at that time, now 10. The requested age difference was not based upon any scientific premise; it just felt to us, as parents, to be the right thing to do so as not to displace our youngest child too much. Subsequently, I have discovered research that proposes that families are finely balanced units where a state of equilibrium has been achieved over time and that placement success is more likely where a foster child is at least two or three years younger than the youngest natural child (Pugh, 1996). The introduction of another child into this unit could have a destabilising effect, especially where biological children experience perceived competition for parents' attention, leading to jealousy, anger and animosity towards the foster child. These negative perceptions could increase if the foster child is the same sex as the biological child and within three years of their age (Sinclair, 2005; Oosterman *et al*, 2007).

With this error rectified, our next foster-child, which just happened to be a new-born baby, arrived. The child's mother, a foreign-national, had a serious medical condition that required hospitalisation. She had no family or social networks in the area and, similar to our previous placement, this child was placed on a short-term basis with us. When the mother returned home, her baby went with her. In both these instances, we as a foster family were fully aware that the children would be returned at the first available opportunity to their birth family, this being generally accepted as being the optimum place for a child in which to grow and develop. Similarly, both placements were very short: the former almost two weeks, while the latter was 10 days. Given these facts, it is no major surprise that no major attachment appeared to have formed between the children and us. In the case of the latter child, we did keep in touch with the mother, becoming a part of her informal support network, developing a strong friendship with her and were subsequently asked to be her child's Godparents, an honour we readily accepted.

Moving On

Not long after this baby had left our home, our link worker discussed the possibility of a local child, aged 2, who was coming into care on a long-term care order, being placed with us in the not too distant future. As this would be our first 'real' experience of foster care, being a long-term placement, we were very excited at the prospect, as were our daughters. Just prior to the placement being made, it was agreed upon by the local social work team that, in the best interests of the child, it would be better to place this child outside the townland, where contact with the natural family could be supervised. The child was placed elsewhere, which was very disappointing for us, at that time; however, we accepted it was the right thing to do.

It was some time after this disappointment that we then were contacted by our link worker to ascertain our feelings about providing day foster care for two young children aged 2 and 4, who were considered a "bit wild" and "out of control", to use her words. Day foster care is where foster carers provide care for a child in their own family home and the child returns to the natural family at the end of the day. This type of foster care may be used to alleviate stress a parent might be experiencing where a child exhibits challenging behaviour and where there is no support network to assist them. My wife was on a computer course and I worked a shift pattern that was not conducive to providing such care, thus we were not in a position to facilitate this request. It was agreed by the local social work team that the best course of action would be that the boys remain in the family home and that family supports would be put in place.

About a month later we were asked if we could provide care for two other young boys, on a short-term basis, who were coming into care on a voluntary care order, as their mother had indicated to the Social Work Department that she was struggling to provide care for them and did not have adequate family or social networks to assist in care provision. We agreed without hesitation. The following week, these two young children were placed with us. They arrived on our doorstep, accompanied by their mother and their social worker. Here appeared to be two normal children, who presented as typical boys of their age, who played on the green outside our house with the family dogs and the two younger girls in the family.

We set about trying to assist the two children adapt to their new surroundings. The younger of the two appeared to settle into this placement from the off; however some minor challenging behaviour such as using foul language was displayed by the older sibling. In time, these behaviours were replaced by new, more appropriate behaviours, reinforced through praise and encouragement. Within a couple of weeks, these two young children appeared very settled within the family home. Being so young, they were the centre of attention for all family members as well as visiting relatives, friends and neighbours. They appeared to enjoy every minute of it.

All was well in the world – or so it would seem – until we were notified by our link worker that the boys would be returning home to their mother. While one of our primary reasons for becoming foster carers was the hope that we could make some difference in a child's life, however small, we felt that as a family we had already made a difference in the lives of these children and hoped their mother would be in a position to care for them. We understood that, in general, the best place for a child to be raised is in their own family home with their own family; however, we were anxious about their welfare and the mother's capacity to care for them. While we could empathise with this parent who was struggling, we felt that the children's welfare was of paramount importance and should be safeguarded by the HSE. As they had been placed in care under a voluntary care order, this could be rescinded at the request of the parent, as happened in this case. The two children went back to their mother's house. Over the next few weeks, my wife encountered them on an *ad hoc* basis, and was seen by them. The reaction of the younger one, lifting arms out to be picked up, calling to her, was, according to her, "heart-breaking". The older of these siblings appeared so angry, shouting expletives, using foul gestures directed at her, which she also found very upsetting. We began to question our ability to provide foster care. If we were going to feel this way every time a child returned home, which is where ideally they should be raised, how could we be good foster parents? It was something we discussed with our link worker and other foster carers.

Two weeks later, we were asked if we would be willing to take these two small children back into our home as they were coming into care on an interim care order. We did not have to be asked twice. Upon their return, there were some notable changes: the older sibling appeared very angry and resentful of being placed with us again, while the younger of the two followed my wife everywhere, shadowlike, appearing unwilling to let her out of his sight. It took some time to re-establish a routine with these two so they felt a part of the household, especially with the older of the two. It was achieved over time by showing that we understood why they were angry and acting out; being patient; including them in family activities and in general just being there for them at all times. This proved successful and a stable placement was established for both these children within the family home.

Challenging Behaviour

In our experience, being a foster carer brings many challenges, many which only become apparent during a placement and no amount of training can adequately prepare you for. However, support from the social work team, as these challenges arise, is imperative if the placement is to succeed. Dissatisfaction with support agencies and inability to cope with the perceived needs of the foster child are contributory factors in placement breakdown and the decision to cease fostering (Murray *et al*, 2011). The greater the levels of motivation among foster carers to make the placement work, the greater the probability of success (Riggs *et al*, 2009). Foster carers may experience demotivating factors, such as allegations by the foster child, the natural family or others, which could lead to placement disruption or foster carers ceasing to foster (Farmer *et al*, 2004).

Many of the children who enter the care system present with challenging behaviours (Brown *et al*, 2007). There appears to be a dearth of statistics relating to the Irish care system; however, international studies estimate this figure to be as high as 80%, depending upon the nature of the circumstances under which they have entered the care system (Chipungu and Bent-Godley, 2004). In a study carried out into the factors that contributed to placement breakdown in Spain, 81% of breakdowns investigated were attributed to the challenging behaviour of the foster child (Lopez *et al*, 2011). Similarly, many foster children will experience mental health problems such as depression, anxiety disorders, suicidal ideation and sexual disorders (Crum, 2010). They are also more likely to have less social skills, to be more withdrawn than their peers and perform less well in school (Crum, 2010). In our experience, the majority of the children who have been placed with us have exhibited challenging behaviour, which has manifested in various forms including overly aggressive behaviour, irrational emotional outbursts, destruction of personal property, intentional disregard for house rules. However, it should be noted that such behaviour is not always exhibited, rather it tends to appear during times when the child is stressed or challenged and it is at this time that support from social work teams and allied professionals is very important to ensure placement stability. As foster parents, both of us are 100% committed to the child placed in the family home. Commitment to a placement and the foster child, understanding reasons behind challenging behaviour, willingness to fight for services and patience are all qualities of foster parents that can assist with placement stability. This motivation to succeed may be reciprocated by a foster child where they are aware of the commitment of the foster carers (Sinclair *et al*, 2005).

Placement Disruption/Breakdown

Placement breakdowns, the premature ending of a foster care placement, generally unplanned and sudden, can occur for a number of reasons:

- Attachment issues;
- Behaviour of child;
- Lack of motivation on the part of the foster child or foster family for the placement to succeed;
- Mismatched placements, where the family has not been accurately assessed to ensure they are capable of meeting the often complex needs of the foster child;
- Influences of birth family, as well as lack of support from social work teams (Sinclair, 2005).

International studies into the factors that contribute to placement breakdown highlight the primary cause as being the challenging behaviour exhibited by the foster child (Lopez *et al*, 2011). This rate increases where foster parents perceive a possibility of danger to themselves or other family members (Gilbertson and Barber, 2003). It is estimated that between 30% and 80% of children in the foster care system will exhibit behavioural challenges due to the nature of the circumstances under which they have entered care or from being a foster child (Chipungu and Bent-Godley, 2004). Many children, especially substance-exposed ones, come into care presenting with challenging behaviours (Brown *et al*, 2007). It is inevitable that many placements will breakdown: 20% in the 1st year and up to 40% by year 5 (Hollins and Larkin, 2011). Placement breakdown can be traumatic (Hollins and Larkin, 2011), interpreted as failure by all stakeholders (Guishard-Pine *et al*, 2007) leaving 'a lasting and corrosive impression' (Rostill-Brookes *et al*, 2010, p.121). It can cause role dissatisfaction and increase burnout among foster carers and social workers, affecting retention rates (Brown and Bednar, 2006; Fisher *et al*, 2000). It might be perceived as being let down by foster parents (Crum, 2010) and could exacerbate the development of behavioural problems in foster children, which could jeopardise future placements for that child, this behaviour becoming 'self-perpetuating' (Rich, 1996, cited in Rostill-Brookes *at al*, 2010).

Our first experience of this phenomenon was not totally unexpected, taking into consideration the preceding events, but it was very traumatic for all members of our household, including the foster child concerned. It involved a 16 year old who had lived with us for over five years. In the latter part of the placement, this child began to push accepted family rules and boundaries such as respecting curfews, drinking alcohol, disagreeing with decisions and being generally argumentative. Such behaviour often appears to be the norm for the youth of society throughout history, ancient philosophers including Socrates and Plato noting that younger generations 'challenge' and 'disrespect' their elders. Here the greatest challenge was not just the challenging behaviour being exhibited, but the apparent support from some members of the child's natural family in undermining our attempts in maintaining boundaries that impacted upon the placement stability.

A care order was in place whereby the child was to remain in this placement until the age of 18. Recently, all other family members had been 'treading on eggshells', endeavouring to avoid confrontation with this child who could become verbally aggressive or hostile towards them with little or no provocation. We felt that, if we let this placement breakdown, we had failed. Quitting was NEVER an option when we commenced fostering. We were determined to see this through to the end. We have always striven to parent all children consistently, without bias, accepting all unconditionally but upon reflection we felt we were making additional allowances for these behaviours, so that the situation that existed would not be intensified and the placement maintained, which was unfair to the other children in the home. The 'straw that broke the camel's back' took the form of a serious incident that occurred in the home whereby the safety of a family member was threatened, this threat being reinforced by the presence outside the family home of numerous members of the child's family. Events had transpired so rapidly that we were speechless. We were devastated.

Yes, we knew that the end was approaching and that our efforts to maintain this placement were like trying to prevent the tide coming in, yet it was only when we accepted that we were unable to ensure the safety of this child, and the safety of others in the family home, that we finally recognised that this was the end. Personally, at the time, I felt we had failed. My wife concurred. Unfortunately, when a foster child wishes to leave a placement, they may manipulate events to achieve this objective (Sinclair, 2005). Immediately after this incident, the child left in the company of those relatives gathered outside our home only to return some days later, accompanied by her social worker, to remove her belongings. Personally, I would compare the emotions we experienced going through this placement breakdown to be similar to those experienced when a loved one dies, the major difference being that in the latter case people are more empathetic and understanding as the loss is more tangible.

Since then, we have experienced another placement disruption, which manifested so rapidly that it caught us by surprise. In the space of a few weeks, a very stable secure placement in place for nine years, commencing when this child was four, transformed almost overnight into one where the child became very angry and destructive, destroying much of their own belongings and furniture, so much so that we felt they had become a danger to themselves and others in the family. It was evident that this child did not want to be in the placement any longer; however, taking into consideration our previous experience, we acknowledged the inevitability of placement disruption and co-ordinated immediately with the local social work team to find a respite placement for this child, which the child also agreed upon. This decision was taken in the best interests of the child, our family and other foster children in the family home. In a situation where all relevant parties acknowledge that an alternate placement is in the best interests of the child, there may be less negative impact than if the child remains in the current placement (Sinclair *et al*, 2005). While acknowledging that an alternate placement was in the child's best interest, it was a very emotional time for all our family, this child having been part of our family for almost 10 years.

Such a roller-coaster of emotions is not unusual among foster families. In a small piece of research carried out in 2013 in partial fulfilment for a Master's Degree in Counselling and Psychotherapy by myself, numerous often conflicting emotions were experienced by foster carers after placement breakdown including failure, sadness, heartbreak, guilt, relief, anger, grief, indecision, devastation, conflicted and worry. Having gone through such experiences personally, we can say that we have experienced all these emotions, many simultaneously, at different stages of placements.

On the Bright Side!

When we commenced our journey into fostering, we had little knowledge of the path that lay ahead. In this chapter, I have listed some of the greatest challenges we have encountered personally. However, we feel the positives far outweigh all the negative experiences to date and in our opinion would require separate volumes, never mind a single chapter to describe them.

How can I put a price on watching the joy on the face of and listening to the excited squeals of delight of a 7 year old child, on board an aeroplane for the first time ever, as it hurtles down a runway heading off on a family holiday? How can I describe the pride I personally have felt standing on the sidelines of a rugby match watching a child carry opponents on their back, 'Bull' Hayes like, as they drive towards the try line? The preparation for that first day at school. Meeting the first boyfriend or girlfriend. The excitement during the build up to Christmas. Helping write that letter to Santa. The simple things like reading a bedtime story or tucking them in to bed at night can have so much meaning. It is very difficult to describe the emotions, the pride, joy, excitement, happiness, I personally have experienced over the past 14 years because these children have been a part of our family and I look forward to many more of these mixed emotions in the future.

A Positive Outcome

Over the last 14 years, many people have told us they think we are great for providing a service as foster carers. While the sentiment is appreciated, we really don't think so – Mother Teresa, Martin Luther King, Gandhi: they are great people. We are doing something we enjoy, something we feel we are good at and something we hope we will be permitted to do for the foreseeable future. We are just one of the many hundreds of individuals and families in Ireland voluntarily looking after the children of others and I am optimistic that this chapter might provide some small insight into their lives, through our experiences, as foster carers.

The following is a brief synopsis of an event that occurred some years after the very turbulent placement breakdown described earlier in this chapter. I encountered this former foster child while out socialising with one of my daughters while abroad. As we walked into a local establishment, within a few seconds I noticed someone running towards me. As I recognised this child charging towards me, like a bull charging a matador, I was initially very apprehensive as to what the next action would be until they let out a shout of "DAD!", and welcomed me a with a 'bear hug'. I felt somewhat emotionally overawed. I was speechless – which as anyone who knows me will attest – is not something that happens to me very often. Even as I write this, I am so proud that this young person did not let past events influence their attitude towards me that night. In recent times, a positive relationship has been re-established between this child and their former foster family. My wife and I have been thanked by this child for providing them with the appropriate skills and values necessary for ensuring their independence. This is what we set out to do from the start – try to make a small difference in the life of a child – and it is what continues to drive us as foster carers.

References

Beek, M. and Schofield, G. (2004). *Providing a Secure Base in Long-Term Foster Care*, London: British Association of Adoption and Fostering.

Brown, J.D, Bednar, L.M. and Sigvaldson, N. (2007). 'Causes of Placement Breakdown for Foster Children Affected by Alcohol', *Child and Adolescent Social Work Journal*, Vol.24, No.4, pp.313-32.

Brown, J.D. and Bednar, L.M. (2006). 'Foster Parent Perceptions of Placement Breakdown', *Children and Youth Services Review*, Vol.28, No.12, pp.1497-1511.

Chipungu, S.S. and Bent-Goodley, T.B. (2004). 'Meeting the Challenges of Contemporary Foster Care', *The Future of Children*, Vol.14, pp.75-93.

Crum, W. (2010). 'Foster Parent Parenting Characteristics that Lead to Increased Placement Stability or Disruption', *Children and Youth Services Review*, Vol.32, No.2, pp.185-90.

Department of Health and Children (2003). *National Standards for Foster Care*, Dublin: Government Publications.

Department of Health and Children (2004). *Preliminary Analysis of Child Care Interim Dataset,* Dublin: Government Publications.

Farmer, E., Moyers, S. and Lipscombe, J. (2004). *Fostering Adolescents,* London: Jessica Kingsley Publishers.

Fisher, P., Mannering, A., Stoolmiller, M., Takahashi, A. and Chamberlain, P. (2011). 'Foster Placement Disruptions Associated with Problem Behaviour: Mitigating a Threshold Effect', *Journal of Consulting and Clinical Psychology,* Vol.79, No.4, pp.481-87.

Fisher, T., Gibbs, I., Sinclair, I. and Wilson, K. (2000). 'Sharing the Care: The Qualities Sought of Social Workers by Foster Carers', *Child and Family Social Work,* Vol.5, pp.225-34.

Gilbertson, R. and Barber, J.G. (2003). 'Breakdown of Foster Care Placement: Carer Perspectives and System Factors', *Australian Social Work,* Vol.56, No. 4, pp.329-39.

Government of Ireland (1991). *Childcare Act, 1991,* Dublin: Government Publications.

Guishard-Pine, J., McCall, S. and Hamilton, L. (2007). *Understanding Looked-after Children: An Introduction to Psychology for Foster Care,* London: Jessica Kingsley Publishers.

Hollins, G. and Larkin, M. (2011). 'The Language and Policy of Care and Parenting: Understanding the Uncertainty about Key Players' Roles in Foster Care Provision', *Child and Youth Services Review,* Vol.33, No.11, pp.2198-206.

Irish Foster Care Association (2012). *Fostering is Caring,* available at www.hse.ie/eng/services/Find_a_Service/Children_and_Family_Services/Fostering/Fostering_is_caring_.pdf, accessed 11 December 2013.

Kelly, F. (1988). *A Guide to Early Irish Laws,* Dublin: Dublin Institute for Advanced Studies.

Lopez, M., del Valle, J. and Montserrat, C. (2011). 'Factors Affecting Foster Care Breakdown in Spain', *The Spanish Journal of Psychology,* Vol.14, No.1, pp.111-22.

Morgan, K. and Baron, R. (2011). 'Challenging Behaviour in Looked-After Young People, Feelings of Parental Self-Efficacy and Psychological Well-Being in Foster Carers', *Adoption and Fostering,* Vol.35, No.1, pp.18-32.

Munn, P. and Dunn, J. (1989). Temperament and the Developing Relationship between Siblings', *International Journal of Behavioural Development,* Vol.12, pp.433-51.

Murray, L., Tarren-Sweeney, M. and France, K. (2011). 'Foster Carer Perceptions of Support and Training in the Context of High Burden of Care', *Child and Family Social Work,* Vol.16, pp.149-58.

Ó Cionnaith, F. (2011). '1600 children put in care by HSE South', *Irish Examiner,* available at www.examiner.ie/ireland/1600-children-put-in-care-by-hse-south-168516.html.

Oosterman, M., Schuengel, C., Slot, N., Bullens, R. and Doreleijers, T. (2007). 'Disruptions in Foster Care: A Review and Meta-analysis', *Children and Youth Services Review,* Vol.29, pp.53-76.

Pugh, G. (1996). 'Seen but Not Heard? Addressing the Needs of Children Who Foster', *Adoption and Fostering,* Vol.20, No.1, pp.35-41.

Rich, H. (1996). 'The Effects of a Health Newsletter for Foster Parents on Their Perceptions of the Behaviour and Development of Foster Children', *Child Abuse and Neglect*, No.20, pp.437-445.

Riggs, D.W., Augoustinos, M. and Delfabbro, P.H. (2009). 'The Role of Foster Family Belonging in Recovery from Child Maltreatment', *Australian Psychologist*, Vol.44, No.3, pp.166-173.

Rostill-Brookes, H., Larkin, M., Toms, A. and Churchman, C. (2010). 'A Shared Experience of Fragmentation: Making Sense of Foster Placement Breakdown', *Clinical Child Psychology and Psychiatry, Online First*, June, pp.1-25.

Schofield, G., Beek, M., Sargent, K. and Thoburn, J. (2000). *Growing Up in Foster Care*, London: British Association of Adoption and Fostering.

Sinclair, I. (2005). *Fostering Now: Messages from Research*, London: Jessica Kingsley Publishers.

Sinclair, I., Wilson, K. and Gibbs, I. (2005). *Foster Placements: Why They Succeed and Why They Fail*, Philadelphia, PA: Jessica Kingsley Publishers.

Stone, N.M. and Stone, S.F. (1983). 'The Prediction of Successful Foster Placement', *Social Casework*, Vol.64, pp.11-17.

Strijker, J., Knorth, E.J. and Knot-Dickscheit, J. (2008). 'Placement History of Foster Children: A Study of Placement History and Outcomes In Long-term Family Foster Care', *Child Welfare*, Vol.87, No.5, pp.107-25.

Conclusion – A New Deal for Parents, A New Deal for Society

Colm O'Doherty and Ashling Jackson

The Politics of Parenting

In the **Introduction**, we outlined that this book would be a reflection on general parenting issues in Ireland and parenting for a variety of 'new' emerging parent groups. In 21st century Ireland, responsibility for the co-production of reasonable citizens rests with parents and the state. The public service dimension of parenting co-exists with the interpersonal world of the family. This is an uneven and contingent arrangement. While some parenting forms are prioritised as social assets, others are seen as a bundle of problems to be regulated and monitored.

Belief in the rule of the market and a social order that is underwritten by its logic has gone hand-in-hand with a belief in trickle-down parenting. As the economy grows stronger, so runs the theory, a flow of positive parenting is the reward. Parents in turn are responsible for channelling this flow and their uncertainty in the face of this task leads them to self-blaming and soul-searching. Under the 'new politics' of parenting in Ireland, 'parents become the guarantors not only of the "good child" but also of the "good society"' (Lawler, 2014) and 'political divisions over family form have given way to political consensus around the need to address the quality of family relationships' (Macvarish, 2014).

This is not all bad news because, as has been made clear throughout this book, new and diverse family forms have transformed Irish social relations. However, in Ireland, as is the case in many other countries, ambiguity still exists around the tasks and responsibilities of parenting – is parenting a public rather than a private concern? There is always a danger that long-standing social issues are seen as a consequence of poor parenting behaviours and that the state therefore has a responsibility to improve parenting but not necessarily to address the structural circumstances that are the root cause of the issues. The intimate world of family relations, in all its forms – one-parent families, lesbian, gay and bi-sexual parenting, and grand-parenting, for example – is seen through the lens of parental determinism. Social problems, such as anti-social behaviour and mental health concerns, are determined by poor or faulty parenting practices. However, parental malfunctioning can be addressed through forms of social action that are focused on cultural and intimate contact. This is translated into:

> … a genuine belief in policy circles that all families need support at some time and that parenting requires a set of skills which *all* parents can enhance (Macvarish, 2014).

Parenting is then professionalised, with commentary on what parents ought to do supplied by nurses, social workers and psychologists. Parenting experts and practitioners deliver evidence-based training that critics such as Lee (2014) argue privileges expert knowledge and authority over learning by experience and instinct. Smeyers (2010), cited in Lee (2014), suggests that this approach replaces a diversity of approaches with a narrow 'one size fits all' recommended pathway that removes practical judgements from parenting and turns the task of raising the next generation into a skill set prescribed by so called 'parenting experts'. In turn, parenting expertise becomes a marketable commodity, 'sold by a particular type of person, both to parents individually and also to the media' (Lee, 2014). Furedi (2005) links the rise of parent training, with its intense focus on individual behaviour, to the state's failure to produce wider social change.

Parenting and Wider Social Change

This book has examined and explored the everyday practices and concerns of different parenting forms in modern Ireland. The dispersal of what were once social control functions of state and civil society institutions (the Church, the education system) to individual parents is not, however, synonymous with a loss of state power. In an age of uncertainty, where raising children is a trade-off between choice and risk, the state has delegated some of the responsibility for the maintenance of social order to parents. Yet, parenting takes place within a welfare state context of care. This means that those who need care/protection, however that manifests in individual lives, should receive that care/protection. Chapters in this book have highlighted where the state's policy and practices fall short of meeting the needs of parents in modern Ireland. For example, effective active fatherhood policies are required to encourage and support men as parents. Working fathers should be given the chance to play a bigger role in parenting through an entitlement to parental leave. Structural barriers to employment experienced within one-parent families, such as the lack of affordable childcare, need to be tackled. Universal non-stigmatising parenting support should be available to all. Real 'change and integration' policy and practice is fundamental to the achievement of a truly multicultural society that respects and supports migrant parenting in modern Ireland. Our overarching goal for Irish society should be happier parenting. To achieve this goal, we need an agenda for social renewal fashioned around the creation of a parent-centred society.

The three pillars of a parent-centred society are:

- **Equality in social relations:** This is manifested through acceptance of diverse family forms;
- **Economic security for parents:** Parents need sufficient income to allow them to live free of hardship and stigma. Articles in *The Irish Times* (O'Brien, 2014a, 2014b) highlighted the problems for parents in low-wage jobs who are paying some of the highest childcare costs in the EU. As Thomas Piketty (2014) contends, unfettered capitalism is accumulating wealth for the already wealthy to such an extent that states such as Ireland can no longer guarantee the set of fundamental social rights to which its citizens are entitled: education, childcare and welfare;
- **Inter-generational solidarity requires strengthening in modern Ireland:** Overreliance on expert-driven parent training runs the risk of reducing parenting to a series of tasks and skills and losing sight of the importance of relationships, context and instinct in childrearing. Bristow (2014) suggests that:

  > … a more progressive parenting culture than the one we have presently would make two matters central. The first is active support for parental authority and judgement. The second is community 'friendliness' towards children, acknowledging general adult responsibility in everyday life for the care and socialisation of children (p.102).

Writing in the context of getting fathers into parenting programmes Panter-Brick *et al* argue that 'we need to comprehensively understand *the community of care* provided to children, and the sensitivity of children to a range of caregiving contexts' (2014). They point to the body of cross-cultural research that highlights the importance of alternative caregivers – grandparents, other blood relatives, community neighbours – with a stake in the everyday responsibilities of parenting.

In September 2014, OCS Consulting and the Society of St Vincent de Paul published an exploratory research study on parenting in one-parent families. It was conducted using one-to-one interviews and online survey research with one-parent families assisted by St Vincent de Paul and St Vincent de Paul members, as well as focus groups with St Vincent de Paul Conference members involved in home-visitation work. Overall, the research documents the parenting challenges experienced by one-parent families (OCS Consulting and the Society of St Vincent de Paul, 2014). Many of these have been explored already in this book. The point of referring to this particular publication here is that it is entitled *It's the Hardest Job in the World*. Such a description of parenting can be applied to any parent in any family form. The challenges facing all parents cannot be overstated.

> There are times as a parent when you realise that your job is not to be the parent you always imagined you'd be, the parent you always wished you had. Your job is to be the parent your child needs, given the particulars of his or her own life and nature. (Waldman, n.d.)

As we have seen in the various chapters in this book, parents must learn as they go, adapt and then re-adapt to changing personal, family, economic and social circumstances, in a world where uncertainty and unpredictability have become the norm.

In such a context, there can be no job description. Neither, can there be a universal handbook. For that reason, we chose *Learning on the Job: Parenting in Modern Ireland* as the title for this book, because that is exactly what parents do. It is an organic learning process.

We fervently hope that this book will locate a path forward for a new understanding and appreciation of the hardest and most important job in the world. We also hope that it will contribute to the emerging discourse on parenting in Ireland. All our tomorrows ultimately depend on the development of a more progressive social contract for parents.

References

Bristow, J. (2014). 'Who Cares for Children? The Problem of Intergenerational Contact' in Lee, E., Bristow, J., Faircloth, F. and Macvarish, J. (eds.), *Parenting Culture Studies*, Basingstoke: Palgrave Macmillan

Furedi, F. (2005). *Politics of Fear: Beyond Left and Right*, London and New York: Continuum.

Lawler, S. (2014). *Identity: Sociological Perspectives*, Cambridge: Polity Press.

Lee, E. (2014). 'Experts and Parenting Culture' in Lee, E., Bristow, J., Faircloth, F. and Macvarish, J. (eds.), *Parenting Culture Studies*, Basingstoke: Palgrave Macmillan.

Mcvarish, J. (2014). 'The Politics of Parenting' in Lee, E., Bristow, J., Faircloth, F. and Macvarish, J. (eds.), *Parenting Culture Studies*, Basingstoke: Palgrave Macmillan.

O'Brien, C. (2014a). 'The Living Wage', *The Irish Times*, 27 September.

O'Brien, C. (2014b). 'The Living Wage', *The Irish Times*, 29 September.

OCS Consulting and the Society of St Vincent de Paul (2014). *"It's the Hardest Job in the World": An Exploratory Research Study with One-parent Families*, Dublin: OCS Consulting.

Panter-Brick, C., Burgess, A., Eggerman, M., McAllister, F., Pruett, K. and Leckman, J.F. (2014). 'Practitioner Review: Engaging Fathers –Recommendations for a Game Change in Parenting Interventions based on a Systematic Review of the Global Evidence', *Journal of Child Psychology and Psychiatry*, Vol.5, No.11,pp.1185-296.

Piketty, T. (2014). *Capital in the Twenty-first Century*, Cambridge and London: Harvard University Press.

Smeyers, P. (2010). 'State Intervention and the Technologization and Regulation of Parenting', *Educational Theory, Vol.*60, No.3,pp. 265-70.

Waldman, A. (n.d.). *Parenting Quotes*, retrieved 8 December 2014 from www.brainyquote.com/quotes/quotes/a/ayeletwald506397.html#VuIbitDmDcWckkbc.99.

Index

OAK TREE PRESS

Oak Tree Press develops and delivers information, advice and resources for entrepreneurs and managers. It is Ireland's leading business book publisher, with an unrivalled reputation for quality titles across business, management, HR, law, marketing and enterprise topics. NuBooks is its recently-launched imprint, publishing short, focused ebooks for busy entrepreneurs and managers.

In addition, through its founder and managing director, Brian O'Kane, Oak Tree Press occupies a unique position in start-up and small business support in Ireland through its standard-setting titles, as well training courses, mentoring and advisory services.

Oak Tree Press is comfortable across a range of communication media – print, web and training, focusing always on the effective communication of business information.

Oak Tree Press, 19 Rutland Street, Cork, Ireland.
T: + 353 21 4313855 F: + 353 21 4313496.
E: info@oaktreepress.com W: www.oaktreepress.com.